Beginning
C# 3.0

An Introduction to Object Oriented Programming

Beginning
C# 3.0
An Introduction to Object Oriented Programming

Jack Purdum

Wiley Publishing, Inc.

Beginning C# 3.0: An Introduction to Object Oriented Programming

Published by

Wiley Publishing, Inc.
10475 Crosspoint Boulevard
Indianapolis, IN 46256

www.wiley.com

Copyright © 2007 by Wiley Publishing, Inc., Indianapolis, Indiana

ISBN: 978-0-470-26129-3

Manufactured in the United States of America

10 9 8 7 6 5 4 3 2 1

Library of Congress Cataloging-in-Publication Data:

Purdum, Jack J. (Jack Jay)
    Beginning C# 3.0 : an introduction to object oriented programming / Jack Purdum.
       p.   cm.
    Includes index.
    ISBN 978-0-470-26129-3 (paper/website)
      1. Object-oriented programming (Computer science)   2. C# (Computer program language)   I. Title.
    QA76.64.P88   2008
    005.13'3—dc22

2008011056

To my children: Katie and John

About the Author

Dr. Jack Purdum started his programming career on an IBM 360 mainframe as a graduate student in the 1960s. In the mid-1970s, he became interested in software development for microcomputers, and he founded his own software development company (Ecosoft, Inc.) in 1977. The company's main product was a statistics package (Microstat) that he wanted to rewrite in a new language called C. Lacking a suitable C compiler, Dr. Purdum's company developed its own MS-DOS-based C compiler and other programming tools. He has been involved with language instruction ever since. Dr. Purdum has authored 15 texts and numerous programming articles and has received several teaching awards. He is currently on the cusp of retirement from Purdue University's College of Technology.

Credits

Acquisitions Editor
Chris Webb

Development Editor
Ed Connor

Technical Editor
Caleb Jenkins

Production Editor
William A. Barton

Copy Editor
S. B. Kleinman

Editorial Manager
Mary Beth Wakefield

Production Manager
Tim Tate

Vice President and Executive Group Publisher
Richard Swadley

Vice President and Executive Publisher
Joseph B. Wikert

Project Coordinator, Cover
Lynsey Stanford

Proofreaders
Jeremy Bagai,
Josh Chase,
David Fine,
Word One

Indexer
Robert Swanson

Acknowledgments

No book is written without massive work by others. Ed Connor, Chris Webb, and a group of editorial people too numerous to mention have all made this a better book.

A large group of other people also contributed to this book, providing everything from encouragement and support to ideas for examples. First, thanks to my students who served as guinea pigs for virtually everything used in this text. Others who played various roles include Tom Bangert, Jay Crannell, Issy Cwynar, Ann Dotson, Don Dudine, Doug Felkins, Bill Jones, Mark Keenan, Jim McAllister, Bob McFarling, John Marsh, Katie Mohr, Jeff Nelson, Alice Parker, Larry Powers, Bill Shaw, Mike Shore, Jim Spuller, John Strack, and John Wilson.

Contents

Contents

Contents

Contents

Introduction

Over the past 25 years I've written 15 books on various programming topics. You might wonder why so many . . . Didn't I get it right the first time? Well, no, I didn't . . . not really. When I wrote my first book over 25 years ago, object-oriented programming (OOP) was obscure at best and unknown to most. Like so many others, I had to go through the OOP learning process before I could appreciate what OOP was all about. I have a feeling that there are a lot of people out there who still feel that way.

Each time I teach a programming class, I learn new and better ways to explain things. When I look out across a classroom filled with students and it looks like a still-life painting, it's time to back off, retool, and try a different approach to whatever concept it is I'm trying to teach. Every class I've taught has offered new perspectives on how I teach and how students learn. Changing my examples and the techniques I use to teach programming concepts is one of the reasons I came back to teaching after so many years away . . . I missed the learning experience.

A number of the books I wrote were concerned with languages other than C#, but that too provides for an enriching experience for me as an instructor. The strengths and weaknesses of a language can be appreciated only if you've grappled with some other less-than-perfect languages. The fact that programming languages continue to evolve supports the conclusion that I'm not the only one who is still learning. After all this time, the one thing that I have learned with absolute certainty is that whatever I know today will likely be out of date tomorrow.

Perhaps the real question you should be asking yourself is, Why should I buy this book instead of someone else's book? Good question . . . and a really short answer won't work. A number of factors come into play, but only one really makes a difference. I have absolutely no doubt that there are programmers out there who can write better code than I can. When I had my own software company, my lead programmer, Tim, could code circles around me. He was an amazing coder. But if you asked Tim to explain something, he fell back toward the end of the line. Indeed, there were times when I thought he fell off the planet.

The thing that makes this book different from many others is the fact that I've tried the techniques, examples, and approach to teaching the various programming concepts on literally thousands of students. I know what works and what doesn't. I've suffered through many deer-in-the-headlights examples, refined and reworked them to the point where I can actually see some students have an epiphany during the class. So many authors today are, no doubt, brilliant coders, but they haven't had to stumble through the bad examples and teaching methods that simply don't work. What works for you, the writer, rarely works for everyone else. Writing good code does not necessarily equate to writing good books. Some charmed people are capable of both (I think P.J. Plauger, Jon Bentley, Brian Kernighan, and Steve McConnell are examples), but they are rare and far between. Alas, you've noticed I did not place myself on the list. However, what I may lack in coding skills is (I think) overcome by my teaching experience. Obviously, you'll be the final judge.

I think you will find this book informative, clear in its examples, and perhaps even entertaining in its narrative. I hope you'll give it a chance . . . I think you'll enjoy the book. Even more important, however, is that you will come to appreciate all that object-oriented programming and C# can do for you.

Who This Book is For

The book assumes no prior programming experience. That does not mean, however, that the book is "dumbed down" in any way. I build slowly, placing you on solid ground before the next topic is introduced. I encourage you to write your own programs and do the exercises at the end of each chapter. If you try to take shortcuts, you're actually shortchanging yourself. You should type in every line of code in this book yourself and experiment with it. Do so and you will pick up the language twice as fast and with greater understanding than if you don't do the examples. (You can download the code from the Wrox website. Details are provided later.) You can learn programming only by writing programs and I encourage you to do so at every possible opportunity.

If you have some programming experience, that's fine too. This book will likely be an easy read for you. However, I still think you will learn some things along the way. If you have never programmed before . . . perfect! You don't have the bad programming baggage so many bring to the experience when they learn a new language.

I think this is the perfect book for someone who knows a programming language but learned that language before object-oriented programming techniques came into existence. I think there are a lot of "old-timers" like myself who would like to retrain themselves in OOP techniques and gain a full appreciation of what OOP brings to the table. I believe this books suits that need perfectly.

Unlike other books, I don't recommend skipping chapters if you already know a programming language or have some other prior programming experience. If you're familiar with symbol tables, lvalues and rvalues, and the Bucket Analogy, good — but it won't hurt you to read about them again from a different perspective. No shortcuts, remember.

What This Book Covers

This text begins with a non-programming-language introduction to object-oriented programming. The goal of that chapter is to present the concept of objects first and then ease into how objects may be viewed in C#.

Throughout the book I have tried to use common, easily understood examples to introduce new programming concepts. I have covered most of the C# programming language, although there are a few less common topics that I have not covered. I do not feel these omissions are important to the task at hand, which is to teach you OOP using C#. When you have completed this book, you should feel comfortable writing complex OOP programs of your own design.

How This Book is Structured

The sequencing of the chapters was dictated by what I use when I teach this class to freshmen students. The sequence makes logical sense, and each chapter builds upon the information contained in the previous chapters. While you could skip around, I think this would detract from the learning experience. I have my own way of explaining things and some are unusual . . . but they work.

Each chapter has several exercises at the end of it. You are encouraged to work through those examples before you progress to the next chapter. As I said earlier, you can only learn programming by writing programs. It's easy to get lulled into a false sense of security by reading code and saying, "Yeah, I got that." Perhaps . . . perhaps not. Writing your own programs is the *only* way to know for sure.

What You Need to Use This Book

All the examples in this book were written using Visual Studio 2008's C# Express edition. Instructions in Chapter 1 tell you how to download and install C# Express from Microsoft at no charge. It is an incredible piece of software and has most of the functionality of the full Visual Studio. There are some nice tools missing from the Express edition, but there is enough there for you to experience most of what Visual Studio and C# have to offer. Chances are, after you've used C# for a while, you'll want to spring for the entire Visual Studio package. I think you'll find it worthwhile.

You should use a Pentium-based system (although emulators also exist for the Mac and Linux and they appear to work well) with at least 1G of memory and 1G (or more) of hard disk space. After those requirements, the system you use is pretty much a matter of taste.

Conventions

To help you get the most from the text and keep track of what's happening, we've used a number of style conventions throughout the book. What follows is a list of the book's style conventions. (I also use a number of programming conventions, and these are introduced as needed throughout the text.)

Try It Out

The *Try it Out* is an exercise you should work through, following the text in the book.

1. They usually consist of a set of steps.

2. Each step has a number.

3. Follow the steps through with your copy of the database.

How it Works

After each *Try it Out*, the code you've typed will be explained in detail.

> Boxes like this one hold important, not-to-be forgotten information that is directly relevant to the surrounding text.

Notes, tips, hints, tricks, and asides to the current discussion are offset and placed in italics like this.

As for styles in the text:

❑ We *italicize* new terms and important words when we introduce them.

❑ We show keyboard strokes like this: Ctrl+A.

❑ We show file names, URLs, and code within the text like so: `persistence.properties`.

❑ We present code in two different ways:

```
We use a monofont type with no highlighting for most code examples.
We use gray highlighting to emphasize code that's particularly important in
the present context.
```

Also, Visual Studio's code editor provides a rich color scheme to indicate various parts of code syntax. That's a great tool to help you learn language features in the editor and to help prevent mistakes as you code. While this text does not use the colors that are available, it should in no way detract from the readability of the source code found in the book.

Source Code

As you work through the examples in this book, you may choose either to type in all the code manually or to use the source code files that accompany the book. All the source code used in this book is available for download at `http://www.wrox.com`. Once at the site, simply locate the book's title (either by using the Search box or by using one of the title lists) and click the Download Code link on the book's detail page to obtain all the source code for the book.

Because many books have similar titles, you may find it easiest to search by ISBN; this book's ISBN is 978-0-470-26129-3.

Once you download the code, just decompress it with your favorite compression tool. Alternately, you can go to the main Wrox code download page at `http://www.wrox.com/dynamic/books/download.aspx` to see the code available for this book and all other Wrox books.

Errata

We make every effort to ensure that there are no errors in the text or in the code. However, no one is perfect, and mistakes do occur. If you find an error in one of our books, like a spelling mistake or faulty piece of code, we would be very grateful for your feedback. By sending in errata you may save another reader hours of frustration and at the same time you will be helping us provide even higher-quality information.

To find the errata page for this book, go to `http://www.wrox.com` and locate the title using the Search box or one of the title lists. Then, on the book details page, click the Book Errata link. On this page you can view all errata that have been submitted for this book and posted by Wrox editors. A complete book list, including links to each book's errata, is also available at `www.wrox.com/misc-pages/booklist.shtml`.

If you don't spot "your" error on the Book Errata page, go to www.wrox.com/contact/techsupport .shtml and complete the form there to send us the error you have found. We'll check the information and, if appropriate, post a message to the book's errata page and fix the problem in subsequent editions of the book.

p2p.wrox.com

For author and peer discussion, join the P2P forums at p2p.wrox.com. The forums are a Web-based system for you to post messages relating to Wrox books and related technologies and to interact with other readers and technology users. The forums offer a subscription feature to e-mail you topics of interest of your choosing when new posts are made to the forums. Wrox authors, editors, other industry experts, and your fellow readers are present on these forums.

At http://p2p.wrox.com you will find a number of different forums that will help you not only as you read this book, but also as you develop your own applications. To join the forums, just follow these steps:

1. Go to p2p.wrox.com and click the Register link.

2. Read the terms of use and click Agree.

3. Complete the required information to join, as well as any optional information you wish to provide, and click Submit.

4. You will receive an e-mail with information describing how to verify your account and complete the joining process.

You can read messages in the forums without joining P2P, but in order to post your own messages you must join.

Once you join, you can post new messages and respond to messages other users post. You can read messages at any time on the Web. If you would like to have new messages from a particular forum e-mailed to you, click the Subscribe to this Forum icon by the forum name in the forum listing.

For more information about how to use the Wrox P2P, be sure to read the P2P FAQs for answers to questions about how the forum software works as well as to many common questions specific to P2P and Wrox books. To read the FAQs, click the FAQ link on any P2P page.

Part I
Getting Started

Getting Started

Welcome to the world of object-oriented programming and C#! The primary goal of this book is to use the C# programming language from Microsoft to teach you object-oriented programming, or OOP. This book assumes that you have no prior programming experience in any language and that you know nothing about OOP.

If you do have programming experience and some familiarity with OOP, that's fine. Having that experience makes things easier for you. However, I still encourage you to read the book from start to finish for a number of reasons. First, this book represents the distillation of 25 years of programming and teaching experience. I have a good idea of what works and what doesn't work when it comes to explaining complex topics so that they're easy to understand. Reading each chapter gives you the tools to understand the next chapter. Second, I may introduce topics in one chapter and then rely heavily on those topics in a much later chapter. In other words, the process used to learn OOP and C# is one that introduces new topics based upon ones that were introduced earlier. Obviously, it's important to master the earlier content before tackling the later content. Finally, the programming examples I use also build on concepts presented in earlier program examples. It will be easier for you to understand the later program examples if you've experimented with those programs introduced earlier in the book.

One more thing: You cannot learn programming by just reading about it. You have to dig in and start programming yourself. For that reason, there are exercises at the end of each chapter designed to help you hone your programming skills. The learning process is even more interesting if you try to create your own programs based upon some real problems you'd like to solve. Don't worry if things don't fall together instantly on the first try. You should plan to make a ton of "flat-forehead" mistakes . . . you know, the kind of mistake where, upon discovering it, you pound the heel of your hand into your forehead and say: "How could I make such a stupid mistake!" Not to worry . . . we've all been there. Such mistakes are just part of the process of becoming a programmer and you should expect to make your fair share. However, stick with it, read the book, and you'll be surprised at how fast things will come together. Indeed, I think you'll find programming to be a truly enjoyable pastime.

In this chapter, you will learn about

❑   Downloading Visual Studio .NET's C# Express

❑   Installing C# Express

❑   Testing C# Express to ensure it was installed correctly

With that in mind, let's get started.

A Short History of Object-Oriented Programming (OOP)

Many people believe that OOP is a product of the 1980s and the work done by Bjarne Stroustrup in moving the C language into the object-oriented world by creating the C++ language. Actually, SIMULA 1 (1962) and Simula 67 (1967) are the two earliest object-oriented languages. The work on the Simula languages was done by Ole-John Dahl and Kristen Nygaard at the Norwegian Computing Center in Oslo, Norway. While most of the advantages of OOP were available in the earlier Simula languages, it wasn't until C++ became entrenched in the 1990s that OOP began to flourish.

C was the parent language of C++ and it was often said that C was powerful enough to shoot yourself in the foot multiple times. C++, on the other hand, not only was powerful enough to shoot yourself in the foot, but you could blow your entire leg off without too much difficulty. Most programmers admit that C++ is a very powerful language and it is still in widespread use today. However, with that power comes a lot of complexity. Language developers wanted a simpler and perhaps less complex language for OOP development,

The next step in the development of OOP started in January of 1991 when James Gosling, Bill Joy, Patrick Naughton, Mike Sheradin, and several others met in Aspen, Colorado, to discuss ideas for the Stealth Project. The group wanted to develop intelligent electronic devices capable of being centrally controlled and programmed from a handheld device. They decided that OOP was the right direction to go with the development language, but felt that C++ was not up to the job. The result was the Oak programming language (named after an oak tree outside Gosling's window), which eventually morphed into the Java programming language. (Oak had to be renamed because the team discovered that a language by that name already existed.)

Java quickly grew in popularity, spurred by the growth of the World Wide Web. In both cases this rapid growth was in part due to the fact that the "guts" necessary to run Java programs on the Web quickly became an integral part of various web browsers. With the improved Web functionality augmented by Java, the Web hit light speed.

To many programmers, C# is Microsoft's answer to Java. Some would even say that C# is the result of Microsoft's stubbornness in refusing to promote a language it did not develop. That sentiment is a bit too harsh. Microsoft had good reasons for developing C#, not the least of which was that it wanted what are known as type-safe programs that run in a managed environment. You're not ready to appreciate exactly what that means right now, but it will become clear as you learn C#.

Suffice it to say that C# provides you with a robust object-oriented programming language and an impressive set of tools to tackle almost any programming task. Whether you wish to develop desktop, distributed, web, or mobile applications, C# can handle the task.

As you become familiar with C#, you will appreciate its relatively few keywords, its crisp syntax, and its easy-to-use development environment. You'll discover that pieces of programs you write in C# can be reused in other programs. Finally, you might appreciate the fact that there are many job opportunities for programmers who know C#. (In fact, in the writer's locality as this text is being written, there are more job openings for C# programmers than in any other language.)

Installing C#

If you have already purchased and installed Visual Studio 2008 and C#, you can skip this section. If you haven't installed C#, this section tells you how to download and install the C# Express version of Visual Studio. C# Express is a modified version of C# that is available from Microsoft at no charge. While the Express version of C# is missing some features found in the commercial version of Visual Studio, you should be able to compile and run all the sample programs in this book using C# Express. Once you are convinced that you should do all your development work in C# (and you will be), you can purchase the full version of Visual Studio.

Downloading C# Express

At the time that this book is being written, you can go to: `http://msdn2.microsoft.com/en-us/ express/future/bb421473.aspx` to download C# Express. The web page looks similar to what is shown in Figure 1-1. As you can see if you look closely at the figure, the book was written using Visual C# Express Edition Beta 2. (By the time you read this book, it is quite likely that the "Beta 2" part of the title will have changed.) Now click the IMG file link to download the file.

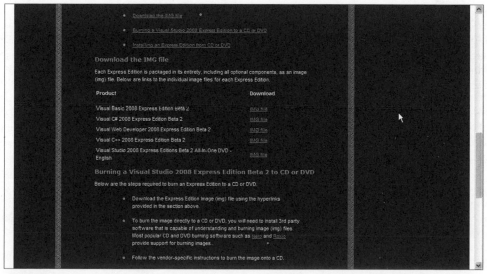

Figure 1-1

Depending upon the speed of your Internet connection, the file should be saved on your system within a few minutes.

Installing C# Express

After the download completes, click the executable file that was supplied (the file was named `vcssetup.exe` when I installed it, but it could change). You should see a screen similar to that shown in Figure 1-2, the C# Express Edition installation screen.

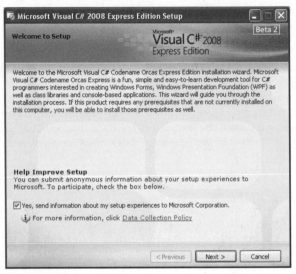

Figure 1-2

Selecting the Installation Options

Click the Next button to proceed to the next phase of the installation. In short order you will see a screen similar to the one in Figure 1-3, showing Visual C# Expression Edition installation options. This screen presents a number of installation options from which to pick. Unless you have some disk space limitations, I suggest that you install all the components in the list. Note that the file sizes mentioned are compressed file sizes. When those files are expanded, their disk space footprint is substantially larger. (Figure 1-3 suggests that a little over 76MB is the download file size. However, just before you press the Install button you can see the actual download file size compared to the expanded file size. When I installed C# Express, I was informed that the download file size was 135MB and the expanded disk storage requirement was 1.2GB.)

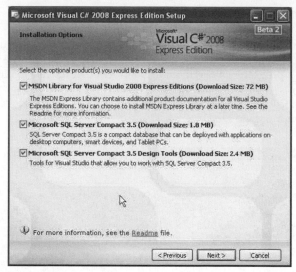

Figure 1-3

Microsoft SQL Server and its associated tools are also useful, especially if you plan to do any web development in the future. Unless you have some severe disk space constraints, you should install all the components. You can always uninstall components later if you need to.

Once you've decided on which components you wish to install, click the Next button and go fix yourself a sandwich . . . it's going to take a while for things to get installed.

> While I was working through the installation process, the install software sensed that some of the Windows software on my system was outdated. I was asked if I wanted to install the updates and patches that had come out since I last updated my system. Because the list also included several patches to Visual Studio, I said yes. It took almost two hours to download and update my software. However, when the updates were finished, the C# Express installer picked up right where it had left off and the installation continued without a hitch. While it does take some time, you should update your software if the installer offers you that option.

Eventually, the installation process ends . . . honest! If you updated your system software as part of the installation process, the installer will ask you at some point if you wish to restart your computer. Answer yes if you are asked. After the system restarts and the software has been installed, you should see a new icon on your desktop labeled Microsoft Visual C# 2008 Express Edition. You should be able to double-click the new icon and launch C# Express.

A Test Program Using C# Express

While things may appear to have been installed properly, you can't be certain until you actually write a program and try to run it. That's the purpose of this section of the chapter. The program is about as simple as we can make a program while remaining confident that the installation was successful.

After you double-click the C# Express icon on your desktop, you should see a C# Express startup screen similar to the one shown in Figure 1-4.

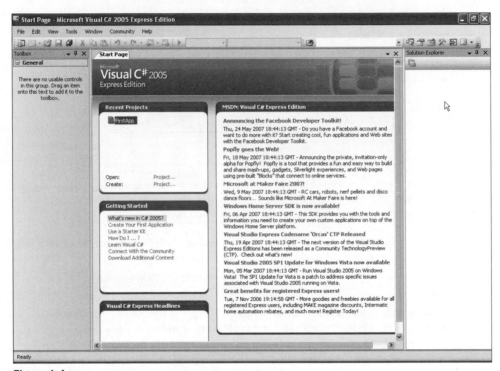

Figure 1-4

Creating a Project

Move the cursor to the upper left-hand side of the screen and select the File menu option from the main program menu bar. Your screen should look like what is shown in Figure 1-5.

Select New Project from the menu. Your program screen changes as shown in Figure 1-6.

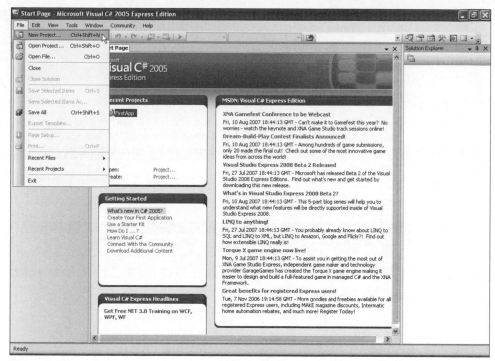

Figure 1-5

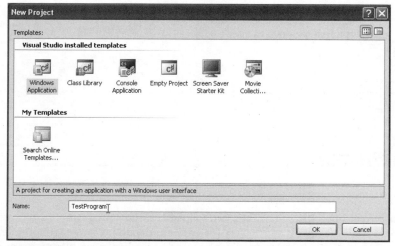

Figure 1-6

In Figure 1-6 you are given a number of predefined project templates from which to choose. These templates define the types of programs that you can develop with C#. When you select one of the templates, Visual Studio creates that type of project for you as well as writing some *stub code* for you.

Stub codes are predefined pieces of code that Visual Studio writes for you as a background process. From the templates shown in Figure 1-6, select the Windows Application template. You should also type in the name you wish the program to have. I have typed in `TestProgram` for our example. Click OK after you've entered the program name you wish to use.

The C# Integrated Development Environment

You should now see something like Figure 1-7 on your screen. Figure 1-7 shows you where you'll be spending a lot of your programming time as you read this book. It's called the *Integrated Development Environment*, or *IDE*, because virtually every programming tool you need to write C# programs is available to you there.

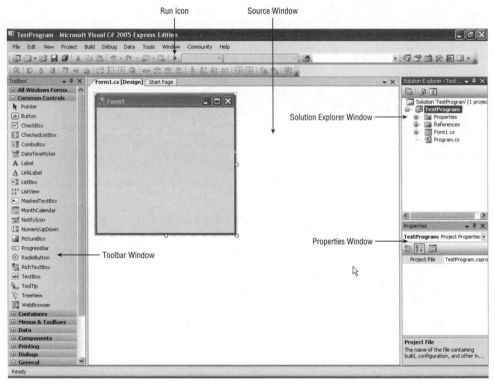

Figure 1-7

Back in the Dark Ages of programming, you had to load and run a programming editor to write the program's source code. Next, you had to close the editor and load the language compiler program to check the program's statements for errors. Then you had to load an assembler program to convert the source code to assembly language. Finally, you had to load and run a linker program to combine all the elements of your program into an executable program. The Visual Studio IDE provides all of these functions within a single program. This makes it much easier to write and test the programs you create.

The Major IDE Windows

The IDE shown in Figure 1-7 divides the screen into three *windows*. The left window shows the Visual Studio Toolbox, which, by default, shows some of the objects Visual Studio makes available to you. If you look closely you can see that the Toolbox presents a smorgasbord of objects you can use in your programs, including textboxes, labels, buttons, and other controls you will find useful as you develop your programs.

The middle window is referred to as the Source window and currently shows an unadorned Visual Studio form object. As presented in Figure 1-7, the form has no other objects placed on it . . . yet. That is, you haven't added any other objects (such as textboxes or buttons) from the Toolbox onto the form. You will change this later in this chapter.

The right side of the IDE currently shows two subwindows. The subwindow on top shows the Solution Explorer. Simply stated, the Solution Explorer shows the current development state of your project. It shows the forms the program has and its references, plus other information that we'll discuss in later chapters.

Below the Solution Explorer window is the Properties window. The purpose of the Properties window is to show you the properties associated with the object currently in focus in the Source window. If you look closely at the form in the Source window in Figure 1-7, you'll notice that it has a couple of small white boxes along its edge. These are called *sizing boxes* and their purpose is to enable you to alter the size of the objects to which they are attached. However, the sizing boxes also show which object in the Source window currently has the attention, or *focus*, of Visual Studio. Whatever object has the focus in the Source window is also the object that the Properties window displays. In Figure 1-7 the properties shown in the Properties window apply to the form shown in the Source window. Visual Studio always maintains this relationship between the object in focus in the Source window and the information displayed in the Properties window.

Using the Source Code Window

If you click Form1.cs in the Solution Explorer window, you can move to the Solution Explorer menu bar and click the source code icon to view the code that Visual Studio has written for you thus far. Figure 1-8 shows you the location of the source code icon in the Solution Explorer window. (When you hover the cursor over the source code icon a small textbox opens and displays the words "View Code," as shown in Figure 1-8.)

Figure 1-8

The code associated with clicking the source code icon shown in Figure 1-8 is shown in Figure 1-9. When you click the source code icon, notice that another tab is added at the top of the Source window. One tab has form1.cs (Design) on it, while the other tab has form1.cs. The first tab is for the view of the form in the design mode. (The design mode is shown in Figure 1-7.) The second tab is the source code mode and shows you the code for the program under development. Even though you haven't written any code yourself, Visual Studio has already written some for you behind your back! You can see the TestProgram C# source code in Figure 1-9.

```
using System;
using System.Collections.Generic;
using System.ComponentModel;
using System.Data;
using System.Drawing;
using System.Text;
using System.Windows.Forms;

namespace TestProgram
{
    public partial class Form1 : Form
    {
        public Form1()
        {
            InitializeComponent();
        }
    }
}
```

Figure 1-9

It's not necessary that you understand the code shown in Figure 1-9 at this time. All you're trying to do at this point is write a very short program to see if the installation was done correctly. However, you will be spending a lot of time in the source code window as you write your own programs.

Adding an Object to a Windows Form

A form with nothing on it isn't terribly interesting. Let's change the form so that, when the program runs, it displays the message, "My first program." You need to add a label to the form object shown in the Source window in Figure 1-7 to hold your program message. There are two ways to add a label object to a form. First, as shown in Figure 1-10, you can click the label object in the Toolbox and, while holding the left mouse button down, drag the label over to the form and release the mouse button. Second, you can simply double-click the label object in the Toolbox. The mouse double-click causes Visual Studio to place a label object near the upper left-hand corner of the form shown in the Source window.

You can click the label in the Source window while holding the left mouse button down and drag the label to wherever you want it to appear on the form object. When you have positioned the label object where you want it on the form, simply release the mouse button.

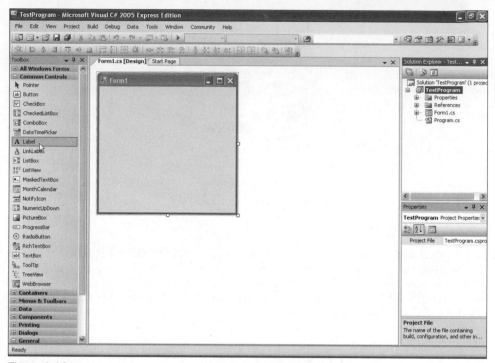

Figure 1-10

Changing the Text of a Label Object

After you position the label object on the form, you can set the text for the label. One of the things that Visual Studio does automatically is size the label to be just big enough to accommodate the label's text. Given the default font size used by Visual Studio, the default height for a label is 13 pixels. (A *pixel* is one dot, or point of light, on the screen of your display device.) If you change the font size of the label object, the height of the label is automatically adjusted for you.

Actually, I am not a big fan of automatic sizing of labels. For that reason, I turn off the auto-sizing feature. To turn off auto-sizing, change the AutoSize property from True, as shown in Figure 1-11, to False. You may have to scroll down in the Property window to be able to see the AutoSize property displayed in the Properties window. Click the down arrow at the right end of the textbox to display the choices you have for the property. In this case you can choose only True or False. Select False. The auto-sizing of the label object is now turned off.

Figure 1-11

After you set `AutoSize` to `False`, you can resize the label object in the Source window by clicking the white sizing boxes that appear on the ends and corners of the label object. In Figure 1-12, I have increased the width of the label by clicking the middle sizing box on the right edge of the label object and dragging the edge to the right until I got the desired size. I then released the left mouse button to end up with the label object shown in Figure 1-12.

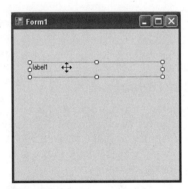

Figure 1-12

After you have set the size of the label object, you can change the text property of the label object to whatever you want to appear in the label. In your example, you want the text "My first program." At the present time, the text property of the label object is `label1` . . . not what you want. Scroll the contents of the Property window down to the `Text` property for the label object and change it to `My first program` and press the Enter key. Changing the `Text` property for the label object is shown in Figure 1-13. Notice how the first line below the Property window's title bar shows the name of the object currently in focus in the Source window (`label1` in Figure 1-13).

Figure 1-13

(Figure 1-13 is only large enough to show the last word typed into the Text property in the Property window. When you look at the label in the Source window, all three words appear in the label object.)

By default, the text of a label object is positioned so it appears in the upper left-hand corner of the label. If AutoSize is set to True, you can't position the text with the label object; it's set for you automatically. However, because you turned off auto-sizing, you can position the text within the label wherever you wish. Figure 1-14 shows how to do this using the TextAlign property. If you look closely at Figure 1-14, you can see that TextAlign is currently set to TopLeft. There are nine positions where you can place the text in a label that you can resize. You want to right-justify your text in the center of the label object. If you look where the cursor is positioned in Figure 1-14, clicking that box right-justifies the text in the label object.

Figure 1-14

After you have positioned the text within the label at the right place, the form should look like what is shown in Figure 1-15. Notice how the text in the label object is now centered.

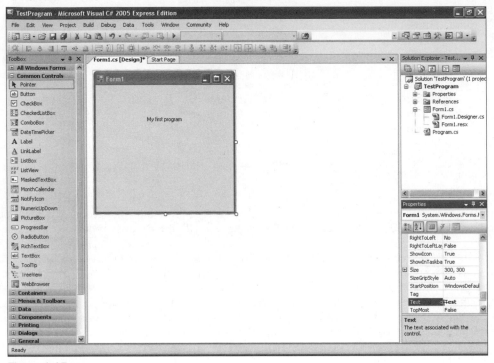

Figure 1-15

Running the Program

This is all that you want to do at the present time to test your C# installation. If you can run the program at this point, it's pretty certain that you have installed C# correctly. There are two simple ways to run a program. The easiest is to press the F5 key. If you do that, the program should appear on the screen in a few moments with our message centered in the label object.

The second way is to click the Run Program icon. If you look carefully at Figure 1-15, right below the Window menu option near the top of the form you can see a small triangle. (On your screen, it appears green. The Run icon is also labeled in Figure 1-7.) Click that green triangle and the program begins execution.

If your program does not run correctly and you're not getting an error message from within Visual Studio, go back to the start of the installation process and check to make sure you followed each step correctly. Likewise, if you are getting an error message from Visual Studio, you performed some step in the coding process incorrectly. Just go back to the beginning of the "A Test Program Using C# Express" section of this chapter and check each step to make sure you followed the correct sequence.

Summary

In this chapter you learned how object-oriented programming got its start over four decades ago. This chapter also showed you how to download and install Visual Studio's C# Express Edition. Finally, you wrote a simple program to test the installation to make sure it was done correctly. So, now what?

You could immediately proceed to the next chapter and start reading. Not a good idea. Now that you have a simple program up and running, this is the perfect time to experiment a little. For example, your program doesn't have any text in the program's title bar. Surely C# provides a property that enables you to change the title bar. (Hint: It does provide such a property!) Play around with some of the other properties and see what they do. For example, change the foreground property and see what happens. Each chapter in this book has a set of exercises at the end of the chapter that you should do before reading the next chapter. I realize that you're anxious to move on to the next chapter, but resist the temptation and do the exercises. They'll help crystallize what you've learned in the current chapter and better prepare you for the content of the next chapter. You can find the solutions in Appendix A.

Programming should be fun, and some of that fun comes from discovering what happens if you change this to that. If you see smoke coming out of your computer, don't make that change again. (Just kidding . . . you can't hurt your computer if you make an incorrect change to a property.) Experiment and have fun!

Understanding Objects

As you learned in Chapter 1, programming with objects has been around for over four decades. However, it's only in the last 15 years or so that object-oriented programming has become the norm rather than the exception. In this chapter I present a simple example of how objects might be used in an everyday situation. You then expand on the concepts presented in that example to an actual program you build using Visual Studio .NET and the objects it provides for you.

In this chapter, you will learn:

- ❑ What an object is
- ❑ What the term *state* means with respect to objects
- ❑ What a class is
- ❑ What it means to instantiate an object
- ❑ What properties are
- ❑ What methods are
- ❑ How to use some of the objects provided by Visual Studio .NET

Understanding Objects

Suppose you are the personnel manager for a company and you need to hire someone to fill an important position. After sifting through dozens of résumés, you select one candidate to call for a face-to-face interview at your company offices. You call her (let's say her name is Issy) on the phone and chat for a few minutes and confirm that she appears to be the right person for the job. You (we'll pretend your name is Jack) make arrangements for Issy to fly to your location, stating that you will meet her at the airport. Figure 2-1 shows arranging a job interview.

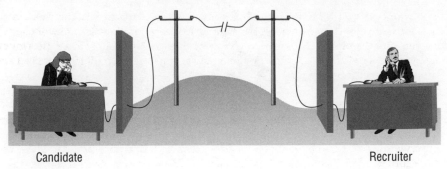

Candidate   Recruiter

Figure 2-1

However, since the two of you have never met before, you start asking a few questions so you can recognize each other at the airport. Issy says she's short with blonde hair and that she will be wearing a black business suit and carrying a tan leather briefcase. You then describe yourself as six feet tall with brown hair and say that you'll be wearing a gray suit. You then set a date and time for the flight and everything's ready for the interview.

Everyday Use of Objects

Perhaps without realizing it, both of you used *objects* in the course of your conversation. (An object is just a simplification of something that you wish to use in your program. In this example, you are creating a list of properties that will be used to describe a person object.) First, you implicitly created a person class during the phone call. A *class* is a template used to describe an object. As such, a class is an abstraction or simplification of some object you observe in the real world. You can break a class down into two basic components: 1. those *properties* that describe the object, and 2. those *methods*, or actions, that you wish to associate with the object.

Class Properties

The class properties are the data that you want to record and associate with an object. If you wanted to create a class person object, a list of properties might include those shown in Table 2-1.

Table 2-1: clsPerson Properties

name
gender
height
build
hairColor
eyeColor
clothing
accessories

It's important to notice that, prior to the phone conversation, the properties list for the class person named Issy is virtually empty. In fact, all you were able to fill in from her résumé were her name and gender. However, after the phone conversation you were able to fill in almost all of the properties for the class person object named Issy. (You might scare her away if you tried to fill in the Build and eyeColor properties over the phone.)

While you were filling in a class person object named Issy, she was doing the same thing for a class person object named Jack. Prior to the phone call, the class person object Issy created to be associated with the name Jack may have been totally empty, because Issy had no idea who might be calling her about a job interview. However, the dialog on the phone enabled each party to fill in at least some of the property values for the other. From Issy's point of view, her class person object went from a totally nondescript object to (at least) a partially identifiable object after the phone call was completed. By changing the values of the class properties, you are able to change the state of the object. The *state of an object* is determined by the values of the properties used to describe the object. In our example, the properties used to describe the state of a class person object are those shown in Table 2-1.

While people don't change their names very often, it happens occasionally. Likewise, people do gain and lose weight, dye their hair, wear tinted contacts, change clothes, and alter their accessories. If any of these property values change, the state of the object also changes. Just keep in mind that anytime the value of a property changes, the state of the object — by definition — also changes.

Class Methods

Just as there are property values that define the state of an object, there are usually class methods that act on the properties. For a class person object, you would want that object to be able to talk, wave his or her arms, walk, change clothes, and so forth. In short, the *class methods* determine the behaviors the object is capable of performing. Methods are used to describe whatever actions you wish to associate with the object. Methods often are used to manipulate the data contained within the object.

We can depict the phone conversation between Issy and Jack as objects of the person class as shown in Figure 2-2.

Often, class methods are used to take one or more property values, process the data those properties contain, and create a new piece of data as a byproduct of the method's process. For example, you might create an invoice object that has priceEach and quantityOrdered (among others) as properties of an Invoice class. You might then create a method named salesTaxDue() as a class method that would compute the sales tax due for the invoice. In fact, you might have another Invoice property named salesTax that gets filled in automatically as part of the code contained in the method named salesTaxDue().

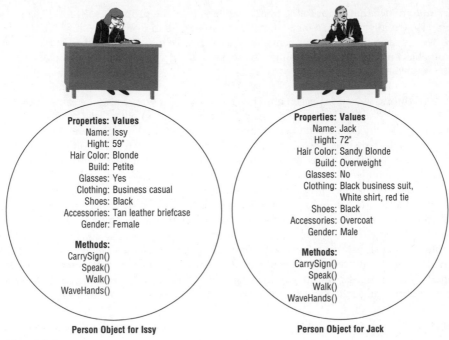

Properties: Values
Name: Issy
Hight: 59"
Hair Color: Blonde
Build: Petite
Glasses: Yes
Clothing: Business casual
Shoes: Black
Accessories: Tan leather briefcase
Gender: Female

Methods:
CarrySign()
Speak()
Walk()
WaveHands()

Person Object for Issy

Properties: Values
Name: Jack
Hight: 72"
Hair Color: Sandy Blonde
Build: Overweight
Glasses: No
Clothing: Black business suit,
White shirt, red tie
Shoes: Black
Accessories: Overcoat
Gender: Male

Methods:
CarrySign()
Speak()
Walk()
WaveHands()

Person Object for Jack

Figure 2-2

If you think about it, a class property may be viewed as a noun: a person, place, or thing. Class methods, on the other hand, often behave like verbs, denoting some kind of action to be taken on the data.

How Many Properties, How Many Methods?

One question that you must grapple with as a programmer is how many properties and methods you should have in a class. For example, in our class person object, you could also include a photograph of the person, fingerprints, a retinal scan, blood type, DNA sample, dental records, plus hundreds of other things that may be part and parcel of a person object. Likewise, you can create methods to simulate talking, running, writing, walking, digestion, elimination, sleeping, dreaming, and a bunch of other actions humans are capable of doing. So where do you stop? What is the proper number of properties and methods?

Classes Are Simplifications of Objects

Keep in mind that for every property and method you add, you are going to have to write program code to implement that property or method. As a general rule, the less code a program has, the fewer things there are to go wrong. From a programmer's perspective, writing less code is a good thing, provided the code accomplishes the task at hand. In other words, when you design a class, you need to strike a balance between minimizing the code you write and fulfilling the design goals for the class.

Simply stated, the proper number of properties and methods in a class is the minimal number of properties and methods that gets the job done. The number of properties and methods in a person class the FBI needs to find criminals is going to be vastly different from the number of properties and methods in the person class you might create to write an address book to keep track of your friends. You'll also find that if you omit unnecessary details in a class, there's a greater likelihood that you can reuse that same class code in some other project. This *code reuse* is one of the main advantages of object-oriented programming. The more generic the object is, the easier it is to reuse the object. In a sense, therefore, you might want to define your classes as the minimal abstraction necessary to describe an object in a way that fulfills your needs.

Always keep in mind that if there is a simple way and a complex way to accomplish the same goal, simple is almost always the best choice. Some programmers get a kick out of writing really clever code that no one else can understand. That's probably okay, as long as no one else has to work with their code. In a commercial setting, however, clever, obfuscated code is rarely a good thing. Given alternatives, stick with the code that is easily understood.

What Do I Do After I've Defined a Class?

As mentioned earlier, a class is a template for an object. In that sense, a class is like a cookie cutter that enables you to shape specific cookie objects. By this release of Visual Studio, Microsoft has buried within the .NET Framework about 4,000 available classes. This means you have about 4,000 cookie cutters already hanging on the wall ready for you to use. (We'll use some of these classes later in this chapter.) Part of your job as a fledgling programmer is to learn about those classes that already exist. After all, there's no reason for you to reinvent the wheel.

Visual Studio as an IDE

As pointed out in Chapter 1, Visual Studio is an IDE that incorporates numerous programming tools. Prior to the advent of IDEs, programmers had separate programs for writing the course code (an editor), compiling the program (a compiler), assembling the program (an assembler), and combining the program into an executable program (a linker). With an IDE, all of these disparate functions are combined into a single package.

A huge part of the functionality of Visual Studio comes from the .NET Framework, including all those cookie cutters. As you write your code, components within the IDE combine your code with elements from the .NET Framework and produce Microsoft Intermediate Language (MSIL) code. It is this MSIL code, passed through the Common Language Runtime (CLR) component of Visual Studio, that actually gets your program to run.

Rather than make the distinction between each of the "pieces" that comprise Visual Studio when some specific function is performed, you simply say something like: "Visual Studio takes your code and" . . . whatever. If a situation arises where the distinction is important, use the proper nomenclature. For now, just remember that, as an IDE, Visual Studio is composed of a lot of different components acting in concert to make your life easier.

Most of the time you must write some of your own classes in addition to those provided for you by Visual Studio. This means that, after you are finished writing your class, you now have 4,001 cookie cutters hanging on the wall, each one of which is capable of creating an object of that class's type. But note: Just because you have defined a class (or a cookie cutter) does not necessarily mean you have an object (or a cookie). As I said before, a class is just a template for the object. Just as a cookie cutter works to cut specific shapes out of cookie dough, a class is used to carve out chunks of memory that are used to hold objects of that class. Until you've used the class template to actually carve out an object, that object does not yet exist.

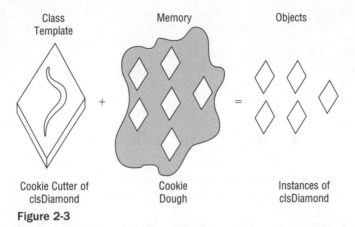

Figure 2-3

The relationship between a class and the objects you can instantiate from that class is depicted in Figure 2-3. The class is depicted as a diamond-shaped cookie cutter. I've named the class `clsDiamond`. You can think of the properties of `clsDiamond` as holding the values that determine the exact shape of the cookie cutter. In other words, the state of the properties make the class look like a diamond rather than some other shape (e.g., a spade). To get an object of the class, you must press the cookie cutter (class template) into the cookie dough (computer memory) in order to get an actual cookie (object). An object is an *instance* of a class. An object, therefore, is something that you can actually use in a program. Just as you can't eat a cookie cutter, you can't directly use a class. You must use the class to instantiate an object of the class in memory before you can use it in your program.

Naming Objects

Throughout this text, I have adopted a convention under which you prefix the name of certain objects with a specific combination of letters. For example, use `cls` before class names, `txt` before the names of textbox objects, `btn` before button objects, and so on. You will discover other examples as you read this text. This convention is a form of what is called Hungarian notation, but not its "pure" form. At the extreme, Hungarian notation prefixed every data item with its data type, such as `iHatSize` for an integer variable, `cLetter` for a character variable, `fWage` for a floating-point variable, `objMyData` for a data object, plus many other similar variations. This notation has lost followers simply because what it brought to the table in terms of code clarity wasn't worth the effort. So why do I continue to use a modified version of Hungarian notation?

One reason is that I feel our version is definitely worth the effort. The major reason is that the prefixes reinforce the object type being used in the program. That is, at a glance you can see that `txtName` is a textbox object and that it's different from `lblName`, which is a label object.

A second reason is the way Visual Studio looks at your program data as you type in program code. For example, if you have three textboxes in your program, all prefixed with `txt`, Visual Studio knows about these objects and can open up a small "look-ahead" window the instant it sees you type in that prefix. You can then select the appropriate textbox object in the window, press the Tab key, and Visual Studio fills in the rest of the object's name for you. If you didn't prefix the textbox names with `txt` and you couldn't recall anything about the object (even its name) other than it's a textbox object, the names would be scattered throughout the look-ahead window, thus making the look-ahead feature less useful.

Because I find this look-ahead feature a real time-saver, I tend to use prefixes for objects in our program examples. If you don't feel it's worth the effort, feel free to use your own style.

Instantiating an Object of a Class

To help explain what is taking place with these statements, consider the simplified memory map of your computer system shown in Figure 2-4.

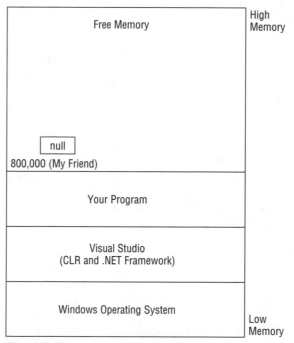

Figure 2-4

Now consider the following program statement:

```
clsPerson myFriend;
```

Simply stated, this statement says: "Go to the cookie cutter wall and look for a cookie cutter named clsPerson. When you've found it, take it down from the wall and label it myFriend." The end result is that .NET asks the Windows operating system for four bytes of memory where it can store the variable named myFriend. Assume that the Windows Memory Manager finds four bytes of free storage at memory address 800,000. For the moment, you haven't done anything with the memory at this address, so its current value is null. (The word null means the variable has nothing useful currently stored in it.)

What you have at this point is a cookie cutter named myFriend just waiting around at memory address 800,000 for something useful to happen. Things start to happen with the next program statement:

```
myFriend = new clsPerson();
```

Words that have special meaning in a programming language are called *keywords*. The new keyword in C# means that you want to set aside enough memory to hold a clsPerson object. Let's further assume that it takes 2,000 bytes of memory to hold the data associated with a clsPerson object. (.NET figures out how many bytes it needs for an object by examining the program code of the class.) If you verbalize what is happening with this programming statement, you might say: "Hey, Windows! It's me . . . Visual Studio. My programmer wants to create a clsPerson object. Do you have 2,000 bytes of free memory available for such an object?" The Windows Memory Manager then looks through its table of available memory and probably finds 2,000 bytes of free memory somewhere in the system. Assume the 2,000-byte memory block starts at address 900,000. The Windows Memory Manager then sends a message back to Visual Studio and says: "Hey, VS! It's me . . . the Windows Memory Manager. I found 2,000 bytes of free memory at address 900,000." Visual Studio says "Thanks," and proceeds to set things up to use the clsPerson object named myFriend.

When Visual studio is finished with the statement, the memory map now looks like the one shown in Figure 2-5.

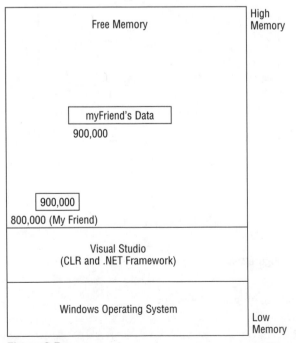

Figure 2-5

Notice what's happened. The value associated with the variable myFriend has changed from null to that of the memory address where the data associated with myFriend is stored. You have now carved out a clsPerson object that you can access via the variable named myFriend. The purpose of the myFriend variable is to tell us where to find the data associated with the myFriend object. The correct programming term is that you have *instantiated* a clsPerson object referenced by the variable myFriend. An instantiated object is an object that you can use in your program.

Repeating our two programming statements (I'll explain the purpose of the slashes in the statements below in Chapter 4):

```
clsPerson myFriend;          // Grab a specific cookie cutter from the wall
                             // and name it myFriend
myFriend = new clsPerson();// Use the cookie cutter to make a clsPerson
                             // cookie and refer to it as myFriend
```

The first statement means that you intend to create an object of clsPerson and refer to that object using the variable named myFriend. The second statement says you carried through with your intent and instantiated an object of a clsPerson type and associated it with myFriend. You reference the object's data for the remainder of the program using the variable named myFriend. Using our cookie cutter analogy, the cookie cutter (that is, the reference) is found at memory address 800,000, but the cookie itself (that is, the object's data) is found at memory address 900,000.

You can combine the two statements into a single statement if you wish:

```
clsPerson myFriend = new clsPerson();
```

The interpretation is exactly as before. You have simply collapsed the two statements into one. Because programmers prefer less code to more code, you will see the abbreviated form used more often.

I Have an Object . . . Now What?

You now have instantiated an object of the clsPerson type. The obvious question is: "So what?" At the present time, the object named myFriend is fairly nondescript. None of the information presented in Table 2-1 has been filled in for the myFriend object. What you need to do is change the faceless myFriend object into one that has some meaningful information in it. You can change the object by changing the information contained in the properties defined within it. From Table 2-1, you might do the following:

```
myFriend.Name = "Issy";
myFriend.Gender = "F";
myFriend.Height = 59;
myFriend.Build = "Petite";
myFriend.hairColor = "Blonde";
myFriend.eyeColor = "Blue";
myFriend.Clothing = "Business casual";
myFriend.Accessories = "Tan leather briefcase";
```

Notice what these statements do. They change the faceless myFriend object into one that gives you some impression of what this particular clsPerson object looks like. In these statements, the equals sign (=) is called the *assignment operator*. The assignment operator takes the information on the right side of the assignment operator and copies that information into the variable on the left side of the assignment operator. What this means is that, somewhere near memory address 900,000, the Name property has been changed from null to Issy. Similar changes have occurred for the other myFriend properties.

In programming terms, the assignment statements change the *state* of the object from a faceless person to an attractive female named Issy.

Object Syntax

It is important to note the syntax associated with changing the state of an object. The *syntax* of a programming language refers to the rules governing the use of the language. The general syntax for using the property of an object is as follows:

```
objectName.Property
```

Note the period, or dot, between `objectName` and `Property`. The period that appears between the object name and the property (or method) name is called the *dot operator* in C#. If you think of an object as a steel shell surrounding the properties inside the object, the dot operator is the key that unlocks the object's door and lets you inside the object to gain access to the object's properties and methods. In the statement —

```
myFriend.Name = "Issy";
```

— the computer processes the statement from right to left. You might verbalize the process implied by the statement as the following sequence of steps:

1. Place the word Issy in a wheelbarrow.
2. Go to the object named myFriend.
3. Insert your key (the dot operator) into the door of the shell.
4. Open the door of the shell.
5. Guide your wheelbarrow over to the Name property.
6. Dump the letters Issy into the Name property.

You can visualize these steps as shown in Figure 2-6.

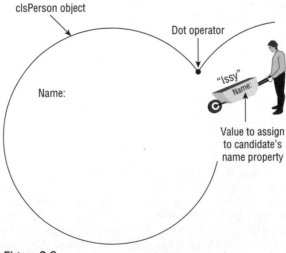

Figure 2-6

Now that you've followed these steps, the object associated with the myFriend variable has a name assigned to it. This also means that the state of the myFriend object has changed from an object with no name to one with the name Issy.

The object may be used "in the opposite direction," too. For example, suppose you have assigned Issy's name to the myFriend object. Later in the program you want to display her name in a textbox object on a form. If the textbox object is named txtName, you could write:

```
txtName.Text = myFriend.Name;
```

Again, because the assignment statement is processed from right to left, the code causes the program to do the following:

1. Go to the myFriend object.
2. Insert the key (the dot operator) into the steel shell.
3. Open the door of the myFriend object.
4. Push an empty wheelbarrow over to the Name property of myFriend.
5. Make a copy of the bytes stored in that property (that is, Issy).
6. Place the copy into the wheelbarrow.
7. Come out of the object's shell (the door closes automatically!).
8. Push the wheelbarrow over to the textbox object named txtName.
9. Insert the key (the dot operator) into the txtName's shell.
10. Open txtName's door in its shell.
11. Push the wheelbarrow over to the Text property of the txtName object.
12. Dump Issy into the Text property.

You can visualize these steps as shown in Figure 2-7.

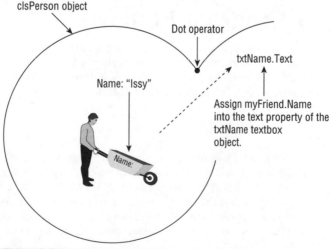

Figure 2-7

This sequence of steps illustrates two important concepts to remember:

❑   You *did not change* the state of the object associated with myFriend. You simply went inside the object, copied its contents, and left. Because you didn't alter the contents of any of the properties (data) of myFriend, its state remains unchanged.

❑   You *did change* the state of the txtName object. This is true because you went into the txtName object and assigned the copy of Issy's name to the Text property of the txtName object. Because the Text property's data changed, the state of the txtName object was changed.

You can make two generalizations from these observations:

❑   If an object's property appears on the right-hand side of the assignment operator (equals sign, =), you are simply reading the property of the object, not changing its state.

❑   If an object's property appears on the left-hand side of the assignment operator, you *are* changing the data of one of its properties and, therefore, changing that object's state.

While there are a few exceptions to these generalizations, they will serve you well most of the time.

Why Hide the Data Inside an Object?

In an oversimplified way, the discussion in this section describes how objects work and how properties, or the object's data, should be hidden inside an object. Why hide the properties? You hide them for the same reason that kings used to hide their daughters in the castle tower . . . to keep other people from messing around with them.

By encasing the properties (data) of the object inside a steel shell, you can restrict access to those properties by forcing everyone to have a proper key (the object's dot operator) to gain access to the properties. Stated differently, you bury the data inside an object in an attempt to protect the data from accidental changes by other parts of the program. The process of hiding data within an object is called *encapsulation*. Encapsulation is one of the cornerstones of OOP. I will have a lot more to say about encapsulation and the other elements of OOP in later chapters.

Developing a Program Plan

Let's put what you've learned thus far to use designing a program. Of necessity, we'll leave out some code that would make your little program more bulletproof simply because you haven't learned how to do that yet. (You will learn how to make programs more bulletproof soon enough.) The goal here is to show you how to start writing a program to solve a specific task.

Where to Start?

Without a doubt, the hardest thing for beginning programmers to figure out is where to begin writing a program. As a general rule, students start solving a program problem by dragging and dropping controls from the toolbox onto a form as the first step in writing a program. Wrong! Don't confuse movement with solutions. If you start dragging and dropping objects all over the place without a coherent plan, you're in for some unexpected disappointments. Inevitably, you'll end up backtracking and developing a plan of attack for the task at hand, so you may as well start out with a plan in the first place.

Indeed, to write good programs you must have a plan. Central to a programming plan is an algorithm. An *algorithm* is simply a step-by-step recipe, or plan, for how you want to solve the programming problem at hand. A good place to start a program plan is with the Five Program Steps.

The Five Program Steps

As a broad generalization, you can describe all programming problems in terms of five steps.

Step 1: Initialization

This step involves those things that are done before the user sees anything displayed on the screen. For example, some programs "remember" the last four or five files that you worked on with the program and tack those file names on to the end of the File menu. Microsoft Word, Excel, PowerPoint and other programs do this. Clearly, those programs must read that information from somewhere before the program can display the File menu on the screen. Likewise, a program might establish a network connection, initialize a printer, connect to a database, or do all kinds of other activities before the user sees anything on the screen. All of these activities are lumped under the initialization step.

Simply stated, the initialization step is responsible for establishing the environment in which the program is to be run. The activities of the initialization step take place before the user sees anything appear on the screen.

Step 2: Input

If you think about it, all programs take some kind of input into the program, process it in some way, and then display some variation of the data that was derived from the original inputs. This step, therefore, is concerned with getting those inputs into the program.

Most of the time you tend to think of program input as coming from the keyboard or mouse. However, input can come from many other input sources. Some examples are an engine sensor, bar-code reader, retinal scanner, network connection, fire or smoke alarm sensor, or a host of other input devices. The important aspect of the input step, however, is that data in some form is collected by the program.

It's always a good practice to validate the input data. Users do make mistakes when entering data, network connections sometimes do weird things, and other unexpected occurrences can make the data invalid. You will learn more about data validation in later chapters. For now, I have assumed a really bright user who never makes a typing mistake! (This assumption enables you to concentrate on the essence of the objects being used in the program.)

Step 3: Process

This is the step in which you take the program inputs and process them in some way. You might perform some kind of mathematical operation on them, or perhaps the inputs are the name and account number of a customer and this step reads a database to calculate a bill to be sent to the customer. In a jet aircraft, the inputs might be the current airspeed and GPS coordinates to calculate when the plane will touch down at a specific airport. In all cases, the process step involves taking the inputs, acting upon them, and producing some form of result or answer.

It is important to remember that often a variety of methods can be used to take the same inputs, process them, and produce the same answer. Just as you can find a variety of ways to fly from New York to

Los Angeles (such as nonstop, or through Chicago, or Denver, or Houston), the result's the same: You end up in L.A. Likewise, you can use different algorithms to take the same inputs into a program, process them differently, but generate the same results. For example, there are dozens of ways to sort data using a computer. However, as you shall see in subsequent chapters, some algorithms are more efficient than others. Always keep your mind open to ways to accomplish old tasks in new ways.

Step 4: Display

This step is responsible for displaying the results produced in the process step. Usually, this means showing the results on the display screen, but other options exist. Perhaps it means skipping the display screen and simply printing a bill and mailing it to a customer. Or perhaps the program is responsible for updating a customer record in a database. In fact, there are many programs that run themselves (called *batch programs*) and don't display anything on the screen or ask for any inputs from the user as they run. Instead, batch programs often start automatically at a predetermined time (perhaps at one a.m. when no one else is using the system), read the input information from some input source (like a database), and generate reports based on the input information.

The display step doesn't always result in your "seeing" a result displayed on a screen. Sometimes the result of the program is passed on to another process, or a database, or even a web site. The key is that you have used the inputs to produce something new and you want to "see," "use," or "save" that new result. However, for most of the programs you write while using this book, the display step does show some information to the user via the display device.

Step 5: Termination

Termination doesn't necessarily mean that you simply end the program. It also means "cleaning up" after the program has finished. For example, if the initialization step reads the four latest files used in the program and appends them to the File menu, this step needs to update those file names to reflect what the user has done during the current session of the program. If the initialization step sets up a printer or database connection, this step should close that connection.

Quite often, whatever is done in the initialization step is undone in the termination step. Finally, the termination step should provide a graceful exit from the program, even if an error occurred while the program was running.

Creating a Simple Application Using Objects

Now let's use the five program steps you just learned to write a simple program. The goal of the program is to gather address information about the user and then simply redisplay that information as if it were a mailing label. For the time being you won't actually do anything with the information, but after you get a little more C# programming under your belt, you could use this program as an input process for some larger programming task, like creating a customer account or writing your own personal mailing list. The primary objective here, however, is to get you familiar with using a few of the objects that are provided to you as part of Visual Studio and .NET.

Using the Program Steps to Create a Program Plan

Your first task is to develop a plan for solving the task at hand. A good place to start the plan is with the five program steps presented earlier.

Step 1: Initialization

This is a simple program and you don't really have any fancy initialization to do. Any necessary initialization tasks are done automatically for you by Visual Studio. We'll take a look at the Visual Studio's background handiwork a little later.

Step 2: Input

This is the step where you must ask yourself, "What information do I need to solve the programming task at hand?" Because you want to arrange user information the way a mailing label does, you need to know the user's:

1. Name
2. Street address
3. City
4. State
5. Zip (or postal) code

You could write the program and "hard-code" values in for each piece of data into the program. When you *hard-code* a value into a program, it means that you make that value a permanent part of the program itself. If you hard-code the data for this program, you write program code that embeds the user's name and address as data directly into the program. However, hard-coding values directly into a program makes the program less flexible than it might otherwise be. For example, each time you wanted information about a new user, you'd need to write new data values into the program's code before you could display the information. Not good.

A more flexible approach is to ask the user to enter his information while the program is running and to display the information as a mailing label when he is finished. After he has entered his information, you can arrange the data for display on the screen. The easiest way to code this approach to the solution is to use label and textbox objects for each piece of information you wish to collect. When the user is satisfied that he has entered the requested information, he will click a button to display the information as a mailing label.

Designing a Program's User Interface

In this program, you decide to use labels and textboxes to collect the information from the user. The labels help to inform the user about the data you are requesting, and the textboxes provide a means for him to type in his responses. These labels and textboxes become part of the user interface of your program. A program's *user interface* simply refers to how the program interacts with the user running the program. In this program the user interface consists of labels, textboxes, and buttons arranged on a form.

Entire books have been written about how to design a good user interface. While I can't possibly do justice to the subject of user interface design, I can offer the following guidelines:

❑ Follow the KISS (Keep It Simple Stupid) Principle. What this means is that you should make the user interface as simple as possible yet still acquire the information you need. Resist the urge to add objects to a form if they don't contribute to the functionality of the program.

❑ Use familiar interfaces. For example, in this program you are asking the user for address information. Chances are good that the user has filled in a tear-out magazine subscription form or filled in a driver's license form that asks for address information. Try to model your interface in a way that the user might already be familiar with, or do your best to make an unfamiliar user interface easy to understand.

❑ The user interface should have a natural flow to it. In a Windows program, the Tab key is used to advance from one input field to the next. It wouldn't make much sense to have the user type in his name and, after he presses the Tab key, to jump to the Zip Code field, have him enter its value, and then jump back to the Address field. The flow would make more sense to the user if the program went from the Name field to the Address field to the City field to the State field, and so forth. Likewise, English-speaking users read from top left to bottom right, while Chinese readers progress from top right to bottom left. Therefore, even language and cultural factors can influence the flow of the user interface. Simply stated, the flow of a user interface should be intuitive and make sense to the user.

❑ Don't use the Gee-Whiz Factor. The Gee-Whiz Factor refers to any user interface change you might make that doesn't serve any purpose other than to get the user to say, "Gee whiz!" Beginning programmers often change the background color for labels and textboxes, change the font color from black to purple, and make other changes that add nothing useful to the interface other than to show that they know how to make them. The fact remains, however, that Microsoft has probably spend more money on research that tests the colors, shapes, and other default property values for objects than you or I will make in a lifetime. As a result, there are not many good reasons not to accept the results of that research.

Always keep in mind that goal of a user interface is to make it easy for the user to run your program. Try to make the user interface intuitive and simple from the user's point of view.

Step 3: Process

This is the step where you devise the algorithm that produces the desired result of the program. The desired result of this program simply is to display the user information in a mailing-label format. The input step provides you with the information you need via the user interface you designed. Therefore, to actually begin the process step you need to have a button (such as a Display button) so the program knows when the input data has been entered and it can begin to address the task at hand.

Microsoft Windows programs are event-driven. An *event-driven* program means that some agent (such as the user) must generate an event of some type in order for the program to perform the next program task. For example, in this program, if the user does not interact with the program in some way, the program will obediently sit there and wait until he does. In your program, the user must click the Display button to trigger the tasks associated with the process step.

The process step for this program is simply to arrange the information entered by the user in the form of an address label.

Step 4: Display

In this program, you simply display the user's name and address information.

Step 5: Termination

Because you didn't write any code to do anything tricky in the initialization step, you don't need to do anything in the termination step to clean up and gracefully end the program. Instead, you can simply have a button object (such as an Exit button) that the user can click to end the program.

Now you have a plan based upon our five program steps. All you need to do now is implement your plan.

Using C# to Implement Our Program Plan

Now you need to write a program to solve the task at hand. You're going to do this by using the objects provided by Visual Studio and .NET in concert with your own program logic using C#. It won't be difficult for you to do this because . . . you have a plan! The fact that you started with a plan rather than by just dragging and dropping objects onto a form puts you light years ahead of most beginning programmers.

True, you too will be dragging and dropping objects onto a form soon enough, but your approach to the problem is different. There's a method to your dragging and dropping . . . it is guided by "the plan." Too often beginning programmers start dragging labels and textboxes onto a form without a plan. They do this because they really don't know what to do first, and because the user interface is the easiest thing to create, they equate movement (dragging and dropping) with solving the problem. However, movement without a plan generates more heat than light. Therefore, the lesson to learn is: *Never* start coding a program without a plan. You can try to code a program without one but, ultimately, you are going to have to think through the problem and develop one. Because you're going to have to create a plan anyway, you may as well begin by developing a plan in the first place. Creating a plan first saves you time in the long run.

While you have performed some of the steps presented in the next few sections in Chapter 1, I didn't take the time to explain why you were doing those steps. Also, you are going to do things a little differently now that you have some understanding of OOP. So let's begin.

Try It Out   Creating a New C# Project

Your first task is to create a new C# project for the mailing label program. Use the same File ⇨ New Project menu sequence you used in Chapter 1 to display the New Project dialog box, as shown in Figure 2-8.

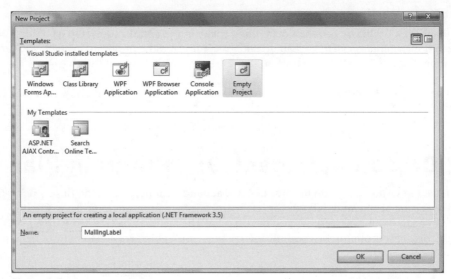

Figure 2-8

If you look carefully at Figure 2-8 you can see that I did *not* select the Windows Application template as I did in Chapter 1. Instead, you should select the Empty Project template. You do this because using the Empty Project template causes Visual Studio to generate less code "behind your back" than does the Windows Application template. That's the good news. The bad news is that using the Empty Project template does require you to do a little more work up front than you might otherwise have to do.

While it may seem stupid to ask you to write code that Visual Studio can write for you, using the Empty Project template serves our purpose better. The goal in this (and subsequent) chapters is to teach you how to write object-oriented programs. Visual Studio already knows how to do that and I assume you don't! In other words, using the Empty Project template enables me to better teach you how to write your own programs. My philosophy is that you learn more if you have to do it yourself.

Type MailingLabel into the Name textbox (near the bottom of the dialog box) for the project name and click the OK button. Visual Studio will create the project for you, using the default file location for the project (such as `C:\Documents and Settings\yourUserName\Local Settings\Application Data\Temporary Projects\MailingLabel`). You should now see the project listed in the Solution Explorer window. If you don't see the Solution Explorer window, use the View ⇨ Solution Explorer menu sequence. (You can also use the keyboard shortcut for displaying the Solution Explorer window by pressing the Control (Ctrl) and W keys at the same time and then pressing the S key.)

Adding Program References to Your Project

I mentioned earlier in this chapter that .NET has almost 4,000 classes available that you can use in your programs. While all of these classes are available to you, you don't really need to use all 4,000 in a single project. For that reason, Visual Studio enables you to specify the categories of classes that you do want to use in your program. In this section I show you how to select those groups of classes that you wish to include in your current project.

Use the Project ⇨ Add Reference menu sequence to show the Add Reference dialog box. Figure 2-9 shows you what the Add Reference dialog box looks like.

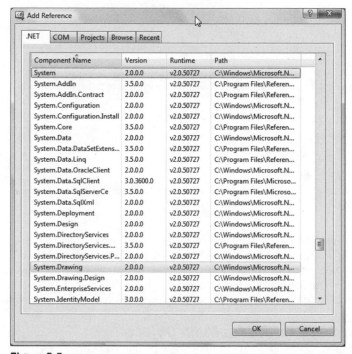

Figure 2-9

Note how I have highlighted two reference objects (`System` and `System.Drawing`) for inclusion in this project. You can select multiple references from the list by holding down Ctrl and then clicking those references you wish to include in the project. The references you need are:

1. `System`
2. `System.Drawing`
3. `System.Windows.Forms`

After you have selected these three references, click the OK button. You should see the references you selected under the References heading in the Solution Explorer window. If you don't see all three references, go back to the Add Reference dialog box and select the missing reference(s).

Adding a New Item to the Project

Now you need to create a form object that is going to hold the (label and textbox) objects that you want to use in your program. Use Project ➪ Add New Item to display the Add New Item dialog box. This dialog box is shown in Figure 2-10.

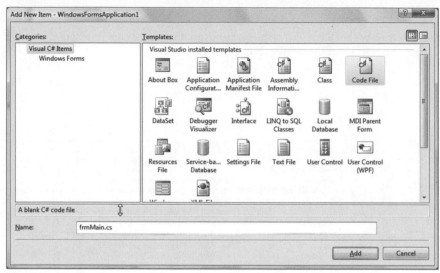

Figure 2-10

Select Code File from the list of available templates and enter frmMain.cs in the Name textbox at the bottom of the dialog box, as shown in Figure 2-10. Click the OK button. You should now see frmMain shown in the Solution Explorer. Also note that the Source Window now has a tab labeled frmMain.cs. The Source Window currently is blank. This shows that the file you just created named frmMain.cs does not yet contain any program code in it. You are about to change that.

Adding Program Code to the frmMain Object

Virtually every program you create while reading this textbook begins with exactly the same program statements. These program statements are shown in Listing 2-1:

Listing 2-1

```
using System;
using System.Windows.Forms;

public class frmMain : Form
{
    #region Windows code
    private void InitializeComponent()
    {
    }
    #endregion

    public frmMain()
```

```
    {
        InitializeComponent();
    }

    public static void Main()
    {
        frmMain main = new frmMain();
        Application.Run(main);
    }
}
```

You should type the program statements shown here into the frmMain.cs tab of the Source Window, as shown in Figure 2-11. Note that C# is case-sensitive, which means you need to pay attention to whether a letter is used in upper- or lowercase when you write program code. I will explain what this code means shortly. For now, however, simply type the code shown into the frmMain.cs tab.

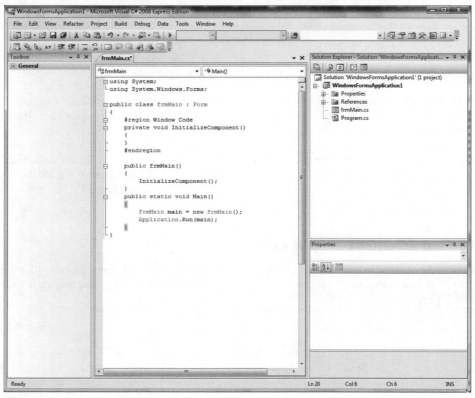

Figure 2-11

Making a Copy of the C# Program Code

Because every program uses the program code shown in Figure 2-11, you should make a copy of it for later use. To make a copy of the code, click the Windows Start button at the lower left-hand corner of the display screen and select Run from the menu options. When the Run dialog appears, type in:

```
notepad.exe
```

Click OK. This opens up the Notepad text editor that comes with Windows. Leave the Notepad program open and running, but switch back to Visual Studio.

After you have typed in the program code, place the cursor at the start of the first program line in the Source Window and, while holding down the left mouse button, drag the mouse cursor to the bottom of the Source Window. This action highlights all the program code you just typed in. Press Ctrl+C. This keystroke sequence copies the highlighted lines of text from Visual Studio's Source Window into the Windows copy buffer. (A *buffer* is just a section of memory that holds data.)

Now switch back to the Notepad program, making sure the program cursor is showing in the Notepad edit window. Press Ctrl+V to insert the contents of the Windows copy buffer into the Notepad edit window. Notepad should now have an exact copy of the program code lines you typed into the frmMain.cs file.

Click the File ⇨ Save As menu option in Notepad to save these program statements. I suggest that you save the file using the name C#CodeTemplate.txt and save it in a convenient place on your system, such as the desktop.

The next time you want to start writing a new program, you can just double-click this file name and Notepad will open up with the program lines in the edit window. All you have to do for the new program is copy the program code lines from Notepad into your new C# project. This copy-and-paste shortcut should save you about a bazillion keystrokes over time.

Setting the Project Properties

You should now set the properties that govern the environment in which the program will execute. Select Project ⇨ MailingLabel Properties to activate the MailingLabel tab in the Source window, as shown in Figure 2-12.

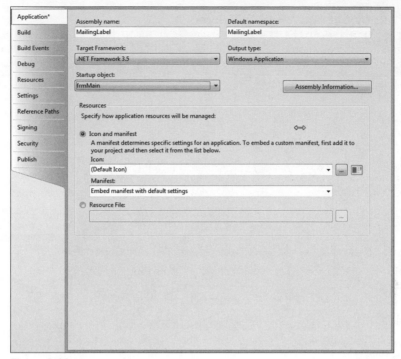

Figure 2-12

Because you want your program to run as a Windows application, select Windows Application from the output type choices. Next, set the startup object to be the object that contains the Main() method for the application. As I mentioned in Chapter 1, every C# program must have a Main() method, as it is this method that tells Visual Studio where to begin executing the program. As you can see in Figure 2-11, it is the frmMain object that contains the Main() method. Select frmMain from the list of startup objects.

Adding Objects to the frmMain Object

If you have followed the directions correctly, your screen should look similar to Figure 2-11. Highlight the frmMain.cs file in the Solution Explorer window and then click on the View Designer icon. (The View Designer icon is just to the right of the View Code icon shown in Figure 1-8 of Chapter 1.) You should now see an empty form object in the Source Window.

You can now add the various program objects to the form. Table 2-2 presents the object and property values for each of the objects you should place on the form. Because the program does not manipulate

Table 2-2: Object and Property Values

Object Name	Property Name	Property Value
frmMain	Text	Mailing Label Program
	StartPosition	CenterScreen
label1	Text	Name:
	AutoSize	False
	BorderStyle	Fixed3D
	Size	75, 20
label2	Text	Address:
	AutoSize	False
	BorderStyle	Fixed3D
	Size	75, 20
label3	Text	City
	AutoSize	False
	BorderStyle	Fixed3D
	Size	75, 20
label4	Text	State
	AutoSize	False
	BorderStyle	Fixed3D
	Size	40, 20
label5	Text	Zip
	AutoSize	False
	BorderStyle	Fixed3D
	Size	40, 20
txtName		Default values for all properties
txtAddress		Default values for all properties
txtCity		Default values for all properties
txtState		Default values for all properties

Object Name	Property Name	Property Value
txtZip		Default values for all properties
txtResult	MultiLine	True
	ReadOnly	True
btnDisplayOutput	Text	&Display
btnExit	Text	E&xit

the property values of the label object in the program, you can leave their names unchanged from the default names supplied for labels by Visual Studio. However, because you do want to manipulate and use the information contained in the textboxes, you should give them meaningful names, as suggested in Table 2-2.

Notice that the btnExit text property has an ampersand imbedded in it after the E. This allows the user to use the Alt+X keystroke sequence in lieu of using the mouse to click on the Exit button. In this example, the letter X is the "hot key" alternative to clicking the Exit button. Hot keys allow the user to run the program using just the keyboard in the absence of a mouse device. The same interpretation applies to the letter D in the btnDisplayOutput button. That is, the user can press Alt+D instead of clicking the Display button.

A programming style convention is to start object names with specific prefixes. For example, textbox names begin with txt and button names start with btn. Such a prefix is followed by a name that describes the object, such as txtName for the user's name, txtAddress for the address, and so on. Note that the object name used after the prefix is capitalized. The practice of using an uppercase letter for the subnames within object and variable names is called *camel notation*. You can see the use of camel notation in the object names shown in Table 2-2 (such as btnDisplayOutput). Camel notation makes it easier to read and understand object and variable names.

When you have finished adding the objects to the form and setting their property values, your form should look similar to the form object shown in Figure 2-13.

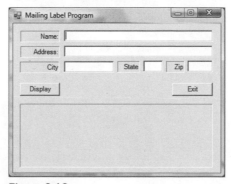

Figure 2-13

43

If you look closely at Figure 2-13, you can see the 3D border effect created with the Fixed3D BorderStyle with the label objects. Strictly speaking, Windows programs normally do not use borders on label objects. Given that borders are nonstandard, why do I use them in this example? There are two reasons. First, it reinforces the purpose of an object's properties. Changing an object's property values changes the state of the object. In this case, changing the state of the BorderStyle property changes the way the label looks on the screen. The second reason for using borders on the labels is that I think they look kind of cool. If you want to follow the strict Windows style or don't like the way label borders look, don't use them. After all . . . it's your program.

Adding Program Code for the Process Step

When the user runs your program, she is expected to fill in the various textboxes and click the Display button. The button click generates an event message that causes the code tied to the btnDisplayOutput click event to be executed. With the form visible in the Source Window, double-click the Display button and add the following program code to the btnDisplayOutput click event:

```
private void btnDisplayOutput_Click(object sender, EventArgs e)
{
        String buffer;

        buffer = "Mailing Label:" + Environment.NewLine +
                Environment.NewLine;
        buffer = buffer + "   Name: " + txtName.Text +
                Environment.NewLine;
        buffer = buffer + "Address: " + txtAddress.Text +
                Environment.NewLine;
        buffer = buffer + "   City: " + txtAddress.Text +
                    " State: " + txtState.Text +
                    " Zip: " + txtZip.Text;
        txtDisplayOutput.Text = buffer;

}
```

Now run the program and fill in the textboxes with the appropriate information. A sample run of the program is shown in Figure 2-14.

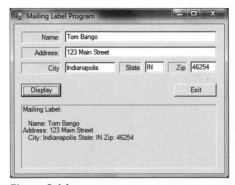

Figure 2-14

How It Works

The program begins by building the form in memory, placing the various objects on the form where you told them to be placed when you constructed the user interface described in Table 2-2. Anytime you move an object on the form, Visual Studio adjusts the code to reflect the new position. If you change a property of an object using the Property Window, Visual Studio makes the appropriate changes to the code for you.

Constructing the User Interface Object

You can examine the code Visual Studio wrote for the user interface by looking at the statements in the InitializeComponent() method. Because the code is fairly lengthy and very repetitive, only the first few statement lines are shown here.

```
private void InitializeComponent()
{
    this.label1 = new System.Windows.Forms.Label();
    this.txtName = new System.Windows.Forms.TextBox();
    this.txtAddress = new System.Windows.Forms.TextBox();
    this.label2 = new System.Windows.Forms.Label();
    this.txtCity = new System.Windows.Forms.TextBox();
    this.label3 = new System.Windows.Forms.Label();
    this.label4 = new System.Windows.Forms.Label();
    this.txtZip = new System.Windows.Forms.TextBox();
    this.label5 = new System.Windows.Forms.Label();
    this.btnDisplayOutput = new System.Windows.Forms.Button();
    this.btnExit = new System.Windows.Forms.Button();
    this.txtDisplayOutput = new System.Windows.Forms.TextBox();
    this.txtState = new System.Windows.Forms.TextBox();
    this.SuspendLayout();
    //
    // label1
    //
    this.label1.BorderStyle = System.Windows.Forms.BorderStyle.Fixed3D;
    this.label1.Location = new System.Drawing.Point(12, 18);
    this.label1.Name = "label1";
    this.label1.Size = new System.Drawing.Size(75, 20);
    this.label1.TabIndex = 0;
    this.label1.Text = "Name:";
    this.label1.TextAlign = System.Drawing.ContentAlignment.MiddleRight;
    //
    // txtName
    //
    this.txtName.Location = new System.Drawing.Point(93, 18);
    this.txtName.Name = "txtName";
    this.txtName.Size = new System.Drawing.Size(297, 20);
    this.txtName.TabIndex = 1;

       // More statements follow
}   // End of the InitializeComponent() method
```

Consider the first program line:

```
this.label1 = new System.Windows.Forms.Label();
```

This statement uses the exact syntax rules I discussed earlier in this chapter for instantiating an object. The word `this` in the statement is a C# keyword and refers to the currently active object. For your program the currently active object is `frmMain`. Remember that the *new* keyword means that you are about to instantiate an object named `label1`. If you look at the code in your `frmMain.cs` file, you will find that `label1` is a label object. A label object is one of the cookie cutters you can use to instantiate an object. In this case you are creating a cookie named `label1`, and a few lines later Visual Studio wrote the following code:

```
this.label1.BorderStyle = System.Windows.Forms.BorderStyle.Fixed3D;
this.label1.Location = new System.Drawing.Point(12, 18);
this.label1.Name = "label1";
this.label1.Size = new System.Drawing.Size(75, 20);
this.label1.TabIndex = 0;
this.label1.Text = "Name:";
this.label1.TextAlign = System.Drawing.ContentAlignment.MiddleRight;
```

This code changes a number of properties (like `BorderStyle`, `Location`, `Name`, `Size`, `TabIndex`, `Text`, and `TextAlign`) for the `label1` object. Because the object's properties appear on the left side of the assignment operator, the code changes the values for each of the properties shown. This also means that the state of the `label1` object has been changed.

Code similar to that shown here is generated for the other objects you placed on the form. In each case the state of the object is changed according to the properties you changed while constructing the user interface.

The btnDisplayOutput Click Event Code

Let's examine program code found in the btnDisplayOutput click event method. The first statement in the method is:

```
String buffer;
```

This line simply creates a program variable named `buffer`. As you will learn in the next chapter, a variable is nothing more than a name for an area of computer memory used to hold a piece of program data. The keyword `String` denotes a specific type of variable that is capable of storing textual data. (You will read more about variables and data types in Chapter 3.) As you are using it here, `buffer` is used to hold some textual characters you've hard-coded into the program (such as Mailing Label) plus some textual characters that the user has supplied via the textbox objects.

The next program line takes the characters `Mailing Label:` and adds two newline characters (as stored in the `Environment.NewLine` property of the `Environment` object) to the end of the sequence of characters:

```
buffer = "Mailing Label:" + Environment.NewLine +
         Environment.NewLine;
```

A newline character causes subsequent characters to print on the next line. Because you have used two newline characters, this has the effect of displaying a blank line in the output. You can see the blank line in Figure 2-14.

The next line of program code takes the current value of buffer and adds the characters Name: to it:

```
buffer = buffer + "    Name: " + txtName.Text +
            Environment.NewLine;
```

The statement then accesses the txtName object and uses the dot operator to access the data stored in the Text property of the txtName object. Using the data shown in Figure 2-14, the Text property of the txtName object currently holds the name Tom Bango in it. This data is then added on to the end of buffer to produce the following:

❑   Mailing Label:

❑   Tom Bango

This is the sequence of characters currently stored in buffer. This sequence of actions on the txtName object is similar to what is depicted in Figure 2-7. Lastly, a newline character is added to buffer so that any additional characters added to buffer appear on a new line in the display.

You can summarize the statement as a series of steps, with the step number appearing in parentheses below its associated action:

```
buffer = buffer + "    Name: " + txtName.Text + Environment.NewLine;
 (5)      (1)         (2)          (3)                (4)
```

This may be read as the following sequence of steps (recall that statements on the right side of the assignment operator (=) are processed first):

1.   Take the original content of buffer (Mailing label:) that existed prior to the execution of this statement.

2.   Add the characters Name: after Mailing label: and the two newline characters.

3.   Use the dot operator to fetch the characters stored in the Text property of the txtName object.

4.   Add a newline character at the end of the characters.

5.   Assign this new sequence of characters back into buffer so buffer contains the old plus the new characters.

After the statement has been processed, buffer now contains the first three lines displayed in Figure 2-14.

The remaining program code statements add the address, city, state, and zip code entered by the user, and work the same way the first two program lines did. The end result of the program statements that assign data into buffer is what you see displayed in the textbox at the bottom of the form. The following program statement simply moves the characters stored in buffer into the Text property of the txtDisplayOutput object:

```
txtDisplayOutput.Text = buffer;
```

Because this changes the value of the Text property of txtDisplayOutput, the state of the object is changed, which causes the display to change and look like what is shown in Figure 2-14.

Critique of the btnDisplayOutput Click Event Code

The program code found in the btnDisplayOutput click event is an example of what is known as RDC . . . Really Dumb Code. This is true for a number of reasons. First, there is no validation of the contents that have been typed into the various textboxes by the user. To make the program code smarter, you should add code to verify that something was typed into the textbox and that the data is appropriate for the information desired. For example, if you want to validate the content of the Text property for the zip code textbox object, perhaps you should check to see if only digit characters are entered. Or, if there is a mixture of alpha and digit characters, perhaps you should check to make sure exactly six characters were entered. This way you would be able to allow Canadian postal codes too, as those codes use both alpha and digit characters.

A second improvement would make the output a little easier to read. If you look closely at the output in Figure 2-14, you'll notice that the fields don't line up properly. This is true even though you made an effort to align the Name, Address, and City fields in the program statements by using an appropriate number of spaces before each field. Why didn't this work?

The reason is that label objects have their Font property set to the Microsoft Sans Serif font. This is what is called a TrueType font. A TrueType font is a variable font. What that means is that each character takes up only as much screen space as it needs to be seen on the display device. The letter *I*, for example, takes up less space on the screen than does the letter *W*. Therefore, because different letters take up different amounts of space, it is difficult to get letters on different lines to align with each other.

You can solve this alignment problem by changing the font to a fixed font. With a fixed font, each letter takes up exactly the same amount of space. If you change the Font property of the txtDisplayOutput object to the Courier New font, which is a fixed font, the letters align perfectly. You can see the result of the font change by comparing the display output in Figure 2-14 with that in Figure 2-15.

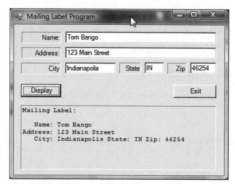

Figure 2-15

Summary

You covered quite a bit of ground in this chapter. You learned:

- What a class is

- What the properties and methods within a class are

- How a class serves as a template from which you can instantiate objects of a class

- How to use the dot operator to read or write the object's property values or invoke an object's method

- What a user interface is and how to design one

- The five program steps

- How to create a new C# project

Finally, you wrote a short program that built a user interface and interacted with the objects that are part of that user interface.

The remainder of this book builds upon the basic concepts presented in this chapter. You should spend enough time with the material presented here to be comfortable with all the terms introduced in this chapter (such as class, object, property, method, dot operator, instantiate, and so on.) A little time spent now learning these concepts will generate huge rewards in later chapters. Take your time, experiment, and have fun.

Part II
Understanding C# Syntax

Understanding Data Types

As you learned in Chapter 2, computer programs often input data in one form, process it, and then show the new data on the computer screen. This kind of invites the question: What is data? Simply stated, data is information. Computer data is information that is stored in a variable for use in a program. In a broad sense, there are two basic kinds of computer data: 1) numeric data and 2) textual data.

Numeric data is any kind of data that can have arithmetic operations performed on it. You can add, subtract, multiply, and divide numeric data. You can perform other operations on numeric data, like finding a square root, a sine, or a cosine of a numeric quantity, and so on. You will also hear numeric data types referred to as *value types.* The precise meaning of this term is discussed in Chapter 5. For now, however, you can think of them as those data types whose variables can have data stored directly into them.

Textual data are character representations of data. Your name is a piece of data that can be represented in a program in a textual fashion. Some students get confused when you ask them whether a zip code is numeric or textual information. Because zip codes are usually not manipulated in mathematical expressions (for example, you wouldn't need to multiply or divide a zip code), they are usually treated as textual information.

This chapter discusses the different data types C# provides to you. In this chapter, you will learn about the following:

❑ Integer data types

❑ The range of values for different data types

❑ Floating-point data types

❑ Which data type should be used to represent financial data

❑ The Boolean data type

❑ When to use one data type versus another

❑ Intellisense

When you finish this chapter you will have a good understanding of why C# offers you such flexibility when it comes to selecting a data type.

Integer Data Types

An *integer data type* is any numeric value expressed as a whole number. Integer values cannot have a fractional component associated with them. If you try to assign a fractional value to an integer variable, C# truncates the value. For example, if `val` is an integer data type, the statement

```
val = 6.9999;
```

assigns the value of 6 to `val`. This means that integer operations do not round values. If an integer data type has a fractional value, C# simply throws away the fractional component.

Table 3-1 lists the various integer data types that you can use in your programs.

Table 3-1

Type Specifier	Bits	Range	Data Suffix
byte	8	0 through 255	
sbyte	8	−128 through 127	
short	16	−32,768 through 32,767	
ushort	16	0 through 65,535	
int	32	−2,147,483,648 through 2,147,483,647	
uint	32	0 through 4,294,967,295	U, u
long	64	−9,223,372,036,854,775,808 through 9,223,372,036,854,775,807	L, l
ulong	64	0 through 18,446,744,073,709,551,615	UL, ul

Range of Integer Data Types

Each of the integer data types has a range of values that it can accommodate. Consider the `byte` data type, which uses eight bits. A *binary digit*, or *bit*, is the smallest unit of computer storage and may assume the value of on (1) or off (0). This means that the most basic unit of information in a computer — the bit — only has two possible states: on and off. Because there are only two possible states, information is stored in a computer in a binary, or base-two, format. While you and I perform mathematic operations using a base-ten numbering system, the computer prefers base-two numbers.

From an engineering standpoint, it is more convenient to group the bits into a larger unit called a byte. A *byte* is a collection of eight bits. Because each bit has two possible values, a byte can have 2^8, or 256, combinations. If you refer to Table 3-1, you can see that a `byte` data type can represent the values 0 through 255.

Understanding Binary Numbers

Wait a minute! I just said eight bits can be used to represent 256 values, not 255. So why is the range of a byte limited to 255? The reason is that eight bits can represent 256 unique values, and one of those values is zero. Therefore, if all bits are turned off, the byte has a value of 0. If all bits are turned on, the byte has the value 255. The relationship between bits and their associated numeric values is further illustrated in Table 3-2.

Table 3-2

Bit Position		7	6	5	4	3	2	1	0
Base 2 Representation		2^7	2^6	2^5	2^4	2^3	2^2	2^1	2^0
Value		128	64	32	16	8	4	2	1
10	=	0	0	0	0	1	0	1	0
73	=	0	1	0	0	1	0	0	1
132	=	1	0	0	0	0	1	0	0
255	=	1	1	1	1	1	1	1	1

As you can see in Table 3-2, the numeric value of a byte depends upon which bits are turned on. For example, for the value 73, you see:

```
01001001
```

which is interpreted as

$$0 + 64 + 0 + 0 + 8 + 0 + 0 + 1$$

If you sum up the values, you'll find the total is 73. If all of the bits are turned on, the byte appears as this:

```
11111111
```

which becomes this:

$$128 + 64 + 32 + 16 + 8 + 4 + 2 + 1$$

and totals 255.

Signed Integer Values

Given this information, why is the sbyte data type limited to a maximum value of 128? The reason is that the sbyte data type is a *signed* byte. Because it is signed, sbyte data may be positive or negative. The highest bit of the byte (bit position 7) is used to store the sign of the number. For signed numbers, the high bit is called the *sign bit*. If the sign bit is turned on, it is a negative number. If the sign bit is turned off, it is a positive number. Because of the sign bit, only 2^7 combinations are available, instead of 2^8. Because 2^7 is 128, only 128 unique values are possible and, because 0 is one of those values, the maximum value is 127. If the sign bit is turned on, you still have 128 unique values available, all of which can be negative. This is true because you have already accounted for the value 0 in the positive range of values. This means the negative range extends from -1 to -128.

If you look at Table 3-1, you can see that if the range of permissible values begins with 0, that integer data type does not use a sign bit. If the range includes negative values, it does use a sign bit. You can also see that integer data types that do use a sign bit have a maximum value that is about half that of their corresponding unsigned data types. The reason, of course, is that the highest bit is reserved for the sign of the number.

Which Integer Should You Use?

One problem beginning programmers face is deciding which integer data type to use. There is no single correct answer. I can, however, list a few factors to keep in mind:

❑ **Range of values:** If you are interested only in counting the number of healthy teeth in a person's mouth, the byte data type will work. On the other hand, if you are measuring the day's high temperature, even an sbyte may not have enough range if your sample site includes both Death Valley and Juneau, Alaska. Always err on the high side so you have sufficient range to accommodate your needs.

❑ **Memory limitations:** For most of the applications you write, you probably have at least half a gigabyte of memory available to you. If you select a long data type instead of an int, chances are the four extra bytes aren't going to mean much. However, if you're writing programs for a toaster or an engine sensor, it could be that memory limitations for the device are very restrictive. In such cases you would want to select the smallest data type with sufficient range to do the job.

❑ **Processor considerations:** Each computer has a central processing unit, which is the heart of a computer. Back in the late 1970s, CPUs had internal storage units, called *registers*, which were capable of processing data in one-byte (eight-bit) chunks. Later on, the CPU registers had 16-bit registers, then 32-bit registers, and finally 64-bit registers. Integer data types that can snuggle neatly into a register without adding or losing bits may have a slight speed advantage for some of the operations a CPU performs on the data. What this means is that a 32-bit CPU may actually process a 32-bit integer faster than a 16-bit integer even though the 16-bit integer is smaller. While the performance hit on a single mismatch is very small, this could make a difference when millions of calculations are being performed.

❑ **Library considerations:** I already mentioned that the .NET Framework provides thousands of classes for you. Some of these classes have methods you might use quite heavily. For example, the math class includes a square root method. You send a data value to the method and it sends that value's square root back to you. Most of the math methods (such as sqrt(), cos(), and pow()) ask that you send a double data type (discussed later in this chapter) to it, and the method returns the answer as a double. If that's the case, it would make sense to have all the data types be double if they interact with the math classes.

❑ **Convention:** Sometimes convention (a nicer word for "habit") determines the data type used with certain programming constructs. For example, in Chapter 8 I discuss program loops that use a variable to control the loop. Convention finds that an int data type is most often used to control program loops. While there may well be other reasons for using an int to control the loop (such as processor considerations), most programmers simply define an int to control the loop without a whole lot of thought. Convention doesn't necessarily make a choice of data type right, but it may explain why so many programmers tend to use certain data types with certain programming constructs.

In the final analysis, the range of values is probably the most important factor to consider when selecting an integer data type. With a little experience, you develop a knack for selecting the proper data types for the task at hand.

Try It Out   A Program Using Integer Data

Let's write a simple program that accepts two values from the keyboard and performs a mathematical operation on the two values. As always, you need a plan to follow to guide you as you write the program. The basis for the plan is always the Five Program Steps. Because this is a simple program, it doesn't need any special initialization step code beyond what Visual Studio does for you automatically. The Input Step suggests that you want to collect two values from the user. The Process Step states that you want to perform some math operation on the data values entered by the user. Let's assume you want to divide the two numbers. Because Windows programs are event-driven, you need to add a Calculate button to begin the processing of the data. The Output Step assumes that you want to show the user the end result of the math operation, division in your program. There's nothing special for you to do in the Termination Step, so you can just provide an Exit button to end the program.

Sequence of Steps to Create a New Project

The sequence of steps you must follow to create the integer-division program is exactly the same as you used in Chapter 2. The details of each step can be found in Chapter 2, but here I present an outline of the steps to create a new programming project:

1. Select New ⇨ Project from the main menu.

2. Select Empty Project from the Template Window (make sure it's for C# if you have the full Visual Studio).

3. Type in the name and location for the new project.

4. Select Project ⇨ Add References, selecting `System.dll`, `System.Drawing.dll`, and `System.Windows.Forms.dll` (or click the Recent Tab and select from there).

5. Select Project ⇨ Add New Item and select Code File, and name the file `frmMain.cs`.

6. Place the cursor in the Source window and copy the C# template code you saved in a file from Chapter 2 into `frmMain.cs`.

7. Select Project ⇨ Properties ⇨ Application. Set Output Type to Windows Application and set Startup Object to `frmMain`.

8. Highlight the `frmMain.cs` file in the Solution Explorer window and click the View Designer icon.

If you have done these steps correctly, an empty form should be visible in the Source window and you will be ready to design the user interface for your program. You can design your user interface to look just about any way you wish it to look, but keep in mind some of the things I suggested in Chapter 2 (such as that most people read from left to right and from top to bottom).

Designing the User Interface

The Input Step suggests you need two textboxes to input the values. You should have one label for each of these textboxes to make clear what each textbox is expecting to be entered. Your interface also needs a Calculate button to initiate the Process Step. The Display Step requires you to have either a label or read-only textbox to display the result of the integer division. The Termination Step requires you to have an Exit button to end the program. (As an optional exercise, try adding a Clear button that, when clicked, clears the contents of all textboxes and places the cursor in the first textbox, ready to accept new input for a different calculation.)

Within the confines of a good user-interface design, you are free to make the user interface looks however you would like it to look. The user interface design I chose is shown in Figure 3-1.

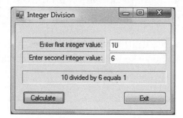

Figure 3-1

You can set labels, textboxes, buttons, and the form's title bar caption using the guidelines presented in Table 2-2 in Chapter 2.

Code for the Process Step

Because you have already copied in the code from the C# template file I discussed in Chapter 2, the essence of the program code is found in the btnCalc() click event. This code is as follows:

```
private void btnCalc_Click(object sender, EventArgs e)
{
  bool flag;
  int operand1;
  int operand2;
  int answer;

      //                    Input Step
      // Check first input...
  flag = int.TryParse(txtOperand1.Text, out operand1);
  if (flag == false)
  {
    MessageBox.Show("Enter a whole number", "Input Error");
    txtOperand1.Focus();
```

```
      return;
    }

        // Check second input...
flag = int.TryParse(txtOperand2.Text, out operand2);
if (flag == false)
{
  MessageBox.Show("Enter a whole number", "Input Error");
  txtOperand2.Focus();
  return;
}

    //                        Process Step
answer = operand1 / operand2;

    //                        Display Step
txtResult.Text = operand1.ToString() + " divided by " +
                 operand2.ToString() +
                 " equals " +answer.ToString();
txtResult.Visible = true;


}

private void btnExit_Click(object sender, EventArgs e)
{
  Close();
}
```

How It Works

You begin the code for the btnCalc() click event by defining a Boolean variable named flag, followed by the definitions for three integer variables of type int. A *variable* is simply a name you give to a specific piece of data. Back in the dark ages of programming, you might store an integer value at memory address 900,000. In those days there were no variable names. You simply typed in 9000000 anytime you wanted to reference that integer value. It didn't take long before programmers started writing programming tools that let them use symbolic names (such as operand1) for memory addresses, which made the act of writing programs much easier and less error-prone, hence the advent of variable names.

Variable Naming Rules and Conventions

A variable name, also called an *identifier*, has several rules you must follow in order to keep the Visual Studio compiler happy. These rules are as follows:

❑   Variable names may only begin with an alpha character (a through z, A through Z) or an underscore character (_).

❑   Punctuation characters are not allowed.

❑   The variable name cannot be a C# keyword.

❑   Digit characters are allowed after the first character (for example, Apollo5).

While it is not a rule, you should always try to use variable names that make sense in the context in which they are used. In the preceding code, operand1 is a better name than o1 even though Visual Studio accepts either name. A second convention, called *camel notation,* is that long variable names start with lowercase letters and that each following word in the name is capitalized, as in myHatSize. Camel notation makes it easier to read the variable names. I have followed these rules and conventions for naming the flag, operand1, operand2, and result variables.

Using the TryParse() Method

The next statement in the program is this:

```
flag = int.TryParse(txtOperand1.Text, out operand1);
```

The statement may seem rather formidable, but it really isn't.

The purpose of the TryParse() method is to examine what the user entered from the keyboard and see if that input can be converted into an integer data type. Keep in mind that anything the user types into a textbox is entered as textual data. Your program wants to manipulate numeric data in the form of integers. Simply stated, the purpose of TryParse() is to convert apples (textual data) into oranges (numeric data).

Sometimes users do make typing errors and the conversion doesn't go smoothly. If you look at your keyboard, you can see it's not too hard to accidentally hit the o (oh) key when you meant to hit the 0 (zero) key. What TryParse() does is examine each character the user typed into the txtOperand1 textbox to make sure it was a digit character.

Let's simplify what comprises the TryParse() statement:

```
flag = int.TryParse(txtOperand1.Text, out operand1);
```

This is actually nothing more than what you've seen before:

```
flag = Object . MethodName(argument1, argument2);
```

As you can see, you have an assignment operator (=) with two operands. The operand on the left is a Boolean variable named flag and the operand on the right is an object named int. You are using the dot operator to get inside the object and use the TryParse() method buried inside the int object. TryParse() needs two pieces of information, called *arguments,* sent to it in order to perform its job. In this example, the TryParse() method wants the Text property of the txtOperand1 object and an integer variable you defined as operand1 sent to it. Why does TryParse() need this information? Simply stated, argument1 supplies the method with the textual data to examine and argument2 gives the method a place to store the numeric result of the conversion if everything goes well. The flag variable simply holds the value that TryParse() returns when it's done doing its thing. If the conversion was completed successfully, it returns true. If things didn't go so well, it returns false. You can then test the value of flag to see how the conversion faired with an if statement, as was done here.

Now refer to the original code you typed in for the TryParse() statement. If TryParse() finds that the user did in fact type in all digit characters, it converts those digit characters (which are textual data) into numeric data of type int. It takes that new numeric value and places it into operand1. Because the conversion of the textual data in the Text property of the txtOperand1 object was successful, it returns the Boolean value `true`. This value (`true`) then gets assigned into `flag`. Therefore, a successful call to the `TryParse()` method converts the textual data of the `Text` property of the `txtOperand1` object. Because you are using the `TryParse()` method found inside the `int` object, the data are converted to an `int` data type and copied into the `int` variable named `operand1`.

Calling a Method

The term *calling a method* refers to the process of sending program control to a method to perform some particular task. You will also hear the term *caller* used in conjunction with calling a method. A caller is a point of execution in a program, not a person or thing. In the `btnCalc_Click()` code presented earlier, the first line after the data definitions of `operand1`, `operand2`, and `result` is a call to the `TryParse()` method of an `int` object. To refer to the process of calling the `TryParse()` method, a programmer might say: "btnCalc calls `TryParse()`." Another programmer might say: "`flag` calls `TryParse()`." Either phrase simply means that program control jumps away from the current sequence of executing the program statements in the `btnCalc_Click()` method to execute those statements found in the `TryParse()` method.

When the program finishes executing the statements in `TryParse()`, program control is sent back to the point at which `TryParse()` was called. This process of sending control back to the point at which the method was called is associated with the phrase "return to the caller."

If the method returns some form of data, such as the Boolean value `true` or `false`, as part of its task, you might hear the phrase: "The method returns `true` to the caller." In our example, `TryParse()` is designed to return the Boolean value of either `true` or `false` to the caller. The way to visualize what happens is to look at the state of the information just before the `TryParse()` method is called:

```
flag = int.TryParse(txtOperand1.Text, out operand1);
```

This shows the information that is about to be sent to `TryParse()`. When `TryParse()` has finished its job of examining the contents of `txtOperand1.Text`, it returns `true` or `false` to the caller. Assuming the user typed in only digit characters, `operand1` contains the numeric value of the user's input and `true` is returned to the caller. Therefore, when program control returns to the caller, the statement appears to be the following:

```
flag = true;
```

This means that `TryParse()` has done its job and converted the user's textual input into a numeric value now stored in `operand1` and returned `true` to the caller.

I will use the terms and phrases introduced here throughout the text.

If the user typed in something other than digit characters into the textbox, `TryParse()` cannot successfully convert the textual characters into a numeric value. In that case `TryParse()` sets operand1 to 0 and returns the value false. The return value (false) is then assigned into the Boolean variable named flag.

An example might help reinforce what's being done. Suppose the user enters 1234 for the input into the txtOperand1 textbox object. The statement line looks like this:

```
flag = int.TryParse(txtOperand1.Text, out operand1);
```

It becomes this:

```
?   = int.TryParse("1234", out ?);
```

I have shown the flag and operand1 values as unknown because, at the moment, they could contain unknown garbage values. After `TryParse()` examines the string of input data from the txtOperand1 textbox object (1234), it decides that it can successfully convert those digit characters into a numeric value of type int. Because the conversion is successful, `TryParse()` sets operand1 to the new value and returns true to the caller. In this case, the caller is the assignment operator that takes the return value (true) and assigns it into the flag variable. The end result is as follows:

```
true = int.TryParse("1234", out 1234);
```

The keyword out in the second argument to `TryParse()` is necessary and tells Visual Studio it's okay to use operand1 as an argument even though it hasn't yet been given a meaningful value.

The code that follows the `TryParse()` method call tests the flag variable to see if the conversion was successful or not. If the conversion failed, the if statement sees that flag is false and the program executes the code controlled by the if statement. (I discuss if statements in detail in Chapter 7.) The following statements are only executed if the flag variable is false:

```
if (flag == false)
{
  MessageBox.Show("Enter a whole number", "Input Error");
  txtOperand1.Focus();
  return;
}
```

The program then creates a MessageBox object and uses its Show() method to display an error message on the screen. After the user reads and dismisses the error message, the program calls the Focus() method of the txtOperand1 object to place the cursor back into its textbox. The *return* keyword causes the program to leave the btnCalc click event code and redisplay the frmMain form object. The cursor will be sitting in the txtOperand1 textbox waiting for the user to enter a proper integer value.

The same check is performed on the contents of the txtOperand2 textbox object. The `TryParse()` method performs the same checks on the textual data held in the Text property of txtOperand2.

Processing and Displaying the Result

After both operands are assigned values from their associated textboxes, you are ready to perform the division operation. The code to perform the calculation and display the results is shown below.

```
answer = operand1 / operand2;

txtResult.Text = operand1.ToString() + " divided by " +
                 operand2.ToString() +
                 " equals " +answer.ToString();
txtResult.Visible = true;
```

Because you want to use the division operator, the first statement divides the integer `operand1` value by the `operand2` value. The assignment operator then assigns the result of the division into the variable named `answer`.

All you need to do now is display the answer for the user to see. However, once again you have the "apples and oranges" problem. That is, `operand1`, `operand2`, and `answer` are all numeric data, but you need to display them in a textbox that expects the data to be in textual form. While you're not quite ready for the complete answer yet, each value type (like an integer data type) can be viewed as being wrapped in an object with certain methods available to it. One of those available methods is `ToString()`. The purpose of the `ToString()` method is to take the current numeric value of the integer object and convert it into textual data. In this example, `ToString()` simply takes the numeric value of the variable and converts it into the appropriate sequence of digit characters.

After all three values have been converted into text, each text representation of the value is concatenated to the next piece of text by means of the concatenation operator (the + operator). After all the text is concatenated together, the combined text is assigned into the `Text` property of the `txtResult` object. (*Concatenation* is a fifty-cent word that means to "append to.")

The last thing the program does is set the `Visible` property of the `txtResult` object to `true`. I do this because, when I designed the user interface, I set the `Visible` property to `false`. Therefore, when the user runs the program, he or she cannot see the textbox that ultimately displays the results. While this program is pretty simple and doesn't have a lot of "clutter" on the form, this technique of hiding the display step objects until they contain something useful may help to "de-clutter" the user interface while the user is performing the input step.

You might want to experiment with your program a bit. Try changing the math operator from division to addition (+), subtraction (–), multiplication (*), and modulo divide (%). (*Modulo divide* gives you the remainder of division.) Another interesting thing to do is enter input data that "breaks" the code. For example, what happens if you enter a zero as the second operand in the current program? What happens if you enter huge values that you know exceed the range of the data type you selected? Breaking your code is a great way to discover the limitations of the data and the kinds of problems you run into out there in the "real world."

Floating-Point Data Types

A floating-point data type is a numeric data type, but it is capable of representing fractional values. The floating-point data types and their associated ranges are shown in Table 3-3.

Table 3-3

Type Specifier	Bits	Range	Data Suffix
float	32	$\pm 1.5 \times 10^{-45}$ to $\pm 3.4 \times 10^{38}$	F, f
double	64	$\pm 5.0 \times 10^{-324}$ to $\pm 1.7 \times 10^{308}$	D, d

Table 3-3 shows that the range of values for either type of floating-point number is quite large. Usually you select floating-point values when 1) you need the data to reflect fractional values, and 2) you need to use very small or very large numbers in your program.

Try It Out   A Program Using Floating-Point Numbers

You can modify your program that used integer numbers to work with floating-point numbers fairly easily. First, try changing the statement lines

```
int operand1;
int operand2;
int answer;
```

to this:

```
float operand1;
float operand2;
float answer;
```

Then run the program. You will get the following error message:

```
The best overloaded method match for 'int.TryParse(string, out int)'
has some invalid arguments.
```

What this error message is telling you is that TryParse() is confused because it expects the second argument to be an integer, but you've passed operand1 as a float data type. This isn't a serious problem, because each of the data types has its own version of TryParse(). Change the TryParse() method calls in the program to the following:

```
flag = float.TryParse(txtOperand1.Text, out operand1);
```

Now compile and run the program. When you ran the integer version of the program and supplied the two input values as 10 and 6, the answer was 1. The reason for this is that integer math doesn't allow a fractional component. The integer version of the program simply truncated the result to 1. If you use those same inputs in the float version of the program, the result becomes 1.666667. This result can be seen in Figure 3-2.

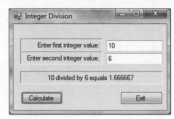

Figure 3-2

Floating-Point Precision

Now change all the `float` keywords in the program to `double`, recompile, and rerun the program with the same inputs. Now the result is `1.66666666666667`. Notice there are more digit characters in the answer using the `double` data type version than when you used the `float` version. This is because the precision of a `float` is limited to seven digits while the precision of a `double` is 15 digits. The *precision* of a number refers to the number of significant digits that a data type can represent. From Table 3-3, you can see that a `float` can represent a number with a value as large as e^{38}. That's a number with up to 38 digits. However, because the precision of a `float` is limited to only seven digits, only the first seven digits of that number are significant. The remaining 31 digits are simply the computer's best guess as to the rest of the digits in the number.

Search and Replace in Visual Studio

In the `float` version of the program under discussion, you were directed to change all instances of the keyword `float` to `double`. You could search through the program code yourself looking for each occurrence of the `float` keyword and change it to `double` yourself. However, this is exactly the type of no-brainer task perfectly suited for the computer to do for you.

If you want to search the entire program for a specific word or phrase, place the cursor at the top of the program in the Source window and press Ctrl+F. You should quickly see the Find and Replace dialog box. There are two options immediately below the title bar. Select the Quick Replace option. Now type in what you are looking for (such as `float`) and then enter what you wish to replace it with (such as `double`). The Find and Replace dialog box should look like what is shown in Figure 3-3.

Figure 3-3

You should now click the Find Next button to find the next occurrence of the word `float` in the program source code. If you wish to change that occurrence of the word `float` to `double`, click the Replace button. The word `float` is then replaced with `double` and the program proceeds to the next `float` keyword it finds in the program.

There is a tremendous temptation to click the Replace All button, which goes through the entire source code file and automatically makes the replacements without asking you to click the Replace button. Don't cave in to this temptation! Search and Replace has the innate intelligence of a box of rocks. Suppose you want to change from an `int` to a `double`. You type those inputs into the dialog box and hit Replace All. Now, when you look at your source code, you find the old program line:

```
int changeStint;
```

has been changed to:

```
double changeStdouble;
```

This is probably not what you wanted to do. The sad thing is that your code very well may still execute correctly because all instances of `changeStint` were faithfully changed to `changeStdouble`. However, your effort to pick a meaningful variable name has been tossed out the window.

My suggestion: never *ever* use Replace All. Use the Find Next and Replace buttons only.

When you changed the data type to double, you increased the precision to 15 digits. While the answer could go on for up to 308 digits for a double, the computer gave up after 15 digits and said: "The heck with it, 1.66666666666667 is as good as it gets."

Which Floating-Point Data Type Should You Use?

Obviously, the increased precision for a double is possible because C# uses twice as much memory to store a double as a float. This invites the question…again: Which floating-point data type should you use? Once again, the answer is: It depends. The same factors that influence your choice of integer data types (memory limitations, processor and library considerations, convention, and so on) play a part in making the right data type choice. The processor and library considerations, however, are especially important when you're dealing with floating-point data.

First, Intel's Pentium-class CPU has a math coprocessor built into it. The math coprocessor is specifically designed to make floating-point math operations as fast as possible. Using the math coprocessor involves no special coding work on your part. Floating-point data is automatically routed to the math coprocessor when your program performs math operations on floating-point data.

The math coprocessor is designed to work with 64-bit data (a double). If you pass a float to the coprocessor, it must expand its 32 bits to 64 bits, perform the floating-point operation on the data, and then shrink the result of the operation back down to 32 bits and move it into your float variable. This expanding and shrinking of the float data takes time. True, the time difference is very small, but if your program is doing millions of floating-point operations, the user may notice the delay if a float data type is used instead of a double.

Second, almost all the methods in the Math class (sqrt(), pow(), log(), cos(), and so on) expect to use the double data type. Again, if you pass a float data type to the sqrt() method of the Math class, code must be executed to expand the data value from 32 to 64 bits. The process of expanding a data value from a smaller to a larger number of bits is called *data widening*. After sqrt() has done its job, code must be executed to shrink the result back to the 32 bits your float data type demands. The process of shrinking a data value from a larger to smaller number of bits is called *data narrowing*. The code associated with data narrowing and data widening can be avoided if you use a double data type when using the methods found in the Math class.

Finally, the two floating-point data types give you different levels of precision. The double data type has more than twice the number of significant digits of a float data type. Unless there are severe memory limitations and given the other advantages of using a double data type, most of the time you should use the double data type for floating-point operations.

Monetary Values: The Decimal Data Type

It might seem that the double data type would also be a good choice for monetary values. The only problem is that even 15 digits of precision may not be enough to represent important monetary values. To overcome the problems associated with limited precision in financial calculations, C# created the decimal data type. The details of the decimal data type are presented in Table 3-4.

Table 3-4

Type Specifier	Bits	Range	Data Suffix
Decimal	128	$\pm 1.0 \times 10^{-28}$ to $\pm 7.9 \times 10^{28}$	M, m

The greatest advantage of the decimal data type is that is has 28 digits of precision — almost twice the precision of a double. This means that, even in financial calculations involving very large amounts, you can keep track of the pennies. The disadvantage of the decimal data type is that each variable takes 16 bytes of memory to store its value.

You can modify the program you've been using to test the various data types by simply changing the int keywords in the code listing presented for the btnCalc_Click() method with the decimal keyword. Now run the program, using the same input values of 10 and 6 for the two operands. What happened? The output for the program is shown in Figure 3-4. (I did not change the input prompts for the two label objects or the text for the frmMain object, so the word "integer" is a little misleading in the figure. Change them if you wish.)

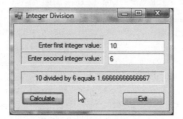

Figure 3-4

As you can see in Figure 3-4, the enhanced precision of the decimal data type is so large the answer doesn't fit in the space allocated for it. Because nobody likes to throw money away, the expanded precision of the decimal data type is a good thing in financial calculations.

Using Intellisense to Locate Program Errors

After you've changed the variable's data types to the decimal data type, try inserting the following program statement into the program just after the definition of answer, but before the call to the TryParse() method:

```
operand1 = .5;
```

When you compile the program, a squiggly blue line appears under .5 in the statement. The blue line is pointing out that Visual Studio sensed an error in the statement line where the squiggly blue line appears.

Syntax Rules and Error Messages

Intellisense is the name Microsoft has given to the part of Visual Studio responsible for checking your statements to make sure they obey the syntax rules of C#. A *syntax rule* simply refers to the language rules C# expects you to follow in order to form a valid C# program statement. (More details on language rules are found in Chapter 4.) Just as the English language expects a sentence to have a noun and a verb, C# has rules it expects you to follow when you write program statements.

If you break (or bend) the syntax rules of C#, Intellisense draws a squiggly blue line under the offending part of the statement. If you move the cursor over the blue line, Intellisense provides you with some information about the error. This information about the nature of the error is presented in the form of an *error message*. In the preceding statement, the error message is as follows:

```
Literal of type double cannot be implicitly converted to type
'decimal'; use an 'M' suffix to create a literal of this type
```

In other words, Visual Studio is confused about what .5 is. You have defined operand1 as a decimal data type, but you are trying to assign the value .5 into it. Unless told otherwise, whenever Intellisense sees a fractional value like .5 in the code, it assumes you want to use a double data type. (A pure number like .5 in a program's source code is called a numeric *literal* because a variable is not used to store the value. Instead, the numeric value is "literally" part of the program's source code.) Therefore, Intellisense sees your program statement attempting to take a double data value (.5) and put it into a decimal data type (operand1). This is like trying to make a person who wears a size-four shoe walk around in a size eight . . . It just doesn't fit right. The error message is saying the same thing, only a little more formally. In its own way, the Intellisense error message is saying this:

```
The literal .5 looks like a double to me and I cannot convert it to type
'decimal' for you; use an 'M' suffix to create a literal of this type
```

Okay . . . that makes sense. Now, let's follow its recommendation, correct the statement, and see what happens. The corrected line should be:

```
operand1 = .5M;
```

Using the information in Table 3-4, you can make the meaning of the literal .5 crystal-clear to Intellisense by placing the decimal data type's suffix, M, after the literal. After you make this change, *voila!* . . . the squiggly blue line disappears.

As a general rule, whenever you see the dreaded squiggly blue line, move the cursor over the blue line and read the error message Intellisense gives you. Sometimes the message may appear a bit cryptic, but with a little experience you'll begin to interpret the error messages correctly.

The Disappearing Squiggly Blue Line

When Intellisense finds an error, it does its best to pinpoint what it thinks is the exact line number of the program error and to draw the squiggly blue line. Most of the time Intellisense does a great job of nailing the exact statement in which the error occurred. Other times, however, the nature of the error is such that Intellisense doesn't realize an error has occurred until it has examined several more lines. In situations where the line with the squiggly blue line appears to be syntactically correct, look at the lines immediately above it for a statement that is amiss.

Note that the squiggly blue line does not always disappear when you correct the error in the statement line. The best way to determine if a program change does fix an error is to recompile the program and see if the error message and dreaded squiggly blue line disappear.

Finally, the squiggly line may also appear red. The red squiggly line is often associated with a missing statement element. For example, if you typed in the following:

```
int i
```

a red squiggly line would appear at the end of the line to inform you that you forgot to add a semicolon at the end of the line.

The Boolean Data Type

Of the two fundamental types of data, numeric and textual, thus far I have limited the discussion to numeric data types. (You will read more about textual data types in Chapter 6.) The Boolean data type is one of those gray areas that don't exactly fit into either a numeric or textual data type. While it is not a precise fit, I discuss the `bool` data type with the numeric data types because it is used to reflect the state of a piece of data, rather than some textual representation of that data.

One of the elemental features of a computer is that it can make decisions based upon the data it processes. You have seen this decision-making ability many times in our sample programs. For example, in the integer-division program you wrote earlier in this chapter, you had the following program statements:

```
flag = int.TryParse(txtOperand1.Text, out operand1);
if (flag == false)
{
  MessageBox.Show("Enter a whole number", "Input Error");
  txtOperand1.Focus();
  return;
}
```

The variable named `flag` that was set by the call to `TryParse()` was used to decide whether the user had typed in a valid integer number into the `Text` property of the `txtOperand1` textbox object. If the user input could be converted successfully into an integer value, `flag` was set to `true` and the value of `operand1` was set to the value entered by the user. If the user entered text that could not be converted to an integer (such as the letter o instead of the zero digit character, 0), `flag` was set to `false` and `operand1` was set to 0. In that case, an error message is displayed and the user is given another chance to enter the data.

In the preceding code snippet, `flag` is a Boolean variable. Boolean variables are defined by the `bool` keyword. (You can see the definition of `flag` in the `btnCalc_Click()` method shown earlier in this chapter.) Table 3-5 shows the relevant information for a `bool` data type.

Table 3-5

Type Specifier	Bits	Values	Data Suffix
bool	8	true, false	None

As you can see from Table 3-5, there is no "range" for a Boolean variable. A `bool` data type can hold only two possible values: `true` or `false`. Therefore, a Boolean variable is used to hold the state of the variable, not a specific value.

If you've ever had a logic course, you've been exposed to truth tables where conditions are stated as either true or false. Quite often those conditions are presented with 1 representing true and 0 representing false. You cannot, however, use 1 and 0 to represent `true` and `false` in a C# program. First of all, `true` and `false` in C# are keywords and Intellisense knows that these are the only two values you can store in a `bool` variable. If you typed in the statement

```
flag = 0;
```

Intellisense issues an error message stating

```
Constant value '0' cannot be converted to a 'bool'
```

This message tells you that Visual Studio is unhappy with your attempt to assign a zero (an integer literal) into the Boolean variable named `flag`. If you change the zero to `false` and recompile the program, the error message goes away because `flag` now is assigned the proper type of data.

Don't Use a bool for the Wrong Purpose

Because a `bool` data type can only reflect the states `true` or `false`, it cannot be used to count data. A `bool` variable should be used only when the information associated with the variable truly can only have only two states. For example, I know of a programmer who was hired to write a program to track information about the members of a club. One of the variables, named `Status`, was implemented as a `bool` with the interpretation that `true` meant the person was an active member of the club and `false` meant the person was not an active member. After the program was written, the club noticed that the program didn't properly handle a member who had been granted a temporary leave of absence. This little change by the club caused the program to fail because the Boolean `Status` variable was now being asked to record three states: 1) active member, 2) inactive member, and 3) member on leave of absence. The programmer had to go back into the code and change `Status` from a `bool` to an `int`.

The lesson is simple: use a `bool` only when you are absolutely certain that the only possible values for the variable are `true` and `false`.

Summary

The discussion in this chapter concentrated on the various value types of data that you can use in your C# programs. More specifically, I emphasized the numeric data types you can use. Any time you wish to manipulate data in a mathematical way, you will likely use one of the numeric data types discussed in this chapter. I also included the `bool` data type in this chapter because it is a value type, although it is not often manipulated in a mathematical sense. (I excluded the `char` value type from this chapter even though it is a value type. Because its use is associated with textual data, I have postponed discussing it until Chapter 6.)

You should now be comfortable discussing the following:

❑   Integer data types

❑   Floating-point data types

❑   The `bool` data type

❑   Factors to consider when selecting a data type for a given task

❑   The purpose of Intellisense

In the next chapter you will expand on your understanding of the basic value types and how they are used in a program. Make sure you understand what the different value types are and how they may be used in a program before advancing to Chapter 4.

Exercises

1. Take the integer program presented earlier in the chapter and modify it so that it performs multiplication instead of division. Make sure you test with extremely large and small numbers to see if you can get the answer to fall outside the intended range of the data type you use.

2. Write a program that converts Fahrenheit temperatures to Celsius using the equation $Tc = 5/9 * (Tf-32)$, where Tc = temperature in degrees Celsius and Tf = temperature in degrees Fahrenheit. What data type did you use and why?

3. Have the user enter a value, and display a message telling the user whether the integer number entered was odd or even.

Understanding C# Statements

This chapter concentrates on the basic building blocks C# provides you for writing programs. In this chapter, you will learn about the following:

❑ Operators and operands

❑ Expressions

❑ Statements

❑ lvalues and rvalues

❑ What a symbol table is and how Visual Studio uses it

❑ How Visual Studio interacts with Windows

❑ The Bucket Analogy

❑ Using the Visual Studio debugger

❑ Magic numbers and why to avoid them

Most beginning books do not discuss many of the topics presented in this chapter. This may cause you to wonder why you need to understand them. There are several reasons. First, once you have mastered these topics, many of the other elements of C# (and programming in general) will become clearer and more intuitive. Memorizing certain rules is one approach to learning a language: once you've memorized (and obeyed) a rule, you can avoid some of the error messages that Visual Studio might throw at you. However, truly understanding *why* a rule exists in the first place is a vastly superior way to learn. It is this higher level of understanding that we seek. If you understand the material presented in this chapter, finding and correcting program errors becomes easier. Error detection becomes easier because you will have a deeper understanding of what C# is doing "under the hood." Finally, your knowledge of the material presented here will be portable. That is, the concepts and techniques discussed in this chapter apply to all programming languages, not just C#. If you decide to learn another programming language later, these concepts will help you learn the new language.

Basic Building Blocks of a Programming Language

While the specific rules of a programming language differ from one language to another, the underlying foundation upon which all programming languages are built is pretty much the same. There is a hierarchy that all languages follow. This hierarchy is:

Programs ⇨ Statements ⇨ Expressions ⇨ Operands and Operators

You can verbalize this hierarchy like this: "Programs consist of one or more statements. Statements consist of one or more expressions. Expressions consist of one or more operands in conjunction with one or more operators." Therefore, to write a program you must understand operands and operators. We begin our journey into the innards of C# by learning about operands and operators.

Operands and Operators

In Chapter 3 you wrote a program that used two variables to store the information that was entered by the user. The program was designed to divide the first number by the second number. Suppose the user typed in 10 for the first number and 6 for the second. You've been doing this kind of math since you were in grade school. We can write the process of dividing 10 by 6 as:

```
10 / 6
```

This simple math process involves taking the value 10 and dividing it by 6. In this example, 10 and 6 are called *operands*. An operand is simply a piece of information. The information associated with an operand might be stored in a variable, or it may be one literal value divided by a second literal value, as shown above.

To make the program more flexible, however, you created variables to store the values in the program. In the program discussed in Chapter 3 you defined two variables named operand1 and operand2. If operand1 has a value of 10 and operand2 has a value of 6, you can write the same process like this:

```
operand1 / operand2
```

The essence of the division process remains the same. All I have done is replaced the literal values 10 and 6 with the variables operand1 and operand2.

Sandwiched between the two operands is the division sign (/) that tells us what to do with the two operands. The division sign is the *operator*. An operator specifies what should be done with the operand(s). In this example we simply want to divide operand1 by operand2. This leads to the following generalization for a math process:

```
operandOne operator operandTwo
```

For all math operations (add, subtract, multiply, divide, modulo), the math operator (+, -, *, /, %) requires two operands to perform its function. Because the math operators require two operands, they are called *binary operators*. Indeed, any operator that requires two operands to perform its task is a binary operator. If an operator requires only one operand, it's a *unary operator*. Finally, if an operator requires three operands, it is a *ternary operator*. Most of the C# operators are binary operators.

Expressions

An *expression* is simply one or more operands and their associated operator treated as a single entity. For example, in the integer division program in Chapter 3, you wrote the following line:

```
answer = operand1 / operand2;
```

This line uses the two operands and the division operator to calculate the result of dividing operand1 by operand2. Because an expression is simply one or more operands and operators treated as a unit, you can visualize this program statement as

```
answer = Expression1;
```

with the understanding that Expression1 consists of operand1 divided by operand2. But, if you generalize the statement

```
answer = Expression1;
```

it can be rewritten as this:

```
operand4 = operand3;
```

where answer is replaced with operand4 and Expression1 is replaced with operand3. The only thing that's different is that the operator has changed to the assignment operator (=). From this, you can also conclude that the assignment operator is a binary operator.

Suppose operand1 equals 10 and operand2 equals 5. Notice the sequence we followed in processing the program line:

```
answer = operand1 / operand2;
answer = 10 / 5;
operand4 = 10 / 5;
operand4 = 2;
2;
```

The process of calculating the result of the division involves little more than using each operator and its operands to generate the proper result. When the chain of events is finished, Expression2 holds the result of the division.

Statements

In C#, a program statement is one or more expressions terminated by a semicolon. However, because expressions are comprised of operands and operators, it follows that this is a program statement:

```
answer = operand1 / operand2;
```

This program statement actually contains two operators (the division operator and the assignment operator) and three operands (`answer`, `operand1`, and `operand2`) terminated by a semicolon.

You can make program statements as complex as you wish, as long as they end with a semicolon. For example, you could take the following program lines:

```
part1 = v + w;
part2 = x + y;
solution = part1 * part2;
```

and write them as a single statement:

```
solution = v + w * x + y;
```

Let's apply some values to the variables in the preceding statement. Assume $v = 2$, $w = 3$, $x = 4$, and $y = 5$. You can view the program statement as the following:

```
solution = 2 + 3 * 4 + 5;
```

The question is, what does `solution` equal? Is the answer 25 or is the answer 19? If you look back at the original set of three program statements, `part1` equals 5 after its statement is processed, while `part2` resolves to 9. The third statement multiplied `part1` by `part2` and assigned the result into `solution`. Because `part1` resolves to 5 and `part2` resolves to 9, `solution` is 45, not 25 or 19. What happened? Why did our collapsed statement version produce the wrong answer?

Operator Precedence

Any time a program statement involves multiple operators, like the one you just saw, there has to be a set of rules that enables us to properly process the operators and operands in the expressions. Table 4-1 presents the precedence, or order, in which operators are processed.

Table 4-1

Order	Type	Symbol
1	Multiply, divide, modulus	*, /, %
2	Add, subtract	+, -
3	Assignment	=

Table 4-1 says that the multiply, divide and modulus operations should be performed before you perform any addition or subtraction operations. Given this information, the order of processing in the program statement

```
solution = 2 + 3 * 4 + 5;
```

is performed in the following order:

```
    (4)        (2) (1) (3)
 solution = 2 + 3 * 4 + 5;
```

This means that C# expects the multiplication operation (3 * 4) to be performed first, followed by the addition of 2 to the result, followed by the addition of 5 to that result and, finally, the value's being assigned into `solution`. We can show the operator precedence in action in the following steps:

```
solution = 2 + 3 * 4 + 5;
solution = 2 + 12 + 5;
solution = 14 + 5;
solution = 19;
```

How did we know to add 2 and 12 together first and then add 5? Any time two math operators have the same precedence level, you process them from left to right. You resolve the order of execution of operators of equal precedence by the operators' *associativity* rules. When ties are resolved by processing from left to right, the operators are called *left-associative*. If ties are broken by the right-most operator's being processed, the operators are said to be *right-associative*.

As you can see from the program sequence's using the precedence order from Table 4-1, the math operators are left-associative. The assignment operator, however, is right-associative. Because the assignment operator is right-associative, everything on the right-hand side of the assignment operator is resolved before anything is assigned into the operand on the left-hand side of the assignment operator. In the preceding statements, these precedence and associativity rules insure that the answer assigned into `solution` is 19.

Overriding the Default Precedence Order

Suppose you really do want the `solution` value to be 45 instead of 19. This would be the same as writing the following:

```
part1 = 2 + 3;
part2 = 4 + 5;
solution = part1 * part2;
```

What you actually want, therefore, is the final statement to resolve to this:

```
solution = 5 * 9;
```

The preceding code assigns a value of 45 into `solution`. However, you saw earlier that

```
solution = 2 + 3 * 4 + 5;
```

resolves to a `solution` value of 19, not 45. How can you get the desired result?

You can override the default precedence order by using parentheses. If you change the statement to

```
solution = (2 + 3) * (4 + 5);
```

the *parentheses* tell C# to perform the operations inside the parentheses before any other operations. The parentheses cause the following sequence to be performed:

```
solution = (2 + 3) * (4 + 5);
solution = 5 * 9;
solution = 45;
```

The end result is that `solution` equals 45. Parentheses are left-associative.

You now know the basic rules necessary to writing program statements in C#. Writing even the most complex program simply boils down to stringing the right sequence of operands and operators together to form expressions that are then used to form program statements. What I need to do next is provide you with a thorough understanding of how variables are defined so you can use them as operands in an expression.

Defining Variables

Some programmers see a statement like

```
int val;
```

and think that the program is defining or declaring a variable named `val`. Many programmers use the terms *define* and *declare* interchangeably. Those programmers are wrong. Defining a variable is very different from declaring a variable. Let's see why the two terms are actually quite different.

Defining a Variable from the Compiler's Point of View

Suppose you write the statement

```
int i;
```

in a program. In your mind, you are simply telling the program that you wish to create an integer variable named `i` for use in your program. To Visual Studio, however, things aren't quite that simple. Let's see what Visual Studio has to do just to process this simple statement.

Step One: Preliminary Syntax Checking

First, Visual Studio must check the statement for syntax errors. A syntax error occurs anytime you write a program statement that does not obey C# syntax rules. For example, you know that a variable name cannot begin with a digit character or contain punctuation characters. If you tried to create a variable with either of these conditions, Visual Studio would issue an error message. You learned in Chapter 3 that if you make a syntax error in a program statement, Intellisense places a squiggly line under the offending statement. Because we know the syntax of our program statement is correct, there is no squiggly line and Visual Studio moves to the next step.

Step Two: Symbol Table Checking

Just because you got the syntax for the statement right doesn't mean there can't be other problems. Therefore, the next thing Visual Studio does is examine its *symbol table* to see if you have already defined a variable named `i`. A symbol table is a table internal to Visual Studio that it uses to keep track of the data you want to use in your program. Table 4-2 shows a hypothetical symbol table. (While a "real" one might have dozens of columns in it, the simplified symbol table shown in Table 4-2 will serve our purpose nicely.)

Table 4-2

ID	Data Type	Scope	lvalue	. . .
hatSize	double	0	650,000	
k	int	0	630,480	

In Table 4-2, column one (ID) shows the names of the variables that have already been defined. (Variable names are often referred to as *identifiers,* hence the column header name, ID.) The second column of the symbol table tells Visual Studio the data type of the variable. We will explain the meaning of the third column shortly. The fourth column, lvalue, is where in memory each variable is located. In other words, the lvalue for hatSize is 650,000. Simply stated, if Visual Studio needs to use the value associated with hatSize, it must access memory address 650,000 to find its value.

In this step, Visual Studio scans the ID column to see if you have already defined a variable named i. Because there is no variable in the symbol table with an ID of i, Visual Studio proceeds to step three. If you had already defined a variable named i (at the same scope level), you would get an error message like this:

```
A local variable named 'i' is already defined in this scope
```

If Visual Studio enabled you to define another variable named i at the same scope level, it would not know which i to use when you try to use the variable in some other statement. This particular error message is called a *duplicate definition* error message and is telling you that it is illegal to have two variables with the same name at the same scope level.

However, because you know you can't have two variables with the same name, i does not appear in the symbol table. Therefore, Visual Studio knows it's okay to add i to the symbol table. Table 4-3 shows the state of the symbol table after you add the variable named i.

Table 4-3

ID	Data Type	Scope	lvalue	. . .
hatSize	double	0	650,000	
k	int	0	630,480	
i	int	0		

Notice that the lvalue column for variable i does not have a value in it. You can also represent the state of variable i as shown in Figure 4-1.

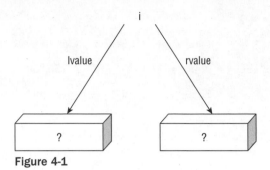

Figure 4-1

lvalues and rvalues

Figure 4-1 shows variable i with two "legs" extending from it, labeled lvalue and rvalue. The *lvalue* of a variable refers to the memory address where the variable is stored. The lvalue for a variable is always interpreted as a memory address. (The term "lvalue" was coined decades ago when programmers used assembly language to write their programs. The lvalue of a variable was an abbreviation for its "location value.") We have shown the lvalue as a question mark for the moment, because we do not presently know its lvalue.

The *rvalue* of a variable refers to the actual value currently stored in the variable. (The rvalue term also had its roots in assembly language programming and stood for "register value.") Normally you use the assignment operator to set the rvalue of a variable. For example, the statement

```
i = 10;
```

assigns the value of 10 into the rvalue of variable i. However, because we are still checking the symbol table entries at this point, nothing is presently associated with the rvalue of variable i. Therefore, we also show the rvalue for i in Figure 4-1 as an unknown value as represented by a question mark.

Step Three: Defining a Variable

Because Table 4-2 does not have another variable named i in it, Intellisense gives the syntax for the statement a clean bill of health. Visual Studio is now ready to associate a memory address with variable i. However, assigning memory addresses is not Visual Studio's job. It is the responsibility of the operating system to find enough memory for a variable. Therefore, Visual Studio sends a message to the operating system (we'll assume it's the Windows operating system) and says, "Hey, Windows! It's me . . . Visual Studio. My programmer wants to define an integer variable for use in a program. Can you find 4 bytes of free memory for me?"

Recall from Chapter 3 that each integer variable requires 4 bytes (32 bits) of storage. Upon receiving the message from Visual Studio, Windows routes the message to the Windows Memory Manager, because the Memory Manager is responsible for fulfilling memory requests.

The Windows Memory Manager scans its list of free memory and probably does find the requested 4 bytes. We'll assume that the Windows Memory Manager finds the 4 bytes starting at memory address 900,000. Having found the requested memory, the Windows Memory Manager sends a message back to Visual Studio: "Hey, Visual Studio! It's me . . . the Windows Memory Manager. I found you 4 bytes of free memory for variable i starting at memory address 900,000." Visual Studio gets the message and immediately puts that memory address into the symbol table for variable i. The symbol table now looks like Table 4-4.

Table 4-4

ID	Data Type	Scope	lvalue	...
hatSize	double	0	650,000	
k	int	0	630,480	
i	int	0	900,000	

Notice how the lvalue in the symbol table records the memory address of where the variable named i resides in memory. We can reflect this change in Figure 4-2.

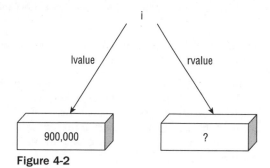

Figure 4-2

The rvalue remains unchanged but the lvalue reflects the fact that variable i is stored starting at memory address 900,000.

You can now state that you have defined variable i. A variable is *defined* if, and only if, the lvalue column for that variable in the symbol table has a memory address assigned to it. When you *declare* a variable, the lvalue column in the symbol table for that variable does not contain a memory address. (You will see examples of data declarations later in the book.) Whenever we say that a variable is defined, it means that variable appears in the symbol table and it has a specific memory address (lvalue) associated with it.

Using a Variable in a Program

Now that you understand what a symbol table is and the information it contains, let's examine how Visual Studio processes something as simple as an assignment. Assuming that you have defined an integer variable named i, suppose you write the following statement:

```
i = 10;
```

The program statement seems simple enough, but let's examine the steps Visual Studio has to perform to process the statement.

1. **Syntax checking:** As before, Visual Studio must first make sure that the program statement obeys the syntax rules of the C# language. Because Intellisense doesn't find anything wrong with the statement's syntax, Visual Studio progresses to the next step.

2. **Symbol table checking:** Because the statement wants to assign the value 10 into a variable named i, Visual Studio needs to verify that variable i has been previously defined. Two things could go wrong in this step. First, the programmer may have forgotten to define a variable named i. If you forgot to define variable i, Visual Studio issues the following error message:

```
The name 'i' does not exist in the current context
```

The second possible problem is that a variable named i was defined, but at a scope level that the current context cannot reach. Without going into details at this moment, the scope of a variable refers to its visibility at each point in a program. As I mentioned in Chapter 3, hiding data is a basic principle of encapsulation and a cornerstone of object-oriented programming. The fact that a variable may not be in scope is a good thing in many cases because it means that you can't inadvertently change that variable's value. A variable must be in scope for you to be able to alter its value. If variable i is not in scope, you get the same error message that was issued when the variable was not defined.

Because our variable is defined at the current scope level, Intellisense is happy and no squiggly line appears.

3. Get the lvalue of variable i. Because the statement wants to assign the value of 10 into variable i, Visual Studio needs to know where to store the value 10. You already know that the lvalue of variable i, as found in the symbol table, tells us where the value 10 should be stored in memory. Visual Studio dutifully creates a binary representation of the value for 10 (i.e., 00000000000000000000000000001010) and moves the value to the 4 bytes of memory starting at memory address 900,000. The change in the value for variable i is shown in Figure 4-3.

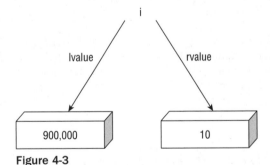

Figure 4-3

The rvalue of variable i has been changed from the question mark seen in Figure 4-2 to the value 10. Because the rvalue has changed, you can also say the *state* of variable i is changed by the assignment statement.

The Bucket Analogy

The Bucket Analogy will help you remember what lvalues and rvalues are all about and reinforce your understanding of what a data definition is. Suppose you write the statement

```
int val;
```

You will recall that Visual Studio checks the syntax of this statement and then searches the symbol table to make sure `val` has not already been defined at the current scope. Assuming those checks are passed and Intellisense is happy, Visual Studio sends a message to the Windows Memory Manager asking for 4 bytes of free memory for the `int` you wish to define. Assuming all goes well, the Windows Memory Manager sends back the memory address at which `val` will be stored. Let's assume that the memory address is 750,000. That memory address is then entered into the lvalue column in the symbol table.

The Bucket Analogy assumes that you have a pile of empty buckets lying around. The buckets come in different sizes. Some are big enough to hold one byte of data, some can hold two bytes of data, and some buckets are big enough to hold 16 bytes of data. Because you want to define an `int` data type, you select a bucket that is big enough to hold an `int` data type. As you learned in Chapter 3, an `int` takes 4 bytes of memory, so the bucket you select is a 4-byte bucket.

Now, paint the variable's name, `val` in this example, on the bucket so you can distinguish it from other buckets that might be stored in memory. Now, pretend you can physically take the bucket inside your computer and place it at memory address 750,000. When you are finished, you might see something like what is shown in Figure 4-4.

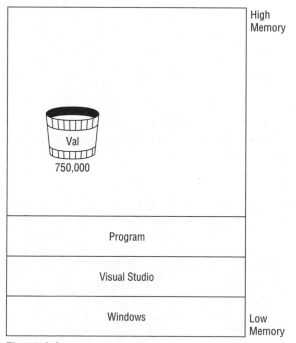

Figure 4-4

The Bucket Analogy relates to a data definition in the following way:

1. The lvalue of a bucket tells you where to find the bucket in memory.

2. The rvalue of a bucket tells you what is stored in the bucket.

3. The data type of the item (such as `int`) tells you how big a bucket is (in this case 4 bytes).

I use the Bucket Analogy again in Chapter 5 to help explain some additional concepts associated with data definitions and how the data are used in a program. For now, simply remember the three major points of the Bucket Analogy. Those points should help you understand the content of later chapters, and make it easier to detect, isolate, and fix program errors.

Types of Program Errors

There are three basic types of program errors. Obviously, your objective is to write programs that are totally free of program errors. Program errors are also referred to as program *bugs*. (The term "bug" was created because one of the earliest program errors ever detected involved a moth flying into the computer and short-circuiting the electronics. The process of removing program errors is called *debugging*.) While that goal is laudable, every programmer, no matter how seasoned, writes programs that contain errors. A skilled programmer, however, can detect, isolate, and correct program errors more quickly than a less skilled programmer. Also, experienced programmers do make fewer programming errors simply because of their experience. The lesson here is that you should expect to make a lot of program errors in the beginning . . . every beginner does.

In the beginning you will start off with the "flat-forehead" type of programming error. Those are the kind of errors that, when you do find them, you slam the heel of your hand into your forehead while mumbling, "How could I make such a silly mistake?" Relax. We've all made those mistakes…and still do! The key is not to get discouraged. View each program error as a challenge and learn from the experience. Alas, as your programming skills advance, so will the type of errors you make. While there will be fewer errors as you gain experience, those errors you do make tend to become more sophisticated and harder to isolate and fix.

Let's take a quick overview of the three types of program errors. I will have a lot more to say about errors and debugging in later chapters. For now, however, let's just categorize the types of program errors.

Syntax Errors

The first type of error is a syntax error. You already know that syntax errors are caused when you don't obey the syntax rules of C#. A common syntax rule you might make in the beginning is forgetting to terminate each program statement with a semicolon.

Intellisense does an excellent job of catching syntax errors. While you may hate the squiggly line that Intellisense displays, it's a lot easier for Intellisense to detect and isolate syntax errors than it is for you to do it yourself.

Semantic Errors

A *semantic error* occurs when you obey the syntax rules of the language but are using the statement out of context. For example, a sentence in English is expected to have a noun and a verb. Consider the sentence "The dog meowed." This sentence does obey the rules of having a noun and a verb, but the context of the sentence is out of whack. Dogs don't meow, therefore the context of the statement is incorrect.

The error message I showed you earlier:

```
The name 'i' does not exist in the current context
```

refers to a type of semantic error. There may well be a variable named i defined somewhere in the program, but it is not currently in scope. That is, you are trying to use i when it is out of scope. Intellisense does a good job of detecting semantic errors.

Logic Errors

Logic errors are those errors that remain after all the semantic and syntax errors have been removed. Usually, logic errors manifest themselves when the result the program produces doesn't match the result your test data suggest it should produce. Most of the time, logic errors are found in the Process Step you studied in Chapter 3. Logic errors occur when you implement the algorithm for solving the problem incorrectly.

The key to fixing logic errors is to be able to reproduce the error consistently. A repeatable logic error is much easier to track down and fix than an error that appears to be occurring randomly. (In Chapter 5 you will learn the details of using some of the tools Visual Studio provides to help you detect and isolate program bugs.)

The Visual Studio Debugger

Visual Studio provides a number of tools to help you detect errors in your programs. Intellisense is one of those tools that sits in the background carefully examining your program code as you type it into the Source window. Intellisense does a great job of finding syntax and semantic errors, but is less helpful in finding logic errors. Because the computer has no intelligence of its own, it blindly follows whatever instructions you give it even if those instructions are wrong. Once you have the syntax and semantics of your program stated correctly, you need a different tool to help you out if the program produces incorrect results. The next line of defense in fixing program errors is the Visual Studio debugger.

The Debugging Process

A *debugger* is a programming tool designed to help you fix program errors. Visual Studio has a powerful program debugger built into its IDE. The process of removing program errors is called *debugging*. There are four steps in the debugging process:

1. **Detection:** Obviously, to be able to correct a program error you have to know the program contains an error in the first place. Detection requires that you have a set of data you can use to test whether the program is working properly. Quite often the test data set is generated by hand or is an input data set known to produce a correct result.

2. **Stabilize:** Once you suspect that there is a program error, the next task is to stabilize the error. By stabilizing an error, I mean arrange it so that you can repeat the error consistently. A *stabilized error* occurs when a consistent set of input data yields a consistent incorrect result. The worst kind of program error is one that acts randomly — that is, one for which some program runs yield correct results while other runs show an error.

3. **Isolation:** When the program bug first makes itself known, you may feel that you have no idea where in the program to begin looking for it. If you followed my suggestion of using the Five Program Steps to design the program, test each step starting with the Initialization Step. Most of the time you will discover the bug in the Input and Process Steps. Obviously, you need to examine the data to make sure it's correct and then watch how that data is transformed during the Process Step. The Visual Studio debugger makes this step much easier than it would be otherwise.

4. **Correction:** Once you have isolated the bug and know what caused it, it usually only takes a few minutes to make the correction. Make sure you understand the bug before you correct it. Too many students take the attitude, "Let's change this statement and hope that fixes the bug." This is the shotgun approach to debugging and it is rarely successful. Stumbling onto the exact program line that causes the bug and then blindly typing in the precise form for the statement to fix the bug is about as likely as winning the lottery. Study the bug and understand *why* it is giving you incorrect results. Only then can you truly fix it.

Making Repetitious Debugging Easier

If your program has a particularly nasty bug, chances are that you will have to rerun the program many times. Frequently, this repetition also requires you to type in the same data set each time the program is rerun. Retyping the data into the textboxes each time you run the program gets very tedious in a hurry. If you feel that correcting the bug is going to take several repeated runs of the program, you may want to consider using the Properties window to set the Text property of each of the input textbox objects to its associated test value. This will save you from having to retype the input data each time you rerun the program. After you have fixed the bug, be sure to remove the test data from the Text property of each textbox object.

Using the Debugger

The Visual Studio debugger becomes active whenever you run a program within the IDE. To learn how to use the debugger, load in the integer division program you wrote in Chapter 3. Although that program is so simple there's not much that can go wrong, we can use it to illustrate some of the features of the Visual Studio debugger.

Setting a Breakpoint

A basic feature of any debugger is the ability to set a *breakpoint* in the program. A breakpoint is simply a point in the program at which you would like to pause the execution of the program. Because program execution pauses at the breakpoint, you can use the debugger to inspect the state of various program variables as they exist at that point.

There are two ways to set a breakpoint. First, you can place the cursor on the program line at which you want to pause the program and press the F9 key. This causes the debugger to highlight that line in red and place a red dot in the extreme left margin of the Source window, as shown in Figure 4-5.

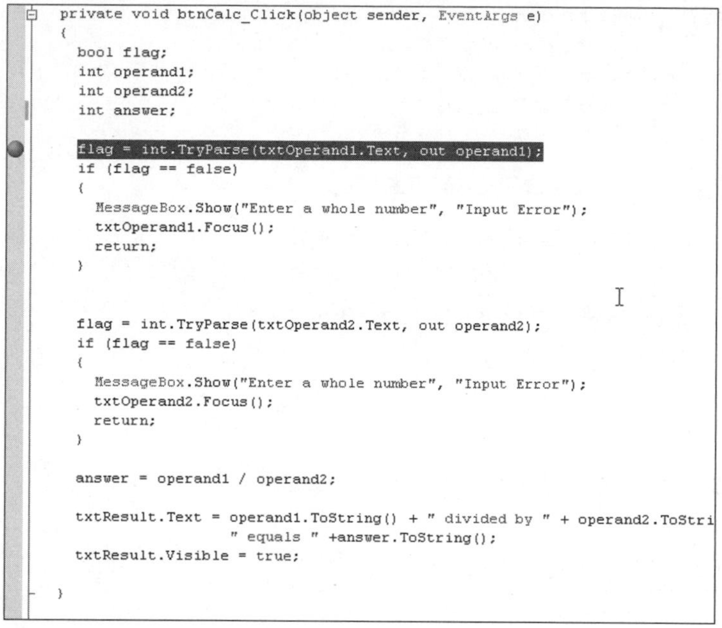

```
private void btnCalc_Click(object sender, EventArgs e)
{
    bool flag;
    int operand1;
    int operand2;
    int answer;

    flag = int.TryParse(txtOperand1.Text, out operand1);
    if (flag == false)
    {
        MessageBox.Show("Enter a whole number", "Input Error");
        txtOperand1.Focus();
        return;
    }


    flag = int.TryParse(txtOperand2.Text, out operand2);
    if (flag == false)
    {
        MessageBox.Show("Enter a whole number", "Input Error");
        txtOperand2.Focus();
        return;
    }


    answer = operand1 / operand2;

    txtResult.Text = operand1.ToString() + " divided by " + operand2.ToStri
                        " equals " +answer.ToString();
    txtResult.Visible = true;


}
```

Figure 4-5

A second way to set a breakpoint is to click the mouse while it's located in the extreme left margin and even with the program line at which you want to pause the program. (The extreme left margin is where the red dot appears in Figure 4-5.)

To remove a breakpoint, move the cursor to the red line of the breakpoint to be removed and press the F9 key again. You can use the F9 key to toggle a breakpoint on and off for a particular line. Likewise, you can click the extreme left margin a second time to remove a breakpoint.

Using a Breakpoint to Examine Variables

After you have set a breakpoint, run the program until it stops there. When the breakpoint is reached, Visual Studio switches to the Source window and displays the line where the breakpoint was set. Figure 4-6 shows the state of Visual Studio at the point where the breakpoint was set.

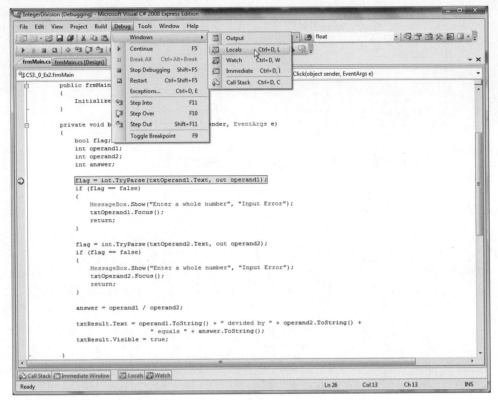

Figure 4-6

While it doesn't show in Figure 4-6, the breakpoint line has changed its background color from red to yellow. Also note that the red dot now has an arrow in it, pointing to the line at which the breakpoint was set.

To examine the variables at that point in the program, use the Debug ⇨ Windows ⇨ Locals menu sequence to activate the Locals window. Visual Studio should look similar to what is shown in Figure 4-7.

The Locals window appears near the bottom of Figure 4-7 and shows you those variables with local scope. Variables that have local scope are those variables that are visible within the current method. In Figure 4-7 the program is paused in the btnCalc_Click() method. Therefore, the Locals window enables you to examine those variables with local scope relative to the btnCalc_Click() method.

Figure 4-8 presents an enlarged view of the Locals window for the breakpoint shown in Figure 4-7.

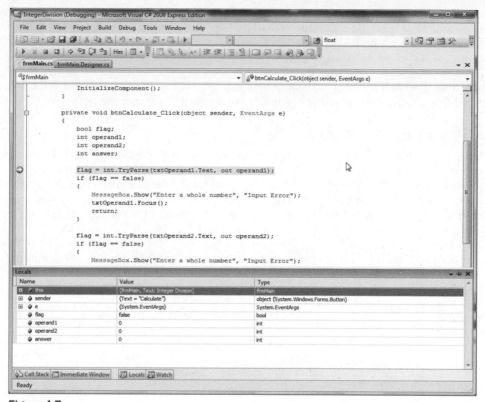

Figure 4-7

Figure 4-8

In Figure 4-8, the C# keyword `this` refers to the currently active object. In the current program, `frmMain` is the currently active object. If you click the plus sign shown in the left margin of the Locals window of the `this` entry, you can see the other objects associated with `frmMain`. When you click the plus sign, the window displays details about the entry and a minus sign is shown where the plus sign used to be. If you click the minus sign, the image reverts back to its previous state. Therefore, clicking a plus sign in the Locals window expands the window to present additional information while clicking a minus sign restores the previous (collapsed) state of the window.

The next two lines in Figure 4-8 display information about the sender and e parameters, respectively. These two variables provide information about the event that caused the program to execute the btnCalc_Click() method. Finally, the last four lines provide information about the flag, operand1, operand2, and answer variables, respectively.

You can also observe the value of a variable by moving the cursor over the variable in the Source window. This action causes Visual Studio to display the current value of the variable.

Single-Stepping the Program

In Figure 4-7 the breakpoint line has changed from red to yellow. The fact that the line is yellow is the debugger's way of telling you that it is about to execute the breakpoint line. This means that the debugger has stopped the program *before* executing the breakpoint line. This is exactly what you want. Because you set a breakpoint at a place in the program where you think a particular statement is causing a problem, the yellow line means that you can examine the state of the variables just before the line is executed.

Now, press the F10 key. Notice how the yellow line advances to the next program line and the original breakpoint line reverts to its red background color. The arrow drawn in the margin has moved down to the line that is about to be executed, and the red dot has reverted to its original state. You can see the changes produced by the F10 key in Figure 4-9.

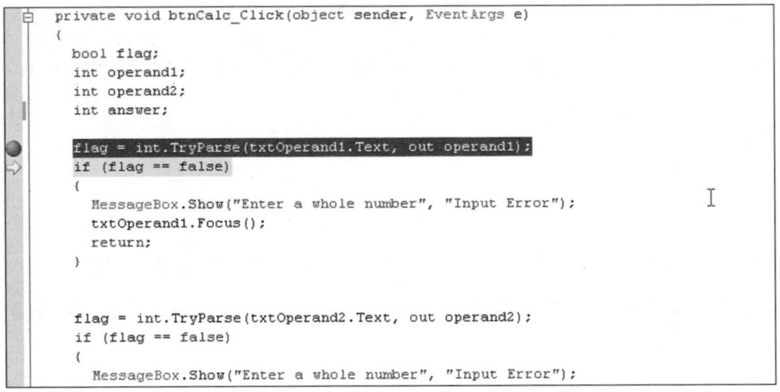

```
private void btnCalc_Click(object sender, EventArgs e)
{
    bool flag;
    int operand1;
    int operand2;
    int answer;

    flag = int.TryParse(txtOperand1.Text, out operand1);
    if (flag == false)
    {
        MessageBox.Show("Enter a whole number", "Input Error");
        txtOperand1.Focus();
        return;
    }

    flag = int.TryParse(txtOperand2.Text, out operand2);
    if (flag == false)
    {
        MessageBox.Show("Enter a whole number", "Input Error");
```

Figure 4-9

The process of advancing the program one line at a time is called *single-stepping* the program. Because the program has advanced to the next line, you can now examine the values of the variables to see if executing the statement in which the breakpoint was set changed these values in the desired way. If not, something in the breakpoint line caused a problem. If the values of the variables are as expected, you can continue to press the F10 key to execute additional lines or set another breakpoint at some other place in the program and run the program to that breakpoint.

To restart the program so it runs "at full speed," simply press the F5 key or click the Run icon. (See Figure 1-7.) If you have set another breakpoint that is executed at a later point in the program, the F5 key causes the program to execute normally until the new breakpoint is reached. You can continue to set additional breakpoints until you find the statement line that is causing the error. Once you have located the source of the error, correcting it is usually fairly simple.

As you can see, the debugger is a powerful tool when you're trying to perform the isolation step of the debugging process. You will use many other debugger features in later chapters. However, simply being able to set a breakpoint, examine the values of variables, and single-step the program will go a long way toward correcting program errors.

Defensive Coding

The best way to avoid program errors is to write perfect code. Since that's not going to happen anytime soon (I've been waiting for over 30 years), the next best thing is to write your code with the expectation that something may go wrong. The first step in this defensive strategy is simple:

> Write your code so someone else can easily understand it.

Consider the following list of things you can do in your program source code to make it easier to understand.

Use Program Comments

A program comment is simply a message you leave in the program to help the reader understand the code. There is an art to using comments. Too few comments force the reader to take more time to understand what the program is doing. Too many comments can actually get in the way of the code by adding unnecessary clutter. Commenting every line in a program is almost never necessary. At the other extreme, I've seen instances where the code is so complex that it was easier to put in the name and page numbers of a book than to explain it ourselves. Try to use comments for those statement(s) that do something unusual or are critical to processing the data. Simply stated, a comment should make it easier for the reader to understand your code, and not get in the way of that understanding.

There are two types of program comments: single-line comments and multi-line comments. Always keep in mind that comments are ignored by the compiler, so they have no impact on the performance of the program. (There goes one excuse for not having comments in a program!)

Single-Line Comments

You have seen single-line comments before. These are comments introduced with a pair of slashes followed by the comment. The comment must fit on one line. For example:

```
answer = operand1 / operand2;      // This is the Process Step
```

This line uses a comment to identify that this statement performs the process step in the program.

One issue is whether to place the comment as shown in the preceding example or to have the comment precede the line, as here:

```
// This is the Process Step
answer = operand1 / operand2;
```

If you are working for a company writing commercial code, there may be a company policy that dictates the style of comments used. Otherwise, which one you select is a matter of personal preference.

My choice is dictated by the comment itself. If the comment can fit at the end of a line without the reader having to scroll the Source window to read it, I prefer to place the comment at the end of a program statement. Doing this means that I can see one more line of source code in the Source window over the alternative style. If the comment is fairly long and would require scrolling to read it, I place the comment above the program statement. Either way, remember that everything on the line after the double slash character pair (//) is ignored by the compiler.

Multi-Line Comments

Multi-line comments are introduced with a backslash-asterisk combination of characters and terminated with a slash-asterisk. For example:

```
/* Purpose: The btnCalc-Click() event method is used to
 * calculate the result of dividing two integer values.
 */
private void btnCalc_Click(object sender, EventArgs e)
```

Anything that appears between the comment pairs /* and */ is treated as a comment and ignored by the compiler. The asterisk at the start of the second line of the comment was automatically supplied by Visual Studio. The asterisks help make the comment lines stand out in the code. The most obvious use for the multi-line comment is when you need to place a long comment in the code. As a rule, you should make each line short enough that it doesn't require horizontal scrolling to read it.

However, you can do more with multi-line comments than add lengthy comments to a program. There will be times when you have a section of code that is giving you a problem and you'd like to try an alternative algorithm. Because you're not sure the new algorithm will work and you don't want to retype the original code if the change fails, the easiest way to remove the code from the program yet still have it available is to surround it with a multi-line comment. For example:

```
/*    This is the original code
 * x = y * .33 - (m * g);
 * z = x % 2 + sigma;
 */
// Start new code...
x = y * .45 - (m * g);
z = x % 3.2 + sigma;
// End new code
```

In this example I have commented out the original two lines of code by surrounding them with the multi-line comment pairs. My style is to precede the trial code with a single-line comment marking the start of the new code, followed by the new trial code, followed by a second single-line comment marking the end of the trial code. If the trial code doesn't work properly, it's easy to restore the program to its original state by removing the trial code and uncommenting the original code.

Program comments are useful in documenting what the code is doing and also for trying alternative code. Because comments have no impact on the performance of the program and make it easier for others to read and understand your code, you should use them often.

Use Meaningful Variable Names

Just because you've followed the C# rules for creating variable names does not mean you've implemented a good variable name. A good variable name has two properties:

1. The variable name reflects the purpose or use of the data in the program. If you are writing a program that converts Fahrenheit to Celsius temperatures, the variable names `t1` and `t2` aren't really helpful to the reader of your code. Select variable names that help the reader understand the code.

2. The variable name is long enough to indicate its use, but short enough that you don't get tired of typing it. While `t1` and `t2` are too short to be helpful, changing them to `currentFahrenheitTemperature` and `convertedCelsiusTemperature` is probably overkill. Trust me, you'd get tired of typing in such long variable names.

Try to strike a balance between names that are long enough to be helpful and names that are tedious to type.

Avoid Magic Numbers

Suppose you read the following line in a program:

```
f = 125 + (s - 1) * 10;
```

It might take a bit of head-scratching to figure out what the statement means without additional information. Now contrast that statement with this:

```
speedingFine = MINIMUMSPEEDINGFINE + (observedSpeed - speedLimit) *
               DOLLARSPERMILEOVERLIMIT;
```

Symbolic Constants

The new statement makes more sense because you have used better variable names and replaced the magic numbers with symbolic constants. A *constant* is simply a variable whose value cannot be changed while the program runs. A *symbolic constant* is a constant that has a name that reflects the constant's function in the program. Convention finds symbolic constants rendered entirely in uppercase.

Symbolic constants are usually defined near the top of the class in which they appear. For example:

```
public class frmMain : Form
{
  const decimal MINIMUMSPEEDINGFINE = 125M;
  const decimal DOLLARSPERMILEOVERLIMIT = 10M;
  // Rest of the class code appears below...
```

The C# keyword `const` in front of a data type means that you are defining a constant of that data type. Because it is a constant, you must initialize the constant at the point where you define it in the program, as shown in the preceding code. Once these values are initialized, they cannot be changed while the program is running.

You gain another advantage from using symbolic constants. Suppose you didn't use MINIMUMSPEEDINGFINE for the minimum fine. Instead, suppose you used the magic number 125 throughout the program. Let's further assume that that identical value is also the minimum fine for overweight trucks and motorcyclists who don't wear a helmet. Finally, let's assume that these three amounts are scattered several dozen times throughout the program. Now some politician decides to raise the minimum speeding fine to $150. The truck and helmet fines stay the same. They now hand you the program and say, "Fix it!"

You can't just do a global search-and-replace for 125 in the program. That would change the truck and helmet fines, too. You are forced to find each program occurrence of 125, decipher the code to see whether the 125 relates to a speeding fine, and then either make the change or leave the line alone. This is a slow process just waiting for something to go wrong.

Suppose instead you had originally written the program like this:

```
const decimal MINIMUMSPEEDINGFINE = 125M;
const decimal TRUCKOVERWEIGHTFINE = 125M;
const decimal NOHELMETFINE = 125M;
```

This way, you avoid the use of magic numbers in the code. Not only is your code easier to read, simply changing one line in the program to

```
const decimal MINIMUMSPEEDINGFINE = 150M;
```

and recompiling the program makes all the necessary changes to the program automatically. Using a symbolic constant permits you to make the necessary program change in seconds and still be absolutely certain that the correct values are used the next time the program is run.

Symbolic constants make your programs easier to read and change when necessary. Avoid magic numbers in your code and use symbolic constants often. They will save you time in the long run.

Summary

In this chapter you learned what you need to do to define a variable for use in a program. While the approach taken here may seem like using an H-bomb to kill an ant, understanding what Visual Studio is doing with something as simple as a data definition will ultimately make you a better programmer. Having studied this chapter, you should now understand the following:

❑   Operators and operands

❑   Binary, unary, and ternary operators

❑   Expressions

❑   Statements

❑   lvalues and rvalues

❑   What a symbol table is and how Visual Studio uses it

❑   How Visual Studio interacts with Windows via messages

❑   The Bucket Analogy

❑   Several aspects of the Visual Studio debugger

❑   The advantages of using symbolic constants in your programs

Make sure you understand completely what lvalues and rvalues are and how they relate to data definitions. We will use those terms often in subsequent chapters.

Exercises

1.   Using a program that you've previously written, set several breakpoints in the program and single-step through the program. Are there any points in the source code where you cannot set a breakpoint?

2.   Rewrite the program from the exercise at the end of Chapter 3 that converts Fahrenheit temperatures to Celsius. Use symbolic constants to make the program easier to understand.

3.   What is an lvalue and what is an rvalue? How can they be used to explain the difference between a data definition and a data declaration?

4.   When you use the Bucket Analogy to explain lvalues and rvalues at your next cocktail party (hey . . . it could happen), what determines the size of the bucket? What are the key elements of the Bucket Analogy?

Understanding Reference Data Types

In Chapter 3, you learned about the different value data types that C# makes available for use in your programs. This chapter concentrates on the other major type of data in C#: reference data types. In this chapter, you will learn:

- ❑ What a reference data type is
- ❑ How reference data types differ from value data types
- ❑ How the Bucket Analogy can be applied to reference data types

You will also learn about the following:

- ❑ String variables
- ❑ Verbatim string literals
- ❑ DateTime variables
- ❑ Constructor methods
- ❑ Overloaded methods
- ❑ Method signatures

In a very real sense, object-oriented programming owes much of its popularity to the power that reference data types bring to the programming table. Reference types are fundamental to object-oriented programming and you will use them a lot.

String Variables

You already know that data used in a computer program falls into two broad categories: 1) numeric data and 2) textual data. Chapter 3 presented the value types that are used to store numeric data in a program. *String variables* are used to store textual data.

Data entered by a user into a program's textbox object is textual data. However, if you want to manipulate the user's input, you must first convert the textual data to numeric data by using the data type's `TryParse()` method. For example, if you want to convert the content of the `txtOperand1` textbox object into an `int` data type, you use the following statement:

```
flag = int.TryParse(txtOperand1.Text, out val);
```

This statement converts the textual data typed into the `txtOperand1` textbox object into an `int` data type, storing the integer result in variable `val`. What you may not have realized is that the `Text` property of the textbox object is actually a string variable! The purpose of the `TryParse()` method is to convert the string data into a numeric data type.

In this chapter, I want to discuss string variables as places to store textual data. Textual data, as a general rule, are not meant to be manipulated mathematically. Instead, you want to keep the data in a text format by storing it in a string variable. It's common to use textual data for storing names, addresses, phone numbers, zip codes, customer IDs, and so on. Note that some textual data actually are pure numbers, such as a zip code. How do you decide when to store something as a string or as a numeric data type? The rule is simple: If you are not going to manipulate the data in some mathematical way, store the data as a string.

Defining a String Reference Variable

Suppose you want to store the name `"Hailey"` in a program. Placing the double quotation marks around a sequence of text marks everything between the quotes as a *string literal*. Stated differently, you "literally" want to assign the word `"Hailey"` into the `name` variable. The double quotation marks that surround the string literal are not part of the literal. The quotation marks simply serve to tell Visual Studio the starting and ending points for the textual data.

You can assign the string literal `"Hailey"` into `name` with the following two lines of code:

```
string name;
name = "Hailey";
```

Intellisense parses each of these two lines and finds the syntax to be correct . . . There is no dreaded squiggly line. So far, so good.

Let's consider the details of what Visual Studio is doing with the first statement line. Because there are no syntax errors in the first line, Visual Studio inspects the symbol table in the way we discussed in Chapter 4. Table 5-1 shows a simplified symbol table similar to what you saw in Chapter 4.

Table 5-1

ID	Data Type	Scope	Lvalue	...
hatSize	double	0	650,000	
k	int	0	630,480	

Because the variable name is not in the symbol table, Visual Studio sends a message to Windows requesting enough memory for a reference variable. All *reference variables* use the same amount of storage: 4 bytes. Provided the Windows Memory Manager can find 4 bytes of free memory, Windows returns the memory address for the reference variable name. We have assumed that the memory address for name is 670,000. Visual Studio makes an entry into the symbol table, as shown in Table 5-2.

Table 5-2

ID	Data Type	Scope	Lvalue	...
hatSize	double	0	650,000	
k	int	0	630,480	
name	string	0	670,000	

Using the diagrams you studied in Chapter 4, we can show the lvalue and rvalue values for name as depicted in Figure 5-1.

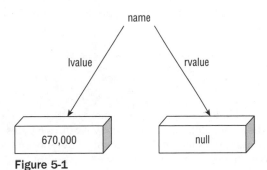

Figure 5-1

The interpretation of the lvalue of name in Figure 5-1 is exactly as it was in Chapter 4. That is, the lvalue is the memory address where the string reference variable name is stored in memory.

The Meaning of null

Once Visual Studio has received the reference variable's lvalue from the Windows Memory Manager, it immediately assigns null into the rvalue of name. null is a keyword in C# and is used to signify that no useable data is currently associated with the variable. Anytime a variable has an rvalue that is equal to null, Visual Studio knows there is nothing useful associated with that variable. A memory map for the current state of the name reference variable is shown in Figure 5-2.

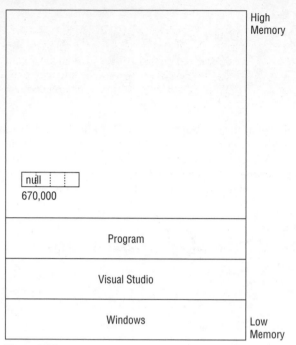

Figure 5-2

Using the Bucket Analogy from Chapter 4, you can verbalize the information in Figure 5-2 like this: "The bucket for the name reference variable is stored at memory location 670,000 (its lvalue) and the content (rvalue) of its 4-byte bucket is null."

Now consider what happens when the second line is executed:

```
name = "Hailey";
```

Each textual letter in the name Hailey takes one byte of storage. (See the sidebar " Unicode Versus ASCII.") This means that the string literal Hailey actually requires 6 bytes of storage. However, you just read that the Windows Memory Manager returned only 4 bytes of storage for the rvalue of name. You are probably saying to yourself, " Wait a minute! How do you hold 6 bytes of data in a 4-byte bucket? " Answer: You don't!

Unicode Versus ASCII

The need for a standard way to code computer information was recognized as early as the 1960s. The result was the American Standard Code for Information Interchange, or ASCII character set. The codes spanned 128 characters and included alpha and digit characters and punctuation, plus some non-printing codes. Because there were only 128 characters, the entire ASCII set could be represented in one byte (i.e., $256 = 2^8$) with room to spare.

> Problems began to arise as computing took on a more international flavor. Many languages and systems, such as the Kanji system for writing Japanese, have thousands of characters. The World Wide Web also pushed the need for a universal character set to the forefront. The result is the Unicode character set. The Unicode character set uses two bytes per character and permits over 65,000 individual characters to be represented. C# uses the Unicode character set by default.

Why Reference Types are Different from Value Types

This is the really cool part about reference variables: Reference variables can be associated with as much or as little data as necessary. The value data types you studied in Chapter 3 all have fixed storage requirements. For example, a `byte` data type requires one byte of storage but a `long` data type requires eight bytes of storage. For value data types, the number of bytes required to hold the rvalue is etched in stone for each one. While using a fixed number of bytes for value types works fine, it won't work for things like string data. After all, the string might be used to hold a name like Hailey, but some other string variable in the program might be used to store the Declaration of Independence. Clearly, reference data types have to work differently to accommodate the varying lengths of data that can be associated with them. The way C# (and other programming languages) manages this is elegantly simple.

With a reference variable, the second line of code:

```
name = "Hailey";
```

causes Visual Studio to send a *second* message to Windows. In essence, the message is, "Hey, Windows! It's me, Visual Studio . . . again. I need 6 bytes of free memory to store some data. Can you help me out?" Notice that Visual Studio doesn't say anything about the nature of the data other than how many bytes it needs for storage. When we discussed the value types in Chapter 3, we just assumed that Windows knew how many bytes are associated with the various value types. With reference types, Visual Studio can't assume Windows knows anything about the number of bytes needed because the storage requirements can be fairly short (`"Hailey"`) or very long (the Declaration of Independence).

Assuming there's some free memory available in the system, the Windows Memory Manager sends a message back saying: "Hey, Visual Studio! I found the storage you need starting at memory location 725,000. Now leave me alone for a while . . . I'm busy." Memory Managers get cranky from time to time because they have other programs making similar requests too. After all, there could be other programs running at the same time that you're running Visual Studio. Because you just asked it for a place to store `name`, it's not real happy to hear from you again so soon for this 6-byte storage request. (Not to worry . . . the Memory Manager will get over it.)

When Windows returns the memory address 725,000 to Visual Studio, Visual Studio immediately takes the name `"Hailey"` and moves it into memory starting at address 725,000. The state of the memory map for `name` now appears as shown in Figure 5-3.

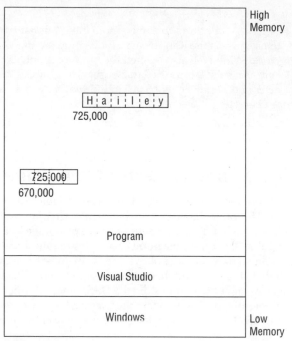

Figure 5-3

Reference Variable Rules

Compare Figures 5-2 and 5-3. First, note how the rvalue of name has changed from its previous value of null to the memory address where the data are stored. Second, you can see that the 6 bytes starting at memory location 725,000 now hold the string literal "Hailey". These observations illustrate the following rules for reference variables:

1. The rvalue of a reference variable can have only one of two values: 1) null or 2) a memory address.

2. If the rvalue of a reference variable is null, the reference variable contains no useful data.

3. If the rvalue of a reference variable is not null, it contains the memory address where the data associated with the reference variable is stored.

The first rule confirms several things about reference variables. First, unlike a value type, which has an rvalue that holds the data you're interested in, a reference variable does not hold the actual data you want to use in a program. Second, because the rvalue of a reference can hold only null or a memory address, the size of a reference variable is *always* 4 bytes. This means that the size of a reference variable's bucket is always the same regardless of the actual data that might be associated with it. When this topic comes up at your next party, you can look really smart by saying, "The state of a reference variable is either null or a valid memory address." (This sentence is quite flexible and can be used either as a pickup line or an icebreaker at a party.)

The second rule affects the way Intellisense enforces the syntax of C# statements that use reference variables. If you try to perform some type of string operation on a reference variable whose rvalue is null, Intellisense complains and issues an error message. For example, if you try to pass name to a method when it contains a null rvalue, Intellisense will say something like this:

```
Use of unassigned local variable 'name'.
```

Intellisense does this because it knows the null rvalue means the program has no useful data associated with the variable.

The third rule is the most important. If a reference variable contains a non-null value, that value is the memory address where the data are stored. Indeed, this is why they are called reference variables. The *non-null rvalue* of a reference variable refers you to the memory location at which the data are stored.

Reference Type Variables Versus Value Type Variables

Consider the interpretation of the Bucket Analogy as it relates to the two types of variables. With value type variables, you look in the bucket and you immediately find the data you are interested in stored in the variable's rvalue. Also, with value types, the size of the bucket varies according to the type of data being stored in the bucket. That is, the bucket size for an int data type is 4 bytes while the bucket size for a decimal data type is 16 bytes. Therefore, you are interested in the size of a value type's bucket because it gives you a clue as to the type of data being stored there.

With a reference type variable, you look into the bucket and find either null or a memory address. If you find a null in the bucket, the variable has nothing interesting associated with it. On the other hand, if you look into the bucket and see something other than null, you must jump to that memory address to inspect the data.

The conclusion is simple: Value types have an rvalue that *is* the data. Reference types have an rvalue that either refers you to the data (a memory address) or does not reference any data (null).

Why Do Reference Variables Work the Way They Do?

Why did the people who designed C# make reference variables work the way they do? Consider the way value types work. Suppose you write a method that squares the number entered into the program by the user. After you convert the user's input into a value type, like an int, you now want to pass that value to a method you plan to write named SquareIt(). The purpose of the SquareIt() method is to take that value, square it, and return that squared value to the caller. To do this, Visual Studio makes a temporary copy of the value of the number, calls your SquareIt() method, and tells it where that temporary copy of the number is located. Because an int uses only 4 bytes of storage, the process of making a copy of the int is very fast and doesn't use up much additional memory for the temporary copy.

Now suppose you have a program with a string variable that refers to the text of three chapters of a book. (Perhaps you read the data from a disk file into the program.) This means that the string variable might point to a block of memory with hundreds of thousands of bytes in it. Now suppose that you write a method whose purpose is to search those hundreds of thousands of bytes looking for a specific word. If the method call works as it does for value types, Visual Studio has to copy those hundreds of thousands of bytes into a temporary memory location. Copying hundreds of thousands of bytes has two disadvantages. First, it's fairly slow relative to copying just a few bytes as with a value type. Second, the temporary copy of the chapters would take up another huge chunk of memory, possibly causing the program to run out of memory.

C# solves these performance and memory-limitation problems by simply passing the *address* of the memory location where the data are stored. Because the rvalue of a reference variable tells Visual Studio where to find the data, the 4-byte rvalue of a reference variable is all the method needs to find the data. Visual Studio doesn't need to copy the data. The method can find the data by just jumping to the memory location it receives from the reference variable's rvalue. This approach saves both time and memory.

That's the good news.

Pass by Value versus Pass by Reference

The bad news is that the method that uses a reference variable has direct access to the data. Recall that a method that uses a value type receives a *copy* of the user's value, not the value itself. This means that the method cannot permanently change the user's value. After all, with value types there are two buckets in memory: the original bucket and the bucket containing the copy. The method can alter the copy's rvalue but has no clue where the original bucket is stored. Therefore, this *pass by value* way of sending data to a method protects the original data because only a copy of the data is seen by the method. With a reference variable, you are sending the actual memory location of where the data are stored. Passing the actual memory location is called *pass by reference.* This means that the method has direct access to the original data, not to a copy of it. It also means that, if the method wants to, it can permanently affect the data associated with the reference variable.

The old saying, "There's no such thing as a free lunch," applies to programming too. You can use reference variables when writing a method to improve its performance and conserve memory. However, the price you pay is that you expose the data to the possibility of contamination because the method has direct access to it. This is sort of like a medieval king who takes the time to hide his daughter away in the castle tower, but then turns around and hands out her room key to every knight in the kingdom . . . probably not a good idea. Similarly, making the effort to hide data isn't terribly worthwhile if you tell everyone where it's hidden. Chapter 10 revisits these (encapsulation) issues and offers ways to cope with them.

A Little Efficiency Gain

As discussed earlier, the following statements caused Visual Studio to send *two* memory requests to the Windows Memory Manager:

```
string name;
name = "Hailey";
```

The first was to find storage for `name` and the second was to find storage for `"Hailey"`. Anything you can do to lessen the number of messages sent between Windows and Visual Studio is probably a good thing. This is because exchanging messages between Visual Studio and Windows takes time. You can accomplish the same thing and save some time by collapsing the two statements into one:

```
string name = "Hailey";
```

In this case, only one message needs to be sent to the Windows Memory Manager. That message might be stated as, "Windows . . . wake up! I need a reference variable capable of storing 6 bytes of data." Windows knows a reference variable requires four bytes of storage. Assuming it responds with the information shown in Figure 5-3, the message sent back might be, "Hey, Visual Studio! I've stored your reference variable at memory address 670,000 and set its rvalue to 725,000 . . . You're welcome." Visual Studio then proceeds to store `"Hailey"` starting at memory address 725,000, as shown in Figure 5-3.

Note that the end result is exactly the same regardless of whether you use the one- or two-line version for assigning the string literal. The one-line version, however, accomplishes the same task with one less message being sent to Windows. True, doing away with one Windows message isn't going to make much of a performance difference. However, if your program repeats a message thousands of times, the user might notice the difference. Obviously, either way works just fine. However, you are likely to see experienced programmers use the second form more often. If you do see the shorter version, it could well be that program speed has nothing to do with it. The programmer may have chosen it simply because it requires less typing!

Using String Variables

String variables are reference variables that enable you to store and manipulate textual data. While most people associate computers with number crunching, a large part of the work done by computers involves manipulating textual data, not numbers. Indeed, database programs are often pushing around huge amounts of textual data, often even more than numeric data.

String Concatenation

We used string concatenation in an earlier program, but I didn't say much about it. Simply stated, *string concatenation* is the process of taking one string and adding another string to it to form a new string. For example:

```
string name = "Hailey";
name = name + " Mohr";
```

In the preceding statements, name is assigned `"Hailey"`, as explained earlier. The second line concatenates the string literal `" Mohr"` (there is a space before `Mohr"`) to form the new string `"Hailey Mohr"`. This new string is then assigned into name. As you can see, string concatenation is little more than adding one string onto another string. In this example, the string concatenation takes the first and last names and concatenates them into a full name.

Shorthand Assignment Operators

Taking one value and adding a second value to it is such a common task in programming that C# provides a number of shorthand assignment operators for the basic math and string concatenation operators. For example, suppose variable name currently holds the string `"Hailey"` as you saw just now. You can take the original line shown earlier:

```
name = name + " Mohr";
```

and rewrite it, using a shorthand concatenation operator, as

```
name += " Mohr";
```

The result is exactly as before: `"Hailey Mohr"`. In the statements

```
int i = 10;
i += 5;
```

the value of i is now 15. Therefore, the "+=" assignment operator serves a dual purpose: It performs string concatenation when string variables are used, or it can be used for addition when value type variables are used. Table 5-3 presents a list of the shorthand assignment operators.

Table 5-3

Operator	Example	Interpretation
+=	val += days;	val = val + days;
-=	val -= days;	val = val - days;
*=	val *= days;	val = val *days;
/=	val /= days;	val = val / days;
%=	val %= days;	val = val % days;

Of the operators shown in Table 5-3, only the concatenation operator (+) makes sense when you're working with string data. All the operators in the table, however, may be used with value types. Obviously, the shorthand operators don't give you anything you didn't already have. However, programmers usually don't like to type more than they have to, so experienced C# programmers use the shorthand operators often.

String Manipulation

You already know that a string is a reference data type. You also know that reference types and value types are different. The rvalue of a value type variable is the data value of the variable. For reference type variables, however, the rvalue is either null or the memory address where the data reside. All reference types in C# behave as objects of a class. As such, reference types can have properties and methods just as textboxes, labels, and buttons do. What we want to do in this section is introduce you to some of the more common properties and methods found in the string class.

String Length

One common task when working with string data is to verify that the string contains the proper data. For example, if you ask a user to enter a zip code, you may want to verify that the user typed exactly five characters into the textbox object used to collect the zip code string. (Yeah, I know there can be nine-digit zip codes, but we'll ignore that for the moment.) For example, suppose you've written a program that uses txtZipCode to collect the zip code from the user. Your next task might be to determine if the user typed five characters into the textbox. One of the properties provided by the string class is the Length property.

```
int length;
string zip = "80122";
length = zip.Length;
```

In the code fragment above, zip is assigned the literal value "80122". The integer variable length is then assigned the value of the Length property of the zip string object. In our example, the zip.Length property has a value of 5. Therefore, the length variable has an rvalue of 5 after the assignment statement in the last line of the preceding code is executed.

Letting Intellisense Show You Properties and Methods

You might ask, "Are there other properties or methods in the string class?" Yes, there are a bunch of them. Any time you want to find the properties or method of an object (string or otherwise), let Intellisense give you the list. For example, in Figure 5-4 I defined a string variable named `temp`. A few lines later you want to find out what property you might use to determine the length of the string. To do this, all I did was type in the name of the string variable followed by the dot operator. Intellisense immediately presented me with a listbox containing all the properties and methods for the current object, a string named `temp` in this case. (See Figure 5-4.)

```
{
    bool flag;
    int index;
    int length;
    int start;
    int end;
    string temp;

    lblIndexOf.Text = "";

    // Find length
    txtLength.Text = txtInput.Text.Length.ToString();
    length = temp.
    // Change c  ≡● LastIndexOf
    txtToUpper.  ≡● LastIndexOfAny    ext.ToUpper();
                 ● Length         int string.Length
    txtToLower.  ≡● Normalize      Gets the number of characters in the current System.String object.
                 ≡● PadLeft
    // Index of  ≡● PadRight
    index = txt  ≡● Remove         of(txtSearchChar.Text, 0);
```

Figure 5-4

If you look closely at Figure 5-4 (or better yet, write some test code of your own), you can see the `Length` property in the listbox object. If your eyes are really good, you can see that the icon to the left of the word `Length` in the listbox object is a hand pointing to a page of code. The *hand icon* is used to denote an object property. If you look to the right of the listbox object, you can see that Intellisense also gives you a brief description:

```
int string.Length
Gets the current number of characters in the current System.String object.
```

The first word (`int`) of the first line tells you that `string.Length` is an `int` data type. (This is why we made `length` an `int` data type in the preceding code fragment). The second line simply provides a brief description about the property (or method).

Finally, if you look at the last item in the listbox object shown in Figure 5-4, you can see a 3D purple box next to the word `Remove`. Because `Remove` has a 3D box icon next to it, it is a method. If you had selected `Remove` from the list, the screen would show something like Figure 5-5.

```
(
    bool flag;
    int index;
    int length;
    int start;
    int end;
    string temp;

    lblIndexOf.Text = "";

    // Find length
    txtLength.Text = txtInput.Text.Length.ToString();
    length = temp.
    // Change c        LastIndexOf
    txtToUpper.        LastIndexOfAny        ext.ToUpper();
                      Length
    txtToLower.        Normalize             ext.ToLower();
                      PadLeft
                      PadRight
    // Index of       Remove
    index = txt                             string string.Remove(int startIndex)  (+ 1 overload(s))
```

Figure 5-5

Note that the nature of the message from Intellisense has changed. It now says this:

```
string string.Remove(int startIndex) (+ 1 overload(s))
```

The first word (string) says that the method returns a string data type. The phrase
string.Remove(int startIndex) says that the Remove() method is part of the string class and
that it expects an integer value to be supplied with it. (I provide a complete example of how to use
Remove() later in this chapter.) Finally, (+ 1 overload(s)) indicates that there are multiple "flavors"
of this method. We're not ready to discuss what that means . . . yet, but we will later in this chapter.

Using an Intellisense Option

Intellisense wouldn't present you with all of the options in a listbox if you couldn't use the listbox. For
example, Figure 5-4 shows the Length property highlighted. If you now press the Tab key, Intellisense
automatically fills in the word Length in your source code. You can use the same technique for object
methods, too. The bad news is that if you select a method rather than a property, Intellisense does *not*
automatically supply the parentheses for the method. You must type the parentheses in yourself.

An Important Distinction Between Properties and Methods

Keep in mind that properties are variables associated with an object. As such, they do not require
parentheses to follow their names. On the other hand, all methods *must* have parentheses following the
method name. Violating these rules evokes a squiggly-line nastygram from Intellisense.

Thinking About Object Properties and Methods

You have just seen that the string data type offers you a host of properties and methods from which to
choose. It's important that you think about string data as an object. Drawing on the discussion from
Chapter 1, a string variable is actually an object with a shell that you can open up using the dot operator.
The dot operator then makes that object's properties and methods available to you. This can greatly
simplify using reference type data because Visual Studio has already written the code for many
properties and methods for you. When you see Intellisense open up a listbox with that object's properties
and methods listed, take a moment to scroll through the list, highlighting each property and method. As
you highlight each option in the listbox, Intellisense gives you a brief description of the purpose of that
property or method. In the process of doing this, you may discover that the very task you need to
accomplish has already been done for you.

Try It Out   Using String Class Methods and Properties

Figure 5-4 shows that numerous properties and methods are associated with strings. In this section, you will write a program that exercises some of those properties and methods. Figure 5-6 shows the user interface for the program.

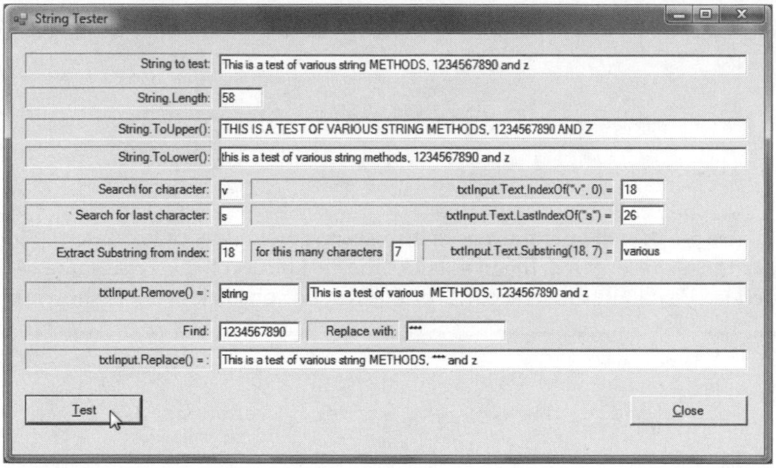

Figure 5-6

Table 5-4 presents the names of the textboxes shown in Figure 5-6, from top to bottom and left to right.

Table 5-4

Textbox name	Description
txtInput	The textual data to be used.
txtLength	The length of the input data.
txtToUpper	The result of converting the data to uppercase.
txtToLower	The result of converting the data to lowercase.
txtSearchChar	A character in the data to search for.
txtSearchIndex	The position where the character was found.
txtLastChar	Find the last occurrence of this letter.
txtLastIndexOf	The position where the last occurrence was found.
txtStartIndex	Start from this position within the string.
txtEndIndex	Copy this many characters from the string.
txtSubstringResult	The substring that is copied.

(continued)

Textbox name	Description
txtRemove	The text to remove from the string.
txtRemoveResult	The string after the text has been removed.
txtReplaceChars	Find this sequence of characters within the string.
txtReplaceWith	Replace the preceding sequence with this sequence of characters.
txtReplaceResult	The resultant string after the replacement.

How It Works

You can see in Figure 5-6 that the program asks the user to enter a line of text into the top textbox (txtInput). After the text is entered, the user clicks the Test button to exercise some of the many string methods provided by Visual Studio. The code for the Test button click event is shown in Listing 5-1.

Listing 5-1

```
private void btnTest_Click(object sender, EventArgs e)
{
  bool flag;
  int index;
  int start;
  int howMany;
  string temp;

  lblIndexOf.Text = "";

  // Find length
  txtLength.Text = txtInput.Text.Length.ToString();
  // Change cases
  txtToUpper.Text = txtInput.Text.ToUpper();

  txtToLower.Text = txtInput.Text.ToLower();

  // Index of
  index = txtInput.Text.IndexOf(txtSearchChar.Text, 0);
  lblIndexOf.Text = "txtInput.Text.IndexOf(\"" + txtSearchChar.Text + "\",0) = ";
  txtSearchIndex.Text = index.ToString();

  //LastIndexOf
  index = txtInput.Text.LastIndexOf(txtLastChar.Text);
  lblLastIndexOf.Text = "txtInput.Text.LastIndexOf(\"" + txtLastChar.Text + "\")
                         = ";
  txtLastIndexOf.Text = index.ToString();

  // Substring
  flag = int.TryParse(txtStartIndex.Text, out start);
  if (flag == false)
```

```
        {
          MessageBox.Show("Improper numeric input. Re-enter.");
          txtStartIndex.Focus();
          return;
        }
        flag = int.TryParse(txtEndIndex.Text, out howMany);
        if (flag == false)
        {
          MessageBox.Show("Improper numeric input. Re-enter.");
          txtEndIndex.Focus();
          return;
        }
        lblSubstring.Text = "txtInput.Text.Substring(" + start.ToString() + ", " +
                            howMany.ToString()+ ") = ";
        txtSubstringResult.Text = txtInput.Text.Substring(start, howMany);

        // Remove
        temp = txtInput.Text;
        index = temp.IndexOf(txtRemove.Text);
        if (index > 0)
        {
          txtRemoveResult.Text = temp.Remove(index, txtRemove.Text.Length);
        }

        // Replace
        temp = txtInput.Text;
        txtReplaceResult.Text = temp.Replace(txtReplaceChars.Text,
                              txtReplaceWith.Text);


    }
```

For the sample test run shown in Figure 5-6, we typed in the following string:

```
    This is a test of various string METHODS, 1234567890 and z
```

For the sections that follow, we repeat specific lines of code relative to the method or property under discussion.

The Length of a String: Length

The Length property stores the number of characters of a string. This count includes everything in the string, including blank spaces, punctuation, and digit characters. The code shown in Listing 5-1 for the Length property is:

```
        // Find length
        txtLength.Text = txtInput.Text.Length.ToString();
```

You're probably saying, "Hold on a minute! Why so many dot operators in the statement?" Good question. Let's break apart the right-hand side of the expression first. Suppose you type in the following in the Source window of Visual Studio:

```
txtLength.Text = txtInput.
```

In Chapter 2, I told you that the dot operator is used to separate an object (the txtInput textbox object in this example) from the properties and methods available to that object. In other words, the dot operator "opens the shell" of the object to give you access to the properties and methods of that object. (See Figure 2-2 in Chapter 2.) The instant you type in the period after the name of the txtInput textbox object, Visual Studio displays the listbox shown in Figure 5-7.

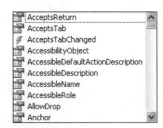

Figure 5-7

The listbox shown in Figure 5-7 actually contains over 200 properties and methods associated with a textbox object. In this particular case, you are interested in the Text property of the txtInput textbox object. So you type in Te and the listbox automatically scrolls down to the Text property of the txtInput textbox object. Press the Tab key and Visual Studio fills in the rest of the word Text for you. So far, so good.

Now ask yourself this question: What kind of data type is the Text property? Well, if the Text property is storing textual data, the data must be stored in a string data type. Because the Text property of a textbox object is a string variable, it also means the Text property is a string *object*. Therefore, you should be able to type in another dot operator to see what's available in that string object. So you type in the dot operator:

```
txtLength.Text = txtInput.Text.
```

Once you've done that, Visual Studio presents you with a listbox containing the properties and methods associated with a string object. This new list is shown in Figure 5-8.

Figure 5-8

If you scroll through this list, you find there are a lot of methods for string objects, but only one property: `Length`. You can either scroll down to the `Length` property or type in the first few letters and let Visual Studio scroll you to the `Length` property. If you press the Tab key, Visual Studio fills in the property name for you. Your statement now looks like this:

```
txtLength.Text = txtInput.Text.Length
```

Now you have a problem. The length of a string is stored as an `int` data type. The problem is that you want to assign a numeric integer value (`txtInput.Text.Length`) into a textual property that is a string data type (`txtLength.Text`). The bad news is that you have an apple on one side of the assignment operator and an orange on the other side. The good news is that C# can treat value types as objects when it needs to . . . like right now. (See the "Data Wrappers" sidebar.) Therefore, because `Length` is an `int` value type that can be treated as an object when necessary, we add another dot operator to the expression:

```
txtLength.Text = txtInput.Text.Length.
```

Visual Studio immediately senses that you want to treat `Length` as an object, so it presents you with a list of properties and methods associated with value data types. The list of methods for value data types is shown in Figure 5-9.

Figure 5-9

As illustrated in Figure 5-9, Visual Studio provides only six methods for value types. However, one of those six is the `ToString()` method, which is exactly what you need. You now complete the statement:

```
txtLength.Text = txtInput.Text.Length.ToString();
```

Now your problem has disappeared. You have a string data type property (`Text`) on the left-hand side of the assignment operator and a string data type on the right-hand side, because you use the `ToString()` method to convert the integer value of `Length` into a string. Ta-da! You can now see the input string's length properly displayed in the `txtLength` textbox object. (See Figure 5-6.)

This rather lengthy explanation may seem like an H-bomb to kill an ant, but it is important that you understand that one object (such as a textbox) can have another object (such as a string) stored as a property inside it. Further, that string object (`Text`) can also have a property (such as `Length`) that may be treated as an object too. All value types have the six methods shown in Figure 5-9 available should you need them. In this example, you needed to use the `ToString()` method of the `Length` property so you could convert the integer value of `Length` into a string for display in the `txtLength` textbox.

Data Wrappers

In non-OOP languages, value types and reference types suffer the old oil-and-water problem . . . they don't mix well. C#, on the other hand, was designed to be an object-oriented programming language from the very start. The designers knew, therefore, that there would be times when the programmer would like to treat the value type data as though it were an object. For that reason, C# has a wrapper class that envelops the value type. While it's a bit of a simplification, you can think of a value type wrapper class as having one property (its value) and six methods (see Figure 5-9). Of the six methods, the ToString () method is used most often and enables you to convert the value of the data type to a string.

Changing the Case of a String: ToUpper() and ToLower()

Sometimes certain tasks can be simplified if the textual data is all in the same case. For example, one person may write her last name as "Van d'Camp" while another person writes it as "van d'Camp." If you were searching a list of strings that contain peoples' names, you might miss the person you were looking for because you didn't enter the name using exactly the same case the user did. To avoid problems like this, you could change the string to a single case and use that case during the search process. The following statements change the input string shown in Figure 5-6 to all uppercase letters using the ToUpper () method:

```
txtToUpper.Text = txtInput.Text.ToUpper();

txtToLower.Text = txtInput.Text.ToLower();
```

The resulting changes are shown in their respective textbox objects. The second statement changes the string to all lowercase letters. The right-hand side of the preceding assignment statements may be verbalized as, "Find the txtInput textbox object, locate its Text property, and, because it's a string variable, use its ToUpper () or ToLower () methods to change the Text property to upper- or lowercase, respectively." You can find both of these methods by scrolling the listbox shown in Figure 5-8.

Finding a Specific Character: IndexOf()

Suppose you want to find a specific character in a string. In Figure 5-6, we typed in the character v and used the IndexOf () method to find the first occurrence of that character. The next textbox (txtSearchIndex) on the same line has the number 18 displayed in it. This means that the IndexOf () method found the letter v at index number 18 in the string. If you count the number of letters and spaces up to the letter v, you'll discover that the v is the 19th character. What?

The reason the value is 19 is that programming languages start counting characters in a string referencing the first position as position zero, not position one. If you count the number of characters and spaces beginning with zero, you will find that the v is, indeed, at position 18. Programmers use the word *index* to refer to the zero-based position of a character in a string.

The code that accomplished the search is found in the following statements:

```
// Index of
index = txtInput.Text.IndexOf(txtSearchChar.Text, 0);
lblIndexOf.Text = "txtInput.Text.IndexOf(\"" + txtSearchChar.Text + "\",0) = ";
txtSearchIndex.Text = index.ToString();
```

Let's examine the first statement. The right-hand side of the assignment operator says, "Get the Text property of the txtInput textbox object and use the Text's method named IndexOf()." Unfortunately, IndexOf() can't do its job without two additional pieces of information. First, IndexOf() needs to know what character you wish to find. The character to find is the letter the user typed into the txtSearchChar textbox object. (It's the textbox with the v in it in Figure 5-6.) You retrieve that character using the txtSearchChar.Text property. Second, IndexOf() wants to know the index where you wish to begin the search. In your case, you want the search to start at the beginning of the string, so you use the index value 0. (The first character in a string is at position zero, remember?) These two pieces of information are called the arguments of the IndexOf() method. Simply stated, *method arguments* are information that you pass to a method so the method can perform its task. Method arguments can be in the form of variables, like txtSearchChar.Text, or literal values, like the second argument, 0.

Once you have entered the proper method arguments for IndexOf(), the program transfers program control to the program code for the IndexOf() method. Simply stated, the IndexOf() code starts examining itself (after all, IndexOf() is part of the Text property, so it knows what the string is) starting at the index you passed to it. Because you passed a zero to the IndexOf() method, it begins its search with the first character in the string, which is at position 0. The code examines the first character and compares it to the character you passed to it, the v. Because there is no match, it looks at the second position. It continues this process until it finds a match, which it finds at position 18. Okay . . . now what?

The IndexOf() method was successful in finding a match at index 18, but it needs a way to convey that information back to the point in the program where we invoked the IndexOf() method. While we cover the technical details of how the value 18 is passed back to the point in the program that needs it in a later chapter, for now, simply think of the right-hand side of the assignment expression

```
index = txtInput.Text.IndexOf(txtSearchChar.Text, 0);
```

as being replaced with this:

```
index = 18;
```

After all, the reason for using the txtInput object was to get to the Text property so we could use its IndexOf() method to locate a specific character. Because the object (txtInput) and its property (Text) and method (IndexOf()) have all done their jobs, the code was able to determine the exact location of the v character in the string. In formal language you would say, "The IndexOf() method returned the integer value of 18." When the statement is complete, the variable index now has an rvalue of 18 assigned into it.

"Calling" a Method

It's quite common to refer to the variable on the left-hand side of an assignment statement as the *caller* when a method is being used to resolve an expression. That is, index is invoking, or "calling," the IndexOf() method so it can have a proper position value assigned into itself. Likewise, you'll often hear something like, "IndexOf() returns the value 18 to the caller." The interpretation is that the value determined by the IndexOf() method is assigned into the caller — index in this example.

What happens if the string doesn't contain the character you're looking for? In that case, IndexOf() returns the value –1 to the caller. If IndexOf() returns a negative value, you know the search failed. One more thing. While we illustrated IndexOf() as searching for a single character, the first argument to IndexOf() can also be a string with more than a single character. In that case, IndexOf() returns the index of the first character in the string where the match occurred. If IndexOf() cannot find an exact match for the character sequence of the string passed to it, it returns a –1.

Searching for the Last Occurrence of a Character: LastIndexOf()

The IndexOf() method enables you to search for the first occurrence of a particular character in a string. Now suppose that there are a half-dozen occurrences of that character, but you're interested in the position of the last one. You could call IndexOf() five times, having the method return an index for each (unwanted) position. That is, you could then call IndexOf() again, using the index plus one as the second argument in the method call. (Think about what that means.) However, it's more efficient to use the LastIndexOf() string method instead.

The code for the LastIndexOf() method is this:

```
index = txtInput.Text.LastIndexOf(txtLastChar.Text);
lblLastIndexOf.Text = "txtInput.Text.LastIndexOf(\"" + txtLastChar.Text + "\")
                       = ";
txtLastIndexOf.Text = index.ToString();
```

There is only one argument to LastIndexOf() and it is the character for which you are searching. It doesn't need a second argument for the starting position for the search because LastIndexOf() automatically starts the search at the end of the string, searching backward towards the start. The method returns the (zero-based) index of the character if the search is successful and –1 if no match is found. The remaining two lines of code have virtually the same interpretation as the IndexOf() code fragment. (Refer to Figure 5-6 to see what the contents of the label look like.)

Searching for a Substring

If you have ever used a word processor and searched a document for a specific word, chances are the word processor was using a method similar to the Substring() method. The code that uses the Substring() method is shown here:

```
lblSubstring.Text = "txtInput.Text.Substring(" + start.ToString() + ", " +
                    howMany.ToString()+ ") = ";
txtSubstringResult.Text = txtInput.Text.Substring(start, howMany);
```

We have ignored the `TryParse()` method calls to set the values for `start` and `howMany` because you have already studied those. Suffice it to say that the two `TryParse()` method calls in Listing 5-1 simply convert the digit characters entered by the user in the two textbox objects into integer variables named `start` and `howMany`.

In Figure 5-6, the `start` position is set to position 18 (`start` = 18). Again, because string positions are always referenced from position 0, you are actually going to start the substring with the 19th character in the string. If you count 19 characters (including spaces and punctuation) in the string, you find that the 19th character is the `v` in the word `various`.

The `howMany` variable might have a different meaning than you think. The value of `howMany` tells the `Substring()` method how many characters to copy, beginning with position `start`. The variable `howMany` does *not* set the ending index value for `Substring()`. In Figure 5-6 you can see that we set the value for `howMany` to 7. Therefore, the statement

```
txtSubstringResult.Text = txtInput.Text.Substring(start, howMany);
```

becomes

```
txtSubstringResult.Text = txtInput.Text.Substring(18, 7);
```

which functionally results in

```
txtSubstringResult.Text = "various";
```

This means that the substring we wanted to copy from the string was the word `various`. You can see the result in Figure 5-6. You should experiment with the program and try different start and end values to see the impact it has on the substring.

Removing a Substring

Suppose you have a string that is actually a memo to a colleague who has botched a job you asked him to do. You find that your memo uses the word "idiot" several times and your secretary suggests that it might not be politically correct to call him an "idiot" since he's your boss's son. You decide to remove the word "idiot" from the memo. The editor you use to remove the word "idiot" probably works like the `Remove()` string method.

The statements for using `Remove()` from Listing 5-1 are as follows:

```
// Remove
temp = txtInput.Text;
index = temp.IndexOf(txtRemove.Text);
if (index > 0)
{
  txtRemoveResult.Text = temp.Remove(index, txtRemove.Text.Length);
}
```

First, we made a copy of the original string entered by the user so we don't permanently change the string as it appears in the first textbox. Next, we use the `IndexOf()` method to find the position where the "target string" is located. In the discussion above, the target string would be the word "idiot." In Figure 5-6, the target string is the word "string." In the code, the target string is whatever the user types into the txtRemove textbox object as stored in the Text property. The code then calls IndexOf() to locate the target string. Note that IndexOf() is capable of searching for a string with a single character, as you saw in the IndexOf() discussion section earlier, or it can locate a string with multiple characters in it.

If the search is successful, variable index is assigned the starting position of the string. If the search fails to find a match, index is assigned –1 (as explained earlier). The if statement prevents an unsuccessful search from calling the Remove() method.

Figure 5-6 shows that we searched for the word string when exercising the Remove() method. The target string starts at an index position of 26. This value becomes the first argument in the call to the Remove() method. The second argument is the number of characters you wish to remove. You know that string has six characters in it, so you could "hard-code" the literal value 6 into the second argument. However, that's not very flexible. Anytime you wanted to find a different string, you'd likely have to adjust the second Remove() method argument. Because the txtRemove textbox object holds the string you wish to remove, you can always use the Length property to adjust the second argument to the proper value. Therefore, the statement

```
txtRemoveResult.Text = temp.Remove(index, txtRemove.Text.Length);
```

becomes

```
txtRemoveResult.Text = temp.Remove(26, 6);
```

which resolves to

```
txtRemoveResult.Text = "This is a test of various  METHODS, 1234567890 and z";
```

The new string is then displayed in the txtRemoveResult textbox object by assigning its Text property to the new string. (Note: There is a little hiccup in this code. Because we removed only the word string from the original string, there are now two blank spaces between the words various and METHODS where there should only be one space. How would you fix this problem?)

Replacing a Substring

Sometimes you need to change one word in a larger string with a replacement word. For example, suppose your boss tells you to send the program specifications to Gene, which you obediently do, only to find out that Gene is actually Jean. In this case, you need to replace the word Gene with Jean. This task is exactly what the Replace() string method is designed to do.

Figure 5-6 suggests that we wish to replace the substring 1234567890 with ***. The statements that accomplish this task are the following:

```
// Replace
temp = txtInput.Text;
txtReplaceResult.Text = temp.Replace(txtReplaceChars.Text,
                        txtReplaceWith.Text);
```

The first line simply copies the input string so we don't permanently change the Text property of the txtInput textbox object. The Replace() method requires two arguments. The first argument is the string you wish to have replaced. The second argument is the string you wish to substitute for the first argument. In the example shown in Figure 5-6, the method calls resolves to

```
txtReplaceResult.Text = temp.Replace("1234567890", "***");
```

which means that you wish to replace the digit characters with three asterisks. After the replacement takes place, the statement appears as this:

```
txtReplaceResult.Text = "This is a test of various string METHODS, *** and z";
```

The new string is assigned into the Text property of the txtReplaceResult textbox object. If the target string does not exist in the original string, the original string is left unchanged.

The listbox in Figure 5-4 shows a partial listing of literally hundreds of string methods available to you. Obviously, we cannot show all of the string methods here. However, you may want to spend a few moments scrolling through the list of possible string methods from which you can choose. Chances are pretty good that anything you'll ever want to do to manipulate string data is already in the list.

Strings and Escape Sequences

You've already seen how a string variable can be assigned a literal value, as in

```
string name = "Katie";
```

However, sometimes certain string literals can pose problems. For example, suppose you want to display the following message:

```
John said: "Reach for the sky!"
```

If you try to write this as a normal string literal

```
string message = "John said: "Reach for the sky!"";
```

Visual Studio gets all confused because the double quotation marks are used to delimit the start and end of a string literal, not as part of the string itself.

To solve this problem, C# uses a special *escape character* within the string to signify that what follows is to be treated differently. The special escape character is the backslash character (\). In essence, the escape character says to treat whatever follows it as though it were part of the string literal itself. For example, suppose you rewrite the string literal like this:

```
string message = "John said: \"Reach for the sky!\"";
```

The double quotation mark before the word Reach and the double quotation mark at the end of the sentence are now treated as part of an escape sequence and, therefore, are printed out as part of the string literal. The end result is that the statement displays this:

```
John said: "Reach for the sky!"
```

Table 5-5 presents a list of the special escape sequences.

Table 5-5

Escape Sequence	Interpretation
\"	Display a double quotation mark.
\'	Display a single quotation mark.
\\	Display a backslash.
\0	Null (non-printing).
\a	Alarm (beep terminal alarm).
\b	Backspace (back up one character position).
\f	Form feed (advance to next page).
\n	Newline (advance to next line).
\r	Carriage return (move to left margin).
\t	Tab (advance one tab space, often eight characters).
\v	Vertical tab.

There are other instances where escape sequences come in handy. For example, suppose you want to set the directory path to the C# folder on the C drive. You would need to use the following command:

```
string path = "C:\\C#";
```

With longer path names, the `path` string starts to look rather complex. C# , however, has a way to make it less so.

Verbatim String Literals

Suppose you want to issue a message stating the following:

```
Go to the C:\Programs\Source directory and send a \n character.
```

You would have to write the message as

```
string message = "Go to the C:\\Programs\\Source directory and send a \\n
                   character.";
```

This looks a little ugly. C# provides a way to make such literals a little prettier. You can use the *verbatim string literal character* (@) to tell Visual Studio to build the string exactly as it appears within the double quotation marks. Therefore

```
string message = @"Go to the C:\Programs\Source directory and send a \n
                   character.";
```

displays the message exactly as you have written it without your having to worry about using escape sequences in the proper places. The verbatim string literal character is not needed very often, but it sure comes in handy when you need to pass directory information around in a program.

DateTime Reference Objects

Many business applications need to manipulate dates and times. Banks need to calculate interest payments on loans based on dates. Producing certain products, like bread, requires that specific ingredients be added after so many minutes or hours have passed. Visual Studio provides a DateTime data type to enable you to work with dates and time easily.

The way Visual Studio tracks time is pretty interesting. The Windows operating system maintains a system clock as part of its duties. Most of you can observe the current local time in the lower right-hand corner of your display. Visual Studio uses the system clock to track the number of ticks on the system clock. A *tick* is a unit of time measured in 100-nanosecond blocks. A nanosecond is one billionth of a second. That's a fairly small time slice. In fact, light only travels about 18 inches in a nanosecond.

The DateTime object maintains a count of the number of ticks since midnight, January 1, 0001 A.D., using the Gregorian calendar. That's a whole bunch of ticks to the present! However, by manipulating the tick count, the DataTime object is able to determine all kinds of things relative to times and dates.

Figure 5-10 shows a sample run of a program that uses some of the DateTime methods and properties.

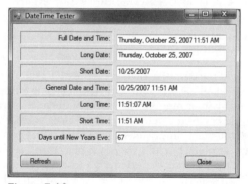

Figure 5-10

DateTime and ToString() Conversions

As I mentioned earlier, all C# data types provide a ToString() wrapper conversion method that enables you to express the data as a string. However, some data types enable you to pass an argument to the ToString() method so the data can be formatted a specific way. Table 5-6 presents the most common formatting characters for use with a DateTime data type. In each case, the letter shown in column one of Table 5-6 becomes the argument to ToString(). For example, myDate.ToString("F") displays the full date and time for the myDate variable. The table example assumes the date is Oct. 25, 2007.

Table 5-6

Conversion Character	Description	Sample Output
`"F"`	Full date and time, including seconds	Thursday, October 25, 2007 12:00:59 PM
`"f"`	Full date and time, without seconds	Thursday, October 25, 2007 12:02 PM
`"D"`	Full date	Thursday, October 25, 2007
`"d"`	Short date	10/25/2007
`"G"`	General date, including seconds*	10/25/2007 12:04:54 PM
`"g"`	General date, without seconds	10/25/2007 12:05 PM
`"T"`	Full time, including seconds	12:05:48 PM
`"t"`	Full time, without seconds	12:05 PM

* The "G" conversion character is the default format if no conversion character is used with `ToString()`.

The first column in Table 5-6 shows the conversion character you may use as an argument to the `ToString()` method when using a `DateTime` variable. The third column of the table presents an example of what the resulting output looks like. As a general rule, an uppercase conversion character presents more detailed information than does its lowercase counterpart.

Try It Out   String Formatting

The program code that produced the output shown in Figure 5-10 is shown in Listing 5-2. Unlike in previous programs, here I present all the program code, less the code automatically generated by Windows. The program begins by informing Visual Studio of the references it plans to use via the `using` keywords. Then the code begins the definition for the class you are writing, named `frmMain`. The `:` `Form` at the end of the statement simply tells Visual Studio that you are going to use the Windows `Form` class as a starting point, but add your own objects to that class and reference them with the name `frmMain`. Next, the program defines the control objects (such as labels, textboxes, and buttons) that you are adding to a generic Windows form (`Form`) to make the new class (`frmMain`) suit your needs. Now things start to get interesting.

Listing 5-2

```
using System;
using System.Windows.Forms;

public class frmMain : Form
{
    private Label label1;
    private TextBox txtLongDate;
    private Label label2;
```

```
private TextBox txtShortDate;
private Label label3;
private TextBox txtGeneralDateAndTime;
private Label label4;
private TextBox txtLongTime;
private Label label5;
private TextBox txtShortTime;
private Label label6;
private TextBox txtDaysToNewYears;
private Label label7;
private Button btnClose;
private Button btnRefresh;
private TextBox txtCompleteDateAndTime;

#region Windows code
#endregion

public frmMain()
{
    InitializeComponent();
    UpdateTimeInfo();          // Update textboxes
}

public static void Main()
{
    frmMain main = new frmMain();
    Application.Run(main);
}

private void UpdateTimeInfo()
{
    int days;
    DateTime myTime = new DateTime();
    myTime = DateTime.Now;
    DateTime newYears = new DateTime(myTime.Year, 12, 31);

    txtCompleteDateAndTime.Text = myTime.ToString("f");
    txtLongDate.Text = myTime.ToString("D");
    txtShortDate.Text = myTime.ToString("d");
    txtGeneralDateAndTime.Text = myTime.ToString("g");
    txtLongTime.Text = myTime.ToString("T");
    txtShortTime.Text = myTime.ToString("t");

    days = newYears.DayOfYear - myTime.DayOfYear;
    txtDaysToNewYears.Text = days.ToString();
}


private void btnRefresh_Click(object sender, EventArgs e)
```

```
    {
        UpdateTimeInfo();
    }

    private void btnClose_Click(object sender, EventArgs e)
    {
        Close();
    }
}
```

How It Works

Listing 5-2 presents the body of code that illustrates a number of different date and time format options. As part of this sample program, I want to discuss a number of topics that are common to all C# programs as well as the program itself.

#region and #endregion

Towards the top of Listing 5-2 are the following lines:

```
#region Windows code
#endregion
```

#region and #endregion are C# program directives that tell Visual Studio to either hide or show a block of code. Assuming you use the C# template presented in Chapter 2 as the starting point for all programs, and then add the control objects to the form, Visual Studio generates a ton of code for you automatically. When you look at your program, the #region directive line has a small plus sign (+) in the left margin of the Source window. If you click on that plus sign, Visual Studio expands the program listing to reveal the code it generated behind your back while you weren't looking! The code looks similar to that shown in Figure 5-11.

```
    private Button btnClose;
    private Button btnRefresh;
    private TextBox txtCompleteDateAndTime;

    #region Windows code
    private void InitializeComponent()
    {
        this.label1 = new System.Windows.Forms.Label();
        this.txtCompleteDateAndTime = new System.Windows.Forms.TextBox();
        this.txtLongDate = new System.Windows.Forms.TextBox();
        this.label2 = new System.Windows.Forms.Label();
        this.txtShortDate = new System.Windows.Forms.TextBox();
        this.label3 = new System.Windows.Forms.Label();
        this.txtGeneralDateAndTime = new System.Windows.Forms.TextBox();
        this.label4 = new System.Windows.Forms.Label();
        this.txtLongTime = new System.Windows.Forms.TextBox();
        this.label5 = new System.Windows.Forms.Label();
        this.txtShortTime = new System.Windows.Forms.TextBox();
        this.label6 = new System.Windows.Forms.Label();
        this.txtDaysToNewYears = new System.Windows.Forms.TextBox();
        this.label7 = new System.Windows.Forms.Label();
        this.btnClose = new System.Windows.Forms.Button();
        this.btnRefresh = new System.Windows.Forms.Button();
        this.SuspendLayout();
```

Figure 5-11

Note how the first several lines after the #region Windows code appear similar to this:

```
private void InitializeComponent()
{
     this.label1 = new System.Windows.Forms.Label();
     this.txtCompleteDateAndTime = new
                             System.Windows.Forms.TextBox();
     this.txtLongDate = new System.Windows.Forms.TextBox();
     this.label2 = new System.Windows.Forms.Label();
     this.txtShortDate = new System.Windows.Forms.TextBox();
     this.label3 = new System.Windows.Forms.Label();
```

This is the code that Visual Studio sneaked into the program for you. Let's look at the first line inside the InitializeComponent() method:

```
this.label1 = new System.Windows.Forms.Label();
```

This statement tells Visual Studio to grab a label cookie cutter and carve out a piece of memory and reference that chunk of memory as label1. The keyword this is a kind of shorthand Visual Studio uses to refer to the current object being used. Because you dragged a label object onto the form named frmMain, the keyword this is actually referring to frmMain. The end result is that Visual Studio creates a new Label object named label1 and places it inside frmMain.

Sliding Down the Object Chain

You should also be able to decipher the meaning of the right-hand side of the statement:

```
this.label1 = new System.Windows.Forms.Label();
```

As you learned in Chapter 2, the new keyword means we want to create a new object of some kind. So you go to the System object and use the dot operator to look inside it. Inside the System object you see a bunch of stuff, including a Windows object. Since that looks promising, you use another dot operator to look inside the Windows object. Inside the Windows object you see some more properties and methods, including one that is a Forms object. Now you're getting close, so you use another dot operator to gain access to the Forms object. Inside the Forms object you find the Label() method that you can call to instantiate a new label object. Perfect! Because that's precisely what you want to do. You call the Label() method to instantiate a new label object named label1.

Don't let the dot operator scare you. Just keep in mind that the dot operator always separates an object (to the left of the dot operator) from a property or method inside that object (to the right of the dot operator). However, because one object can contain another object, you might need to use another dot operator to peek inside *that* object. In the preceding statement the System object evidently has a Windows object inside it. So you use another dot operator to go inside the Windows object and you find a Forms object is defined inside the Windows object. Undaunted, you go inside the Forms object and find there is a Label object. Finally you call the Label() method to instantiate a label object for you in memory. Visual Studio then enters the information about that label object into the symbol table using the ID label1. No matter how complex the statement, if you bump over enough dot operators you'll eventually end up looking at the property or method you're interested in. Even though you had to plow through three objects to get there, eventually you found the method that constructs a new label object for you named label. Piece of cake!

Always remember: Each time you do use a dot operator, Visual Studio displays a listbox of the properties and methods available in the object. You saw this in Figure 5-4. (Some of the properties actually represent classes that can be used to instantiate a new object, but you can still think of them as properties.)

Visual Studio wrote the next line in the `InitializeComponent()` method for you:

```
this.txtCompleteDateAndTime = new
                            System.Windows.Forms.TextBox();
```

This creates a new textbox object, gives it the name `txtCompleteDateAndTime`, and adds it to `frmMain`. This process repeats itself until all the form objects (labels, textboxes, and buttons) have been added. If you look further down the code listing in the `InitializeComponent()` method, you can see the property values you set when you created your user interface. That is, you can see the text you placed in the labels, the locations of each label, textbox, and button after you dragged them onto the form, and any associated properties you may have changed (such as border style, size, AutoSize, and so on).

How a Program Begins Execution

You learned in Chapter 1 that every C# program begins its execution with a special method named `Main()`. Consider the following statements from Listing 5-2:

```
public static void Main()
{
    frmMain main = new frmMain();
    Application.Run(main);
}
```

These statements define the `Main()` method and, because of this, mark the spot where the program starts executing. The first line says you wish to create a new object of the `frmMain` class and give it the name `main`. (Remember that C# is case-sensitive, so `Main` is not the same as `main`.) If you look at the top of Listing 5-2, you can see that the name of the class you are defining is `frmMain`. Therefore, this statement is telling Visual Studio you wish to create an object of type `frmMain`.

Class Constructors

Because the right-hand side of the assignment operator is processed first, the first thing that happens is that the `new` keyword sends a message to Windows asking for enough memory to hold a `frmMain` object. Assuming Windows can find enough memory, the program then calls the `frmMain()` method. Note that the method being called shares the same name as the object you are trying to instantiate. A method that has the same name as its class is called a *class constructor*. The purpose of a constructor is to perform any initialization tasks that need to be done before you use the object of the class. From Listing 5-2, you can see that our constructor looks like this:

```
public frmMain()
{
    InitializeComponent();
    UpdateTimeInfo();        // Update textboxes
}
```

There are several things you need to remember about constructors:

1. Constructors always have the same names as the classes in which they appear.

2. Constructors always use the `public` keyword before their names if you wish to instantiate objects of that class.

3. Constructors can never return a value to their callers.

Inside the constructor for the frmMain class, the first thing that happens is that the code calls the `InitializeComponent()` method. However, as you saw in Figure 5-11, all `InitializeComponent()` does is place all the label, textbox, and button objects in the correct positions on the form and set their properties to whatever values you specified by dragging and dropping the objects on the form when you were creating the user interface.

When the `frmMain()` constructor is finished, your frmMain object is sitting in memory exactly the way you wanted it to look while you were designing it. Now what?

Well, the next thing that happens is that the program calls the `UpdateTimeInfo()` method that you wrote. (We'll discuss that in a few moments.) In essence, all the `UpdateTimeInfo()` method does is fill in the textboxes with date and time information using a variety of format options.

Invoking the Application

Having initialized the object, the program hits the closing curly brace for the `frmMain()` constructor method and knows it's time to return to the caller. Returning to the caller means that program control reverts back to the statement.

```
frmMain main = new frmMain();
```

Your code has now created an image of your frmMain object in memory and associated it with an object named main. The next line says, "Okay, everything's set up and ready to go. Begin executing the program by calling the `Run()` method using the object named main":

```
Application.Run(main);
```

At this point . . . shazam! Your frmMain object named main appears on the display screen and the user actually sees what all your work has accomplished. The output should look similar to what is shown in Figure 5-12.

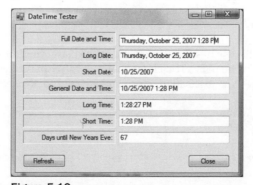

Figure 5-12

129

You should prove these actions to yourself. To do that, place the cursor on the following line and press F9:

```
frmMain main = new frmMain();
```

This sets a breakpoint at that point in the program. (The program line now has a red background.) Now run the program. Very shortly, Visual Studio halts the program on the line where the breakpoint is set, setting the background color to yellow. Think of yellow as a caution, informing you that Visual Studio is ready to execute that line. Now press F11. You will see the yellow line jump to the frmMain() constructor. You can continue to press the F11 key to advance to the InitializeComponent() method. If you continue pressing the F11 key, Visual Studio continues to single-step through each line in the program. If you get bored, hit Shift+F11 and Visual Studio sends you back to the caller, the frmMain() method. Using the debugger to march through the program code is a great way to see what's going on. It's even more informative if, when the first breakpoint is reached, you invoke the Debug ⇨ Windows ⇨ Locals menu sequence. This opens up a debugging window that lets you observe program variables as you single-step through the code. Good stuff.

The UpdateTimeInfo() Method

The code for the UpdateTimeInfo() method is reproduced here for convenience:

```
private void UpdateTimeInfo()
{
    int days;
    DateTime myTime = new DateTime();
    myTime = DateTime.Now;
    DateTime newYears = new DateTime(myTime.Year, 12, 31);

    txtCompleteDateAndTime.Text = myTime.ToString("f");
    txtLongDate.Text = myTime.ToString("D");
    txtShortDate.Text = myTime.ToString("d");
    txtGeneralDateAndTime.Text = myTime.ToString("g");
    txtLongTime.Text = myTime.ToString("T");
    txtShortTime.Text = myTime.ToString("t");

    days = newYears.DayOfYear - myTime.DayOfYear;
    txtDaysToNewYears.Text = days.ToString();
}
```

The method begins by defining an integer variable named days followed by a DateTime object named myTime. Note that the right-hand side of the statement calls a method named DateTime():

```
DateTime myTime = new DateTime();
```

However, because that method shares the same name as the class, you know that the DateTime() method is the constructor for the DateTime class. Therefore, after the statement executes, an object named myTime of type DateTime exists in memory and is ready to be used in the program.

The next statement creates another DateTime object named newYears by calling the DateTime() constructor:

```
DateTime newYears = new DateTime(myTime.Year, 12, 31);
```

Wait a minute! This time it appears that the `DateTime()` constructor has arguments supplied to it, but there were no arguments when we called the constructor for `myTime`. What's going on here?

Overloaded Methods

Earlier in this chapter I stated that a constructor is used to perform any initialization tasks that need to be performed before you use the object. Usually, "performing initialization tasks" means setting the state of the object's properties to some non-default value. When you created the `myTime` object you didn't use any arguments to the constructor. That's because you were satisfied with the default values for the `DateTime` properties (that is, 0 or null). Figure 5-13 uses the same old dot operator technique to get a list of the properties and methods available for a `DateTime` object.

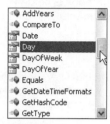

Figure 5-13

As you can see in the listbox, one of the properties is named `Day`. Evidently you were happy assigning the value of 0 to `Day` when `myTime` was instantiated. If you scroll the listbox shown in Figure 5-13, you'll find properties for `Month` and `Year` too. These properties are also initialized to their default values of 0 for the `myTime` object. In fact, if you don't initialize any of the properties for a `DateTime` object, it displays the date and time of Monday, January 01, 0001, 12:00 AM, which is the starting date when the number of ticks is zero!

Suppose we backtrack and type in the statement

```
DateTime newYears = new DateTime(
```

and observe what we see on the screen. You should see something similar to Figure 5-14.

```
        }

    public static void Main()
    {
        frmMain main = new frmMain();
        Application.Run(main);
    }

    private void UpdateTimeInfo()
    {
        int days;
        DateTime myTime = new DateTime(
        DateTime newYears    |◄ 4 of 12 ►| DateTime.DateTime (int year, int month, int day)
                              year: The Year (1 through 9999).

        myTime = DateTime.Now;

        txtCompleteDateAndTime.Text = myTime.ToString("f");
        txtLongDate.Text = myTime.ToString("D");
        txtShortDate.Text = myTime.ToString("d");
        txtGeneralDateAndTime.Text = myTime.ToString("g");
        txtLongTime.Text = myTime.ToString("T");
        txtShortTime.Text = myTime.ToString("t");

        days = newYears.DayOfYear - myTime.DayOfYear;
```

Figure 5-14

131

Your screen actually shows a small box stating 1 of 12 DateTime.DateTime() with up and down arrows surrounding the 1 of 12 part of the message. What Intellisense is telling you is that there are 12 "flavors" of the DateTime() constructor method available to you. Figure 5-14 shows that we want to use the fourth flavor that passes the year, month, and day to the constructor. It also tells you that each of these arguments should be an integer value. In your code you used the constructor with three integer arguments:

```
DateTime newYears = new DateTime(myTime.Year, 12, 31);
```

You are telling Visual Studio you're not happy initializing the newYears DateTime object with its default values. Instead, you want to initialize the state of the newYears DateTime object with the values that correspond to December 31, 2007. (This book is being written in 2007.) This works properly because the statement before the instantiation of the newYears DateTime object is

```
myTime = DateTime.Now;
```

which sets the Year property of the myTime object to 2007. (Now is a property of the DateTime class that holds the current tick value as measured by the Windows system clock. The current tick value also determines the values for the Month and Day properties.)

The end result is that the program now has two DateTime objects it can use. The first object, myTime, holds the current date and time because we used the Now property to assign its state. We initialized the second object, newYears, to December 31, 2007, by using the fourth DateTime constructor and supplying the proper arguments to that constructor.

Given how the two DateTime objects have been initialized, the following two statements use the DayOfYear property to calculate the number of days until New Year's:

```
days = newYears.DayOfYear - myTime.DayOfYear;
txtDaysToNewYears.Text = days.ToString();
```

The rest of the code in the UpdateTimeInfo() method simply illustrates several of the different formatting options available through the ToString() characters presented in Table 5-6.

Method Signatures

When an overloaded method is called, which flavor of the method ends up being called? After all, if a method is overloaded, it means that multiple methods are using the same method name. How does Visual Studio know which one to call? Visual Studio makes the decision based upon the signature of the method.

A *method signature* is everything from the method name through the closing parenthesis of the method. For example, you already know that the DateTime() constructor method has 12 different forms. You have seen two of these. The two forms you have used are these:

```
public DateTime()
public DateTime(int year, int month, int day)
```

The signature for the first constructor is DateTime(). The signature for the second is DateTime(int year, int month, int day). The signatures are different because the parameter lists for the two methods are different. That is, the first version of the constructor does not have any arguments passed to it. The second signature, however, expects three integer arguments to be passed to it. Therefore, the three statements from Listing 5-2 are as follows:

```
DateTime myTime = new DateTime();
myTime = DateTime.Now;
DateTime newYears = new DateTime(myTime.Year, 12, 31);
```

The first statement causes Visual Studio to call the constructor that has no arguments being passed to it. The third statement causes Visual Studio to call the constructor that expects three integer variables to be passed to it. This leads to an important rule about overloaded methods: *Methods* may be overloaded provided no two overloaded methods have the same signature. What this means is that only one overloaded method can have zero arguments passed to it. Likewise, only one overloaded method can have three integers passed to it. An overloaded method can have three other variables passed to it, but they cannot all be integers. For example, you could have an overloaded method named countThis() with the following signatures:

```
public int countThis(int val);
public int countThis(long val);
```

These are perfectly acceptable because their signatures are different. True, both flavors accept one argument, but the data type for that argument is different, therefore the signatures are different. If you scroll through the 12 constructors for the DateTime data type, you will discover that all 12 have different arguments being passed to them.

Overloaded methods are great when you need to write methods that behave differently when different information is passed to them. You will see other examples of overloaded methods in later chapters.

The Refresh Button

The purpose of the refresh button is to update the time aspects of any strings using the time component. The code is simple:

```
private void btnRefresh_Click(object sender, EventArgs e)
{
    UpdateTimeInfo();
}
```

When the user clicks the refresh button (btnRefresh), the code calls the UpdateTimeInfo() method to update the information in the textboxes. Note that we call the UpdateTimeInfo() method in two different places in the program: once in the frmMain() constructor and again in the btnRefresh_Click() method.

The fact that we can call a method illustrates another important feature of methods: They enable you to avoid writing duplicate code. You could, after all, take the following code and shove it into both the frmMain() constructor and the btnRefresh_Click() methods:

```
int days;
DateTime myTime = new DateTime();
myTime = DateTime.Now;
DateTime newYears = new DateTime(myTime.Year, 12, 31);
```

```
txtCompleteDateAndTime.Text = myTime.ToString("f");
txtLongDate.Text = myTime.ToString("D");
txtShortDate.Text = myTime.ToString("d");
txtGeneralDateAndTime.Text = myTime.ToString("g");
txtLongTime.Text = myTime.ToString("T");
txtShortTime.Text = myTime.ToString("t");

days = newYears.DayOfYear - myTime.DayOfYear;
txtDaysToNewYears.Text = days.ToString();
```

But if you did that you'd have twice as much code to write and maintain. By placing the code in a method, you write, test, and debug the code only once, but you can call it from anywhere in the program as many times as you wish. Methods make programming much easier!

Summary

You've covered a lot of ground in this chapter. You've learned what a reference data type is and how it differs from a value data type. You've also learned that reference variables have rvalues that can hold either the value null or a memory address only. You also saw how the Bucket Analogy still applies to reference variables, but in a slightly different way. Business programs process a lot of textual data. For that reason, we spent quite a bit of time discussing string variables and how they can be manipulated by various string methods. We also discussed the DateTime data type and some of its common properties and methods. We used the DateTime variables to introduce you to the concept of constructors and overloaded methods. You should also understand how an overloaded method must have different signatures so Visual Studio knows which method to call. Lastly, you learned how to use various formatting characters for the ToString() method of the DateTime class.

This chapter presented a lot of new information. It is especially important that you understand the difference between reference types and value types before you move on to the next chapter. A little time spent now to understand the concepts presented in this chapter will yield huge benefits later on.

Exercises

1. Explain the difference between a reference variable and a value type variable.

2. Suppose you have a long message that you wrote and stored in a string named message. You have this nagging feeling that you misspelled Friday as Frday somewhere in the string. Write the statement(s) that would find and correct the misspelling.

3. I mentioned that there is an error in the program that uses the Remove() method. The problem is that after the word is removed there are two spaces between the remaining words. How would you fix this bug?

4. What is a constructor and when should it be used?

5. Suppose the user typed her birthday into a textbox named txtBirthday in the form MM/DD/YY and you want to show how old she is in a textbox named txtAge. What would the code look like?

Making Decisions in Code

If computers could not use data to make decisions, they would be little more than very expensive boat anchors. Because it is hard to write a nontrivial program without some form of decision-making ability in it, I have used some decision-making keywords in previous programs. However, I never really explained what those keywords actually do. That changes by the end of this chapter. In this chapter, you will learn about:

- ❑ Relational operators
- ❑ Comparing value types
- ❑ Comparing reference types
- ❑ The `if` and `else` keywords
- ❑ Cascading `if` statements
- ❑ Logical operators
- ❑ The `switch`, `case`, `break`, and `default` keywords
- ❑ Data validation

This chapter also presents some thoughts on coding style. Coding style simply refers to the way you write program code. There are myriad coding styles. Because C# is not form-specific, you are free to use just about any coding style you wish. The author has known brilliant programmers whose code is almost impossible to read or decipher. On the other hand, I've had mediocre students who write code that is a joy to read. True, beauty is in the eye of the beholder. However, experience has taught me that 80 percent of a program's development time is spent in testing, debugging, and maintaining the code, and only 20 percent in writing it. For that reason, anything you can do to make your code clearer and more easily understood is a good idea.

Relational Operators

Making a decision about anything involves comparing one thing against another. It's no different in a computer program. You learned in Chapter 3 that statements are built up from operators and operands. I used the math operators to illustrate how program statements are constructed from those basic building blocks. In this section I want to discuss another set of operators that you have at your disposal: the relational operators. The relational operators are presented in Table 6-1.

Table 6-1

Relational Operator	Relational Tests	Example	Outcome of Example
==	Equal	15 == 20	False
!=	Not equal	15 != 20	True
<	Less than	15 < 20	True
<=	Less than or equal to	15 <= 20	True
>	Greater than	15 > 20	False
>=	Greater than or equal to	15 >= 20	False

In Table 6-1, every example has one operand on the left-hand side of the relational operator (15) and a second operand on the right-hand side of the operator (20). Once again, two operands are associated with the use of a relational operator, so all relational operators are binary operators. Therefore, combining two operands with a relational operator results in a *relational expression*.

Note that each relational expression ultimately resolves to a logic True or logic False state. In C#, logic True and logic False are expressed as Boolean values. The result of a Boolean expression resolves to the C# keywords `true` or `false`. In Table 6-1, each example shown in the third column resolves to the state shown in the fourth column. In the table, I used literal values simply to make the relational expression more concrete. In programming situations, however, the operands in a relational expression are usually variables rather than literals.

Using Relational Operators — The if Statement

Now let's take what you've learned about relational operators and put them to work in a C# `if` statement. While you have seen several examples of the `if` statement in earlier chapters, I haven't actually explained how they work. That's the purpose of this section.

The syntax form for an `if` statement is as follows:

```
if (expression1)
{
    // Logic true: if statement block
}
```

expression1 appears between the opening and closing parentheses following the if keyword. Usually, expression1 represents a relational test to be performed. As you saw in Table 6-1, the outcome of a relational expression is either logic True or logic False. The code that appears between the two curly braces is called the if *statement block*. If expression1 evaluates to logic True, then the if statement block is executed. If expression1 evaluates to logic False, program control skips over the if statement block. You can see how the program flows based upon the outcome of expression1 in Figure 6-1.

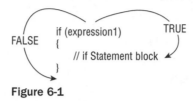

Figure 6-1

Try It Out   Testing for Odd or Even

To illustrate a simple use of an if statement, consider the program shown in Figure 6-2.

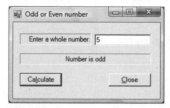

Figure 6-2

The user enters a number and, based upon its value, the program tells whether the number is odd or even. The program should also check that the user entered a valid sequence of digit characters for the number. After all, the letter O is just below the zero digit character (0) and sometimes people in a hurry hit the wrong key.

How It Works

The code that does all the work is found in the button click event method. The code is shown in Listing 6-1.

Listing 6-1

```
private void btnCalc_Click(object sender, EventArgs e)
{
    bool flag;
    int val;
    string output = "Number is even";

    // Convert from text to number
    flag = int.TryParse(txtNumber.Text, out val);
    if (flag == false)
```

```
       {
         MessageBox.Show("Not a number. Re-enter.");
         txtNumber.Clear();
         txtNumber.Focus();
         return;
       }

       // See if odd or even
       if (val % 2 == 1)
       {
         output = "Number is odd";
       }
       // Show result
       lblOutput.Text = output;

     }
```

The `btnCalc_Click()` method begins by defining several working variables. Note how you initialized the string variable named `output` with the string literal `Number is even`. You then used the `TryParse()` method to convert the text entered by the user into a numeric value.

How the TryParse() Method Works

The `TryParse()` method is normally used to convert data from a string format to a numeric format. In this example, the `TryParse()` method is part of the `int` object type, as shown by the `int.TryParse()` method call in Listing 6-1. The `TryParse()` method requires two arguments: 1) the string to be converted, and 2) the variable that will hold the numeric value if the data conversion is successful.

The keyword `out` in the second argument is necessary and must precede the numeric variable name. The data type of the variable (such as `val`) must match the flavor of `TryParse()` you are using (such as `int.TryParse()` in this example). You can think of the `out` keyword as serving two purposes. First, it tells C# that it's okay to use this variable even though it has not been initialized to any known value. Second, the `out` keyword also tells C# that it is the lvalue being passed to the method, not the rvalue. Recall that, by default, arguments are passed by making a copy of the rvalue of the data item. With `TryParse()`, it is the lvalue that gets passed. Using the Bucket Analogy, this means that the `TryParse()` method knows where the bucket for `val` is located in memory. Because this flavor of `TryParse()` is a method for the `int` object type, it also knows the size of the bucket. Given that `TryPrase()` knows where the data resides in memory and its type, `TryParse()` has everything it needs to permanently change the value of the variable being passed to it.

`TryParse()` takes the string of characters from the first argument and tries to format those characters into a numeric data value. If one of the characters is inconsistent with a numeric digit character, the conversion fails. `TryParse()` returns `false` to the caller and moves the value 0 into the rvalue for the variable. `TryParse()` has no problems setting `val` to 0 because it knows where `val` resides in memory and how many bytes it takes.

If the `Try.Parse()` method fails (for example, because the user entered a non-digit character), the variable `flag` is logic False. The `if` statement —

```
     if (flag == false)
```

— checks the state of `flag` using the equality relational operator (`==`). If `flag` is `false` because `Try.Parse()` failed to convert the user's input into an integer value, the expression in the `if` statement is logic True. That is, it is true that `flag` is `false`. (Think about it.) The code then executes the `if` statement block code, which displays a message about the error, sets the program focus back into the textbox object, and then returns back to the caller.

To Clear() or Not to Clear()

The `Clear()` method simply removes any characters that currently exist in the `Text` property of a textbox object. The program statement in the `if` statement block is a little controversial:

```
txtNumber.Clear();
```

This is because some people think you should allow the user to see his mistake after he has viewed the message you displayed by the call to `MessageBox.Show()`, while the other school of thought says that you should clear out the error in preparation for the entry of the new, hopefully correct, value. There is no "right" answer here. You can choose either approach, as long as you use it consistently. Users like consistency, so pick a style and stick with it.

Assuming the user entered a proper numeric value, that number is assigned into `val` by the `Try.Parse()` method. The next `if` statement uses the modulus operator to find the remainder of the user's number:

```
if (val % 2 == 1)
{
   output = "Number is odd";
}
```

Obviously, if you divided a number by two and there is a remainder, the number must be odd. Therefore if

```
val % 2
```

yields a result of `1`, then the `if` test appears as if it were written like this:

```
if (1 == 1)
```

The result of this test is obviously logic True. Therefore, if the number is odd, its remainder is `1` and the `if` test expression is `true`. That means that the code for the `if` statement block is executed and `output` is assigned the string literal `Number is odd`.

Note how you can cause the program to ignore or execute the statements in the `if` statement block based upon the state of the `if` expression. Whenever the expression is `true`, the statement block is executed. Whenever the expression is `false`, the statement block is skipped. As simple as it is to understand, the `if` statement is the major building block that enables computers to have the processing abilities they do.

The absolute *best* way to understand how an `if` statement alters the flow of a program is to single-step through the code using different values for `val`. To do this, place your cursor on the statement that reads

```
flag = int.TryParse(txtNumber.Text, out val);
```

and press the F9 key to set a breakpoint. Now run the program. When the program reaches the breakpoint, single-step the program by repeatedly pressing the F10 key. (You can also use the F11 key, which is even better because it causes the program to single-step through any methods that you wrote as well.)

"use of unassigned local variable"

Sometimes, when you're using the if statement, you may get the following error message:

```
use of unassigned local variable i
```

I can illustrate this error with the following code snippet:

```
int i;

// Some additional lines of code
if (x == MAX)
{
    i = 10;
}
i *= i;
```

Visual Studio issues the error message for the last line, stating that you are trying to use variable i before a value has been assigned to it. The reason Visual Studio acts this way is that it does not know at compile time whether the if statement resolves to logic True to be able to assign the value 10 into i. After all, if the if expression is logic False, variable i has no known value assigned to it. You can fix this problem by simply assigning a default value to variable i. Most of the time, you do this when the variable is defined. Simply change the definition of i to this:

```
int i = 0;
```

This sets the rvalue of i to 0 and Visual Studio is now happy because i now has a known value regardless of the outcome of the if expression.

The if-else Statement

If you look closely at the code in Listing 6-1, you'll notice that I set the output string to the literal Number is even at the moment the string is defined. Therefore, the string is only changed when the number is odd. If you think about it, what I really wanted to do is set the output string based upon whether the number is odd or even. The program works, but it really doesn't reflect what I want to do.

The if-else statement is the perfect solution to clarify our code. The syntax for the if-else statement is the following:

```
if (expression1)
{
    // Logic true: if statement block
}
else
{
    // Logic false: else statement block
}
```

With the `if-else` statement, if (expression1) evaluates to logic True, the `if` statement block is executed. If expression1 is logic False, the statements within the curly braces following the `else` keyword are executed. The group of statements within the curly braces following the `else` keyword is called the *else statement block*. The program flow for the `if-else` statement is shown in Figure 6-3.

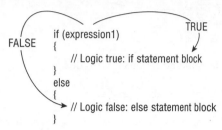

Figure 6-3

As you can see in Figure 6-3, the `if-else` statement creates a "this-or-that" kind of decision. That is, the decision produces one of two mutually exclusive outcomes. Let's revise Listing 6-1 to use an `if-else` construct. First, drop the initializing string literal for `output` and make it simply this:

```
string output;
```

Next, replace the second `if` statement with this:

```
// See if odd or even
if (val % 2 == 1)
{
  output = "Number is odd";
}
else
{
  output = "Number is even";
}
```

Most programmers would agree that this form is easier to understand because the outcomes are clearly stated in one place. With the first form of the program you had to look at a different section of the program (the definition and initialization of `output`) to see what the string was when the number was even.

Shorthand for Simple if-else: The Ternary Operator

Because `if-else` statements are so common in programs, C# has a special operator designed specifically to replace a simple `if-else` statement. C# uses the ternary operator to replace simple `if-else` statements. The syntax for the ternary operator is

```
(expression1) ? trueExpression : falseExpression
```

The statement works by evaluating expression1. If expression1 evaluates to logic True, then trueExpression is evaluated. If expression1 is logic False, then falseExpression is evaluated. The logic can be seen in Figure 6-4.

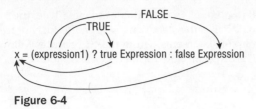

Figure 6-4

For example, our odd-even code could be replaced with this:

```
output = (val % 2 == 0) ? "Number is even" : "Number is odd";
```

The variable `output` is assigned the string literal `Number is even` if `val % 0` is 0. Otherwise, if the modulus operator yields a value of `1`, `output` is assigned `Number is odd`. You may want to type this operator into your sample program to try it out for yourself.

Style Considerations for if and if-else Statements

C# is a format-insensitive language. This means that you could write the `if-else` statement as a single line, like this:

```
if (val % 2 == 1){output = "Number is odd";}else{output = "Number is even";}
```

Visual Studio would process the statements just fine. However, most programmers would find the preceding line much more difficult to read without the line breaks and indentation. Such formatting issues are factors in the style you use to write your code. You do have some choices.

For example, when an `if` or an `else` statement block consists of a single statement, you don't need the curly braces. That is, you could write this:

```
if (val % 2 == 1)
{
  output = "Number is odd";
}
else
{
  output = "Number is even";
}
```

as this:

```
if (val % 2 == 1)
  output = "Number is odd";
else
  output = "Number is even";
```

The program would execute exactly as before. However, when the `if` statement block contains multiple statements, you *must* use the curly braces. For example, suppose you wrote the following code:

```
if (val % 2 == 1)
{
    output = "Number is odd";
    oddCounter++;
}
```

Your intent is to count the number of odd numbers using `oddCounter`. If you write the same code without curly braces —

```
if (val % 2 == 1)
    output = "Number is odd";
    oddCounter++;
```

— your intent may be the same, but without the curly braces what you actually have is this:

```
if (val % 2 == 1)
{
  output = "Number is odd";
}
        oddCounter++;
```

The reason the code functions differently is that without the curly braces, the `if` statement controls only a single statement. The result of this error is that `oddCounter` will always be incremented regardless of the value of the number `val` — probably not what you wanted to do.

So the style question becomes: should I use curly braces when the `if` statement block contains only one statement? I think the answer is yes. Always use curly braces. First, always using curly braces promotes consistency in your coding. Anytime you use an `if` statement, curly braces follow. Second, often what starts out as a single statement in the `if` statement block ends up with multiple statements after testing and debugging. You'll have to add the braces anyway, so you might as well add them from the get-go. Third, most programmers think the curly braces make the statement blocks stand out more and make them easier to read. The lesson learned here is always to use curly braces, even when the `if` statement block only contains one statement.

Another style consideration is where to place the curly braces. For example, because C# doesn't care about statement formatting, you could write the previous code as follows:

```
if (val % 2 == 1){
  output = "Number is odd";
} else {
  output = "Number is even";
}
```

Note that the required curly braces are still where they need to be, but that their location is different. This *K&R style* was made popular by the C programming book written by Brian Kernighan and Dennis Ritchie back in the 1970s (*The C Programming Language*, Prentice Hall, 1978). One reason this style is popular is that it uses two fewer screen lines, meaning that you are making better use of your display's nano-acres. Being able to see more source code without scrolling is usually a good thing.

So which style should you use? Well, obviously C# doesn't care. If you are working on a programming team, such style considerations should be a team (or company) decision. If you are just writing code for yourself, it's your choice. Personally, I really like the K&R style, mainly because C was the first language I really enjoyed using and most C programmers used the K&R style. Also, I find fewer students doing something silly like

```
if (x == 2);
    x++;
```

when they use braces and the K&R style. What this little snippet really is becomes more obvious when braces are added:

```
if (x == 2){
    ;
}
x++;
```

This is probably not what the programmer meant to do. Always using braces helps reduce this type of silliness.

There is no "correct" style. However, whatever style you select, use it consistently.

Nested if Statements

You can have if statements within if statements. For example, suppose you own a bar and on Tuesday nights ladies get drinks at half price. You might have code like this:

```
price = FULLPRICE;
if (age => 21)
{
    if (gender == "Female")
    {
        price *= .5M;
    }
} else {
    MessageBox.Show("Illegal minor.");
}
```

In this example, you take the drink price and multiply it by .5 if the customer is a female age 21 or older. If the gender is male, the full price prevails. Because you have an if statement contained within the if statement block, this is called a *nested if statement*. The else statement block may also contain nested if statements.

You may be asking, "What's with the letter M after the .5?" Recall from our discussion of data types that several value types have suffixes that can be appended to them to make it clear what the data type is. In this case, because you are dealing with the price of a drink (that is, with money), you want to use the decimal data type. If you don't place the M after the .5, C# assumes the literal .5 is a double data type. C# views this as an error and issues an appropriate error message.

Finally, you might ask why we multiply by .5 instead of dividing by two. After all, the results are the same so why not use the conventional divide-by-two approach? There are two reasons. First, multiplying by .5 is a fairly common programming idiom for dividing a number in half. Second, division is the slowest of the four basic math operations. Multiplication is slightly faster than division. While the speed improvement in this example would be unnoticeable, such would not be the case if the operation were being performed in a tight loop doing tens of thousands of iterations. Also, I just wanted you to see an example of this idiom in case you run across it while looking at someone else's code.

RDC

Sometimes you need to do a search that involves multiple values, any of which might be correct depending upon some variable. For example, suppose you have a variable that tells what day of the week it is and you want to perform various tasks based on that value. You might write the following code:

```
if (day == 1)
{
     doMondayStuff();
}
if (day == 2)
{
     doTuesdayStuff();
}
if (day == 3)
{
    doWednesdayStuff();
}
if (day == 4)
{
    doThursdayStuff();
}
if (day == 5)
{
    doFridayStuff();
}
if (day == 6)
{
    doSaturdayStuff();
}
if (day == 7)
{
    doSundayStuff();
}
```

This is what I call *RDC*, or Really Dumb Code. The reason is that the structure shown here often causes unnecessary code to be executed. For example, suppose you want to do Monday's tasks (day = 1). The first if test is logic True, so the code executes doMondayStuff(). That's the good news. The bad news is that, when program control returns after executing the doMondayStuff() method, it then performs six unnecessary if tests on variable day. The tests are unnecessary because you already know that day's value is 1. Therefore, the code executes six unnecessary if tests even though you know they can't be logic True. Once you realize what makes your code RDC, you usually perform a flat-forehead slap and ask yourself why you didn't see it in the first place. Not to worry . . . most good programmers have well-earned flat foreheads! The important thing in becoming a good programmer is to move on to more complex bugs and not repeat the same old ones over and over.

The next section shows you how to get rid of this kind of RDC.

Cascading if Statements

Sometimes there are situations in which you need to perform some action based upon a particular value of a variable. Sticking with our days-of-the-week example from the previous section, you might see something like this:

```csharp
if (day == 1)
{
    doMondayStuff();
} else
    if (day == 2)
    {
        doTuesdayStuff();
    } else
        if (day == 3)
        {
            doWednesdayStuff();
        } else
            if (day == 4)
            {
                doThursdayStuff();
            } else
                if (day == 5)
                {
                    doFridayStuff();
                } else
                    if (day == 6)
                    {
                        doSaturdayStuff();
                    } else
                        if (day == 7)
                        {
                            doSundayStuff();
                        }
```

Code like this is called a *cascading* if statement. As a general rule, cascading if statements perform different tasks based upon the state of a particular variable. In this code snippet, it appears that different methods are called based up on the value of the variable day. If you follow the logic carefully, you'll see that the six unnecessary if tests are no longer executed when the first test is logic True. (Use the debugger to prove this is the case.) The reason the unnecessary code is now skipped is that when an if statement becomes logic True there is no reason to evaluate any further if expressions.

Quite often cascading if statements are a bit clumsy and difficult to read, simply because there are so many if statements and curly braces that things can appear a little confusing. The other problem is that if you use proper indentation with each if expression your code gets pushed farther and farther to the right of the display screen. Eventually, this can force you to use horizontal scrolling, which most programmers dislike. You will see a more effective way to write cascading if statements later in this chapter.

Logical Operators

Sometimes it is necessary to make complex decisions based upon the state of two or more variables. For example, to determine if a year is a leap year, you apply the following test:

If the year can be evenly divided by 4, but not by 100, it is a leap year. The exception occurs if the year is evenly divisible by 400. If so, it is a leap year.

If you try to code this as a series of simple `if` statements, the code gets a little messy. It's actually easier to code the algorithm if you can use a combination of logical operators. The C# conditional logical operators are shown in Table 6-2.

Table 6-2

Item	Meaning	Example
Logical `&&`	Logical AND	`x && y`
Logical `||`	Logical OR	`x || y`
Logical `!`	Logical NOT	`!x`

Because these are logical operators, each one resolves to a `true` or `false` expression. I can show these relationships by using truth tables. Table 6-3 shows the truth table for the logical AND operator.

Table 6-3

Expression1	Expression2	Expression1 && Expression2
True	True	True
True	False	False
False	True	False
False	False	False

The last column in Table 6-2 shows that the logical AND truth table is constructed using two expressions in conjunction with the `&&` operator. Table 6-3 shows the outcome for all possible values for those two expressions and the impact on the logical AND result. For example, if `Expression1` resolves to logic True and `Expression2` resolves to logic False, the result is logic False. This is because a logical AND requires both expressions to be True for the result to be True. All other combinations yield a result that is logic False.

Table 6-4 shows the truth table for the logical OR operator. As you can see in the table, the result of a logical OR statement is True if either or both expressions is logic True. Only when both expressions are False is the result False.

Table 6-4

Expression1	Expression2	Expression1 || Expression2
True	True	True
True	False	True
False	True	True
False	False	False

Finally, Table 6-5 shows the truth table for the logical NOT operator. Unlike the other operators, logical NOT is a unary operator, which means it only uses a single expression. Therefore, Table 6-5 is rather simple.

Table 6-5

Expression1	Expression2
True	False
False	True

As you can see from Table 6-5, the logical NOT operator simply "flips" the current state of the expression.

Using the Logical Operators

Now let's revisit the algorithm for determining if a year is a leap year. The algorithm is: "If the year can be evenly divided by 4, but not by 100, it is a leap year. The exception occurs if the year is evenly divisible by 400. If so, it is a leap year."

You might code the algorithm like this:

```
if (year % 4 == 0 && year % 100 != 0 || year % 400 == 0)
{
  return 1;
}
else
{
  return 0;
}
```

If you examine the algorithm and then the code, you should be able to convince yourself that the single
`if` statement does implement the algorithm correctly.

However, things are not always so simple. You might get something like this:

```
if (x + y < b && z - y == c || z * 5 - b == d)
{
    answer = x * y * z;
}
```

The preceding `if` statement mixes logical, conditional, and math operators all together. So how do you
know what to do to resolve such a complex `if` statement? As you learned in Chapter 4, the precedence
order determines the order in which operators are evaluated. However, because you have added new
operators in this chapter, you need to expand your precedence table to include the new operators. The
new precedence table is presented in Table 6-6.

Table 6-6

Operator	Type
. ++ -- new	Primary
!	Unary
* / %	Math
+ -	Math
< > <= >=	Relational
== !=	Relational
&& ||	Logical
?:	Ternary
= *= /= %= += -=	Assignment
,	Comma

If you're not happy with the order in which a group of expressions are evaluated, you can always force
something to be evaluated out of its natural precedence by containing the expression within parentheses.

Associativity

How is precedence resolved when an expression contains two operators with the same precedence level?
Precedence-level ties are broken by the associativity rules for operators. As a general rule operators are
left-associative, which means they are evaluated from left to right in the statement. Once again, if you

need to override the precedence and associativity rules, you can use parentheses to force your preferred order. Consider the following code:

```
x = 5 + 6 * 10;
```

The answer is 65. This is because multiplication has higher precedence than addition, so the sequence becomes:

```
x = 5 + 6 * 10;
x = 5 + 60;
x = 65;
```

If you actually need the answer to be 110, then you would use parentheses:

```
x = (5 + 6) * 10;
x = 11 * 10;
x = 110;
```

The switch Statement

You learned earlier that you could replace the RDC with a cascading if statement when you wanted to test for a specific day, as in our days-of-the-week example:

```
if (day == 1)
{
    doMondayStuff();
} else
    if (day == 2)
    {
        doTuesdayStuff();
    } else
        if (day == 3)
        {
            do WednesdayStuff();
        }

// The rest of the days are similar to above
```

While this code works just fine, it's difficult to read cascading if statements. That's because you still must match up the proper if statement with its associated day value. Secondly, if the cascade is fairly long, the code starts to scroll off to the right. Programmers hate horizontal scrolling because it wastes time. They would rather be able to read all the code without scrolling. The switch statement offers one way to resolve these drawbacks.

The syntax for the switch statement is as follows:

```
switch (expression1)
{
        case 1:

        // Statements for case 1
```

```
    break;
case 1:

// Statements for case 1

    break;
case 1:

// Statements for case 1

    break;
default:

// Statements for default

    break;
}
```

With a `switch` statement, the value of `expression1` determines which `case` statement block is executed. If `expression1` does not match any `case` statement, the `default` expression is evaluated. The `break` statements are necessary to prevent program control from "falling through" to the next `case` statement. The `break` statement causes program execution to resume with the first statement after the `switch` statement block's closing curly brace. You can rewrite your cascading `if` statements using the following code:

```
switch (day)
{
    case 1:
        doMondayStuff();
        break;

    case 2:
        doTuesdayStuff();
        break;

    case 3:
        doWednesdayStuff();
        break;

    case 4:
        doThursdayStuff();
        break;

    case 5:
        doFridayStuff();
        break;

    case 6:
        doSaturdayStuff();
        break;
```

```
case 7:
    doSundayStuff();
    break;

default:
    MessageBox.Show("We should never get here");
    ErrorLog(day);
    break;
}
```

If you study this code fragment, you will discover that it works like a cascading `if` statement, only it's quite a bit easier to read. Also, you don't have to do horizontal scrolling to see all the code at once.

If variable `day` does not have a value between 1 and 7, the `default` case is executed. (You are not required to use a `default` case, but it's a good idea to include one in each `switch` statement.) In this situation, I elected to display an error message and then pass the value of `day` to an `ErrorLog()` method. This is a fairly common practice. Often, the error log file is just a simple text file that can be read with any word processing program. Because I wrote the value of `day` to the error log file, the person in charge of supporting the program can ask the user over the phone to read the last line in the error log file. The support person would, therefore, have some idea of the value that produced the error.

Summary

This chapter presented the basics of making decisions in a program. The basic building block of computer decision making is the simple `if` statement. From that, I discussed the `if-else` and `switch` statements and showed when it may be appropriate to use them. I also made some comments on programming style. Even though C# doesn't care about your coding style, other people who may have to read your code do. In all cases, try to make your code as easy to read as possible.

Exercises

1. Suppose a movie theatre charges half price for children 12 or under or adults age 65 or older. Write an `if` statement that accounts for this pricing policy.

2. What are the important style considerations when you're writing `if-else` statements?

3. When is it appropriate to use a cascading `if` statement?

4. What errors do you see in the following code snippet?

    ```
    if  (x = y);
    {

        price =* .06;

    }
    ```

5. Suppose a small pizza sells for $6, a medium is a dollar more, and a large is a dollar more than a medium. Assuming that the variable `size` stores the customer's selection, how would you write the code to determine the final price?

Statement Repetition Using Loops

Computer programs are very good at doing repetitive tasks . . . much better than humans, because computers don't get bored. In this chapter, I examine *program loops.* These are simply a means by which a program can repeat the execution of a given set of program statements. In this chapter you will learn the following:

❑   What a loop is and when it should be used

❑   What constitutes a well-behaved program loop

❑   What happens when loops are ill-behaved

❑   What a `for` loop is

❑   What a `while` loop is

❑   What a `do-while` loop is

❑   When to use the `break` and `continue` statements

Most nontrivial programs use some form of program loop. Loops are so useful that C# makes several different types available. Let's see what loops can do for you.

Program Loops

If you're sitting in a public building right now, look at the ceiling. Chances are you can see sprinklers embedded there. In most modern office buildings, each room has one or more sprinklers in it. Modern sprinklers are monitored by software that tests each one to see if it senses a fire. If a building has 500 sprinklers, the program samples the current state of sprinkler one and, assuming everything's okay, goes on to test sprinkler two. This process continues until sprinkler 500 is tested. Assuming all 500 passed the test and no fire is sensed, the program goes back to the start and tests sprinkler one again. The program then moves on to sprinkler two and the entire process repeats itself. It's fairly quick, probably taking less than a few seconds to test all 500 sprinklers.

The process of repeated testing is performed by a program loop within the fire system software. If one of the sprinkler system tests failed, the software would likely branch out of the loop and process code that would sound the alarm, make sure there is water pressure to feed the sprinkler system, and place a call to the fire department. Loops are everywhere around us, in everything from fire alarms to elevators to circuits in your car's engine and safety equipment. Indeed, people who find their lives boring are perhaps caught in endless loops wherein they do the same things over and over again!

Good Loops, Bad Loops

Not all loops are created equal. As you will see in a moment, there are good loops and bad loops. To understand the difference, let's list the conditions of a well-behaved loop. I list these conditions first, and then explain them with a program example.

The Three Conditions of a Well-Behaved Loop

In general, well-behaved loops:

❑   always initialize the starting state of the loop

❑   provide a test expression to decide whether another iteration of the loop is needed

❑   alter the current state of a variable that controls the loop

The first condition means that your code should always start executing a program loop in a known state. Usually this means that you assign the variable that controls the loop some initial value. Failure to initialize a loop variable almost always means that the loop executes an unexpected number of times . . . not good!

The second condition means that you must have some form of test that decides whether another pass through the loop is needed. Usually this means testing the variable that you initialized as part of the first condition against some termination criteria. This condition often means that a relational operator is part of the condition.

The third condition means that some variable must change its value during the execution of the loop. If the state of the loop does not change during execution, there is no condition that can terminate the loop. This produces an *infinite loop,* which is one that continues to execute forever. Most of the time, an infinite loop is the result of an error in the logic of the program.

Infinite Loops

Infinite loops are often unintentional and can "hang" the system. Therefore, any time you are writing code that involves program loops, it's a good idea to save your code before running it. By default, Visual Studio saves your code when you run the program (F5). You can save the project's code explicitly by using the either the File ⇨ Save All menu sequence or the Ctrl+Shift+S key combination. By saving your code before a trial run, you can pick up where you left off if the code enters an infinite loop. Usually you can regain control by clicking the "small blue square" icon or pressing Shift+F5. Sometimes these don't work and you may need to use the dreaded Ctrl+Alt+Delete to regain control of the system when an infinite loop is executed.

To illustrate the three conditions of a well-behaved loop, I begin with the `for` loop.

The for Loop

The syntax for a `for` loop is as follows:

```
for (expression1; expression2; expression3)
{
    // for loop statement block
}
```

expression1 is normally used to initialize the starting value for the loop. expression2 is usually a relational test that determines if another iteration of the loop is needed. Finally, expression3 is often a statement that increments or decrements the variable controlling the loop. A concrete example should help identify these expressions. Suppose you want to generate a table of squares for values from 0 through 100. The `for` loop controlling the processing might look like this:

```
for (i = 0; i <= 100; i++)
{
    // statements to calculate the values
}
```

expression1 is the statement

```
i = 0;
```

This expression sets, or initializes, the initial state of the loop. In this case you are starting the table-of-squares calculations with the value 0. Because the variable i appears in all three expressions, it is the variable that controls the `for` loop. If you wanted to initialize the state of the loop with the value 1, you would change expression1 to be

```
i = 1;
```

The second expression,

```
i <= 100;
```

checks the current value of variable i against the desired ending value of 100. If this expression resolves to logic True, another pass through the loop code is made. That is, the `for` loop's statement block is executed.

The third expression,

```
i++;
```

is responsible for changing the state of the loop during each pass. In this case the code simply increments the value of variable i. Note that you can place any expression statement here, including a decrement if you wish.

Sequencing in a for Loop

There is a well-defined sequence for the order of statement execution in a for loop. This sequencing is illustrated in Figure 7-1.

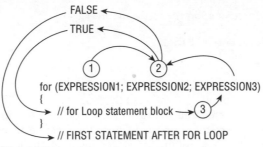

Figure 7-1

In the figure, Step 1 is usually the initialization of the variable that controls the loop. After Step 1 is accomplished, program control is transferred to Step 2. Note that expression1 in Step 1 is never revisited again. The sole purpose of expression1 is to initialize the loop; once that is done, that expression is not executed again.

Step 2 is the relational expression. This means the code normally compares two variables to decide what to do next. As shown in Figure 7-1, if the outcome of the relational test in expression2 is logic True, program control is sent to the statements in the for loop statement block. If expression2 evaluates to logic False, program control is sent to the first statement following the closing curly brace of the for loop statement block, and the loop body is skipped.

Assuming Step 2 is logic True, the code between the opening and closing curly braces is executed. When the last statement of the for loop statement block is executed, Step 3 sends program control to expression3. Normally, expression3 is responsible for changing the state of the for loop. Perhaps the most common statement for expression3 is an increment operation of the variable that was initialized in Step 1.

After expression3 is executed, program control is immediately sent back to expression2. Once again, the code in expression2 is tested to see if another pass through the loop statement block is needed. If the test is logic True, another pass through the for loop statement block is made. This repeated sequence continues until expression2 evaluates to logic False, at which time the for loop terminates.

Now that you understand what each of the three expressions in a for loop does, compare their tasks with the three conditions required of a well-behaved loop. See any relationship? The three expressions needed to use a for loop *are* the three required conditions of a well-behaved loop!

Try It Out   Table of Squares

Let's write a program that produces a table of squares for a series of numbers. Figure 7-2 shows what the user interface looks like for our program.

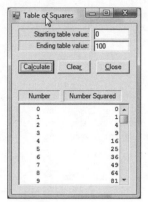

Figure 7-2

The code behind the interface is shown in Listing 7-1. In this example I show all the code, including the template C# code from Listing 2-1 in Chapter 2 that I discussed when you wrote your first program.

Listing 7-1

```csharp
using System;
using System.Windows.Forms;

public class frmMain : Form
{
  private Label label2;
  private TextBox txtStart;
  private TextBox txtEnd;
  private Button btnCalculate;
  private Button btnClear;
  private Button btnClose;
  private ListBox lstOutput;
  private Label label3;
  private Label label4;
  private Label label1;

  #region Windows code

  public frmMain()
  {
    InitializeComponent();
  }

  public static void Main()
```

```csharp
{
  frmMain main = new frmMain();
  Application.Run(main);
}

private void btnCalculate_Click(object sender, EventArgs e)
{
  bool flag;
  int i;
  int start;
  int end;
  string buff;

  //======================= Gather inputs =======================

  // Convert start from text to int
  flag = int.TryParse(txtStart.Text, out start);
  if (flag == false)
  {
    MessageBox.Show("Numeric data only", "Input Error");
    txtStart.Focus();
    return;
  }

  // Convert end from text to int
  flag = int.TryParse(txtEnd.Text, out end);
  if (flag == false)
  {
    MessageBox.Show("Numeric data only", "Input Error");
    txtEnd.Focus();
    return;
  }
      if (start >= end)                        // Reasonable values?
      {
         MessageBox.Show("Start greater than end.", "Input Error");
         txtStart.Focus();
         return;
      }

  //====================== Process and Display ==============

  for (i = start; i <= end; i++)
  {
    buff = string.Format("{0, 5}{1, 20}", i, i * i);
    lstOutput.Items.Add(buff);
  }
}

private void btnClose_Click(object sender, EventArgs e)
{
  Close();
}

private void btnClear_Click(object sender, EventArgs e)
```

```
        {
            txtStart.Clear();
            txtEnd.Clear();
            lstOutput.Items.Clear();
        }
    }
```

How it Works

All of the work is done, as usual, in the click event code for the Calculate button. Several working variables are defined and then the code works on securing the input data from the user interface objects. In this example, the user has typed the starting and ending values into the txtStart and txtEnd textbox objects respectively. (The TryParse() method was discussed in detail in Chapter 6, so we need not go over its purpose here.) If both TryParse() methods perform without error, the user typed in valid digit characters that can be converted into the variables start and end. Note how this also means that you have completed the Input Step of the Five Program Steps discussed in Chapter 2.

Now let's review the code in the for loop:

```
        for (i = start; i <= end; i++)
        {
            buff = string.Format("{0, 5}{1, 20}", i, i * i);
            lstOutput.Items.Add(buff);
        }
```

The first condition of a well-behaved loop is that you must set the initial state of the loop. In this example, expression1 of the for loop (i = start) sets the starting state of the variable controlling the loop (i) to its beginning value (start). (This corresponds to Step 1 in Figure 7-1.) Having done that, the program then moves to expression2 of the for loop, i <= end. Suppose the user typed in 0 for the starting value and 100 for the ending value. Because i has been initialized to 0, the expression:

```
    i <= end;
```

may be viewed as:

```
    0 <= 100;
```

Because 0 is less than 100, the expression evaluates to logic True, which means that the statements in the loop body are executed next.

Formatting String Data

The statement:

```
        buff = string.Format("{0, 5}{1, 20}", i, i * i);
```

is a special formatting method provided for you by the string class. The arguments to the method are the key to its usefulness. The first argument of the Format() method is always a quoted string literal. Within that string is a list of options about how you want the data formatted. The first option I used is {0, 5}. This option says to take the first argument and right-justify it in a field of five characters.

(Keep in mind that programmers reference almost everything from zero, so the first argument is actually argument zero.) The second option is {1, 20}, which says to format the second argument as right-justified in a field of 20 characters. This is why the output lines up in nice columns in Figure 7-2.

Okay, so you know how to format the arguments, but . . . where *are* the arguments? After the quoted format string ("{0, 5}{1, 20}") is a comma followed by a list of the arguments. Notice that the option string indicates there are two arguments. Following the option string are two arguments: i , i * i. Therefore, the first argument is the value of variable i and the second argument is the value of i * i. These two pieces of data are then formatted by the Format() method and placed in the string variable buff.

Some of the Format() method options are shown in Table 7-1. You can use Visual Studio's online help to see other formatting options. The vertical lines in the third column of Table 7-1 show the width of the field being requested in the options string. Note that it is permissible to not specify a field width.

Table 7-1

Format Option String	Argument	Output
{0}	"Katie"	|Katie|
{0, 15}	"John"	| John|
{0, -15}	"Tammy"	|Tammy |
{0,15:C}	5.10	| $5.10|
{0,-15:C}	5.10	|$5.10 |
{0, mm}	9:15	|15|
{0, 5:hh}	12:15	| 12|
{0, 15:hh mm}	12:15	| 12:15|
{0, dddd MMMM}	1/1/2008	|Tuesday January|

If you want to format columns in a listbox, even when using the Format() method of the string class, there are still problems to overcome. If you try the code in Listing 7-1 as it is, the column output in your listbox looks pretty good, but not perfect. Why isn't your output perfectly aligned as in Figure 7-2?

Fonts and Column Alignment

The reason the columns in your program aren't perfectly straight is that the default font for a listbox is Microsoft Sans Serif. This is a TrueType font. What that means is that each character gets only as many screen pixels as are necessary to display the character. Therefore, the digit character 1 may take only three pixels to display while the digit 8 might take seven pixels to display. The result is that the digit characters won't line up exactly right because each digit character in the listbox uses a different amount of pixel real estate.

If you switch from a TrueType font to a *fixed font*, like Courier New, the columns line up perfectly. This is because each character in the Courier New font character set takes exactly the same number of pixels regardless of how wide (or skinny) the character is. Therefore, all you have to do to fix this alignment problem is go to the listbox's font property and change it to Courier New. You can do this by clicking the listbox in the Design window, selecting the Font property, and clicking the ellipsis operator (. . .). Then scroll through the list of fonts in the listbox shown in the font dialog until you come to the Courier New font. You can see the Font window in Figure 7-3.

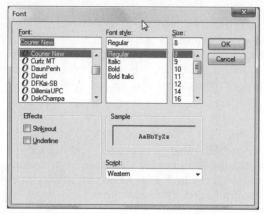

Figure 7-3

After the value of i and i * i have been formatted into buff by means of the Format() method, the code places the string into the listbox object. The statement to add a string to a listbox is simply:

```
lstOutput.Items.Add(buff);
```

You should be able to figure out why there are two dot operators in this statement. The listbox object lstOutput has a property named Items that is itself an object. (Technically, Items is a collection object; you will learn about these in Chapter 8. For now, you can just think of Items as a group of thingies that can store string data.) The code calls the Add() method of the Items object, which results in one line of output being added to the listbox.

After the string data in buff has been added to lstOutput, program control jumps to the third expression of the for loop (i++), as shown in Figure 7-1. This increment expression is the third step in a well-behaved loop: It changes the state of the loop. If you didn't change the state of the loop counter variable, i, you would have an infinite loop. In this case, an infinite loop would not be a good thing.

After i has been incremented by means of the ++ increment operator, program control is transferred to expression2. For our for loop, this expression is

```
i <= end;
```

The second expression, therefore, compares the newly incremented value of i to the variable end to decide whether another pass through the for loop's statement body is warranted. As long as the current value of i is less than or equal to the value of the variable end, another pass through the loop is made. Eventually, after 101 passes through the loop, expression2 becomes logic False and the for loop statement block is skipped. Program execution then resumes with whatever statement follows the closing curly brace of the for loop. You can see in Listing 7-1 that the next statement is actually the closing brace for the btnCalc click event. Therefore, our table of squares is now complete.

When to Use a for Loop

The most common use of `for` loops is to count something or perform a sequence of instructions a specific number of times. That is, the terminating condition as stated in `expression2` of the `for` loop is usually known when the loop is entered. In the preceding program, for example, you knew that the variable `end` determines how many passes should be made through the `for` loop statement block.

You will discover hundreds of situations in which the `for` loop offers the perfect way to solve a given problem. Of the various looping structures C# makes available to you, it is probably the one used most often. A bonus feature of the `for` loop is that all three requirements for a well-behaved loop are specified in the three expressions used in a `for` statement. Having all three requirements for a well-behaved loop in one place makes it pretty difficult to forget any of them.

Nested for Loops

Sometimes you need to solve problems that require a loop within a loop. When one loop appears inside another loop it is called a *nested loop.* Let's modify our table-of-squares program by putting a new twist on it. Many years ago the author discovered, quite by accident, that you can square a number in a different way from simple multiplication. The algorithm is:

The square of a number N is equal to the sum of N positive odd integers, starting with 1.

Reread the algorithm again and think about it. For example, suppose you want to find the square of the number 3. You already know the answer is 9, but let's use the new algorithm to calculate the answer:

```
N² = 1 + 3 + 5
N² = 9
```

Note how I simply added up three positive odd integers, starting with 1, to arrive at the square of 3, which is 9. Suppose you want to find the square of 5:

```
N² = 1 + 3 + 5 + 7 + 9
N² = 25
```

While this is an RDC way of squaring a number, it is an interesting test to see if you can figure out how to implement the algorithm in code.

You should reuse the code from Listing 7-1 as a starting point. (After all, one of the key advantages of object-oriented programming is code reuse!) You still want to generate a table of squares, so the user interface doesn't need to change. However, instead of the simple `i * i` means of squaring the number, you want to implement the new squaring algorithm.

You need to add a few new variables to the original version of the program. The new variables that you need to add to the button click event code are the following:

```
int j;
int square;
int nextOddInteger;
```

The variable j is used to control the new for loop, square is used to hold the squared value, and nextOddInteger is used to create the series of odd integers in the loop. The revised for loop looks like this:

```
for (i = start; i <= end; i++)
{
    nextOddInteger = 1;        // Set first odd integer
    square = 0;                // Always start with square = 0

    for (j = 0; j < i; j++)    // Nested j loop
    {
        square += nextOddInteger; // Sum the odd integer
        nextOddInteger += 2;      // Set the next odd integer
    }
    buff = string.Format("{0, 5}{1, 20}", i, square);
    lstOutput.Items.Add(buff);
}
```

The for loop controlled by variable i is called the *outer loop*. The for loop controlled by variable j is called the *inner loop*. Together, these loops are the *nested loops* mentioned earlier. Note that the outer loop still cycles through all the values you wish to display in the table of squares. Also note that both loops are constructed using our three requirements for a well-behaved loop. Now let's examine the code in the inner loop.

Suppose variable i from the outer loop has a value of 3. This means you want to calculate the square of 3. The code sets nextOddInteger to 1 and clears variable square to 0. Replacing variable i with its current value, the j for loop looks as though it is written like this:

```
for (j = 0; j < 3; j++)    // Nested j loop
{
    square += nextOddInteger; // Sum the odd integer
    nextOddInteger += 2;      // Set the next odd integer
}
```

Because expression2 is j < 3, the code makes three passes through the loop (0, 1, and 2, because expression2 becomes logic False when j = 3). On the first pass, the loop looks like this:

```
for (j = 0; j < 3; j++)    // Nested j loop
{
    square = 1;            // Sum the odd integer
    nextOddInteger = 3;    // Set the next odd integer
}
```

Therefore, after the first pass, square equals 1 and nextOddInteger is increased to 3. The partial result therefore is:

```
square = 1 = 1
nextOddInteger = 1 + 2 = 3
```

On the second pass through the loop, you find:

```
for (j = 0; j < 3; j++)      // Nested j loop
{
     square = 4;              // Sum the odd integer
     nextOddInteger = 5;     // Set the next odd integer
}
```

from the processing of the following code:

```
square = 1 + 3 = 4
nextOddInteger = 3 + 2 = 5
```

On the third and final pass through the loop, you find:

```
square = 1 + 3 + 5 = 9
nextOddInteger = 5 + 2 = 7
```

No additional passes through the inner loop are needed because `expression2` (j < 3) is now logic `False`. Therefore, the next two statements display the output in the listbox as before:

```
buff = string.Format("{0, 5}{1, 20}", i, square);
lstOutput.Items.Add(buff);
```

The only difference is that you replaced `i * i` with the variable `square`. To the user running the program, the output in the listbox looks exactly the same as before. The only difference is that you used a weird algorithm and a nested `for` loop to generate the squares of the numbers.

Use the Debugger as a Learning Tool

The best way for you to see how loops work is to single-step through the program. For example, place the cursor on the following `for` statement:

```
for (i = start; i <= end; i++)
```

Press the F9 key to set a breakpoint at that statement. (The text background changes to red for that statement line.) Now press the F5 key to run the program. Eventually, you'll get to the breakpoint statement. (You may have to click in the Source window to see the breakpoint, which now has the statement displayed with a yellow text background.)

Now start pressing the F10 key to single-step through the program code. Make sure you have the Locals debugger window visible (Debug ⇨ Windows ⇨ Locals, or Ctrl+D, L) so you can see the values of the variables change as you go. Using the debugger is a great way to understand how the flow of the program changes based upon the values of the variables.

while Loops

Another type of program loop is the while loop. The general syntax for a while loop is as follows:

```
while (expression2)
{
    // while loop statement block
}
```

For a while loop to be well behaved, it must follow the same three rules you applied to a for loop. However, unlike the for loop, the while loop does not make all three conditions part of the syntax of the loop structure itself. In fact, only the second condition (expression2) is part of a while loop's syntax. The code from Listing 7-1, rewritten to use a while loop, is presented in Listing 7-2.

Listing 7-2

```
private void btnCalculate_Click(object sender, EventArgs e)
{
    bool flag;
    int i;
    int start;
    int end;
    string buff;

    //======================= Gather inputs =======================

    // Convert start from text to int

    flag = int.TryParse(txtStart.Text, out start);
    if (flag == false)
    {
        MessageBox.Show("Numeric data only", "Input Error");
        txtStart.Focus();
        return;
    }

    // Convert end from text to int

    flag = int.TryParse(txtEnd.Text, out end);
    if (flag == false)
    {
        MessageBox.Show("Numeric data only", "Input Error");
        txtEnd.Focus();
        return;
    }

    if (start >= end)                    // Reasonable values?
    {
        MessageBox.Show("Start less than end.", "Input Error");
        txtStart.Focus();
```

(continued)

Listing 7-2 (continued)

```
        return;
    }

    //====================== Process and Display ==============

    i = start;              // Initialize loop counter: condition 1
    while (i <= end)        // Another iteration:       condition 2
    {
        buff = string.Format("{0, 5}{1, 20}", i, i * i);
        lstOutput.Items.Add(buff);
        i++;                // Change state of loop:    condition 3
    }

}
```

You can see in Listing 7-2 that the first condition for a well-behaved loop is set prior to the while loop's being entered. That is, variable i is initialized to the value of variable start just *before* the while statement. The conditional expression controlling the while loop is exactly the same as expression2 in the for loop (i <= end) in Listing 7-1. This is the second condition of a well-behaved loop.

The while loop body extends from the opening curly brace to the closing curly brace. The loop body is exactly the same as the for loop body in Listing 7-1, except that you must place the third expression within the while loop body (i++). Note that all three conditions for a well-behaved loop are still present, but the while loop scatters them around a bit whereas the for loop had them all in one place. The output from the program is exactly the same as before. This invites the question: Why use a while loop?

Why Have More Than One Type of Loop?

Any code that uses a for loop can be rewritten to use a while loop, so why does C# bother with two kinds? Simply stated, C# gives you a choice of loop types because the nuances of different programming tasks may suit one loop type better than another. For example, there will be many times where you will be looking for a specific piece of data in a list, like a specific customer name in a list of customers, and you don't know exactly where it appears. Most programmers would code such a task as a while loop because they can't be sure of exactly how many iterations it's going to take to find the name. On the other hand, if you need to read 14 sensors on a machine and react to those sensors, you would likely use a for loop.

The ability to choose different loop structures simply makes certain programming tasks easier. While you might be able to contort all your code to fit into a single loop structure, having choices means you don't have to. Multiple loop structures means you have multiple tools at your disposal to attack different programming problems. After all, if the only tool you have is a hammer, it's not surprising that all your problems start to look like a nail. Multiple tools make for more elegant solutions to different programming problems.

do-while Program Loops

C# provides a third loop variation that you can add to your loop toolkit called a do-while loop. The syntax for a do-while loop is as follows:

```
do
{
    // do-while statement block
} while (expression2);
```

The do-while loop variant is similar to the while loop with one major exception: A do-while loop *always* makes at least one pass through the loop statement block. If you look at the other two loop variations, the test of expression2 takes place *before* the loop statement block. With the for and while loop statements, it is quite possible for expression2 to evaluate to logic False at the very start of the loop. If expression2 is false for either the for or while loop, no pass is made through the statements in the loop body.

This is not true for a do-while loop. A do-while loop always makes at least one pass through its statement block. This is because the expression that evaluates whether another pass should be made through the loop is made at the *bottom* of the loop, and is arrived at after the statements in the loop body have been executed at least once. In other words, program control has to pass through the do-while statement block at least one time.

Try It Out   **Generate Random Numbers**

C# provides a class that is capable of generating a series of random numbers. Let's write a program that tests whether that class generates a series of random numbers wherein two identical random numbers are produced "back to back." Listing 7-3 shows the code for the program.

Listing 7-3

```csharp
using System;
using System.Windows.Forms;

public class frmMain : Form
{
    const int MAXITERATIONS = 200000;    // Limit on loop passes

    private Button btnClose;
    private Label lblAnswer;
    private Label label1;
    private TextBox txtMax;
    private Button btnStart;
    #region Windows code

    public frmMain()
    {
        //======================= Program Initialize Step ==============
```

```
        InitializeComponent();
    }

    public static void Main()
    {
        frmMain main = new frmMain();
        Application.Run(main);
    }

    private void btnStart_Click(object sender, EventArgs e)
    {
        bool flag;
        int counter;      // Pass counter
        int max;          // Max value for random number
        int last;
        int current;
        Random randomNumber = new Random();

        //=================== Program Input Step =====================
        flag = int.TryParse(txtMax.Text, out max);
        if (flag == false)
        {
            MessageBox.Show("Digit characters only.", "Input Error",
                        MessageBoxButtons.OK, MessageBoxIcon.Stop);
            txtMax.Focus();
            return;
        }

        //================== Program Process Step ====================
        counter = 0;
        last = (int) randomNumber.Next(max);
        do
        {
            current = randomNumber.Next(max);
            if (last == current)
            {
                break;
            }
            last = current;
            counter++;
        } while (counter < MAXITERATIONS);

        //================== Program Output Step =====================
        if (counter < MAXITERATIONS)
        {
            lblAnswer.Text = "It took " + counter.ToString() + " passes to
                        match";
        } else
        {
            lblAnswer.Text = "No back-to-back match";
        }
```

```
        }
    }

    //======================= Program Termination Step ================
    private void btnClose_Click(object sender, EventArgs e)
    {
        Close();
    }
}
```

A sample run of the program is shown in Figure 7-4.

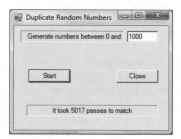

Figure 7-4

The value of 1000 in the textbox object says the program should generate random numbers between 0 and 1000, exclusively. (That is, the random values vary between 0 and 999.) Figure 7-4 shows that it took 5017 passes through the loop before the random number generator produced the same value back to back. Let's take a closer look at the code.

How it Works

The program begins by using the C# template discussed in Chapter 2. Near the top of Listing 7-3 is the statement:

```
const int MAXITERATIONS = 200000;      // Limit on loop passes
```

This statement is used to constrain the maximum iterations of the do-while loop. I did this because it might be possible to make several billion passes through the loop without having two identical values generated in sequence. Using the symbolic constant MAXITERATIONS, you can easily change the limits on the loop without having to change code in the loop itself. True, you could hard-code the value 200000 in the while loop, but then you'd have a "magic number" in the code that doesn't tell us what its purpose is. Using the symbolic constant MAXITERATIONS helps document what the number does. Also, if you decide to change MAXITERATIONS to some other value, simply change it at the top of the program and the new value is used automatically in the rest of the program.

The statement:

```
Random randomNumber = new Random();
```

is used to create a Random object named randomNumber. The program then uses the TryParse() method to construct the range within which the user wants the random numbers to fall. The Random class method Next() is called to produce a random value between 0 and max minus 1. The following code fragment does most of the work in the program:

```
counter = 0;
last = (int) randomNumber.Next(max);
do
{
    current = randomNumber.Next(max);
    if (last == current)
    {
        break;
    }
    last = current;
    counter++;
} while (counter < MAXITERATIONS);
```

Note that the variable named counter is initialized to 0 prior to entering the loop. (This statement serves the purpose of expression1 in a for loop.) This is the variable used to control the loop. The program then uses the Next() method of the Random class to generate a random number and assign it into the variable last. However, because the goal of the program is to compare two random values, you know you must generate another random value before you can test to see if the two are the same. This is why you use the do-while loop: You need to execute the loop body at least once to produce the two random values for the comparison. The second random value is assigned into the variable named current. You now have two random numbers to compare.

The break Keyword in Loops

The if statement compares the values of last and current to see if they are the same. If they are, the if statement is logic True and the break statement is executed. Anytime a break statement is executed within a loop statement block, the break sends program control to the first statement following the closing curly brace of the loop statement block. In this program, control is sent to the

```
if (counter < MAXITERATIONS)
```

statement shown in Listing 7-3.

If the values for the variables current and last are not the same, the break statement is not executed and the program evaluates the expression2 element of the do-while block:

```
while (counter < MAXITERATIONS);
```

The evaluation of this statement determines whether another pass through the loop should be made. At the moment, the symbolic constant MAXITERATIONS is set to 200000, but you could alter the constant if you wish. (Notice how I use this symbolic constant again in subsequent lines to determine the message displayed to the user.) Assuming that counter does not exceed MAXITERATIONS, the while test results in another pass through the loop statement block.

I limited the number of passes made through the loop using the test against MAXITERATIONS for two reasons. First, an integer variable is capable of holding values in excess of two billion, and I felt the user may not want to sit there waiting for the loop to plow through two billion passes. Second, and more importantly, it is possible that it might take *more* than two billion passes through the loop to produce matching values for last and current. This means that the program might produce a value for counter that is too large for an integer variable to store. This could produce what is called a *numeric overflow exception* and our program would die an ungraceful death! (I discuss how to prevent such ugliness in Chapter 9.)

Eventually, either a match for the two variables occurs or counter equals MAXITERATIONS and the do-while loop is terminated. At that point, the final if statement is evaluated and the appropriate message displayed in the lblAnswer label object.

As you might expect, the number of passes required to produce a match increases as the value of max is increased by the user. Indeed, if the user enters a very large value (such as 200000), the program frequently produces a no-match condition.

The continue Statement

Sometimes situations arise wherein you need to do something special within a loop before you continue processing it. For example, you might have a loop that is polling the fire sprinkler sensors I mentioned at the beginning of this chapter. However, instead of breaking out of the loop when a sensor is tripped, perhaps you want to continue reading the rest of the sensors to see how fast the fire is speading. The code might look like this:

```
while (true)
{
    ID++;
    state  = readSensor(ID);
    if (state == true)
    {
        soundAlarm();
        callFireDepartment();
        continue;
    }
    if (ID == MAXSENSORS)
    {
        ID = -1;    // -1 so increment operator sets it to 0
    }
}
```

In this code fragment, you establish an infinite loop by design by stating that the test expression is always logic True. The code increments a sensor identification number (ID) and then reads the appropriate sensor. If the sensor does not return true, the program makes another pass through the loop. If there is a fire and the sensor returns true, the alarm is sounded, the fire department is called, and then the code continues execution at expression2. Because expression2 is always logic True, the loop continues to execute the code. When a while or do-while loop is used, the continue statement always sends control to the expression that determines whether another pass through the loop is necessary (that is, expression2).

The same type of code using a for loop would be the following:

```
for (ID = 0; true; ID++)
{
    state  = readSensor(ID);
    if (state == true)
    {
        soundAlarm();
        callFireDepartment();
        continue;
    }
    if (ID == MAXSENSORS)
    {
        ID = -1;      // -1 so increment operator sets it to 0
    }
}
```

In this situation, if there is a fire, variable state is true and the alarm and fire department methods are executed; then continue is executed. The continue statement sends program control to expression3 (ID++) of the for statement, which increments the sensor ID. Program control is then sent to expression2 to determine if another pass through the loop is needed. Because expression2 is always logic True, the code makes another pass through the loop. You should be able to convince yourself that this is an infinite loop.

Note that, unlike the break statement that transfers program control out of the loop, a continue statement keeps program control in the loop to decide if another pass is warranted.

Summary

In this chapter you learned the necessary conditions for writing a well-behaved loop. You then applied those conditions to writing for, while, and do-while loops. You also learned that for loops are ideally suited for counting operations and that while loops are good for searching for a particular value in a set of values. Finally, you learned how to transfer control out of a loop (break) before its natural termination condition is reached, and how to continue processing a loop statement block (continue).

Exercises

1. Write the loop code necessary to calculate the factorial of a number. For example, 5 factorial is written like this:

```
5! = 5 * 4 * 3 * 2 * 1

5! = 120
```

You may assume that a variable named `num` is defined to hold the number to factor, and that a variable named `i` is used to control the loop.

2. Even though the solution shown for Exercise 1 produces correct answers, it has two hiccups in it. Can you determine what they are?

3. Given that one ounce equals 28.3495231 grams, write a loop that produces a table in a listbox that shows the conversion into grams for weights from one ounce through four pounds.

4. Look at the solution code for Exercise 3. Can you find a minor change that improves the code?

5. Assuming that a monetary asset grows by x percent each year, calculate how much the asset is worth at the end of n years (using simple interest).

Arrays

In this chapter you will learn about arrays, array lists, and collections. As you will learn, these data structures are useful in solving many types of programming problems. In this chapter you will learn about:

- ❏ Arrays
- ❏ Array indexes and elements
- ❏ How to set the size of an array
- ❏ Some of the Array class methods that are commonly used
- ❏ Multi-dimensional arrays
- ❏ Array lists
- ❏ Collections
- ❏ Jagged arrays

When you finish this chapter, you'll have an appreciation of how arrays can make certain programming problems much easier to solve.

What is an Array?

An *array* is a group of identical data types that share a common name. The syntax for defining an array is as follows:

```
typeSpecifier[] arrayName = new typeSpecifier[numberOfElements];
```

where

- ❏ `typeSpecifier` is the data type you want to use,
- ❏ `arrayName` is the name you wish to use for the array, and
- ❏ `numberOfElements` is the number of array elements you want.

Each of these parts is explained in a moment using the following example.

Suppose you have an address book with 100 names in it. Because you want to manipulate those names in some way in your program, each name must be stored in a variable. Because names are textual data, you could use something like this:

```
string name00;
string name01;
string name02;
string name03;
//...Many more variables...
string name98;
string name99;
```

While this would work, it suffers two serious drawbacks. First, you would get really tired of typing in all those variable names. Even worse, think what would happen if the address book had a million names in it! Second, how would you perform the common task of searching the names in the list for a specific person? You'd be forced to plow through 100 `if` statements looking for a particular name:

```
if (name00.Equals(targetName))
{
    index = 0;
}
else
{
    if (name01.Equals(targetName))
    {
        index = 1;
    }
    else    //...and so on...
```

(Remember that when you compare objects like strings, you don't compare rvalue-to-rvalue. Instead, you want to compare what is stored at the memory address contained in the object's rvalue. Therefore, when comparing strings, you should use the `Equals()` method, which is available for all string objects.) Such a programming solution is just not practical, which is precisely why arrays were created.

Instead of using 100 different variables, one for each name, you would define a single string array to hold the names using the syntax you saw earlier:

```
string[] names = new string[100];
```

The program now has a string array variable named `names` that is capable of storing 100 names. You can use what you learned about loops in the previous chapter to simplify the code:

```
for (i = 0; i < names.Length; i++)
{
    if (names[i].Equals(targetName))
    {
        index = i;
        break;
    }
}
```

If you read the code carefully, you can see that on the first pass through the loop, the `if` test compares the first name in the list (`names[0]`) to the name stored in `targetName`. If the test fails, the loop counter variable `i` is incremented by the third expression of the `for` loop (`i++`) and the code makes the next comparison test (`if names[1].Equals(targetName)`). The loop continues until a match is found. At that time, `index` is assigned the value of `i` (so you can reference that person later) and the `break` statement sends program control to the first statement following the `for` loop. If no match is found, `index` is unchanged and the search fails. (Setting `index` to `-1` before entering the loop is a good way to tell if the search failed.)

As you can see, there is a symbiotic relationship between arrays and loops, and they are used together often to solve a myriad of programming problems.

Some Array Details

In my effort to justify the use of arrays, I glossed over a number of important details about them.

Array Element Versus Array Index

An *array element* is a single unit of an array. Consider the following array definition:

```
int[] myData = new int[10];
```

The statement says that you would like to have 10 integers arranged back to back in memory and that you would like to refer to them as `myData`. You can see how this might look in memory in Figure 8-1.

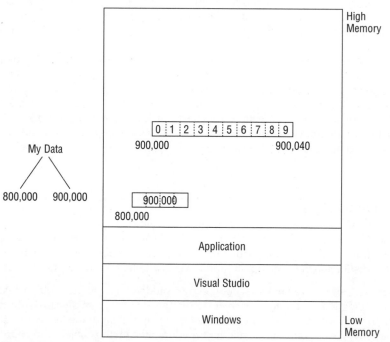

Figure 8-1

Each of those 10 integers is referred to as one element in the array. When you define the size of the array, you always specify the number of elements you want. That number appears between the last set of brackets at the end of the definition statement (`[10]` in this example).

An *array index* refers to the position of a specific element in the array. In the example you requested 10 elements, but the position of the first element is index 0. Like almost everything else, C# counts array indexes starting with 0. Therefore, in

```
val = myData[0];
```

`val` would equal the content of the first element of the `myData` array. This also means that an index of 0 accesses the first element of the array. (In Figure 8-1, `val` is assigned the value stored at the four bytes beginning at memory location 900,000.)

N – 1 Rule

Your definition of the `myData` array requested 10 elements for the array size. This means that the valid indexes for the array run from 0 through 9. This gives us the N – 1 Rule: The *highest index* permitted for an array is one less than the number of array elements.

This is a frequent stumbling block for beginning programmers. Because you asked for 10 elements, it would seem reasonable to be able to use an index of 10 to access the last array element. Not so. Visual Studio will issue an out-of-bounds error if you try to reference an element using something like this:

```
val = myData[10];
```

The reason for the error message is that the statement tried to access an element that doesn't exist within the boundaries of the array. Only elements 0 through 9 are valid array index values. If you get an out-of-bounds error, remember the N – 1 Rule and see if you're trying to index outside the limits of the array.

If you are uncertain about how large the array is, you can always use the following code:

```
size = myData.Length;
```

The `Length` property of the array object returns the number of elements in the array. (It does *not* return the number of bytes in memory occupied by the array.) In this example, `size` would equal 10 after the statement is executed. (Note how I used the `Length` property in the sample `for` loop at the beginning of this chapter.)

Try It Out   Letter Count

Let's write a short program that has the user enter a couple of sentences in a multi-line textbox and then count how many times each letter occurs in that text. You are not interested in punctuation, spaces, digit characters, or the distinction between upper- and lowercase letters . . . just alpha characters.

Given the program design stated in this section, how would you attack the problem? Again, start thinking about solving a programming problem using the Five Program Steps. The Initialization Step is pretty much done for you by Visual Studio. The Input Step is simply the text entered by the user. The Process Step involves examining each letter typed into the textbox object and counting how many times each alpha character occurs. The Output Step simply involves copying the letter counts to a listbox for display. The Termination Step is very simple in this program. You simply end the program with the `Close()` method. Clearly, the real work is done in the Process Step.

Figure 8-2 shows a sample run of the program and the user interface I used to write the solution.

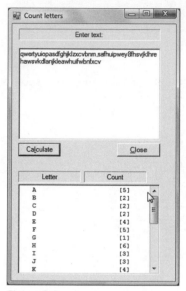

Figure 8-2

How It Works

Our solution for the programming task is shown in Listing 8-1.

Listing 8-1

```
using System;
using System.Windows.Forms;

public class frmMain : Form
{
  private const int MAXLETTERS = 26;                // Symbolic constants
  private const int MAXCHARS = MAXLETTERS - 1;
  private const int LETTERA = 65;

  private TextBox txtInput;
  private Button btnCalc;
  private Button btnClose;
  private ListBox lstOutput;
  private Label label2;
  private Label label3;
  private Label label1;

  #region Windows code
```

```csharp
public frmMain()
{
  InitializeComponent();
}

public static void Main()
{
  frmMain main = new frmMain();
  Application.Run(main);
}

private void btnCalc_Click(object sender, EventArgs e)
{
  char oneLetter;
  int index;
  int i;
  int length;
  int[] count = new int[MAXLETTERS];
  string input;
  string buff;

  length = txtInput.Text.Length;
  if (length == 0)     // Anything to count??
  {
    MessageBox.Show("You need to enter some text.", "Missing Input");
    txtInput.Focus();
    return;
  }
  input = txtInput.Text;
  input = input.ToUpper();

  for (i = 0; i < input.Length; i++)     // Examine all letters.
  {
    oneLetter = input[i];                  // Get a character
    index = oneLetter - LETTERA;           // Make into an index
    if (index < 0 || index > MAXCHARS)     // A letter??
      continue;                            // Nope.
    count[index]++;                        // Yep.
  }

  for (i = 0; i < MAXLETTERS; i++)
  {
    buff = string.Format("{0, 4} {1,20}[{2}]", (char)(i + LETTERA),
           " ",count[i]);
    lstOutput.Items.Add(buff);
  }
}

private void btnClose_Click(object sender, EventArgs e)
{
  Close();
}
}
```

The program begins by defining a series of symbolic constants.

```
private const int MAXLETTERS = 26;            // Symbolic constants
private const int MAXCHARS = MAXLETTERS - 1;
private const int LETTERA = 65;
```

I have already explained why using symbolic constants in a program is a good thing. If nothing else, it prevents you from using magic numbers in the program.

The LETTERA constant needs some explanation. When you press a letter on your keyboard, it completes an electrical circuit in the keyboard matrix, which is decoded and sent to the computer as a single-byte numeric value. The code sent to the computer uses the ASCII character set as explained in Chapter 5. The ASCII value for the letter A is 65. The ASCII value for Z is 90, which means the codes are in alphabetical order. That is, B is 66, C is 67, and so on. Therefore, if you convert the text the user typed into the textbox object to uppercase letters, it's a simple matter to create the proper index into the array that holds the letter counts. The array that holds the counts is defined as follows:

```
int[] count = new int[MAXLETTERS];
```

Because the symbolic constant MAXLETTERS is 26, you are defining an array with 26 elements in it, which means the indexes can have values from 0 through 25. (The ole N – 1 Rule, remember?) Plan to use count[0] to store the count for the A's, count[1] for the B's, count[2] for the C's and so on.

Now suppose the user typed in the word Abe. Because lower- and upper-case letters do have different ASCII values, the first thing you need to do is convert everything to uppercase letters. (Our program design said you don't care about the case of the letters.) The following statements from Listing 8-1 take the input typed in by the user and assign it into the string variable named input:

```
input = txtInput.Text;
input = input.ToUpper();
```

The code then uses the ToUpper() method to convert all of the letters to uppercase. The text is now ABE. Having made the case conversion, you are now ready to count the letters.

The statement

```
oneLetter = input[i];                // Get a character
```

makes use of the fact that you can treat a character string as though it is an array. Therefore, in the for loop, when i is 0, input[i] is the A in ABE. The next statement,

```
index = oneLetter - LETTERA;         // Make into an index
```

resolves to this:

```
index = 'A' - 65;        // Make into an index
```

However, A is actually 65 when it is viewed as an ASCII character. So the expression becomes this:

```
index = 65 - 65;         // Make into an index
index = 0;
```

The next three lines first check to make sure the index that was just calculated falls between 0 and 25. If it doesn't, the character is not an alpha letter and you don't want to count it:

```
if (index < 0 || index > MAXCHARS)   // A letter??
   continue;                          // Nope.
count[index]++;                       // Yep.
```

Since our index is 0, you execute the following statement:

```
count[0]++;
```

This increments the contents of the first integer in the array. (All value-type array elements are initialized to 0 at the moment they are defined in C#. Arrays of objects are initialized to null. I will have more to say about these details later in the chapter.) If you think about it, count[0] corresponds to the letter A . . . which is exactly the element you want! count[0] now equals 1 because the code counted the letter A in ABE.

The processing for the next letters is as follows:

```
index = 'B' - 65;
index = 66 - 65;
index = 1;
```

This means the code increments count[1] to 1, because you counted the B in ABE. Finally:

```
index = 'E' - 65;
index = 69 - 65;
index = 4;
```

Here count[4] is incremented to 1, which counts the letter E. This process continues as long as there are characters in the string left to process. (Note expression2 in the for loop: i < input.Length, which limits the number of passes through the loop.)

You should be able to convince yourself that the final for loop —

```
for (i = 0; i < MAXLETTERS; i++)
{
  buff = string.Format("{0, 4} {1,10}[{2}]", (char)(i + LETTERA),
         " ",count[i]);
  lstOutput.Items.Add(buff);
}
```

— increments through the count[] array and displays the characters in the listbox object as shown in Figure 8-2. Notice how the format string uses an empty string for the second argument and has brackets surrounding the third argument. The expression

```
(char)(i + LETTERA)
```

is necessary in the Format() method because you are taking the sum of the numeric values i and LETTERA, which are int data types of four bytes each, but wish to display them as a char data type of two bytes each. Because you are trying to pour four bytes of data into a two-byte bucket, you must cast the sum of i and LETTERA to a char data type before you can display it as an alphabetic character. Once again, you used the formatting abilities of string.Format() to make the columns line up in the listbox (using a fixed font).

When the program finishes executing, the output looks similar to that shown in Figure 8-2. (Just to get a good distribution of letters, I dragged my finger over all three rows of letters on the keyboard and added a few more letters after doing that.) The two labels above the listbox identify what is displayed in the listbox.

The Listview Object

Formatting columns of data in a listbox is such a common practice that Visual Studio provides a special control dedicated to that specific purpose. It's called the *listview object.* You select the listview object from the Toolbox and drag (or double-click) it onto the form as you would any other control. Indeed, at this juncture, it looks the same as a listbox object. Now the neat stuff begins.

With the focus set to the listview object in the Source window, first scroll to the View property in the Properties window and set it to Details from the list of choices. This enables you to see the impact of property changes for the object as you make them. Now scroll to the Columns property in the Properties window. (If the Properties window is hidden, just press the F4 key.) Click on the ellipsis button of the Columns property. You should see a dialog box similar to that shown in Figure 8-3.

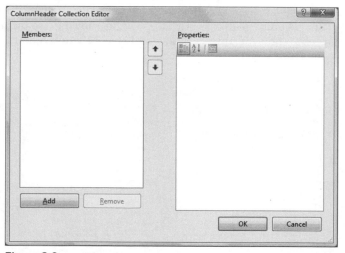

Figure 8-3

Now click the Add button, and the display changes to that shown in Figure 8-4.

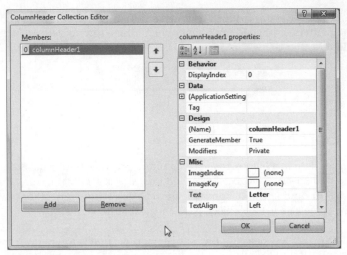

Figure 8-4

On the left side of the dialog box is a box area labeled Members. This area contains the columns you want to define for the listview object. (Because you haven't added any members yet, the box has filled in the default name of `columnHeader1`.) On the right side of the dialog form is a box that presents the properties you can use for each column, arranged by function (in this example Behavior, Data, Design, and Misc). Personally, I don't like this arrangement of ordering by function. At the top of the box is an icon showing the letters A and Z with a downward-pointing arrow next to them. If you click this icon, the list in the box changes to show the properties arranged in alphabetical order. The dialog box now looks like that shown in Figure 8-5.

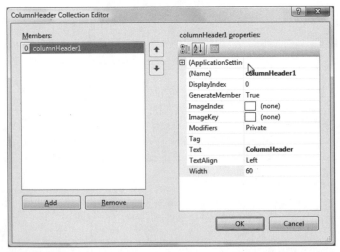

Figure 8-5

The contents of the properties box appears less cluttered than before because the functional area titles have been removed. If you prefer it the other way (as shown in Figure 8-4), simply click the "categorized" icon next to the "alphabetical" icon you just clicked. The rest of the discussion assumes that you, too, prefer the "decluttered" version of the properties list.

Change the Text property for columnHeader1 in the right-hand box to Letter and its Width property to 110, as shown in Figure 8-6.

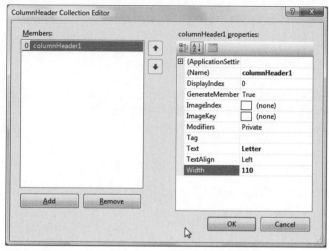

Figure 8-6

Now click the Add button. (Do not click the OK button, as that dismisses the Columns dialog box and you're not through with it yet.) If you drag the Columns dialog box out of the way, you should see the changes you just made reflected in the listview object in the Source window. The dialog box now shows a second column header in the Members box. Set its Text property to Count and its Width property to 115. Now click OK. Your listview object should look similar to Figure 8-7.

Figure 8-7

The Width property is stated in pixels and you may want to experiment with its value until the listview object looks "good" to you. In Figure 8-7 you can see a small gap to the right of the listview column headers. This is for the scroll bar control that appears automatically when there is more data than can be shown in the listview object.

Guesstimating Column Widths

So how did I determine that each column should be 115 pixels wide? Well, after I set the `View` property to `Details`, I noted that our listview object had its `Size` property set to `251, 133`. This means that the width of the listview object is 251 pixels. Because a scroll bar object takes about 20 pixels of display real estate, I simply divided the remaining 231 pixels in half to get approximately 115 pixels for each column. While this approach isn't exact, especially with an odd number of columns, it's close enough for government work.

With the listview object's properties set, you need to modify the code that places the data in the listview object. To do this, remove the following lines from Listing 8-1:

```
for (i = 0; i < MAXLETTERS; i++)
{
  buff = string.Format("{0, 4} {1,10}[{2}]", (char)(i + LETTERA),
         " ",count[i]);
  lstOutput.Items.Add(buff);
}
```

Replace them with this:

```
ListViewItem which;
for (i = 0; i < MAXLETTERS; i++)
{
    oneLetter = (char)(i + LETTERA);
    which = new ListViewItem(oneLetter.ToString());
    which.SubItems.Add(count[i].ToString());
    lsvOutput.Items.Add(which);
}
```

The first statement creates a `ListViewItem` reference variable. You can think of a `ListViewItem` object as a group of data that defines one row of the listview object. The `for` loop remains unchanged from the previous version. The third statement simply constructs the cast you used in the first version and assigns the character that's constructed from the sum of variable i and `LETTERA` into the variable `oneLetter`. When i is 0, the sum is 65, which is then cast to a `char`, which becomes the character A in the Unicode character set and is assigned into `oneLetter`.

A `ListViewItem`, however, prefers to work with `string` data rather than `char` data. Therefore, you use the `ToString()` method for `char` objects to convert `oneLetter` to a string when the code creates the `ListViewItem` object in statement four using its constructor method. This statement has the effect of creating a `ListViewItem` named `which` with its first column initialized to the current letter (in this example A).

The fifth statement takes the count for the current letter as stored in the `count[]` array and adds it to the `ListViewItem` named `which`. Notice that `which` contains an object named `SubItems` and uses its `Add()` method to add this column data to the first column's data. The last statement is virtually the same as the listbox object's `Add()` method, except that you pass it the `ListViewItem` object named `which` instead of a formatted string. The result of these code changes is shown in Figure 8-8.

Figure 8-8

Although you did have to add a few new lines of code and tinker around with the `Columns` property of the listview object, the results do look a little better than the output in Figure 8-2. The biggest visual improvement is that the column headers are more closely tied to the data. (Try modifying the code in the second version to surround the counts with brackets, as the first version does.)

Arrays are Objects

Unlike in some other programming languages, arrays in C# are objects. This means each array object has a set of properties and methods that you can use with it. The code in Listing 8-1 makes use of the `Length` array property to control the number of iterations made through the loop. What is less obvious is that all array objects are derived from the `System.Array` class. Table 8-1 presents a partial list of some of the properties and methods available through the `System.Array` class.

Table 8-1

Example	Description
`System.Array.BinarySearch(count, target)`	Performs a binary search on a sorted, one-dimensional array named `count` looking for `target`.
`System.Array.Clear(count, start, count.Length)`	Clears value type arrays from element `start` through element `Length` to `0`. Reference arrays are cleared to `null`.
`System.Array.Copy(Souce, Dest, Length);`	Copies `Length` elements from the `Source` array to the `Dest` array.
`System.Array.IndexOf(count, val)`	Returns the index in the `count` array where the first occurrence of `val` is found.
`System.Array.LastIndexOf(count, val)`	Returns the index in the `count` array where the last occurrence of `val` is found.
`System.Array.Sort(count)`	Sorts a one-dimensional array named `count` into ascending order.
`System.Array.Reverse(count)`	Reverses the current values of a one-dimensional array named `count`. Note: if you call `Sort()` and then `Reverse()`, it puts the array into descending order.
`count.Rank`	Returns the number of dimensions for the array named `count`.
`count.GetUpperBound(val)`	Returns the highest index number for dimension `val` for the `count` array. For example, if the definition for an array named `test` is as follows: `int[,] test = new int[5,10];` the statement `max = test.GetUpperBound(1);` sets `max` to 9. Remember that a two-dimensional array uses dimensions 0 and 1, and the N – 1 Rule applies! Getting the `Rank` property first would enable you to call this method with valid dimensions if they are unknown.
`count.Initialize()`	Calls the default constructor to set each element. For value data types the value is `0`; for reference data types the value is `null`.

Many of the methods presented in Table 8-1 are overloaded. You can use Intellisense to see what the overloaded parameter lists are for the various array methods.

Once you have defined an array, you can use the properties and methods presented in Table 8-1. For example, if an array named `val` has 100 random values in it and you want them sorted into ascending order, the statement

```
System.Array.Sort(val);
```

reorganizes the values into sorted order. If you then call

```
System.Array.Reverse(val);
```

The values in the `val` array are now in descending order. As you can see, manipulating array data is greatly simplified by the properties and methods in Table 8-1 compared to you having to write the code yourself.

Multidimensional Arrays

So far I've discussed one-dimensional arrays, which are great for describing lists of data. However, data are often organized in tables of rows and columns. For example, you might want to see the distribution of grades in a class where the columns represent the student's class and the rows represent the grades, as shown in Table 8-2.

Table 8-2

Grades	Freshmen	Sophomores	Juniors	Seniors
A	1	4	6	5
B	4	7	11	4
C	11	13	11	3
D	3	4	3	1
F	2	1	0	0

If you wanted to define an array for storing the data shown in Table 8-2, you might use the following code:

```
int[,] grades = new int[5, 4];
```

This definition states that you want to define a table, or matrix, with five rows and four columns. Note the comma within the brackets in the definition. The first comma in the brackets on the left side of the assignment expression simply tells C# that you are about to define a two-dimensional array. The second set of brackets specifies exactly how many elements there are in the table. Because there are two dimensions, you say the `grades` array has a rank of two. That is, the term *rank* refers to the number of dimensions associated with the array.

You can use more than two dimensions if you need them. For example, 3D graphics are drawn using X, Y, and Z coordinates. To define an array with three dimensions, you might use this code:

```
int[,,] images = new int[20, 100, 200];
```

This defines a data cube rather than a table or list. Note that if you want N dimensions (such as three), there are always N – 1 commas (in this case two commas) within the brackets.

You may even need more than three dimensions. If you are writing game software, for example, you might need three dimensions for the placement of the 3D images in the game and a fourth dimension to keep track of the time at which each image should appear. (I tried to think of an example using five dimensions and all I got was a headache.) C# appears to support more ranks than you can ever reasonably be assumed to need.

Try It Out

Let's assume you want to write a program that lets the user enter the number of rows she wants in a table that shows the number, the square of the number, and the cube of the number. The program requires a two-dimensional array with a user-supplied number of rows and three columns. A sample run of the program is shown in Figure 8-9.

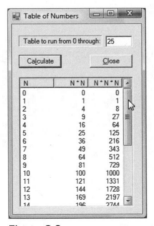

Figure 8-9

(Don't forget to set the listview's `View` property to `Details` before you start working with the listview object. This makes it easier to see the impact of changing the properties as you go.)

How It Works

The code for the program is presented in Listing 8-2.

Listing 8-2

```csharp
using System;
using System.Windows.Forms;

public class frmMain : Form
{
    private TextBox txtMax;
    private Button btnCalc;
    private Button btnClose;
    private ListView lsvTable;
    private ColumnHeader columnHeader1;
    private ColumnHeader columnHeader2;
    private ColumnHeader columnHeader3;
    private Label label1;
    #region Windows code

    public frmMain()
    {
        InitializeComponent();
    }

    public static void Main()
    {
        frmMain main = new frmMain();
        Application.Run(main);
    }

    private void btnCalc_Click(object sender, EventArgs e)
    {
        bool flag;
        int number;
        int i;
        ListViewItem which;

        flag = int.TryParse(txtMax.Text, out number); // check input
        if (flag == false)
        {
            MessageBox.Show("Numeric data only.", "Input Error");
            txtMax.Focus();
            return;
        }
        if (number < 0)          // Make sure it's positive
        {
            number = number * -1;
        }
        number++;    // Do this because of N - 1 Rule

        int[,] myData = new int[number, 3];      // Define array
```

```
    for (i = 0; i < number; i++)
    {
        myData[i, 0] = i;              // first column of table
        myData[i, 1] = i * i;          // second column of table
        myData[i, 2] = i * i * i;      // third column of table
    }

    for (i = 0; i < number; i++)       // Now show it
    {
        which = new ListViewItem(myData[i, 0].ToString());
        which.SubItems.Add(myData[i, 1].ToString());
        which.SubItems.Add(myData[i, 2].ToString());
        lsvTable.Items.Add(which);
    }
}

private void btnClose_Click(object sender, EventArgs e)
{
    Close();
}
}
```

As usual, things get interesting in the `btnCalc_Click()` event code. First, several working variables are defined, including a `ListViewItem` object named `which`. The code draws upon the `TryParse()` method to validate that the user entered numeric data. If she entered a negative number, you force it to be positive. When these checks are complete, the variable `number` holds the number of rows you want to display in the listview object. That value is incremented because you want to display the data through the number the user entered, inclusively. That is, if the user types in 100, you actually want to display 101 values, 0 through 100 . . . it's that pesky N − 1 Rule again.

The statement

```
        int[,] myData = new int[number, 3];      // Define array
```

defines the array that holds the data. The loop simply assigns the values needed for each column of the array:

```
    for (i = 0; i < number; i++)
    {
        myData[i, 0] = i;              // first column of table
        myData[i, 1] = i * i;          // second column of table
        myData[i, 2] = i * i * i;      // third column of table
    }
```

As you can see, variable `i` controls the loop, but also dictates the number of rows in the table. Therefore, variable `i` is used to set the first dimension of the array in the loop, or its row value. The second dimension (0, 1, 2) determines the values for the three columns in the table.

The next `for` loop formats the data into the listview object named `lsvTable`:

```
    for (i = 0; i < number; i++)       // Now show it
    {
        which = new ListViewItem(myData[i, 0].ToString());
```

```
            which.SubItems.Add(myData[i, 1].ToString());
            which.SubItems.Add(myData[i, 2].ToString());
            lsvTable.Items.Add(which);
    }
```

This code is very similar to the code you saw earlier in the discussion of the listview object. The only contextual difference is that there are now three columns instead of the two shown in Figure 8-8.

If you've looked at the code closely you're probably saying, "Hey, doofus! The three expressions controlling the two `for` loops are identical, so why not collapse them into a single `for` loop?" This piece of RDC was done purposely to minimize the "busy-ness" of the code. You can easily move the four statements from the second `for` loop and place them after the three statements in the first `for` loop. You can then do away with the second `for` loop altogether. (Of course, if you do that, you can do away with the array completely and the whole purpose of the program disappears!)

Initializing Arrays

Often you know that certain arrays have specific values and you want to initialize the array elements to those values. For example, you might have an array named `days` that holds a count of the number of days in each month. You could use the following code:

```
days[0] = 31;       // January
days[1] = 28;       // February
days[2] = 31;       // March
```

. . . and so on. As you can see, this is a pretty repetitive task that requires 12 statements that are almost identical. C# provides you with an easier, more direct way, of setting the values of an array. The syntax is shown here:

```
typeSpecifier [] arrayID = new typeSpecifier [elementCount] { val1, val2,
val3,. . .};
```

Using our example of the days in each month, you might use this:

```
int[] days = new int[12] {31,28,31,30,31,30,31,31,30,31,31};
```

This statement sets all 12 monthly values in a single statement. Setting the values of an array as part of the definition of the array is called *initializing* the array. The list of values that appears between the curly braces is often referred to as the *initializer list*.

Variations for Initializing an Array

What's interesting is that C# provides two additional syntax variations for initializing an array. These variations for the same array shown in the previous section are

```
int[] days = new int[] {31,28,31,30,31,30,31,31,30,31,31};
```

or

```
int[] days = {31,28,31,30,31,30,31,31,30,31,31};
```

Note that the first variation does not fill in the element count for the array. The compiler does that automatically by counting the number of values in the initializer list. The second variation does away with the new keyword and the type specifier with brackets.

Which Array Definition/Initialiation Syntax is Best?

Given that you have three ways to accomplish the same task, which should you use? As always, whenever you have options for the way to code a specific task, the important thing is that you be consistent in the option you use. You (or your programming team) should pick one and always use that variation. It makes no difference to C# which one you use.

That being said, I personally would opt for the following definition:

```
int[] days = new int[] {0, 31,28,31,30,31,30,31,31,30,31,31};
```

There are several reasons I would choose this variation. First, the use of the new keyword in the definition reinforces the fact that arrays are objects. Second, there is no good reason for you to fill in the element count for the initializer list. The compiler is very good at counting so you should let it do its thing. Finally, if you need to add or delete elements from the initializer list, the compiler automatically adjusts for the new size when you don't specify the element count. (If you do supply the element count and it doesn't match the initializer list, Visual Studio gets cranky and issues an error message complaining about the rank of the array. This message is a little misleading because the problem is that the number of elements supplied don't match the elements specified.)

Code Like a User

Did you notice that my preferred definition for the days array has 13 elements in it? I added an extra element because of the way users think about this type of data. After all, if you ask someone, "What is the first month of the year?", I doubt too many of them answer, "February!" Yet, element 1 in the array, days[1], has the value 28. True, you as the programmer can always make the mental adjustment when using zero-based arrays. My experience, however, is that programs that work with familiar data sizes (such as days in the month, days of the week, number of holes in a round of golf, and so on) often have fewer bugs when the first value in the array is initialized to 0 to make the data align with a ones-based counting system.

If you do use a ones-based data set, it doesn't hurt to call attention to that fact with a comment:

```
// CAUTION: ones-based array follows:
int[] days = new int[] {0, 31,28,31,30,31,30,31,31,30,31,31};
```

Once again, whatever choice you make about initializing arrays, make that choice and stick with it consistently in your code. Consistency helps to make the code easier to read and understand, which in turn makes debugging easier.

Initializing Multidimensional Arrays

You may also use initializer lists with multidimensional arrays. For example, suppose you want to initialize a two-by-three array (an array with two rows and three columns). You could use this code:

```
int [,] myData = new int[ , ] { {1,2,3}, {4,5,6} };
```

The syntax rule for initializing multidimensional arrays is that the values for each row are enclosed in their own set of curly braces. If you wish to supply the element counts, as in

```
int [,] myData = new int[2 ,3 ] { {1,2,3}, {4,5,6} };
```

you may do so. However, the compiler is very good at doing this for you. Since you already have enough on your plate, why not let the compiler perform those tasks for which it has a comparative advantage?

Some programmers find it useful to use a different style for presenting multidimensional array initializer lists:

```
int [] myData = new int[,] {
                             {1,2,3},
                             {4,5,6}
                          };
```

While this style does reinforce the idea that the data definition establishes a matrix of data values, it also takes up three extra rows of display real estate that I'm reluctant to give up. Still, if you think it makes it easier to understand the data, select this style and apply it consistently in your code.

Initializer Lists for Objects

You can use initializer lists for objects, too. For example:

```
string[] weekDays = new string[] { "Monday", "Tuesday",
                       "Wednesday", "Thursday", "Friday",
                       "Saturday", "Sunday" };
```

The syntax is the same as for value-type data. However, the way in which arrays of objects work is not exactly the same as it is for value-type data. Figure 8-1 shows how the memory map for an integer value type appears in memory. While I've taken a few liberties with the details, you should visualize the memory map for the weekDays array as something like that shown in Figure 8-10.

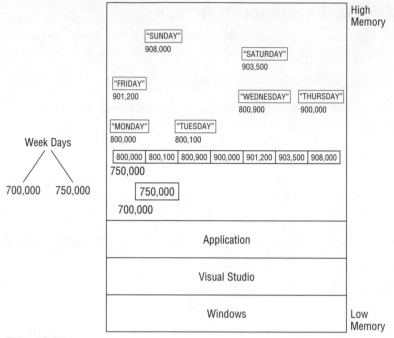

Figure 8-10

The memory map in Figure 8-1 for integer data shows that the actual integer data values are in a contiguous set of bytes starting at memory address 900,000. (The rvalue of myData in that figure is 900,000.) Now compare Figure 8-1 with Figure 8-10.

In Figure 8-10, you can see that the lvalue for weekDays is 700,000 and its rvalue is 750,000. This means that there is an array of memory addresses that begins at memory address 750,000. Because the initializer list contains seven strings, there is enough memory allocated for the weekDays array to hold seven contiguous memory addresses starting at address 750,000. Each element of the array contains a memory address that points to the memory location where its data is stored. For example, the first string object in the array is stored at memory location 800,000. Go to that address and you find Monday stored starting at that memory location. Look at the other values in the array and you will find they are stored in the same manner.

What would the weekDays array look like if you didn't have the initializer list? In Figure 8-10, instead of finding seven memory addresses starting at memory location 750,000, you would find that each element in the array contains the value null. When each element of the weekDays array is assigned a piece of string data to store, the Windows operating system hands Visual Studio a memory address, based upon where the Windows Memory Manager found enough memory for the data item, to replace the null value for that element in the array.

Why doesn't C# just store the data back to back as it does the integer data shown in Figure 8-1? The reason is that the memory requirements for each object in the array can vary. While each integer always takes four bytes, each object in an array of objects can require differing amounts of memory. That is, the memory needed to store Friday is different from the amount of memory needed to store Wednesday.

Because you cannot assume the memory requirements for elements of an object array are symmetrical, C# must store an array of memory addresses (which *are* symmetrical), each element of which points to the memory location of the actual data for that element in the array.

Ragged Arrays

It is this lack of symmetry in object arrays that gives rise to the term *ragged* or *jagged array*. That is, if you were to stack an array of integer elements one on top of the other, they would form a smooth vertical column with a width of four bytes per element. If you take the days-of-the-week array and stack the elements on top of each other, the column would probably be ragged, because each element may have a differing width.

Arrays of value data types are guaranteed always to be symmetrical. That is, you can always think of arrays of value types as being stored in the manner presented in Figure 8-1. Arrays of objects, however, cannot make that guarantee and use the storage mechanism depicted in Figure 8-10.

Defining Ragged Arrays at Runtime

I can illustrate how to define a ragged array at runtime with another example. Suppose you have three people who agree to provide blood samples. The first person hates needles, but agrees to give three samples. The second person isn't bothered by needles at all and agrees to give 10 samples. The third person simply agrees to give five samples. Suppose these sample counts are inputted by the user and maintained in variables count1, count2, and count3 respectively. If you keep in mind that a two-dimensional array is an array of arrays, understanding the following code snippet should be pretty easy.

```
int[][] samples = new int[3][];  // Note last spec empty

// Some code that sets the element counts for each person

samples[0] = new int[count1];    // Person 1
samples[1] = new int[count2];    // Person 2
samples[2] = new int[count3];    // Person 3

for (i = 0; i < 3; i++)          // Set 1st three values to equal i
{
    samples[0][i] = i;
    samples[1][i] = i;
    samples[2][i] = i;
}
```

This code snippet also shows another syntax style for declaring multidimensional arrays. Note how the first statement starts with [][] after the type specifier and ends with the second dimension unspecified in the second set of brackets ([3][]). If you want to leave the second dimension unspecified, you must use the syntax presented here. (Using a comma to separate dimensions does not work.)

The next three definition statements fill in the missing dimensions according to the subjects' desire to provide samples. (The keyword new in the three statements is a tipoff that Visual Studio is having conversations with the Windows Memory Manager.) Finally, the for loop demonstrates how you can assign values into the new array elements. Therefore, the syntax presented here enables you to define ragged arrays at runtime. Always keep in mind, however, that only the last dimension of a multidimensional array can be unspecified.

Collections

A *collection* is a set of objects that share the same characteristics. You can have a collection of strings, as you do with the weekDays array, or you can have collections of complex objects, like a listview or similar control object.

Try It Out   **Squares and Cubes**

Suppose you wish to iterate through the days and weekDays arrays. Because arrays are objects, you can treat them as a collection. A sample run of a test program is shown in Figure 8-11.

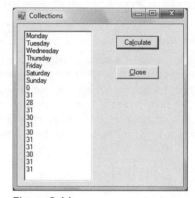

Figure 8-11

Notice how you can place either collection in the listbox object.

How It Works

The code for the program is shown in Listing 8-3.

Listing 8-3

```
using System;
using System.Windows.Forms;

public class frmMain : Form
{
    private Button btnCalc;
    private Button btnClose;
    private ListBox lstTest;
    #region Windows code

    public frmMain()
    {
        InitializeComponent();
    }
```

```
public static void Main()
{
    frmMain main = new frmMain();
    Application.Run(main);
}

private void btnClose_Click(object sender, EventArgs e)
{
    Close();
}

private void btnCalc_Click(object sender, EventArgs e)
{
    int[] days = new int[] { 0, 31, 28, 31, 30, 31, 30, 31, 31, 30,
                31, 31 };
    string[] weekDays = new string[] { "Monday", "Tuesday",
                        "Wednesday", "Thursday", "Friday", "Saturday",
                        "Sunday"};

    foreach (string str in weekDays)
    {
        lstTest.Items.Add(str);
    }
    foreach (int val in days)
    {
        lstTest.Items.Add(val.ToString());
    }
}
}
```

The two arrays are defined in the button click event method. Notice the use of the keyword `foreach` in the loops that iterate through the collections:

```
foreach (string str in weekDays)
{
    lstTest.Items.Add(str);
}
foreach (int val in days)
{
    lstTest.Items.Add(val.ToString());
}
```

A `foreach` loop is designed specifically to iterate through a collection of objects. It is very similar to a standard `for` loop, except that the first expression (`expression1` in a standard `for` loop) is always set to the first object in the collection and the loop iterates through all elements of the array one by one (`expression3` in a standard `for` loop). The data type used in the loop must match the data type in the collection. This is why `str` is a `string` in the first loop and `val` is an `int` in the second loop.

You should think of the `foreach` loop as a read-only loop. That is, you should not use a `foreach` loop to change the value of any of the objects in the collection. Collections provide a convenient way to view objects by iterating through them, but you should not try to change those objects within a `foreach` loop.

ArrayList Objects

The arrays that I have discussed thus far are called *static arrays*. This is because once you have set their element sizes, they cannot be changed. Indeed, you cannot use a static array until its dimension or dimensions have been determined. However, life isn't always that simple. Quite often you have a situation in which you know you need to store the data in an array, but don't have a clue how many elements you might need. For example, you might write a program that records the names and addresses of friends in an object called `Friends`. When you run the program you might need 50 array elements, but another person might only need 20 elements. The issue is: How do you decide how many elements to allocate for the array?

With static arrays, the usual solution is to settle for a worst-case design. A *worst-case design* is one in which you try to guess the largest reasonable value you will ever need for the size of the array and then set the dimension for the array to that size. This can be very inefficient because you will likely overestimate the required size for the array most of the time. The `ArrayList` object overcomes this limitations of static arrays. `ArrayList` objects have the effect of creating dynamic arrays for which you don't have to specify a size. Let's see how this works.

Try It Out   **ArrayList Example**

Let's write a simple program that enables you to add a person's name to a list. Because you have no idea how many names will be added by the user, you decide to use an `ArrayList` object. A sample run is shown in Figure 8-12.

Figure 8-12

The program has the user type in a name after which he clicks the Add button. This process can continue as long at the user wants. When he is finished, he can click the Show button to review the list of names he has entered.

How It Works

The code for the program is shown in Listing 8-4.

Listing 8-4

```
using System;
using System.Windows.Forms;
using System.Collections;

public class frmMain : Form
{
    ArrayList names = new ArrayList();

    private TextBox txtName;
    private Button btnAdd;
    private Button btnShow;
    private Button btnClose;
    private ListBox lstNames;
    private Label label1;

    #region Windows code

    public frmMain()
    {
        InitializeComponent();
    }

    public static void Main()
    {
        frmMain main = new frmMain();
        Application.Run(main);
    }

    private void btnAdd_Click(object sender, EventArgs e)
    {
        if (txtName.Text.Length != 0)
        {
            names.Add(txtName.Text);     // Add new name
            txtName.Clear();             // Clear it out
            txtName.Focus();             // Get ready for another name
        }
        else
        {
            MessageBox.Show("Please enter a name.", "Input Error");
            return;
        }
    }

    private void btnShow_Click(object sender, EventArgs e)
    {
        foreach (string str in names)
        {
            lstNames.Items.Add(str);
        }
    }
```

```
      private void btnClose_Click(object sender, EventArgs e)
      {
          Close();
      }
  }
```

The first thing to notice in Listing 8-4 is that you must add a new using statement:

```
using System.Collections;
```

This new using statement is required because it is part of the Collections class and is not included in a program by default.

Inside the frmMain class, you find the statement

```
ArrayList names = new ArrayList();
```

This statement defines the ArrayList object used to hold the names entered by the user. I defined names outside any method so it has class scope. This means that names is visible at all points in the frmMain class. Even though the ArrayList is used like an array, no dimension size is associated with its definition.

All the work is done in the click event for the Add button:

```
      private void btnAdd_Click(object sender, EventArgs e)
      {
          if (txtName.Text.Length != 0)
          {
              names.Add(txtName.Text);     // Add new name
              txtName.Clear();             // Clear it out
              txtName.Focus();             // Get ready for another name
          }
          else
          {
              MessageBox.Show("Please enter a name.", "Input Error");
              return;
          }
      }
```

The code simply checks to make sure the user typed in a name and then uses the Add() method of the ArrayList object to add the new name to the array list. The program then clears out the name that was just entered from the txtName textbox object and sets the focus back into the textbox object in preparation for another name. The user may continue this process until all names have been entered.

When the user has finished entering the names, he can click the Show button to view the list of names he just entered. The code in the Show() click event uses a foreach loop to iterate through the ArrayList object and add each name to the listbox object. ArrayList objects make it easy to use dynamic arrays in a program.

Also note that `ArrayList` objects have most of the methods and properties shown in Table 8-1 available for you to use. For example, if you want to present the names in sorted order before displaying them in the listbox, just add the statement

```
names.Sort();
```

before the `foreach` loop and the names are displayed in ascending order.

If `ArrayList` objects enable you to create dynamic arrays, why would you ever use a static array? It's just like the old saying: "There's no such thing as a free lunch." The same holds true in programming. The dynamic behavior of `ArrayList` objects adds a fair amount of overhead to them so they tend to consume more memory than static arrays for the same objects. This additional overhead also means there is a slight performance hit during processing for `ArrayList` objects compared to static arrays. Still, the ability to use an "undimensioned" array in a program adds sufficient flexibility that the `ArrayList` is a valuable tool to add to your toolkit.

Summary

In this chapter you learned about arrays and how they make many programming tasks easier by offering a convenient way to organize data. You also learned how to define arrays of differing sizes and how to initialize them. Examples discussed included data lists and data tables. You saw how program loops can be used to set values into an array and read those values from an array. You learned that collections are simply groups of objects and saw how you can use `foreach` loops to observe the items in a collection. Another important topic was how jagged arrays can be defined to meet specific needs, especially when memory limitations might be severe.

Exercises

1. A resent research study suggests that a person's ideal weight is related to his or her height in inches. They said that a person's ideal weight can be calculated from the following equations:

   ```
   Female = 3.5 * height (in inches) - 108

   Male = 4.0 * height (in inches) - 128
   ```

   Write a program that has the user enter a starting and ending height, calculates a table of ideal weights for males and females, and stores the results in an array. The program should then display the table in either a listbox or listview object.

2. In what way are arrays of objects different from arrays of value types?

3. Write a program that stores 100 random values in an `int` array and then displays those values in a listbox. Have a Sort button that, when clicked, sorts the values and redisplays them in the listbox.

4. Modify the program you wrote for Exercise 3 so it displays a bar graph for the data, as shown in Figure 8-13.

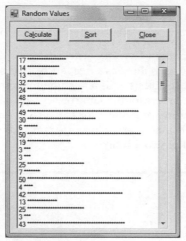

Figure 8-13

5. Given the following statements,

```
string [] str1 = new string[100];
string[] temp;

str1[0] = "Hailey";
// Some more code

temp = str1;
```

What does the rvalue of temp equal?

Part III
Writing Your Own Classes

Designing Classes

In Chapter 2, I stated that classes are like cookie cutters. I went on to point out that Visual Studio provides you with a room full of cookie cutters hanging on the wall that you can use. You have used many of those cookie cutters in the sample programs, including labels, textboxes, buttons, listboxes, and listview objects, all of which are extensions of the basic Windows Forms class. Up to this point, you've been writing code that uses those objects in a single class that I have consistently named frmMain. I called it that because all the programs used a single class containing the Main() method that marks the starting point for all C# programs.

Well, it's time to cut the apron strings.

In this chapter, you will learn how to make your own cookie cutters to hang on the wall. This chapter concentrates on the design considerations you need to think about in order to write "good" code for your own classes. A well-designed class becomes another cookie cutter that you can hang on the wall and use over and over in other programs. Poorly designed classes tend to become use-once-and-throw-away cookie cutters. Given that one of the major advantages of OOP is code reuse, you need to think about class design anytime the opportunity presents itself.

In this chapter, you will learn about:

- ❑ What elements constitute good class design
- ❑ Scope
- ❑ The static storage class
- ❑ Access specifiers
- ❑ Class properties and methods
- ❑ Class components and writing style
- ❑ UML Light
- ❑ General versus helper methods
- ❑ User interfaces

This chapter creates a clsDates class as a reference point for learning about class design. You will add two methods to this class: a leap year method that's a little different from the method offered by the DateTime class, and a getEaster() method for determining the date on which Easter falls. (Easter falls on a Sunday in either March or April, depending on the state of the lunar calendar.)

The next two chapters are probably the two most important chapters in the book. I feel this way because these two chapters reveal two of the major benefits to be derived from OOP: data encapsulation and code reuse.

Class Design

The first thing you need to do is create a project that serves as a test platform for our discussion of class design. As always, you begin by following the steps outlined in Chapter 2. I continue to call this initial class frmMain, as it contains the Main() method that marks where program execution begins. I used ClassDesign as the project name. Figure 9-1 shows the user interface for the project.

Figure 9-1

The user enters the year of interest and your program informs the user if it is a leap year and the date on which Easter falls. Note that there are two labels below the buttons for displaying the output, lblLeapYearResult and lblEasterResult.

Adding a Class to a Project

You are now ready to add a new class to this project. To add the class, use the Project ⇨ Add Class menu sequence (or Shift+Alt+C) and name the new class clsDates. (Visual Studio adds .cs for the second part of the file name.) This selection process is shown in Figure 9-2.

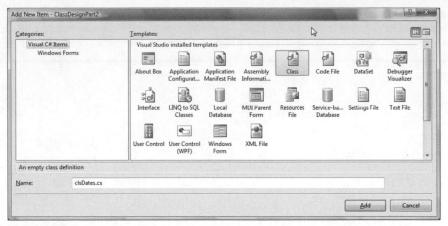

Figure 9-2

Note how the Class template is selected and the new class name is filled in at the bottom of the form. Now click the Add button to add this new class to your project. Your Solution Explorer window should look like Figure 9-3.

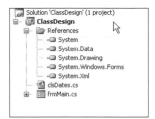

Figure 9-3

There are several things to notice in Figure 9-3. First, the icon to the left of clsDates in the Solution Explorer window is different. While class frmMain has a Windows form icon, clsDates uses an icon that looks like the C# logo on a sheet of paper. This is to reinforce the fact that you just added a class to the project, *not* a new Windows form. Second, you can see that Visual Studio added two new references (System.XML and System.Data) to the project while you weren't looking. While you won't explicitly be using these references, you can simply ignore them for the time being.

Scope

If you look in the Source window, you can see the following code:

```
using System;
using System.Collections.Generic;
using System.Text;

namespace ClassDesign
{
    class clsDates
    {
    }
}
```

This code stub was automatically generated by Visual Studio when you created `clsDates`. For purposes of discussion, I am going to expand it. *You should not make the code changes shown in Listing 9-1.* The code changes shown are being done only to help you understand the concept of scope.

Listing 9-1

```
using System;
using System.Collections.Generic;
using System.Text;

namespace ClassDesign
{

    class clsDates                                  // Namespace scope
    {
        int scopeClass;                             // Class scope

        public int MyFunction()
        {
            int scopeLocal;                         // Local scope

                                                    // Block scope
            for (int scopeBlock = 0; scopeBlock < 20; scopeBlock++)
            {
                // for statement block

            }   // End block scope

        }       // End local scope

    }           // End class scope

}               // End namespace scope
```

The code in Listing 9-1 is not "real" code you are going to use. However, you can use Listing 9-1 to understand an important concept called *scope*. I have mentioned scope a few times before, but never fully explained it. That's about to change.

Simply stated, scope refers to the visibility and lifetime of a variable. As long as a variable is *in scope,* you have access to it and can use it in your code. If a variable is *out of scope,* it's as though the variable doesn't even exist; you cannot use it in your program. Let's investigate the concept of scope in greater detail starting from the "inside" of Listing 9-1.

Block Scope

Consider the definition of `scopeBlock` in the following code:

```
                                            // Block scope
    for (int scopeBlock = 0; scopeBlock < 20; scopeBlock++)
    {
        // for statement block

    }   // End block scope
```

When program control reaches the `for` loop shown in the preceding code, `expression1` of the `for` loop defines a variable named `scopeBlock`. At the moment of its definition, `scopeBlock` becomes available for use in the program. This means that `scopeBlock` is now in scope and can be used in your code. Stated another way, `scopeBlock` has begun its lifetime.

Now let's assume that the `for` loop has made 20 passes through the `for` loop statement block and program control is ready to execute whatever statement follows the closing brace of the `for` loop. Now here's the interesting part: When program control reaches the closing curly brace of the `for` loop, the variable `scopeBlock` ceases to exist in the program. Because the closing curly brace marks the end of the `for` loop and `scopeBlock` is defined within that `for` loop, `scopeBlock` is no longer available for use in the program. Once the closing curly brace of the `for` loop is reached, `scopeBlock` goes out of scope and cannot be used.

The scope of a variable extends from its point of definition to the closing curly brace of the code block in which it is defined.

It follows, then, that *block scope* extends from the point of definition of the variable to the closing curly brace of the statement block in which the variable is defined. To prove the concept of block scope, make the following code changes in the `Main()` method in `frmMain`. The code changes are shown in Listing 9-2.

Listing 9-2

```
public static void Main()
{
    int j = 1;

    frmMain main = new frmMain();
    Application.Run(main);

    if (j == 1)
    {
        int i;      // defined with block scope
        i = 10;
        // pretend more code here manipulates i in some way...
    }               // End of if statement block
    j = i;          // Error will occur here
}
```

Now try to compile the program. You will see the following error message:

```
The name 'i' does not exist in the current context
```

The code fails at the statement wherein the code attempts to assign variable i into j. The reason is that variable i has `block scope`. Variable i is defined within the `if` statement block, so its scope and lifetime extend from its point of definition within the `if` statement block to the closing brace of the `if` statement block. Because the assignment statement is outside the `if` statement block, variable i is no longer in scope and hence cannot be used.

Local Scope

Now let's move up the food chain and examine *local scope*. Local scope variables are defined within a method block, but outside a statement block. (Some programmers may refer to local scope as *method scope*.) Therefore, local scope extends from the variable's point of definition to the closing curly brace of the method in which the variable is defined. Variable j in Listing 9-2 is an example of a local scope variable. Variable j comes into scope at its point of definition within the method named Main(). Variable j goes out of scope and ceases to exist when program control reaches the closing brace for the Main() method in Listing 9-2.

You should be able to see that variable scopeLocal in Listing 9-1 has local scope. When program control reaches the closing brace in Listing 9-1, variable scopeLocal is no longer in scope and can no longer be used in the program:

```
}              // End local scope
```

It is important to notice that local scope variables can be used within a statement block, but the reverse is not true. That is, block scope variables cannot be used outside of the statement block in which they are defined, but local scope variables can be used within statement blocks within the same method.

Class Scope

You have probably figured this out already, but we'll plow through it anyway. Variables with *class scope* are those that are defined within a class, but outside of a method. (Some programmers refer to class scope as *module scope*.) Class scope extends from a variable's point of definition to the closing curly brace for that class. Variable scopeClass in Listing 9-1 is an example of a class scope variable.

Notice that class scope subsumes both method and statement block scope. This means that a variable with class scope can be used at both the method and statement block levels of scope. If you think about it, variables with class scope are the properties of the class. Methods in the class always have class scope.

Namespace Scope

Namespace scope applies to any variable that is defined within the current namespace. Near the top of Listing 9-1 you'll find the following statement:

```
namespace ClassDesign
{
```

You can tell from this statement that the current project under development is named ClassDesign. Because the project is named ClassDesign, it also means that, if you wish to do so, you can reference the program's entry point as the following:

```
ClassDesign.frmMain.Main();
```

Every program you have written thus far has a frmMain.Main() method. Think how confusing it would be to invoke the correct frmMain.Main() method if you didn't know which project you were referencing. One of the primary reasons for namespace scope is to prevent name collisions for classes and methods that exist within that namespace. If two programs both have a clsDatabase class in them, I can apply the correct namespace to use the correct class from the project I wish to use. That means you can have `JonesProject.clsDatabase.ReadOneRecord()` and `SmithsProject.clsDatabase` `.ReadOneRecord()` and the two `ReadOneRecord()` methods will remain distinct from one another even though they share the same class name. Namespace scope subsumes all program elements (such as variables, classes, and methods) within the current project and makes it possible to distinguish program elements that may share a common name.

Visualizing Scope

If you're into imagery, try to imagine a really tall ladder that spans several platforms, like the one shown in Figure 9-4. Place yourself and several friends on the ground at the bottom of the ladder. The only weird thing is that none of you can look up higher than eye level. This is block scope. You can see and interact with your friends provided you are all defined within the same statement block. In the figure, data items with block scope have a field of vision (FOV) that includes only those items with block scope.

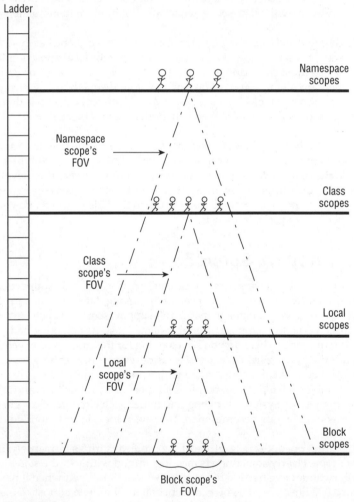

Figure 9-4

Now, climb up the ladder to the second platform. You look around and see some more of your friends on the local scope platform. You can go to the edge of the platform, look down, and see your friends below you as well as those on the same platform. The only difference is that your friends below you can no longer see or interact with you because they can't look up. Because you are now at a higher scope level, you can interact with them only if you climb down the ladder and join them at their *statement block scope level*. That is, any statement that involves you and has local scope must occur within the statement block that defines the statement block variable. For example, if you are variable x with local scope and you have a friend named i with block scope, the statement:

```
x = i;
```

can occur only if you climb back down the ladder to interact with variable i in his statement block. This means the statement must occur within the statement block where i lives. Otherwise, the statement cannot occur, because i can exist only within its own statement block. In terms of Listing 9-2, you can interact with variable i only if you place the assignment statement within the if statement block. Therefore, variables with local scope have a field of vision that includes data items with both local and block scope, but can interact with block scope items only within those items' statement block.

Now climb even higher to the class scope platform. Again, you have friends at this scope level with whom you can interact directly. Looking below you, you can see both your local and statement block friends, but to interact with them you must climb down the ladder to their levels. That is, for you to interact with local variables, any statement involving you must take place within the method in which your local block friend is defined, or the statement block within which your block scope friend is defined. Notice how the FOV for class scope includes data items defined with both local and block scope.

Finally, climb up to the highest platform. Once again you can see some new friends at this level (such as global data items), but looking down you can see everything! All data items in the program are visible to you. To interact with them, however, still means you must climb down to their levels, because they cannot look up and see you. Suppose you are a variable with namespace scope. To interact with variable i in Listing 9-2, you would have to climb all the way down the ladder and make yourself present within the if statement block where variable i exists.

Why Does C# Support Scope?

Most modern (and all OOP) languages support the concept of scope. This support is an attempt to minimize the undesired interaction effects that can occur among data items in a program. Consider what might happen if you were using a language that didn't support scope. In such languages, all variables behave like namespace variables. Suppose a variable named x starts behaving badly and has a value it shouldn't have. Without scope, where do you start looking for the cause of the weird value for x? The entire program is the playing field because x is visible everywhere throughout the program. Any element of the program could be messing around with x and you don't have a clue where it is being contaminated. Debugging such a problem becomes a hit-or-miss proposition, and it's only by chance that you finally locate the bug. Systematic debugging under such circumstances goes out the window and finding and correcting the bug becomes more an issue of luck, incantations, and eye of newt.

With data items that are scoped, the magnitude of the problem shrinks immensely. If x is a variable defined with block scope, clearly something is messing around with x in the statement block where it is defined. After all, x cannot live outside the block in which it's defined when it has block scope. In a large program with 3,000 lines of code, you can immediately eliminate almost all 3,000 and concentrate on the relatively few lines of code that form x's statement block.

If x is defined with local scope, you can still eliminate thousands of lines of code because only the code within the method in which x is defined comes into play. While a local scope variable is likely in scope for a larger number of code lines than a block scope variable, it's still a lot better than no scope at all.

Note that as you climb the scope ladder in Figure 9-4, more lines of code come into play, offering more places for x to get messed up. (This is because of the widening FOV.) Because more lines must be considered as a variable's scope widens, debugging becomes more difficult. For that reason, your program design should try to work with data at the narrowest scope level possible that still makes sense for the task at hand. The process of isolating the data in a program is called *encapsulation*, one of the cornerstones of object-oriented programming. While it may be easier to slap a program design together with little or no thought, you'll pay for it in the long run with more debugging and maintenance time.

Think Before You Write

The lesson to learn: Take the time to *think* about program design before you start writing. I cannot begin to tell you how many times I've given an in-class programming assignment only to have the students immediately start banging on the keyboards and dragging-and-dropping objects onto a form. As I watch the students, there's usually one or two who sit in their seats either doodling something on a piece of scratch paper, or perhaps they just stare at the ceiling. In a few minutes, they eventually start writing their programs. The really great thing is that these doodlers and ceiling-watchers almost always finish their programs before the rest of the class and generally have better program solutions. The reason? The time they spent doodling or ceiling-watching was actually spent creating a program design.

Many students confuse simple movement with problem-solving. That is, they think that because they are dragging and dropping textbox and label objects onto a form that they are working toward the program solution. However, as they get into the problem, it's not uncommon to see them remove the objects they originally thought they needed and replace them with something else. Lots of movement, but no useful work. Such students would be miles ahead if they had just taken a few minutes to think through the problem and come up with a design first, *before* they did anything else.

So . . . how *do* you design a program? This is exactly what you want to examine in the rest of this chapter.

Designing a Program

Perhaps the most difficult task a new programmer faces is knowing where to start when designing a program. Every program is a little different, so each design must be a little different. Given that, where's the best place to start?

While it is true that programs are different, you already know that all programs have at least one thing in common: the Five Program Steps. With that in mind, let's return to the clsDates program that I mentioned at the start of the chapter. The goal of this program is to write a class that can determine the date of Easter and tell us whether the year in question is a leap year or not. Let's see how you can use the Five Program Steps as a starting point for your design.

The Five Program Steps

Let's assume that the user interface shown in Figure 9-1 is good enough for the program. Under that assumption, we'll examine the Five Program Steps from a design perspective.

Initialization Step

For this program, about the only thing the Initialization Step needs to do is properly initialize the objects you've placed on the `frmMain` form and display that form on the screen. Listing 9-3 shows the `frmMain` code as it currently exists after you've followed the instructions at the beginning of the chapter.

Listing 9-3

```
using System;
using System.Windows.Forms;

public class frmMain : Form
{

    private TextBox txtYear;
    private Button btnCalc;
    private Button btnClose;
    private Label lblLeapYearResult;
    private Label lblEasterResult;
    private Label label1;
    #region Windows code

    private void InitializeComponent()
    {
        // Windows initialization code for frmMain form
    }

    #endregion

    public frmMain()                        // Constructor
    {
        InitializeComponent();
    }

    public static void Main()
    {
        frmMain main = new frmMain();   // Programs starts here
        Application.Run(main);
    }
}
```

When the program starts executing, you already know that the origin for its execution is with the method named `Main()`. Within `Main()`, the statement

```
frmMain main = new frmMain();    // Programs starts here
```

says that the first thing the program does is create an instance of an object of the `frmMain` class and name it `main`. To create the object named `main`, the program must first call the method named `frmMain()`. As you learned in Chapter 5, any method that shares the same name as the class in which it is defined is the constructor for that class. If you look at the `frmMain()` constructor in Listing 9-3, you can see that it calls a method named InitializeComponent(). Actually, you have been using these exact code lines for every program you've written, beginning with your first program in Chapter 2!

The purpose of the InitializeComponent() method is to enable Windows to recreate the form that you built while you were dragging and dropping objects onto the empty form. The only difference is that Windows is now rebuilding that form in memory so it can launch your program. If you look at the code that hides between the #region and #endregion directives, you can see the details about how your form is rebuilt each time you run the program.

Once that form is built in memory, control eventually returns to Main() and executes the following statement:

```
Application.Run(main);
```

When the Run() method is executed, Windows displays the form image for the frmMain class as it is currently stored in memory and the screen now looks like what is shown in Figure 9-1. At this point the Initialization Step is complete and the program is waiting for the user to do something.

Input Step

Only two inputs are needed from the user running the program: The year and a click of the Calculate button. Let's assume that the user types in 2008 for the year and clicks the Calculate button. At that point, program control enters the btnCalc_Click() event method. Once program control enters that method, the program needs to convert the textual data for the year into a numeric data type and assign its value into a variable. Because the program needs only the year entered by the user and a click of the Calculate button, the Input Step is very simple.

Process Step

If all goes well, the program now needs to call another method that takes the value for the year entered by the user and determines the date for Easter. Having done that, the program needs to call yet another method to determine if that year is a leap year. You will assume that the date for Easter is returned to you as a string and that the leap year value is returned as an int.

Display Step

Our display requirements are pretty simple: Fill in the Text property of the two label objects on the form with the information from the Process Step.

Termination Step

Because the program hasn't done anything tricky or used any special resources that you need to clean up after, you can simply call the Close() method to end the program.

You can diagram the state of your current design as shown in Figure 9-5.

Initialization Step
    Main() → frmMain() → InitializeComponent()
    Run (Main)

Input Step
    bfnCalc_Click()
    Convert text to year

Process Step
    String Easterday = getEaster(Year);
    int Leap = getLeapYear(Year);

Display Step
    lblEasterResult.Text = easterDay;
    lblLeapYearResult.Text = Leap;

Termination Step
    Close():

Figure 9-5

If you examine Figure 9-5, it should be pretty clear that everything you've done could be placed within the confines of the frmMain class. That is, the Initialization Step sets up the way you want the form to look, the Input Step uses the form to collect the input(s) from the user, the Process Step converts the data into the desired answers, the Display Step shows the results to the user, and the Termination Step simply ends the program. Now, think about the steps shown in Figure 9-5 and how they work.

Look at the Forest, Not Just the Trees

In a very real sense, all the steps are tied to the frmMain class, except the Processing Step. That is, all the steps except the Processing Step interact with visual components represented on the form frmMain. Only the Processing Step has nothing that relates directly to the visual representation or objects of the frmMain form. This means that, if you want to, you can totally isolate the Process Step from the visual state of the form. All the Process Step needs to function properly is a variable that stores the year. Given that fact, you should ask yourself: Will I ever, in my programming lifetime, need to reuse a method that can figure out the date for Easter in a given year or whether that year is a leap year? If you think this answer might be yes, you should consider writing the code for the Process Step as a method in a separate class. Why?

One of the driving forces behind OOP is code reuse. If you can write the code once and use it many times in the future, why reinvent the wheel each time you need to accomplish the same task? While it may take a tiny bit more effort in the short run, the benefits can be huge in the long run. You need to view writing a new class as an investment in the future. Invest a little work time now to get more free time down the road.

Think about how some of those 4,000 cookie cutters that Microsoft wrote have simplified things for you so far. How much more difficult would the programming examples in this book have been if you had to personally rewrite the code that creates a textbox, a label, and button objects for every program? We'd still be back in Chapter 2! Having the ability to use those objects without writing their code has saved you countless hours of typing and debugging time.

Because you just may want to reuse the Easter and leap year methods at some point in the future, you are going to implement those methods as part of a new class named clsDates.

UML Light

The Unified Modeling Language (UML) is a standardized specification language for modeling objects. It evolved from a joint effort by James Rumbaugh, Grady Booch, and Ivar Jacobson in the 1990s. Entire volumes have been written on UML and there is no way that I can do justice to it here. Still, you can make use of a small subset of UML called a *UML class diagram*. This is a visual representation of the parts that comprise a class. Rather than use all the features of UML class diagrams, you use only a small subset, hence the term *UML Light*. (Don't bother Googling "UML Light". . . I made the term up.)

Figure 9-6 shows the general format for a UML class diagram.

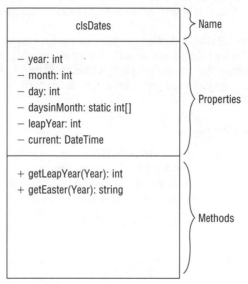

Figure 9-6

A UML class diagram may be viewed as three stacked boxes. The top box holds the name of the class (in this case `clsDates`). This is the name you see on the cookie cutter when it's hanging on the wall. Below the class name box is a box that describes the properties of the class. (Other OOP languages might refer to these properties as *class members* or *class attributes*.) The third box describes the methods that this particular class supports. (The latest version of UML supports a fourth box that describes how the class is *persisted*, or permanently stored, in a disk data file or a database. Our light version ignores this fourth box.)

Access Specifiers

The first line in the properties box contains the following line:

```
- year : int
```

The minus sign at the beginning of the line is used as a symbol to represent the access specifier for this particular property. I discuss only two possible access specifiers here: `private` and `public`. Both of these access specifiers are keywords in C#. The keyword `private` means that this property can only be accessed from outside the class by using its property methods. (I defer the discussion of an object's property methods until Chapter 10.) The minus sign in Figure 9-6 is a UML symbol for the keyword private in C#.

You can also define a property using the public keyword. The keyword public means that the property is directly accessible without the need to use the object's property methods. The UML symbol for the public keyword is the plus sign.

The minus sign appears at the beginning of the line, before the word year. The word year is the name you wish to give to this particular class property. Following the property name is a colon (:). The colon simply serves to separate the property name from the type specifier for the property. In this case, the type specifier is int. This means that year is an int data type. The entire line tells us quite a bit about the property. That is, year is an integer property of the clsDates class and uses the private access specifier.

In Figure 9-6, you can see that all the properties use the private access specifier. There are very good reasons for using this specifier, as I shall show shortly. For now, simply think of the private access specifier as affording more protection for the properties than does the public access specifier. In a very real sense, the private access specifier encapsulates a variable within its class and protects it from contamination by the outside world.

Access Specifiers and Scope

The properties of a class have class scope by default. This means that the class property variables are visible at all points within the class from their points of definition to the closing brace of the class code. The *default access specifier* for class properties is private. Class scope also means that class property variables do *not* have namespace scope. For example, if you define the property year according to the specification shown in Figure 9-6, it appears in clsDates as the following statement:

```
int year;
```

Because the private access specifier is the default storage class, what you are really stating is

```
private int year;
```

Now suppose you create an object named myDate of clsDates in frmMain. As things currently stand, you might try this statement:

```
myDate.year = 2008;
```

Visual Studio gets upset and tells you

```
ClassDesign.clsDates.year' is inaccessible due to its protection level
```

This is Visual Studio's way of telling you that year is not in scope. In other words, the private access specifier you gave to year in the clsDates class affords it some level of protection from the evil forces that lurk in the outside world.

Now change the definition of year in clsDates to

```
public int year;
```

and try to compile the program. Visual Studio no longer gets upset. The reason is that you have done away with the data protection afforded by the private keyword. Now anyone with a clsDates object is free to change year to any value she wishes and there's nothing you can do about it. Not good.

By defining the class property data with the private access specifier, you are acting like the smart medieval king who locks his valuable possessions (data) in the castle keep. Because you have the key to the tower, you control who has access to the possessions and they must play by your rules. On the other hand, if you define class properties with the public access specifier, you might as well make a thousand copies of the key and leave them hanging on the gate next to the moat. Outsiders no longer have to play by your rules and they can change things as they see fit . . . also not good.

In summary, the private access specifier reinforces the OOP design goal of encapsulating data. While there may be some technical reasons to argue for using the public access specifier, those reasons are few and far between. As a general rule, use the private access specifier for all property data.

The static Keyword

What does the line:

```
- daysInMonth : static int[]
```

mean? The word static is a C# keyword that conveys information about how something is stored in a program. In this case, you can verbalize the line like this: "daysInMonth is a private integer array that uses the static storage class." The brackets after the int keyword tell us that daysInMonth is an integer array. The keyword static means several things, but the most important is that, regardless of how many instances of this class you create in a program, you get only one array named daysInMonth.

For example, suppose you write a program that, for some reason, needs a million objects of the clsDates type. Each one of those objects gets its own copy of the year, month, day, leapYear, and current properties shown in Figure 9-6. However, all of the million objects share a single instance of the daysInMonth array. Why only one copy? Because there is no good reason to have more than one, hence you can save several million bytes of storage.

As you will see later in the chapter, the daysInMonth array stores a count of how many days each month has in it, as in 31, 28, 31, 30, and so on. Because these monthly counts aren't likely to change anytime soon, there's no reason to create multiple copies of the array. Such an array is really just a "read-only" array, because there is no conceivable reason to change these values. Therefore, because no object ever has a need to change the content of the array, there's no reason to duplicate it. The needs of the program for the content of the array are such that each class object can share this data.

Another thing about static data items: They are created the moment the program is loaded. You may not have noticed that the method Main() uses the static storage class. This means that a copy of that method exists the moment the program is loaded into memory. If you think about it, this makes sense. After all, if the program didn't immediately create a copy of the Main() method when it loaded, how would you ever get the program to start executing? You need the Main() method to get the program running.

As a general design rule, you should use the static keyword with any data that can safely be shared between instances of the class, or any data that must be present the moment the program is ready to start executing.

UML Methods

The interpretation of the UML class method entries is very similar to that of its properties. Consider this entry:

```
+ getLeapYear(year) : int
```

It states that the `getLeapYear()` method is a `public` method (+) that is passed one argument named `year` and that returns an `int` data type value. The interpretation for `getEaster()` is similar, except that it returns a `string` value to the caller.

Design Intent and Access Specifiers for Methods

Like class properties, class methods may use either `public` (+) or `private` (-) access specifiers. The interpretation of `public` methods is similar to that for `public` properties. However, the *intent* of a `public` access specifier for a method is different from that for a class property. Class properties are data and, as a general rule, you want to hide the class data as much as possible. Again, data hiding is the basis for encapsulation and one of the real benefits of OOP. Class methods, however, are different.

public Methods

Most class methods are designed to perform one specific task on one or more pieces of data. Quite often, those pieces of data are the class properties. Given that class methods are used to manipulate the class data, it seems reasonable to assume that the programmer using the class wants access to that newly transformed data. For example, in a few moments you are going to write a class method that returns the value 1 if a year is a leap year or 0 if it is not. You are writing the method so that whoever calls that method knows whether the year he passed to the method is a leap year or not. Clearly, you want to be able to make that result known outside the class itself. Therefore, you would write the `getLeapYear()` method using the `public` access specifier.

All elements of a class that you give the `public` access specifier become part of the *user interface* for the class. That is, you purposely are designing properties and methods using the `public` access specifier specifically because you want the outside world to have access to them. As mentioned earlier, I take a dim view of `public` properties. However, I am tickled pink about `public` methods. The reason for the disparity is that you want to hide the data (that is, the properties) but make the class useful via the `public` class methods and the functionality those class methods bring to the party.

In fact, sometimes you will hear the term *class API*. This refers to the class Application Programming Interface. Therefore, a class API refers to all of the elements of the class that use the `public` access specifier. This makes sense if you think about it, as the only way the outside world can interact with a class is through its `public` properties and methods.

private (Helper) Methods

Just as a class can have `public` methods, it can also use `private` class methods. By definition, `private` class methods cannot be part of the class API. After all, if the method is `private`, it has class scope and is not visible outside the class in which it is defined.

You're probably asking yourself: If `private` class methods cannot be accessed outside the class itself, what use are they? Good question, and it's best answered with an example.

Suppose you are collecting personal data about people for use in an electronic phone book application you're writing. You decide to collect each person's home phone number as well as his or her cell and work phone numbers. You know that people often make mistakes when entering numbers so you want to verify that the numbers they entered for each phone number uses a format that is valid. Now you have a design choice. You can duplicate your validation code three times, once for each phone number type, or you can write a single method named `validatePhoneNumber()` and call it when it is needed. Hmmm . . . which is a better decision: Write three times as much code and then test and debug it three times, or write the code once and test and debug just that version once? Seems like a no-brainer.

The `validatePhoneNumber()` method exists in the class to make your job of verifying phone numbers easier. Any class method that simply makes your job easier and that you do not wish to make part of the class API should be defined using the `private` access specifier. Quite often, such `private` class methods are called *Helper methods* because they are in the class to make your work as a programmer easier and *do not* form part of the class API that you expose to the outside world.

Class Property and Method Names

When you design a class you have a lot of freedom in terms of what you name your properties and methods. Obviously you cannot use C# keywords for names, but just about everything else is fair game. (The rules for naming classes are the same as for naming variables.) Given that freedom, does it matter what names you give to your properties and methods? Obviously, the names you use within a class do matter or I wouldn't be writing this section of the chapter! Consider the following class-naming conventions as you design your classes.

Use Lowercase Letters for Property Names

First, I suggest that you start the names of your properties with lowercase letters. The full explanation for this decision is deferred until Chapter 10. The brief explanation is that using lowercase letters enables you to implement a naming convention that is common to many C# programmers.

Hint as to Their Functions

Second, select names for your API methods that give a hint as to what their functions are. For example, the method name `SortData()` seems like a good choice, until you realize that the class contains more than one piece of data. A better name might be `SortZipCodes()` because that name gives a better idea of what's about to happen. If you need to sort all the class data based upon the zip codes, you might name that method `SortAllDataByZip()`. Using functional names makes it easier to recall what each method does when Intellisense presents you with a list of the method names available in a class.

Use Action Names for API Methods

Third, because most API class methods interact with the class data, method names often imply an action of some kind and hence are verb-based. For example, `SortZipCodes()` implies an active change in the zip code data from its current state to a sorted state. `CalculateSaleTaxDue()` might be a method in a company sales package that changes the `salesTaxDue` property of the class. By contrast, an API method `Name()` doesn't provide any clue about what the method does, only that it likely has something to do with the `names` data. A better choice would be `getClientName()`, because that suggests what the method does.

API Method Names Should be Implementation-Neutral

Fourth, the API class methods should *not* reflect how the functionality of the methods is implemented. I've seen code in which two API methods were named `SearchLeftTreeNode()` and `SearchRightTreeNode()`. It doesn't take much imagination to figure out that the programmer who wrote the class is probably using a binary tree to search for something. Now suppose that some really bright propeller-head somewhere develops a new, superfast searching algorithm and you want to implement it in your code. Do you change the API class names to reflect the new algorithm, or do you leave them as they are? If you change the API method names, older versions of the code will break because those methods are no longer in the class. If you don't change the names, you're sort of lying about what the methods do to anyone who uses your class. This is a true dilemma: two choices, both bad. The solution is to never have used an implementation-based name in the first place.

Programmers search binary trees because they want to find something, and the API method name should reflect that fact. For example, if the binary tree search is being performed using the client's ID number to find the client's demographic data, a better API method name would be `getClientData()`. This API method name says nothing about *how* you accomplish a task. To the outside world, your API class methods should appear to be black boxes: The user doesn't need to know the specific type of magic that produces a result, only that the magic works. Implementation-neutral method names enable you to change the *way* you accomplish a task without making you feel guilty the next morning. This lack of guilt is the result of the method name being implementation-neutral and making no promises about how things are done within the method.

Think Like a User

One more aspect of class design is to think like the user who ultimately uses the properties and methods of your class. For example, in a few moments I present the code for the `clsDates` class. One of the properties in that class is defined as follows:

```
private static int[] daysInMonth = { 0, 31, 28, 31, 30, 31, 30, 31,
                                      31, 30, 31, 30, 31};
```

If you look at the initialization data for the `daysInMonth` array, it's pretty obvious that the values reflect the number of days in each month. However, closer inspection shows that the first element of the array is 0. Why?

The reason is the way people think, as was mentioned in Chapter 8. If you ask people how many days there are in one month of a year, very few are going to say 28. That is the answer you get, however, if the user of the class passes you the value 1 in a method that is supposed to return the number of days in a given month. True, you can always recall the N − 1 Rule and adjust the value users pass to you when you index into the array. But you too are a "people" and you probably think the same way your user thinks. Debugging a method is easier if the data are organized to match the way you think about the data. Yes . . . I know I've wasted four bytes. Big deal. When each computer now comes with a mega-munch of memory, I don't really think frittering away four bytes is going to make or break the application. Also, the time you save working with logically organized data pays for itself in reduced testing and debugging time.

The lesson is simple: Organize your data in a way that makes sense to you (and to any others who may have to support your code).

The clsDates Design

Now let's use some of our design ideas to implement the design for clsDates. The code for clsDates is shown in Listing 9-4.

Listing 9-4

```
using System;
using System.Collections.Generic;
using System.Text;

public class clsDates
{
    // ============== symbolic constants ==================

    // ============== static members =====================
    private static int[] daysInMonth = { 0, 31, 28, 31, 30, 31, 30, 31,
                                         31, 30, 31, 30, 31};

    // ============== instance members ====================
    private int day;
    private int month;
    private int year;
    private int leapYear;

    private DateTime current;

    // ============== constructor(s) =====================

    public clsDates()
    {
        current = DateTime.Now; // Sets DateTime to right now
    }
    // ============== property methods =====================

    // ============== helper methods =====================

    // ============== general methods =====================

    /*****
     * Purpose: To determine if the year is a leap year. Algorithm
     *          taken from C Programmer's Toolkit, Purdum, Que Corp.,
     *          1993, p. 258.
     *
     * Parameter list:
     *    int year        the year under consideration
     *
     * Return value:
     *    int             1 if a leap year, 0 otherwise
     *****/

    public int getLeapYear(int year)
```

(continued)

225

Listing 9-4 (continued)

```
    {
        if (year % 4 == 0 && year % 100 != 0 || year % 400 == 0)
            return 1;    // It is a leap year
        else
            return 0;    // Nope.
    }


/*****
 * Purpose: To determine the date for Easter given a year. Algorithm
 *          taken from C Programmer's Toolkit, Purdum, Que Corp.,
 *          1993, p. 267.
 *
 * Parameter list:
 *    int year        the year under consideration
 *
 * Return value:
 *    string          the date in MM/DD/YYYY format
 *****/
public string getEaster(int year)
{
    int offset;
    int leap;
    int day;
    int temp1;
    int temp2;
    int total;

    offset = year % 19;
    leap = year % 4;
    day = year % 7;
    temp1 = (19 * offset + 24) % 30;
    temp2 = (2 * leap + 4 * day + 6 * temp1 + 5) % 7;
    total = (22 + temp1 + temp2);
    if (total > 31)
    {
        month = 4;             // Easter is in April...
        day = total - 31;   // ...on this day
    }
    else
    {
        month = 3;             // Easter is in March...
        day = total;        // ...on this day
    }
    DateTime myDT = new DateTime(year, month, day);
    return myDT.ToLongDateString();
    }
}
```

namespace Modifier

If you look closely at Listing 9-4, you'll notice that I removed the following statements from the clsDates code:

```
namespace ClassDesign
      {
      }
```

Why? The reason is that you want your clsDates class to be useable in other programs you might develop, without your having to use the project's namespace as part of the class hierarchy. For example, if you leave the namespace lines in and you wish to create an object named myDate, you have to define it with the following statement:

```
ClassDesign.clsDates myDate = new ClassDesign.clsDates();
```

This syntax seems a little cumbersome. By removing the namespace statements in clsDates, you can define the object with this statement:

```
clsDates myDate = new clsDates();
```

This syntax structure is more commonly employed even though there might be a small risk of namespace collision with another class that might use clsDates as a class name. If you want to leave the namespace in as part of the class definition, that's fine. Just remember to supply the complete hierarchy when you define an object of the class.

Class Organization

In Listing 9-4 you can see how I've added comments to section off various parts of the class. Those parts are (from top to bottom):

❑   Symbolic constants

❑   static members of the class

❑   Instance members

❑   Constructors

❑   Property methods

❑   Helper methods

❑   General methods

There is nothing etched in stone about this organization for a class. It is, however, an organizational structure that has worked for me in my writing of commercial applications over the years. A few comments about the organization are warranted.

static Data Versus Instance Members

First, notice the division of the properties into those that are `static` and those that are not. As I mentioned earlier in this chapter, `static` data are created at program load time. This means that, even if the program never gets to a point where it defines a `clsDates` object, the `daysInMonth` array always exists in memory. Also recall that no matter how many objects of `clsDates` are created, they all share the same `daysInMonth` array. For those two reasons, I place `static` data in its own category.

Instance members is the common term for all the non-`static` properties of the class. Instance members are those class properties that are created for each and every object that is instantiated from the class. Simply stated, each instance of the class gets its own set of the (non-`static`) class properties, hence the term "instance members."

Property and Helper Methods

I set these methods off by themselves for reasons that are explained more completely in Chapter 10. Also, I have purposely kept the code in the current example simple so I don't throw too much at you at one time.

General Methods

The general methods are those methods that become part of your API for the class. As such, all general methods are written using the `public` access specifier.

General Method Headers

For nontrivial general methods, I usually supply a header for the method using the following style, as seen in Listing 9-4:

```
/*****
 * Purpose: To determine if the year is a leap year. Algorithm
 *          taken from C Programmer's Toolkit, Purdum, Que Corp.,
 *          1993, p. 258.
 *
 * Parameter list:
 *    int year       the year under consideration
 *
 * Return value:
 *    int            1 if a leap year, 0 otherwise
 *****/
public string getEaster(int year)
{
```

The header for a method simply states the purpose of the method, the parameter list of data that is passed to it (if any), and the return data type (if any). If the method uses code based on some special algorithm and you think you may want to refer back to it, you place that reference in the method header. Note that I use multiple-line comment characters to block off the header. If you enforce this structure in your team's code, you can use it to create class documentation on the fly. That is, you can write a program that examines the source code files looking for the sequence /*****. You can then copy the text that follows that sequence into a disk data file, ending the copy process when you read one additional line after the sequence *****/. The additional line is copied to get the signature for the method. When you've finished reading all the program source code, you end up with a file that you can print, documenting each method in the source code.

Try It Out   **The clsDates Programs**

Now that you've written the code for the `clsDates` class, let's write the code for a form that can be used to test the class. A sample run is shown in Figure 9-7.

Figure 9-7

The user simply enters the year she wants to use for determining the date for Easter and clicks the Calculate button. The program then displays the results in two label objects.

How It Works

The code for the `frmMain` class is shown in Listing 9-5.

Listing 9-5

```
using System;
using System.Windows.Forms;

public class frmMain : Form
{
    private TextBox txtYear;
    private Button btnCalc;
    private Button btnClose;
    private Label lblLeapYearResult;
    private Label lblEasterResult;
    private Label label1;
    #region Windows code

    public frmMain()
    {
        InitializeComponent();
    }

    public static void Main()
    {
        frmMain main = new frmMain();
        Application.Run(main);
    }

    private void btnCalc_Click(object sender, EventArgs e)
```

```
        {
            bool flag;
            int year;
            int leap;
            clsDates myDate = new clsDates();

            // Convert validate integer
            flag = int.TryParse(txtYear.Text, out year);
            if (flag == false)
            {
                MessageBox.Show("Digit characters only in YYYY format.",
                               "Input Error");
                txtYear.Focus();
                return;
            }
            leap = myDate.getLeapYear(year);
            lblLeapYearResult.Text = year.ToString() + " is " +
                    ((leap == 1)? "":"not ") + "a leap year";
            lblEasterResult.Text = myDate.getEaster(year);
        }

        private void btnClose_Click(object sender, EventArgs e)
        {
            Close();
        }
    }
```

There isn't really much in Listing 9-5 that you haven't seen before. Notice the definition of myDate:

```
        clsDates myDate = new clsDates();
```

Because you removed the namespace attribute from the clsDates code, you can instantiate the myDate object by simply using the class name. The TryParse() and if statement block convert the text stored in the Text property of the txtYear object into an integer and assigns it into a variable named year. The statement

```
        leap = myDate.getLeapYear(year);
```

calls the general method named getLeapYear() in the clsDates class, returns either 1 (a leap year) or 0 (not a leap year), and assigns this value into leap.

Why didn't I write getLeapYear() to return a bool that returns true for a leap year and false otherwise? The reason is that programmers frequently use a leap year calculation to determine the number of days in February for a given year. This enables me to write code like this:

```
        int februaryDays = 28;
        // Some code. . .
        februaryDays += myDate.getLeapYear(year);
```

If I make the code return a `bool`, I cannot use this kind of statement. Returning 1 or 0 better suits the way I think programmers use leap year calculations. (The nice thing about writing the class yourself is that you can change my code if you wish.)

Note that if you type in:

```
leap = myDate.
```

Intellisense is smart enough to present you with a list of methods defined in the `clsDates` class. (In the next chapter, you learn how to have the properties appear in the list as well.)

The next statement is used to build a message string stating whether the year is a leap year or not:

```
lblLeapYearResult.Text = year.ToString() + " is " +
            ((leap == 1)? "":"not ") + "a leap year";
```

That message string is then assigned into the `Text` property of the `lblLeapYearResult` label object. Quite honestly, this statement is an example of SOC, or *Show-Off Code.* It uses the ternary operator to determine how the message string is built. If you study the code for a moment, you should be able to figure out how it works. However, you could also use an `if` statement and accomplish the same thing. (You didn't study the code, did you? If not, go back and study it . . . now!)

The last statement in the click event simply calls `getEaster()` and writes the string that is returned from the call into the `Text` property of the `lblEasterResult` object. Note how easy it was to create this string in the `getEaster()` code in `clsDates`:

```
DateTime myDT = new DateTime(year, month, day);
return myDT.ToLongDateString();
```

Just two lines of code and you have a perfectly formatted date string for Easter. The reason this works the way it does is that you used an overloaded constructor to pass in the month and day as calculated by the Easter algorithm, along with the year supplied by the user. The `DateTime` method named `ToLongDateString()` builds the date string shown in Figure 9-7. The lesson to be learned here is: Life is often easier when you take the time to explore the properties and methods of the class you are using.

User Interfaces Versus User Interfaces

You need to be a little careful when you talk about user interfaces. Care is needed because the terms can be used in multiple contexts. First, most people think of a user interface as being that part of a program with which the end user interacts. This type of user interface has visual objects presented on a form, such as `frmMain` has always used. The user then interacts with textbox, button, listbox, and a host of other types of objects on the form. The user interface, in this instance, serves as the primary means of getting input from and displaying results to the end user.

The second type of user interface does not require a visual representation at all. For example, all the properties and methods that have the `public` access specifier comprise the *user interface for a class.* In this case, the user is actually a programmer. The `public` properties and methods of the class form the API for that class and thus define how the programmer interfaces with it.

When you speak about the user interface in the context of a class, the "user" is a programmer working through the API to interact with the class. When you speak about the user interface in the context of a Windows form that has visual objects on it (such as textboxes and buttons), the "user" is the end user who is actually running the program. If you try to make a concerted effort not to confuse the two, casual conversations with other people can be confusing. The rule of thumb to follow: If you're unclear which user interface is under discussion, ask.

Summary

This chapter discussed the fundamental design factors you need to consider when you start creating your own classes. You learned how to organize your design and use UML class diagrams to help you solidify your design. You also learned about the `static` storage class and how `static` data differs from instance variables in a class. You also were introduced to the concept of creating a user interface for a class by creating a programming API for it.

I continue with additional details about writing and using classes in the next chapter.

Exercises

1. Suppose you are adding the following data items as properties to a class. How would you write them in the class?

   a. A person's last name

   b. A zip code

   c. The days of the week

2. Suppose you want to add a general method to the `clsDates` class that returns the number of days in a given month. How would you write the code?

3. Give a good example of where you would use the `public` access specifier to define a class property.

4. Modify the following SOC code to use an `if` statement instead:

   ```
   lblLeapYearResult.Text = year.ToString() + " is " +
           ((leap == 1)? "":"not ") + "a leap year";
   ```

   Which form would you use in your own code and why?

5. Suppose you overload the `clsDates` constructor so that the following constructor is available. Would you modify your `getLeapYear()` method and, if so, how?

   ```
   public clsDates(int yr)
   {
       year = yr;
   }
   ```

Designing and Writing Custom Classes

In Chapter 9 I initiated a discussion about designing your own classes. I ended that chapter by designing and writing a simple class named clsDates that added two methods: getLeapYear() and getEaster(). This chapter continues the theme of class design, but gets into additional details about writing classes. In this chapter you will learn about:

- ❑ Constructor details
- ❑ Method overloading
- ❑ Cohesion
- ❑ Coupling
- ❑ Property methods
- ❑ Getters and setters
- ❑ Changing the state of an object
- ❑ Sensing an error in a class method

When you finish this chapter, you will have a solid foundation upon which to start writing your own classes. With a little effort, I think you'll find that it is both worthwhile and kind of fun.

Constructors

You should think of *constructors* as methods that are designed to create, or instantiate, an object. The sole purpose of a constructor is to enable you to instantiate an object with a known state. The beauty of C# (and most other OOP languages) is that you get a default constructor automatically.

Default Constructors

To make the creation of a default constructor possible, a constructor always has the same name as its class. For example, if you wish to create an object named myDate of the clsDates class, you would use the following statement:

```
clsDates myDate = new clsDate();
```

I've talked about this syntax before, but let's dig a little deeper now.

First, notice that the leftmost reference to clsDates is simply the name of the class: no closing parentheses follow the class name. In effect, this reference to clsDates is simply telling you which cookie cutter to take from the thousands of them hanging on the wall.

Second, the purpose of the identifier myDate is to enable you to give a name to the *reference variable* that your code uses as a link to the data for the clsDates class. You learned in Chapter 5 that the rvalue of a reference variable is either null or the memory address of the location of the data for the object. For learning purposes, you can think of myDate as having the rvalue of null at this instant in time.

Third, the keyword new should always jog your memory and make you remember that there are going to be some messages exchanged between your program and the Windows Memory Manager. Specifically, new means that you are asking Windows for enough memory to store a clsDates object. Assuming that enough memory is found, the rvalue of myDate instantly changes from null to the memory address of where the object is stored.

Fourth, the final expression in the statement is clsDates(). Note that, unlike the first reference to the class at the beginning of the statement, this reference is followed by parentheses. This means that the code is calling a method. In this case clsDates() is a call to the constructor method. If you don't write your own constructor, C# still calls its own default constructor. When the default constructor is finished executing, all the value data types in the class have the value 0 and all the reference variables have the value null. Note that the default constructor places the object in a known state where value types are 0 and references are null.

Non-Default Constructors

Okay, so when do you need to write a non-default constructor? Under two basic circumstances: 1) when your class design is not happy with the default state of the object when it comes to life or 2) when a non-default constructor makes life easier for the user. (Don't forget: here the term "user" refers to another programmer who uses the class you are creating.)

The first reason means that there is something about starting out with all the class data set to either 0 or null that just isn't the "right" state for the object. For example, in Chapter 9 I changed the default constructor to this:

```
public clsDates()
{
    current = DateTime.Now; // Sets DateTime to right now
}
```

This constructor changes the DataTime data item named current from its uninitialized state to the present date and time. In other words, your design is such that you want to have current start out with its value set to the date and time at which the object was instantiated.

Note that creating a clsDates object with the present date and time already stored in current may make some aspect of the class easier to use. (Right now there's no code in the class that takes advantage of current, but that doesn't mean there won't be!)

Constructor Overloading

I discussed method overloading in Chapter 5. Because a constructor is nothing more than a method that is always called when an object is instantiated, constructors may also be overloaded. For example, you can add the following constructor to the code shown in Listing 9-4:

```
public clsDates(int yr)
{

    year = yr;
}
```

Now you have two constructors. As mentioned in Chapter 5, method overloading is never a problem as long as the method signatures are different. Because this second constructor has an integer parameter (yr) passed to it, the signatures are different. However, you can now use the following statement to instantiate the myDate object:

```
clsDates myDate = new clsDate(year);
```

Now the instance variable named year in the clsDates object named myDate is initialized the moment the object is instantiated. Kinda neat, huh? Well, not really.

Constructor Sloppiness

There's a problem with the way we've written the two constructors. Let's look at them side by side.

```
public clsDates()              // No-parameter constructor
{
    current = DateTime.Now; // Sets DateTime to right now
}

public clsDates(int yr)      // Constructor with parameter
{
    year = yr;
}
```

If I create the myDate object with the statement

```
clsDates myDate = new clsDate();
```

the no-parameter version means that myDate comes to life with the instance member named current initialized to the present date and time. However, if I use the statement

```
clsDates myDate = new clsDate(year);
```

then `current` is not initialized to its (assumed default) state! As a general rule, a non-default constructor (that is, a constructor that has one or more arguments) should always subsume the default state of the object. What this means is that our parameterized version of the constructor should also initialize `current` to the present date and time. As the code stands right now, however, the default (no-parameter) constructor initializes the member named `current`, but the overloaded constructor does not. Not good.

Fixing the Constructor Problem

The solution to our problem seems simple enough: just call the default constructor from within the parameterized constructor:

```
public clsDates(int yr)      // Constructor with parameter
{
    clsDates();              // This won't work!
    year = yr;
}
```

This fix won't work because the compiler gets confused as to how `clsDates` is to be used in this context.

Now try the following form for the parameterized constructor:

Listing 10-1

```
public clsDates(int yr) : this()
{
    year = yr;
}
```

Note the (colon) operator (`:`) and the keyword `this` in the first statement. You've been using the colon operator in every program you've written, but probably haven't thought much about it. For example: pick any program you've written and look at the first statement in the definition of `frmMain`:

```
public class frmMain : Form
```

You can verbalize the colon operator as the phrase "inherits from." In other words, your `frmMain` inherits the basic properties and methods of a common Windows form, but is going to extend it with whatever objects and code you add to `frmMain`.

Now let's examine the following statement:

```
public clsDates(int yr) : this()
```

The `this` keyword is simply shorthand notation for a reference to the instance of the current object. In other words, `this` is a shorthand notation for the `clsDates` object that the program is in the process of constructing. However, because you have followed the `this` keyword with parentheses, the compiler knows that it must call the default (no-parameter) constructor for this class before it does anything else. (If you're ever at a cocktail party and someone mentions *constructor chaining*, this is exactly what that person is talking about.)

Add the code for the second constructor (Listing 10-1) to the code presented in Listing 9-4. Now set a breakpoint on the first line of this new (parameterized) constructor, and then run and single-step through the program. You will find that, upon reaching the breakpoint in the second constructor, the program immediately jumps to the default constructor, initializes current to the proper value, and *then* executes the statement body for the second constructor. This is exactly what you want to happen because both flavors for creating the myDate object —

```
clsDates myDate = new clsDate();
```

and

```
clsDates myDate = new clsDate(year);
```

— leave current in the same state. The parameterized version of the constructor simply initializes an additional member (year) of the class to a known value.

Always Call the Default Constructor

You might be asking yourself: "Why bother calling the default constructor? If I never use the content of current, who cares?" Well, given the way clsDates is written presently, current isn't used, so it really doesn't matter. However, that does not mean you won't add code later on that does assume a default state for current.

More importantly, calling the default constructor gets you into the coding habit of establishing a "base state" for the object. Not starting all objects with the same base state may cause problems later on. For example, you might be writing some form of database class in which the default constructor creates a connection to the database. If an overloaded constructor didn't also establish that database connection, perhaps other methods in the class would not be able to perform their function(s) properly.

Just as you've seen so many times before, the Initialization Step of the Five Program Steps creates the base environment in which the program code is to perform. Calling a constructor is similar to the Initialization Step for a program, but viewed in the more narrowly defined context of a method. That is, the constructor establishes the environment in which a specific *object* is to exist and perform. Therefore, it is always a good idea for all overloaded constructors to call the default constructor so the base state of the object can be safely assumed.

Property Methods

So far you have designed and implemented the property members of the class, and you've also added two constructors to give the user some flexibility when he instantiates a clsDates object. Finally, you've written two General methods, getLeapYear() and getEaster(), that provide some functionality for the class. In the spirit of encapsulation, you defined all of the property methods using the private access specifier. Using the private access specifier makes it much more difficult to inadvertently change the value of a class property. This protection for the class properties exists because the private access specifier limits the scope of the properties to the class in which they are defined. The properties are invisible to the outside world!

Wait a minute. If the properties are invisible to the outside world because of their scope, then there is no way to change them! If the class properties can't be changed, there is no way to change the state of the object. If you can't change the state of an object, you may as well have defined a boat anchor cast in concrete. It is the ability to use and change the state of an object that makes that object useful in a program. After all, how useful can an object be if its properties are always null or 0?

Getters and Setters

Obviously, there's a method to this seeming madness. C# provides you with a program structure known as a *property method*, which is used to access private methods defined within a class. A class property method is built with *property getters* and *property setters*. These are special methods designed for use with class properties. As a rule, you define a set of getters and setters for each private property member.

The syntax for a property getter and setter is as follows:

```
AccessSpecifier   ReturnDataType   PropertyName
{
    get
    {
        return PropertyMember;
    }
    set
    {
        PropertyMember = value;
    }
}
```

An example using the month property of the clsDates class is shown in Listing 10-2. You should write the month property method as follows.

Listing 10-2

```
public int Month
{
    get
    {
        return month;
    }
    set
    {
        if (value > 0 && value < 13)
        {
            month = value;
        }
    }
}
```

Property Method Rules

There are a number of things to notice about property methods. First, *all* property methods use the public access specifier. As you learned in Chapter 9, if a method uses the public access specifier, that method becomes part of the user interface (or API) of the class. Because property methods are public, they become the gateway into the class and provide a means of accessing the `private` property members of the class.

Second, the return data type for the property method *must* match the data type of the property. If you defined the class property to be an `int` (as `month` is), then the property method must return an `int`. If the property member is a `DateTime` data type, the return data type must also be a `DateTime`.

Third, note that a *property method* is different from any other type of method because the name of the property method is not followed by a set of parentheses. A common programming convention is to make the name of the property method the same as that of the property, but to capitalize the first letter of the property name. In this example, the class property named `month` has a class property method named `Month`. (This is also consistent with making the first word of all class property names lowercase.) There will be no confusion between `month` and `Month` because C# is case-sensitive.

Fourth, the keyword `get` is used to mark the block of code within a property method that may be used to retrieve the value of a class property member. Usually, the statement within the `get` statement block is simply a `return` keyword followed by the property name, as shown in the example. You will often hear a `get` statement block referred to as a *getter*.

Finally, the keyword `set` is used to mark the block of code within a property method that may be used to assign a value to a class property member. The `set` statement block should be the only means by which the outside world can change the private property member of a class. (You could change it through a General class method, but that's an ugly way to do it and is discouraged.)

If you look at the `set` statement block in the `Month` property method, you can see that you validate that the value being assigned into `month` is reasonable. Wait a minute! Where did the variable named `value` come from?

The value Keyword

The keyword `value` is an implied variable used as part of the syntax of the `set` statement block. You can think of `value` as a *ghost variable* that holds the data that you wish to assign into the property member. The data type of `value` always matches the return type specifier of the property method. For example, the `Month` property method returns an `int`, so `value` must be an `int`.

There is no formal definition of `value` in a property method. The data type for `value` is implied by the context in which it is used. The type always matches the type specifier for the property method.

How the get Property Methods Work

Suppose you wish to read the value of `month` as it is presently stored in a `clsDates` object. The following code fragment shows how to access the property member named `month`:

```
int myMonth;
clsDates myDate = new clsDates();

// Misc lines of code . . .

myMonth = myDate.Month;
```

The intent of the preceding code is to retrieve the value of month as it currently exists in the myDate object, and assign that value into myMonth. When the last statement executes, program control executes the get statement block of the Month property method in clsDates and returns the value of the property named month. You should type in code similar to the code fragment above into frmMain, set a breakpoint on the last statement in the code fragment, and then use the F11 key to single-step into the Month property method to see how program control works for such statements.

As the property method code in Listing 10-2 presently works, the value returned is 0 because no value has been assigned to the month property. You could modify Listing 10-2 to what is shown in Listing 10-3.

Listing 10-3

```
public int Month
{
    get
    {
        if (month == 0)              // New code
        {
            return current.Month;
        } else
        {
            return month;
        }
    }
    set
    {
        if (value > 0 && value < 13)
        {
            month = value;
        }
    }
}
```

The modification in Listing 10-3 says that, if the class member named month is unassigned (that is, if it has its default value of 0), return the Month value of the DateTime object named current. This returns a nonzero value because the constructor initializes current to the date and time at which the object is created. Notice that, if you had defined the class member named current with the public access specifier, you could not do this kind of checking on current before it was used.

How the set Property Methods Work

Suppose you want to change the month property to 12. You can accomplish that with the following statements in frmMain:

```
int myMonth = 12;
clsDates myDate = new clsDates();

// Misc lines of code . . .

myDate.Month = myMonth;
```

If you set a breakpoint on the last statement of the preceding code and then use the F11 key to single-step into the Month property method, you can see that the set statement block is executed. The code in Listing 10-3 can check the ghost variable named value to see that an appropriate value is recorded for month in clsDates. If you are using the debugger as suggested, you can see that the variable named value has the value of myMonth back in frmMain.

How Does Visual Studio Know Whether to Use the get or set Statement Block?

Visual Studio can determine what your intent is by the context in which you are using the Month property method. For example, in the assignment statement

```
myMonth = myDate.Month;      // A get operation
```

it's obvious that your intent is to fetch the current value of the month property of the myDate object and assign it into myMonth. The statement, therefore, must perform a get operation.

Conversely, in the assignment statement

```
myDate.Month = myMonth;      // A set operation
```

your intent is to use the value stored in myMonth and assign it into the month property of the myDate object. Because you wish to change the month property of myDate, Visual Studio must perform a set operation.

You can generalize these context behaviors into the following two rules for using class property methods:

1. if the property method name appears on the right-hand side of an assignment operator, a get statement is performed.

2. If the property method name appears on the left-hand side of an assignment operator, a set statement is performed.

Always keep in mind that a set operation has the potential to change the state of an object. Also, the set statement block is a good place to write any validation code you deem necessary to ensure that the property doesn't accept bogus or undesired values.

If you see a property method used in an expression that does not involve the assignment operator, such as

```
for (j = 0; j < myDate.Days; j++)
```

the expression is performing a get operation. (Again, the property method appears on the right-hand side of the relational operator (<), so it must be a get operation.)

What to Do if an Error Occurs in a Property Method

There will be times when a bogus value reaches a property method. However, the set statement block is used to change the state of the object and not to return a value to the caller. So how do you communicate to the user that your class code read a bad data value in a property method?

Your first approach might to be to use a MessageBox object to display a message to the user that a bad value for a property was read. The problem with this approach is that the data manipulation is going on in the class, not in frmMain where the end user is interacting. When you are writing code for a class, you should always keep in mind that *your* user is a programmer, not the end user running the program. Because of this, you need to let the person using your class know that something's amiss. (A general style convention is that property methods do *not* use MessageBox objects.)

The main purpose of a set statement block is to change the value of the property associated with the method. Because a change in the value of a class property also means a change in the *state of the object*, the safest thing to do when an error is detected is to leave the state of the object unchanged. For example, if a bogus value for a month reaches the set statement block in Listing 10-3, the new value for month is ignored and the state of the object remains unchanged. It would be the responsibility of the programmer using your class to detect that the set operation failed, as shown by the unchanged state of the object.

Another possibility is to have a state flag as a property member of the class. You could have code similar to this:

```
private int errorStatus = 0;    // Assume no errors for object's state

            // more code for other class members . . .

public int getErrorStatus       // Property method for errorStatus member
{
    get
    {
        Return errorStatus;
    }
}
```

Notice that there is no set statement block for the getErrorStatus property method; it is a *read-only property method*. Because the property method is read-only, the user cannot change the state of errorStatus; only you can change it, in your class code. Given that fact, you could modify Listing 10-3 to what is shown in Listing 10-4:

Listing 10-4

```
public int Month
{
    get
    {
        if (month == 0)             // New code
        {
            return current.Month;
        } else
```

```
        {
            return month;
        }
    }
    set
    {
        if (value > 0 && value < 13)
        {
            month = value;
        } else
        {
            errorStatus = 1;      // Flag as error
        }
    }
}
```

Now any time the user of your class wants to see if a set operation worked properly, she could add code similar to this back in frmMain:

```
myDate.Month = myMonth;
if (myDate.getErrorStatus == 1)
{
    MessageBox.Show("The world is ending. Run for your lives!");
    return;
}
```

This would detect the occurrence of an error in the class. Other possibilities exist, but those shown here are the most direct.

Method Coupling and Cohesion

As you've learned in this chapter, property methods are used to read and write the values associated with the properties in a class. Because they are public, property methods form an important part of the user interface for the class. However, the purpose of a property method (either getting or setting) is correctly constrained to the property itself.

Helper and General methods, on the other hand, are designed to use or act upon the properties of the class. Because Helper methods always use the private access specifier, they do not form part of the user interface (API) for the class. Instead, they serve to reduce the coding burden on you, the programmer of the class. Helper methods are often used for validation purposes. Checking and validating data, like the format of phone and Social Security numbers, is a task often given to Helper methods.

General methods, however, are often used to derive new data from the property data. For example, an inventory class might have a property that records the quantity of an item sold. There might be a General method that takes the quantity sold and multiplies it by a price per item to produce a total purchase amount. A General method for the class might be called getTotalCost(). Another General method named getShippingCost() might use the weight per unit and the quantity sold to calculate the shipping charges. Yet another method named getSalesTaxDue() might calculate the sales tax for the order, and so on.

Cohesion

The important thing to notice about each of these General methods is that each one is geared to a specific and narrowly defined task. These narrowly designed tasks illustrate the concept of *cohesion*. This term refers to the ability to describe what a method does in one or two sentences. If it takes more that a couple of sentences to define its purpose, chances are it is not a cohesive method. A cohesive method does a single task and you should be able to describe its purpose crisply and concisely. If you can't, it's back to the drawing board to rethink the method's design.

Beginning programmers often try to create Swiss Army knives by designing a method that performs multiple tasks. This is usually a bad idea for two reasons. First, methods that attempt to multitask complicate the code. Several simple methods that perform one task each are simpler to write, test, debug, and maintain than one method that tries to multitask. Second, single-task methods have a higher chance of being reused than a complex method that attempts to solve multiple problems at once. The more tasks you try to pack into a single method, the less likely it is that that precise sequence of tasks can be reused in some other program.

Keep your methods crisp, clean, short, and geared to a single task.

Coupling

Coupling refers to the degree of dependency between data elements in a program. *Method coupling* refers to the ability to make code changes in one method without forcing changes in another. The goal is to have zero coupling between methods. That is, changing the code in one method should not force you to change code in another method. Obviously, the smaller the degree of method coupling, the greater the likelihood that you can reuse that method in another program, as its functionality is less dependent on other methods.

Sometimes coupling introduces sequencing issues, too. For example, if you wish to open a disk file for writing data, you must first make sure the file exists or create a new file if it doesn't. Clearly, you need to open the file, write the data to the file, and then close the file. The sequencing might seem to suggest that one method should be used to open, write, and close a disk file. Such a design is bad on two levels. First, the design is not cohesive because it is multitasking. Second, this is coupling to the highest degree because what should be three separate steps are instead rolled into a single method. Because errors can occur at each step along the way, it makes more sense to decouple these tasks and write three methods to attack all three. The code will be simpler and easier to maintain, plus you'll be able to pass back more meaningful error states to the user of the class if one of the methods fails to perform its specific task.

The goal is simple: write simple methods geared to one task and write them so they operate independently.

Class Design for Deck-of-Cards Program

Let's try our hand at a new program to incorporate some of the design elements I've been discussing in the last two chapters. Let's suppose you want to write a program that models shuffling a deck of cards.

Try It Out   Shuffle Cards

The program should simply display the shuffled deck of cards in a listbox object. Figure 10-1 shows a starting point of how you might construct the user interface for the program.

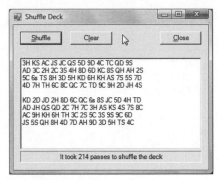

Figure 10-1

The figure shows what the output might look like after two clicks of the Shuffle button. Also note that a label object appears below the listbox to inform the user how many passes it took through the "shuffle loop" to produce a shuffled deck. (More on the shuffle loop in a minute.) Given that Figure 10-1 describes the way you want the user interface to look, how would you design and write the code? Equally important, where do you start the design process?

How It Works

As is almost always the case, you could write the code and stuff it all into frmMain and be done with it. However, is there a chance that at some time in the future you might write a game program that needs a deck of cards? A related question to ask is how much more difficult writing the program would be if you wrote a class to simulate a deck of cards instead of jamming all the code into frmMain. The answer is that there is virtually no appreciable cost to separating the administration of the program from the simulation of the deck of cards.

The program is sufficiently simple that you can keep all but the Process Step (of the Five Program Steps) in frmMain. The Process Step, however, should be the domain of a class that simulates the behavior of a deck of cards.

UML Class Diagram

Figure 10-2 shows our first attempt in designing our card deck class. I've used the UML notation discussed in Chapter 9 to construct the UML class diagram shown in Figure 10-2. You can examine the symbolic constants and properties of the class first.

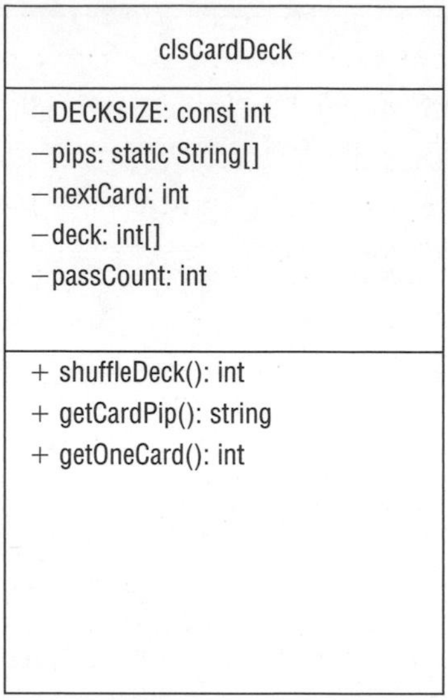

```
                  clsCardDeck

  −DECKSIZE: const int
  −pips: static String[]
  −nextCard: int
  −deck: int[]
  −passCount: int


  + shuffleDeck(): int
  + getCardPip(): string
  + getOneCard(): int
```

Figure 10-2

The first thing to note is that all the properties are prefixed by a minus sign, which means they use the `private` access specifier. Because the properties are not directly visible outside the class, they are not part of its user interface. The second thing to note is that all the methods use the `public` access specifier. Therefore, you know at a glance that all three methods are part of the user interface for the class.

As you can see in Figure 10-2, the property methods are not shown as part of our UML Light class depiction. Those methods are omitted for two reasons. First, property methods always use the `public` access specifier. This also means that *property methods* always form a part of the public user interface for the class. Second, because the property methods align one to one with the properties themselves, it seems redundant to make them part of the UML class diagram.

Good class design almost always makes the properties of the class `private`, but lets the outside world have access to them through their associated property methods. Using this design approach gives you control over what values can be properly assigned into any given property.

Class Constants and Properties

In the UML class diagram shown in Figure 10-2, the symbolic constant `DECKSIZE` represents the number of cards in the deck. While most games use 52 cards in a deck, there are games that don't (such as euchre and canasta). The `pips` variable is a `string` array that holds a non-graphic representation of each card. As you can see in Figure 10-1, the first entry, `3H`, represents the three of hearts, `KS` the king of spades, and so on.

Why is the `pips` array defined with the `static` storage class? The reason is that the contents of the array can be shared regardless of how many objects of `clsCardDeck` are instantiated. Indeed, if you wanted to, you could make this array a `const`, because its state never changes.

The `nextCard` variable serves as an index into the card deck. If `DECKSIZE` is 52, when `nextCard` reaches the value 52 the interpretation is that all cards have been dealt from the deck. This allows the class to track where it is in the deck. Also, if `nextCard` has the value `DECKSIZE`, it's time to shuffle the deck.

The variable `deck` is an integer array and represents the deck of cards. One of the design considerations I discussed earlier is that you should design a class in a way that reflects how a user thinks about the properties and methods of the class. Once again, most people do not think of a zero-based deck of cards. To a user, the first card in the deck is card number one, not card number zero. Therefore, you should set the dimension of the deck to `DECKSIZE + 1`. This allows the largest index for the `deck` array to match the user's ones-based perception of the deck of cards. That is, if the deck size is 52, making the dimension 53 lets us present the valid indexes for `deck` as the set 1 through 52. (It's that pesky $N - 1$ Rule again.)

Finally, `passCount` is an integer variable that stores the number of passes made through the loop that is used to shuffle the deck. While this variable is probably not needed for any card game you might write, it does give you some information about the shuffling algorithm used to shuffle the deck and may be useful for debugging purposes.

Class Methods

Figure 10-2 shows that there are only three General methods in the class. (You know they are General methods because they are all defined with the `public` (+) access specifier. If they were Helper methods, they would have to be defined with the `private` (–) access specifier. While `Property` methods are also `public`, they are only concerned with getting or setting a property.) Because the methods are General methods, they become part of the user interface for the class.

As suggested in Chapter 9, method names should be action- or verb-based. If you have selected the method names well, they should reflect the tasks the methods are designed to accomplish. The methods `shuffleDeck()` and `getOneCard()` should be self-explanatory. The method `getCardPip()` is a little unusual and needs some explanation.

getCardPip()

As mentioned earlier, our design uses two-letter abbreviations for the cards in the deck (3H, KS, and so on). These abbreviations are defined in the `static` array named `pip`. The definition of this array is

```
      private static string[] pips = {"",
"AS","2S","3S","4S","5S","6s","7S","8S","9S","TS","JS","QS","KS",
"AH","2H","3H","4H","5H","6H","7H","8H","9H","TH","JH","QH","KH",
"AD","2D","3D","4D","5D","6D","7D","8D","9D","TD","JD","QD","KD",
"AC","2C","3C","4C","5C","6C","7C","8C","9C","TC","JC","QC","KC"
                         };
```

If you look at the organization of the array, you can see that `pips[1]` is AS, and that `pips[14]` is AH; `pips[27]` is AD, and `pips[40]` is AC. What may be less obvious is that is that if you take the index into the `pips` array divided by the number of cards in each suit (13), the remainder is that suit's card. That is, 1 % 13 = 1, 14 % 13 = 1, 27 % 13 = 1, and 40 % 13 = 1. Therefore, anytime the index modulus 13 is 1, you know you are looking at the ace of some suit. You can determine which suit by looking at the quotient when the index is divided by four (the number of suits). For example, 2C has an index of 41. Dividing that index by 13 yields a quotient of 3, which you can interpret as the clubs suit. It doesn't take too much thought to realize that values 2 through 10 represent those cards for each suit, and values

11 through 13 are the face cards. (The king of each suit has a modulus of 0 and forms a special case that needs to be checked.) Okay . . . so what?

Recall from our design discussion that you don't want to select a class method name that tells the user anything about the implementation details used in the method. However, suppose you want to use the clsCardDeck class to write a card game. Chances are, you're going to need to know the structure that produces the relationship between each card and its suit to make the card game work. Providing the getCardPip() method allows the user to "dump" the card deck and examine its structure. For example, the following loop helps to reveal to the user the organization of the data used to implement the deck:

```
clsCardDeck myDeck = new clsCardDeck();

for (int j = 0; j <= myDeck.DeckSize; j++)
{
     lstCard.Items.Add(myDeck.getCardPip(j));
}
```

In a real sense, therefore, the method named getCardPip() is a Helper method, but written for the user rather than yourself. Simply stated, this method is a debugging aid for the user of clsCardDeck.

Making the method part of the user interface allows the user to have access to data structure specifics that makes her coding tasks easier. I provide this method because I know that the user may need this information in order to implement her card game. Also, with this structure and knowing that she needs the information it provides, I ease her programming burden by doing away with a trial-and-error approach to figuring out the deck's organization.

Now that we have the design done, let's implement the code and see how all the pieces fit together. First, let's examine how the end-user interface is written.

The frmMain Code

Listing 10-5 presents the code that exercises clsCardDeck.

Listing 10-5

```
using System;
using System.Windows.Forms;

public class frmMain : Form
{
    private Button btnShuffle;
    private Button btnClose;
    private Label lblPassCounter;
    private Button btnClear;
    private ListBox lstDeck;

    #region Windows code

    public frmMain()
    {
        InitializeComponent();
    }
```

```
public static void Main()
{
    frmMain main = new frmMain();
    Application.Run(main);
}

private void btnShuffle_Click(object sender, EventArgs e)
{
    int j;
    int cardIndex;
    int deckSize;
    int passes;
    string buff;
    string temp;
    clsCardDeck myDeck = new clsCardDeck();

    passes = myDeck.ShuffleDeck();
    lblPassCounter.Text = "It took " + passes.ToString() +
                          " passes to shuffle the deck";

    deckSize = myDeck.DeckSize;

    for (cardIndex = 1; cardIndex < deckSize + 1; )
    {
        buff = "";
        for (j = 0; j < 13; j++)    // Show 13 cards per line
        {
            temp = myDeck.getOneCard(cardIndex);
            if (temp.Length == 0)
            {
                MessageBox.Show("Error reading deck.",
                                "Processing Error");
                return;
            }
            buff += temp + " ";
            cardIndex++;
        }
        lstDeck.Items.Add(buff);
    }
    lstDeck.Items.Add(" ");      // Add an empty line

}

private void btnClose_Click(object sender, EventArgs e)
{
    Close();
}

private void btnClear_Click(object sender, EventArgs e)
{
    lstDeck.Items.Clear();
}
}
```

As usual, all the action takes place in the btnShuffle_Click() method. The code defines a clsCardDeck object named myDeck and then calls the ShuffleDeck() method to shuffle the deck. The variable passCount is assigned the number of passes the code had to make to complete the shuffle. This information is displayed in the lblPassCounter object.

The statement

```
deckSize = myDeck.DeckSize;
```

is using the DeckSize property method to determine how many cards are in the deck. The return value from the property method is used to control the for loop that is responsible for displaying the deck.

A nested for loop actually displays the cards.

```
for (cardIndex = 1; cardIndex < deckSize + 1; )
{
    buff = "";
    for (j = 0; j < 13; j++)     // Show 13 cards per line
    {
        temp = myDeck.getOneCard(cardIndex);
        if (temp.Length == 0)
        {
            MessageBox.Show("Error reading deck.",
                            "Processing Error");
            return;
        }
        buff += temp + " ";
        cardIndex++;
    }
    lstDeck.Items.Add(buff);
}
```

The outer for loop is controlled by the variable named cardIndex. Note how it is initialized to 1 in the first expression of the for loop. The second expression in the outer for loop simply suggests that all the cards in the deck are shown. The third expression in the outer for loop . . . doesn't exist! What?

While we could have done away with the inner for loop, we elected to display the cards in a format that has 13 cards per row in the listbox object. Therefore, the code simply calls the getOneCard() method 13 times in the inner j loop, concatenating each card's pip representation to the string variable named buff. Note, however, that the code needs to increment cardIndex on each pass through the inner j loop to fetch the next card. Because the increment of cardIndex must be done within the inner j loop, the increment operation normally found in the third expression of the outer for loop is omitted.

After the inner j loop reads 13 cards from the deck, buff contains a string representation of those 13 cards. The last statement in the outer loop adds the row of cards to the listbox object using the Add() method. With a standard deck of cards, four rows are displayed and the program run is complete.

The clsCardDeck Code

The code for clsCardDeck is shown in Listing 10-6.

Listing 10-6

```
using System;

class clsCardDeck
{
    // =============== symbolic constants ==================
    private const int DECKSIZE = 52;   // The number of cards in the deck

    // =============== static members =====================
    private static string[] pips = {"",
"AS","2S","3S","4S","5S","6s","7S","8S","9S","TS","JS","QS","KS",
"AH","2H","3H","4H","5H","6H","7H","8H","9H","TH","JH","QH","KH",
"AD","2D","3D","4D","5D","6D","7D","8D","9D","TD","JD","QD","KD",
"AC","2C","3C","4C","5C","6C","7C","8C","9C","TC","JC","QC","KC"
                                     };

    // =============== instance members ===================
    private int nextCard;         // The next card to be dealth from deck
    private int[] deck = new int[DECKSIZE + 1];   // The deck of cards.
    private int passCount;        // To count loop passes to shuffle deck

    // =============== constructor(s) =====================
    public clsCardDeck()
    {
        nextCard = 1;
    }

    // =============== property methods ====================
    public int DeckSize
    {
        get
        {
            return DECKSIZE;   // How many cards in the deck
        }
    }

    public int NextCard
    {
        get
        {
            return nextCard;
        }
        set
        {
            if (value > 0 && value <= deck.Length)
            {
                nextCard = value;
            }
        }
    }
```

(continued)

Listing 10-6 (continued)

```
public int PassCount
{
    get
    {
        return passCount;
    }
}
// ============== helper methods =======================

// ============== general methods =======================
/**
* Purpose: Shuffle the deck
*
* Parameter list:
*       N/A
* Return value:
*       int      number of passes to shuffle the deck
*/
public int ShuffleDeck()
{
    int index;
    int val;
    Random rnd = new Random();

    passCount = 0; // Count how many times through the while loop
    index = 1;
    Array.Clear(deck, 0, deck.Length);  // Initialize array to 0's

    while (index < deck.Length)
    {   // Add 1 to offset 0-based arrays
        val = rnd.Next(DECKSIZE) + 1;   // Generate values 1 - 52
        if (deck[val] == 0)
        {              // Is this card place in the deck is "unused"?
            deck[val] = index;       // Yep, so assign it a card place
            index++;                 // Get ready for next card
        }
        passCount++;
    }
    nextCard = 1;                    // Prepare to deal the first card
    return passCount;
}

/**
* Purpose: Show a given card in the deck.
*
* Parameter list:
*       int          the index of the position where the card is found
* Return value:
*       string       the pip for the card, or empty on error
*/
public string getOneCard(int index)
```

```
    {
        if (index > 0 && index <= deck.Length && nextCard <= deck.Length)
        {
            nextCard++;
            return pips[deck[index]];
        }
        else
        {
            return "";        // Error
        }
    }


    /**
     * Purpose: Show the abbreviation used for a given card in the deck.
     *
     * Parameter list:
     *      index           an integer for the index position in the deck
     *
     * Return value:
     *      string          the pip for the card, or empty on error
     */
    public string getCardPip(int index)
    {
        if (index > 0 && index <= DECKSIZE)
        {
            return pips[index];
        }
        else
        {
            return "";        // Error
        }
    }
}
```

Let's examine each section of the class code. First, notice that when we created `clsCardDeck`, Visual Studio automatically enclosed the class within the project's namespace. I removed the namespace from the class, just as I did in Chapter 9.

Class Properties, Constructor, and Property Methods

The properties are defined exactly as they were in Figure 10-2. The constructor doesn't do anything other than set the value of `nextCard` to 1. I do this because the first card in the deck is treated as `deck[1]` rather than `deck[0]`. Because the constructor initializes class properties to 0 or `null`, as dictated by the property's type, I initialize `nextCard` explicitly to 1.

Notice that neither the `DECKSIZE` nor `passCount` property method has a `set` statement block. In essence, this makes these read-only properties, which means that nothing outside of `clsCardDeck` can change the size of the deck of cards or the variable that counts the number of passes made to shuffle the deck. As you design other classes, you will find that read-only properties make sense in some situations. For example, if you created a `clsCar` to simulate an automobile, you might want to make the odometer a read-only property. (In some states, if you had a setter for the odometer property, you might find yourself a guest of the state in one of their jails!)

Class General Methods

As you gain more programming experience, you'll often find that a class design evolves as you get further into a project. Gone are the old days of BDUF (Big Design Up Front) program design whereby months were spent creating a design that went up in smoke in less than a week once the project began. Agile modeling, whereby the program evolves through as series of small design steps, seems to better capture the way software is developed.

In clsCardDeck, your design provides for only three General methods. The codes for getOneCard() and getCardPip() are straightforward and you should have no difficulty explaining what they do and how they do it. The way ShuffleDeck() works, however, would benefit from some explanation.

The ShuffleDeck() General Method

There are likely dozens of different ways in which you can simulate the process of shuffling a deck of cards. The method implemented here is based on the following algorithm:

1. Initialize a card counter variable to 0.

2. Generate a random integer number that falls within the range of 1 to DECKSIZE, inclusively.

3. Use that random number as an index into the card deck array and examine that element of the array.

4. If the indexed element of the deck array has the value 0, it is unassigned, so it is safe to assign the index number into that element of the array and increment the card counter by one.

5. If the indexed element of the deck array is not 0, that element of the array has already been used.

6. If the card counter is less than DECKSIZE, repeat Step 2.

The implementation of the algorithm begins with the definition of a number of working variables. The statement

```
Random rnd = new Random();
```

uses Visual Studio's Random class to define an object named rnd. The Next() method of the Random class is used inside the while loop with the following syntax:

```
val = rnd.Next(DECKSIZE) + 1;   // Generate values 1 - 52
```

The method Next() is design to generate a series of pseudo-random numbers that fall within the range of 0 to DECKSIZE. Assuming that DECKSIZE is 52, this means that Next() produces random numbers that fall within the range of 0 to 52. Note that the set of values generated by Next() spans the domain from 0 to — but *not* including — 52. However, because of the way that you have defined the pips array, you need the domain to be from 1 to 53, inclusively. You can generate that domain of values if you add 1 to each random number produced by the Next() method. In the statement above, val has the potential to store the values 1 through 53 . . . exactly what we need.

In Chapter 8 you learned that the statement

```
Array.Clear(deck, 0, deck.Length);   // Initialize array to 0's
```

uses the `Clear()` method of the `Array` class to initialize all elements in the `deck` array to 0. Now let's see how our algorithm works.

The Implementation of the Shuffle Algorithm

The code for the program loop seen in Listing 10-6 is repeated here:

```
while (index < deck.Length)  // Add 1 to offset 0-based arrays
{
    val = rnd.Next(DECKSIZE) + 1;   // Generate values 1 - 52
    if (deck[val] == 0)
    {              // Is this card place in the deck is "unused"?
        deck[val] = index;     // Yep, so assign it a place
        index++;               // Get ready for next card
    }
    passCount++;
}
```

At the start of the `while` loop, the deck array looks like Figure 10-3. The figure shows that none of the elements has been assigned a value. That is, each empty element depicted in Figure 10-3 has the value 0 in it.

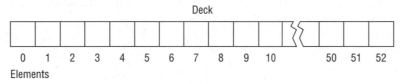

Deck

0 1 2 3 4 5 6 7 8 9 10   50 51 52

Elements

Figure 10-3

To understand what is happening, assume that program control has entered the `while` loop and the first random number assigned into `val` is 5. The `if` statement checks to see if element `deck[5]` is 0. Because this is the first pass through the loop, `deck[5]` is "empty" (that is, its value is 0), so we assign the value of `index` into the fifth element of the array. Because the variable `index` has been initialized to 1, the `deck` array now looks like what you see in Figure 10-4.

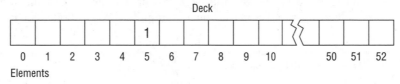

Deck

0 1 2 3 4 5 6 7 8 9 10   50 51 52

Elements

Figure 10-4

If you look at the `pips` array discussed earlier, you should be able to figure out that the fifth card in the deck is now the ace of spades. After the assignment of `index` into the `deck[val]` element of the array, `index` is incremented. Because `index` is less than the size of the element count of the array (in this case 53), another pass is made through the loop.

On this second pass through the loop, let's assume the next random number is 51. Because element 51 is 0 (that is, "empty"), the `if` statement assigns the value 2 into `deck[51]`. You now know that the two of spades is the second-to-last card in the deck. The state of the card deck at this point is shown in Figure 10-5.

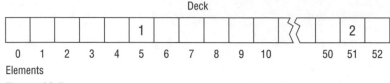

Figure 10-5

On each pass through the loop the code attempts to assign the current value of `index` into an empty element of the `deck` array using `val` as its index. If you think about it, as the arrays fill up, it gets harder and harder to find an empty array element. This is why it may take several hundred passes through the loop to fill up the array with the random card values. The variable `passCount` maintains a count of how many times the loop is executed before the `deck` array is filled. Usually the `deck` array is filled in less than 300 passes through the loop. While there are more efficient card shuffling algorithms out there, the simplicity of the code and its reasonable speed make this version acceptable for our purposes.

When the loop finishes filling the deck array, `nextCard` is assigned the value of 1 and the value of `passCount` is passed back to the caller in Listing 10-6.

If you set a breakpoint on the following statement:

```
temp = myDeck.getOneCard(cardIndex);
```

in the nested `for` loops back in `frmMain` (Listing 10-5) and step into the `getOneCard()` method using the F11 key, you can see how the cards are added to the listbox object. Once again, single-stepping through a program is a great way to understand how it actually works.

Designing a Card Game Using clsCardDeck

Now that you have a class that is capable of shuffling a deck of cards and dealing them out one at a time, let's design a very simple card game. The card game is a simplification of one called "In Between."

Try It Out   **In Between Card Game**

Our variation of this game begins with the dealer (the computer) giving you a hundred dollars to wager. The dealer then deals two cards face up. You may wager nothing on a game, or you may wager up to all of the credit you have. If you don't want to bet, simply click the Deal button again to deal another set of cards. If you make a wager, the dealer deals the next card. If that card falls within the range formed by the other two cards, you win an amount equal to your wager. Your winnings are automatically added to your balance. If the third card falls outside the range of the first two cards, the dealer wins and your balance is reduced by the amount of your wager. If the third card equals either of the two first cards, the dealer wins. Aces are considered to have the lowest value (one) in the deck and the king (13) the highest.

A sample run is shown in Figure 10-6.

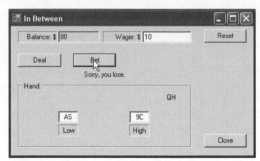

Figure 10-6

For example, if the first two cards are AS and 9H and the third card is QH, the player loses because the third card (a queen, or 12) falls outside the range of 1 to 9. If the third card is an ace or a nine of any suit, the dealer wins because those cards form a tie and the dealer wins ties. If the third card is 5H the player wins because the five falls inside the range of 1 to 9.

Now that the rules have been stated, how would you design and implement the game? Aw, come on. Don't just continue reading. Take the time to draw up whatever class diagrams you think you'll need to make the game work. It's the only way you can really learn this stuff. Come back and start reading again after you've given the program design some real thought.

Design Considerations

If you think about it, games are actions governed by rules. Indeed, it is within the framework of rules that most games are played. Some require third parties to enforce the rules (such as a referee in football) while others may operate with self-enforcement (such as golf). Our card game has rules and it is your program that must enforce those rules. Given that viewpoint, where does our clsCardDeck come into the picture and how do you enforce the rules of the game?

What Kind of Architecture?

If you step back and look at the forest rather than just the trees, our game is similar to a client-server architecture found in many database applications. The client is the player and the server is clsCardDeck, which "serves" cards to play the game. Simple client-server architectures are often called *two-tiered architectures* because the design contains two active elements. However, because there are rules to the game, you need to introduce an intermediary into the program to ensure that the rules of the game are enforced. We can draw this design for the game as shown in Figure 10-7.

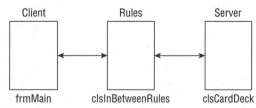

Figure 10-7

In Figure 10-7, we have inserted a class named `clsInBetweenRules` between the client (`frmMain`) and the server (`clsCardDeck`). Because we have introduced another tier over the standard two-tier architecture, the design in Figure 10-7 is a *three-tier architecture*. (Sometimes programmers simply call anything above a two-tier architecture an *N-tier architecture*. We'll stick with the term *three-tier* since it is a little more descriptive.)

Sideways Refinement

Previously we discussed using UML class diagrams to serve as a starting point in the program's design. An alternative and less formal design approach is what I call *Sideways Refinement.* In a nutshell, with Sideways Refinement you list the Five Program Steps on the left side of a piece of paper. Then you write to the right of each Program Step those tasks that each element of the program must address. For example, the following shows the various steps, the tasks to be performed, and where in the architecture they might be addressed:

1. Initialization ⇨   Build and display the form (`frmMain`)

2. Input ⇨   Ask for new cards (`frmMain`)

            Get amount of wager (`frmMain`)

            Ask for bet (`frmMain`)

3. Process ⇨   Deal a hand (`rules`) ⇨   Enough cards left in deck (`clsCardDeck`)

                                          Shuffle (`clsCardDeck`)

                                          Get three cards (`clsCardDeck`)

                                          Figure winner (`clsCardDeck`)

            Adjust player balance (`rules`)

4. Display ⇨   Show two cards (`frmMain`)

            Show third card (`frmMain`)

5. Terminate ⇨   Close

A Sideways Refinement is much less formal than a UML class diagram, but it serves as a good starting point for a program design. (You can always follow a Sideways Refinement with the more formal UML class diagrams.) As I pointed out earlier, all but the Process Step is normally performed as part of the program with which the user interacts. For the programs you've written thus far, `frmMain` is the class that presents the user interface for the program.

The class that sets the rules for the game assumes the processing responsibilities. That is, the game assumes that there are enough cards to deal a hand. If there aren't, the deck needs to be shuffled. The rules then ask for three cards. While you could design the mechanics of the administration of the rules differently if you wish, I decided to determine the winner when the first two cards are requested. That is, when the game displays the two cards and asks the player if she wishes to bet, the third card is already waiting for display and the rules class knows if the player is a winner or not before the third card is displayed. As soon as the user clicks the Bet button, the third card is displayed and the player's game balance is adjusted accordingly.

Note that Sideways Refinement does not necessarily show the sequencing of the program. Rather, it is meant to show the responsibilities each class has in the program relative to the Five Program Steps.

How It Works

The code for the `frmMain` class is shown in Listing 10-7. The nature of the code should be familiar to you now. The variable named `position` needs some explanation, however. The form shown in Figure 10-6 has five labels set across the top of the `GroupBox` object that I've labeled `Hand`. Because those labels have no border or text in them, they are not visible. However, when the rules class determines the winner of the hand, it also determines where the third card is to be displayed in the `GroupBox` object. In Figure 10-6, because the Queen of Hearts (`QH`) is greater than the high card that was dealt (`9C`), `QH` is assigned to the `Text` property of fifth label object. Therefore, the `position` variable is simply used to give a display of the third card relative to the range of the first two cards.

Listing 10-7

```
using System;
using System.Windows.Forms;

public class frmMain : Form
{
    const int TIE = 0;
    const int PLAYERWINS = 1;
    const int DEALERWINS = 2;

    int betResult;
    int wager;
    int balance;
    int position;

    clsInBetweenRules myRules = new clsInBetweenRules();
    string[] cards = new string[3];

    private Button btnDeal;
    private Button btnClose;
    private Label label1;
    private TextBox txtWager;
    private TextBox txtBalance;
    private Label label2;
    private GroupBox groupBox1;
    private Label lblLow;
    private Label label4;
    private Label label3;
    private TextBox txtHi;
    private TextBox txtLow;
    private Label lblMore;
    private Label lblLess;
    private Label lblHi;
    private Label lblMiddle;
    private Button btnBet;
    private Label lblOutcome;
    private Button btnReset;
    #region Windows code

    public frmMain()
```

```csharp
{
    bool flag;
    InitializeComponent();

    txtBalance.Text = myRules.Balance.ToString();    // Grub stake
    txtWager.Text = myRules.Wager.ToString();        // Default bet $10
    flag = int.TryParse(txtBalance.Text, out balance);
    flag = int.TryParse(txtWager.Text, out wager);

    myRules.Shuffle();                               // Shuffle deck
}

public static void Main()
{
    frmMain main = new frmMain();
    Application.Run(main);
}

private void btnDeal_Click(object sender, EventArgs e)
{
    int retval;

    ClearRanges();              // Clear old data
    lblOutcome.Text = "";

    retval = myRules.Balance;    // Money left to bet??
    if (retval == 0)
    {
        MessageBox.Show("You're broke. Game over.");
        return;
    }

    retval = myRules.getCardsLeft();     // Enough cards left??
    if (retval < 3)
    {
        lblOutcome.Text = "Deck was shuffled . . . ";
        myRules.Shuffle();
    }
    myRules.DealHand(cards, ref betResult, ref position);
    ShowHiLow();
}

private void btnBet_Click(object sender, EventArgs e)
{
    bool flag = int.TryParse(txtWager.Text, out wager);
    if (flag == false)
    {
        MessageBox.Show("Dollar bets only. Re-enter.", "Input Error");
        txtWager.Focus();
        return;
    }

    switch (betResult)
```

```
        {
            case TIE:            // This is a tie
                lblOutcome.Text = "Tie. Dealer wins.";
                myRules.Balance -= wager;
                break;

            case PLAYERWINS:
                lblOutcome.Text = "You win!";
                myRules.Balance +=  wager;
                break;

            case DEALERWINS:
                lblOutcome.Text = "Sorry, you lose.";
                myRules.Balance -= wager;
                break;
        }
        txtBalance.Text = myRules.Balance.ToString();
        switch (position)
        {
            case 1:
                lblLess.Text = cards[2];
                break;
            case 2:
                lblLow.Text = cards[2];
                break;
            case 3:
                lblMiddle.Text = cards[2];
                break;
            case 4:
                lblHi.Text = cards[2];
                break;
            case 5:
                lblMore.Text = cards[2];
                break;
            default:
                MessageBox.Show("Results error.", "Processing Error");
                break;
        }
    }

    private void ShowHiLow()
    {
        txtLow.Text = cards[0];
        txtHi.Text = cards[1];
    }

    private void ClearRanges()
    {
        lblLess.Text ="";
        lblLow.Text = "";
        lblMiddle.Text = "";
        lblHi.Text = "";
        lblMore.Text = "";
    }
```

```
        private void btnReset_Click(object sender, EventArgs e)
        {
            myRules.Balance = 100;
            txtBalance.Text = "100";
            txtWager.Text = "10";
            ClearRanges();
        }
        private void btnClose_Click(object sender, EventArgs e)
        {
            Close();
        }
    }
}
```

The code in the constructor simply initializes the textbox objects for play. When the user clicks the Deal button object, several method calls to the `clsInBetweenRules` class are made. The first checks to see if the player has any credit left with which to play the game. If the player is broke, the game cannot continue. The user can click the Reset button to reset her beginning balance. If the player has a balance, the program checks to see if there are enough cards left to play a hand. If not, the player sees a message stating that the deck was shuffled and the game continues. Finally, the hand is dealt and the two cards are shown to the dealer. If you look at the way the code works, the outcome of the bet is already known at this point. The outcome of the hand is simply a matter of whether the player clicks the Bet button or not.

Using the ref Keyword

If the player does decide to play, the `btnBet_Click()` code determines how things are displayed to the user. When the hand was "dealt" by the call to

```
        myRules.DealHand(cards, ref betResult, ref position);
```

the variable `betResult` determines who won the bet and the variable `position` determines where among the five labels the third card is displayed, as explained earlier. The variable `cards` is an array filled in with the three cards for the hand being played. Because C# methods can return only a single value, you cannot use a simple `return` statement within the method to return all the information you need from the call. Instead, you pass the `cards` array to the method along with the `betResult` and `position` variables. However, because the keyword `ref` appears before the two variables in the call, C# knows not to send each variable's rvalue to the method, but sends the lvalue instead. Any time the `ref` keyword prefixes a variable name in a method call, the lvalue of the variable is passed to the method. Recall that arguments sent to methods pass a copy of the variable's rvalue to a method by default. However, when the `ref` keyword is used the lvalue of the variable is sent to the method. Because an lvalue tells the method where the variable "lives" in memory, the method can permanently change the value of the variable. Our code uses this mechanism to permanently change the values of `betResult` and `position`. The two `switch` statements in the `btnBet_Click()` method use these two variables to inform the player of the outcome of her bet.

Listing 10-8 shows the code for the `clsInBetweenRules` class.

Listing 10-8

```
using System;


class clsInBetweenRules
{
    // ============== symbolic constants ==================
    const int TIE = 0;
    const int PLAYERWINS = 1;
    const int DEALERWINS = 2;


    // ============== static members =====================
    // ============== instance members =====================
    private int balance;        // The player's money balance
    private int wager;          // Amount of current bet
    private int lowCard;        // The low card value 1 - 13
    private int lowCardIndex;   // The position of this card in pips
    private int hiCard;         // The high card value 1 - 13
    private int hiCardIndex;    // The position of this card in pips
    private int dealtCard;      // The dealt card value 1 - 13
    private int dealtCardIndex; // The position of this card in pips


    private clsCardDeck myDeck; // A card deck object


    // ============== constructor(s) =====================
    public clsInBetweenRules()
    {
        balance = 100;
        wager = 10;
        myDeck = new clsCardDeck();
    }
    // ============== property methods =====================
    public int Balance
    {
        get
        {
            return balance;
        }
        set
        {
            if (value >= 0)
            {
                balance = value;
            }
        }
    }

    public int Wager
```

(continued)

Listing 10-8 (continued)

```
    {
        get
        {
            return wager;
        }
        set
        {
            if (value > 0)
            {
                wager = value;
            }
        }
    }
}


    // =============== helper methods =========================

    /*****
     * Purpose: Deals out the next three cards and fills in the hand[]
     *          array that was passed in from frmMain. It always arranges
     *          cards so lower of first two cards is displayed on the
     *          left of frmMain.
     *
     * Parameter list:
     *   string[] hand          the three cards for a hand
     *
     * Return value:
     *   void
     *
     *   *****/
    private void SetCards(string[] hand)
    {
        int temp;

        hand[0] = myDeck.getCardPip(lowCardIndex);
        hand[1] = myDeck.getCardPip(hiCardIndex);
        hand[2] = myDeck.getCardPip(dealtCardIndex);

        if (lowCard == hiCard || lowCard < hiCard)       // A tie
        {
            hand[0] = myDeck.getCardPip(lowCardIndex);
            hand[1] = myDeck.getCardPip(hiCardIndex);
        }
        else
        {
            temp = hiCard;                // Swap hi and lo cards
            hiCard = lowCard;
            lowCard = temp;

            temp = hiCardIndex;       // Swap hi and lo indexes
            hiCardIndex = lowCardIndex;
            lowCardIndex = temp;
```

```
        hand[0] = myDeck.getCardPip(lowCardIndex);
        hand[1] = myDeck.getCardPip(hiCardIndex);
    }
}


/*****
 * Purpose: Sets the outcome of the bet and tells where to display the
 *          down card.
 *
 * Parameter list:
 *  ref int outCome      who won the game
 *  ref int position     where to display the down card
 *
 * Return value:
 *  void
 *
 * CAUTION: the two ints are passed in by reference, which means this
 *          method can permanently change their values.
 *  *****/
private void SetWinnerAndPosition(ref int outCome, ref int position)
{

    if (dealtCard == lowCard)    // Dealt and low card equal
    {
        outCome = DEALERWINS;
        position = 2;
        return;
    }
    if (dealtCard < lowCard)      // Dealt card less than low card
    {
        outCome = DEALERWINS;
        position = 1;
        return;
    }
    if (dealtCard > lowCard && dealtCard < hiCard) // Card in range
    {
        outCome = PLAYERWINS;
        position = 3;
        return;
    }

    if (dealtCard == hiCard) // Dealt card equals hi card
    {
        outCome = DEALERWINS;
        position = 4;
        return;
    }
    if (dealtCard > hiCard) // Dealt card equals hi card
    {
        outCome = DEALERWINS;
        position = 5;
        return;
    }
}
```

(continued)

Listing 10-8 (continued)

```
// ============== general methods =====================

/*****
 * Purpose: Gets the first card and treats it as first displayed card
 *
 * Parameter list:
 *  n/a
 *
 * Return value:
 *  void
 *
 * CAUTION: King is a special case since its modulus = 0
 *  *****/
public void getFirstCard()
{
    lowCardIndex = myDeck.getOneCard();
    lowCard = lowCardIndex % 13;
    if (lowCard == 0)                // A King
        lowCard = 13;
}

/*****
 * Purpose: Gets second card and treats it as second displayed card
 *
 * Parameter list:
 *  n/a
 *
 * Return value:
 *  void
 *
 * CAUTION: King is a special case since its modulus = 0
 *  *****/
public void getSecondCard()
{
    hiCardIndex = myDeck.getOneCard();
    hiCard = hiCardIndex % 13;
    if (hiCard == 0)                // A King
        hiCard = 13;
}
/*****
 * Purpose: Gets the last card and treats it as down card
 *
 * Parameter list:
 *  n/a
 *
 * Return value:
 *  void
 *
 * CAUTION: King is a special case since its modulus = 0
 *  *****/
public void getDealtCard()
```

```
{
    dealtCardIndex = myDeck.getOneCard();
    dealtCard = dealtCardIndex % 13;
    if (dealtCard == 0)                // A King
        dealtCard = 13;
}

/*****
 * Purpose: Shuffle the deck
 *
 * Parameter list:
 *   n/a
 *
 * Return value:
 *   void
 *
 *   *****/
public void Shuffle()
{
    myDeck.ShuffleDeck();
}

/*****
 * Purpose: Gets the number of cards left in the deck.
 *
 * Parameter list:
 *   n/a
 *
 * Return value:
 *   int              the number of cards left
 *
 * CAUTION: King is a special case since its modulus = 0
 *   *****/
public int getCardsLeft()
{
    return myDeck.getCardsLeftInDeck();
}

/*****
 * Purpose: Deals out a hand. Note that all three cards are dealth at
 *          once, but the dealt card is not displayed until after the
 *          bet. The results are known before the bet, but not revealed
 *          now.
 *
 * Parameter list:
 *   string[] hand         the three cards for a hand
 *   ref int outCome       who won the game
 *   ref int position      where to display the down card
 *
 * Return value:
 *   void
 *
 * CAUTION: the two ints are passed in by reference, which means this
 *          method can permanently change their values.
```

(continued)

Listing 10-8 (continued)

```
 *   *****/
public void DealHand(string[] hand, ref int outCome, ref int position)
{
    getFirstCard();      // Get first two display cards
    getSecondCard();

    getDealtCard();      // Get down card

    SetCards(hand);      // Rearrange if necessary

                         // Who wins and where to display down card
    SetWinnerAndPosition(ref outCome, ref position);
}


}
```

One thing to notice in the code presented in Listings 10-7 and 10-8 is that `frmMain` knows nothing about `clsCardDeck` (that is, there is no coupling between the two classes). All interaction with the deck of cards is managed by the `clsInBetweenRules` class. This is as it should be. If the game were not played with this enforced isolation between the card deck and the player, it would be like allowing gamblers in Vegas to deal their own hands of blackjack . . . not going to happen!

To accommodate the requirements of the game, we added two new methods to the `clsCardDeck` class. These two methods are shown in Listing 10-9.

Listing 10-9

```
/**
 * Purpose: Get the index of a dealt card. This overloads the method
 *          that returns the string representation of the card.
 *
 * Parameter list:
 *      void
 *
 * Return value:
 *      int        the index into the pips array or 0 if no more cards
 *                 left in deck.
 */
public int getOneCard()
{
    nextCard++;
    if (nextCard <= DECKSIZE)
    {
        return deck[nextCard];
    }
    else
    {
        return 0;
    }
}
```

```
/**
 * Purpose: Returns the number of cards left in the deck.
 *
 * Parameter list:
 *       void
 *
 * Return value:
 *       int        A count of card remaining in the deck.
 */
public int getCardsLeftInDeck()
{
    return DECKSIZE - nextCard;
}
```

The getOneCard() method is designed to return the index of a card rather than its string representation. The getCardsLeftInDeck() method simply returns the number of cards left in the deck. Note how easy it was to make this change for the game at hand. If you think about it, most card games will likely need these methods too.

While this program involves more code than others you've studied, you should be able to follow what each method does. However, to really make sure you do understand what's going on in the code, study it and describe in your own mind what happens as the game is played. When you feel you understand the program flow, rerun the program with breakpoints and single-step through the code to see if your expectations match what actually happens. If they don't, you need to figure out why. This kind of exercise will help you develop your debugging skills . . . the subject of the next chapter.

Summary

In this chapter you learned why constructors exist and why it often makes sense to overload a default constructor. You also learned the details of property methods and how they are part of the user interface for a class. It is the set statement blocks of the property methods that serve as your last line of defense against having a class object put into an undesired state. You should also have a more complete appreciation of how the private access specifier for the class properties helps to safeguard the integrity of the data.

Someone once said, "Practice makes perfect." Well, not really. Perfect practice makes perfect. However, while perfection in writing classes may be your goal, a more reasonable objective right now is to get experience designing and writing classes for objects of your own creation. You are now familiar with the benefits of both UML class and Sideways Refinement design methods. Both are worthwhile tools to hang on your tool belt.

You should spend enough time to answer the exercises at the end of this chapter before moving on to Chapter 11. Having done the exercises, try to think up a few programming problems of your own design. Thinking about programming problems, designing a solution, and then implementing that solution is the *only* way to learn programming.

Exercises

1. Another game similar to the In Between game discussed in this chapter is called acey-deucey. This variant of the game is played exactly the same way, but the high card in the deck is an ace and a two becomes the lowest card. What would you do to implement this variation of the game instead of In Between?

2. If you made the changes suggested in Exercise 1, can you see any improvements that might make the code easier to understand?

3. The game of euchre uses a subset of a standard deck of cards. Specifically, only the nines, tens, jacks, queens, kings, and aces are used. If you wanted to write a program that plays euchre, what problems does clsCardDeck pose?

4. Give the problem stated in Exercise 3, how would you resolve the problem?

5. Modify the program shown in Figure 10-1 to display only those cards that apply to the game of euchre.

Exception Handling and Debugging

It would be wonderful if we didn't even have to write a chapter like this one, but the truth is that problems do arise when programs are developed and run. In this chapter you will learn about

- ❑ The differences among bugs, errors, and exceptions
- ❑ Syntax, semantic, and logic bugs
- ❑ Exception handling
- ❑ Throwing exceptions
- ❑ Using the debugger
- ❑ Debugging windows
- ❑ Bug detection, isolation, and correction

Most experienced programmers agree that approximately 20 percent of program development time consists of writing the program code. The remaining 80 percent is used for testing, debugging, and maintenance of that code. Clearly, anything you can do to reduce that 80 percent figure is going to help you keep on time and on budget.

Overview

It's pretty common for programmers to lump bugs, program errors, and program exceptions into a single concept. Technically, each of these types of errors is different. Let's consider each in a little more detail.

Bugs

A bug is a specific type of error caused by the programmer. Bugs typically fall into one of three general categories: 1) syntax errors, 2) semantic errors, and 3) logic errors.

Syntax Errors

A *syntax error* occurs when a statement does not comply with the rules of the language. Just as English has specific rules, so do programming languages. A sentence in English, for example, is expected to have a noun and a verb. A programming statement is similar to a sentence, and if you don't obey the rules, syntax errors result. A program that has a syntax error cannot be compiled.

Visual Studio's Intellisense does an excellent job of detecting syntax errors the instant you enter a program statement. The dreaded squiggly line tells you the nature of the syntax error that you've made. If you place the cursor over the squiggly line, Visual Studio presents a message informing you of the probable cause of the error. When you first started writing programs, they probably had a ton of squiggly lines in them. However, as you've gained experience with C#, the frequency of your syntax errors likely has decreased. If you're like most programmers, you've moved on to bigger and better errors!

Semantic Errors

Semantic errors occur when you have used the proper language syntax, but the context of the statement or expression is wrong. For example, you could say the following English sentence: "The dog meowed." The syntax is correct because the sentence has a noun and a verb, but the context of the noun and verb is wrong. A program with a semantic error can be compiled, but the results are (usually) wrong.

Consider the following statements:

```
int j;
int answer;

j = 10;
answer = 1 / j;
```

The code generates no error messages from Intellisense and it does compile. However, answer is always 0 for any value of j that is greater than 1. (The code, for example, does produce the correct result if j equals 1.) In this context, you are trying to create a fractional value using integer math. If you write the last statement above as

```
answer = 1.0 / j;
```

Intellisense issues an error message asking if you need to cast the expression. Intellisense can ferret out the proper context now because it knows that 1.0 is a floating-point value. Semantic errors are a little harder to uncover than syntax errors because Intellisense cannot always detect them.

Logic Errors

Logic errors exist when the program compiles, but produces an incorrect result. This makes them sound a lot like semantic errors, but there is a distinction. Semantic errors reflect a bending of the syntax rules of the language. Logic errors, on the other hand, are the result of design errors the programmer makes when manipulating a program's data. The distinction is subtle, but real.

As you gain programming experience, syntax and semantic errors tend to become less and less frequent. Instead, you will spend most of your time tracking down and correcting logic errors in the program. Every programmer makes logic errors and you should expect to make your fair share. The attitude to take is that fixing any kind of bug is a learning experience. It is one of the oddities of programming that the more mistakes you have under your belt, the better you become as a programmer.

Program Errors

In a strict sense, a program error is an error made by the user. Sadly, every end user is smart enough to know that he doesn't have to read the user's manual. It's sort of like guys who refuse to ask for directions when they're lost. Users refuse to admit that they don't know how to run a program. As a result, strange things can happen when the program is run.

How can you reduce program errors? The following programming concepts can help.

Data Validation

Perhaps the most common type of program error occurs when the user provides input into the program, but not input of the correct type. For example, the program might request the user to enter the number of units to purchase and the user might mean to type 10, but because of a fat finger types 1o instead. However, a good programmer anticipates such mistakes by adding validation code to a program. If you wish to validate that the user did correctly enter the quantity to be purchased, you can validate the input using the TryParse() method:

```
bool flag;
int quantity;
flag = int.TryParse(txtQuantity.Text, out quantity);
if (flag == false)              // Things didn't go well
{
     MessageBox.Show("Expected digit characters only. Re-enter.",
                     "Input Error");
     txtQuantity.Focus();
     return;
}
```

This is a common validation routine you've seen in previous programs.

Invalid input data is probably the most common source of program error. One reason this is true is that you cannot totally control what a user types into a textbox object. As a general rule, any time you ask for input from the user using a textbox object, you should validate the response. The general areas of validation include the following:

1. **Type checking:** This is where you would use code like TryParse() to make sure the input characters are consistent with the desired data type.

2. **Consistency checking:** This type of check frequently compares two or more responses to insure that the input data is consistent. For example, if a user states their gender as male and later states they are eight months pregnant, chances are they answered one of the input questions incorrectly.

3. **Range checking:** This check attempts to verify that the input data is reasonable by checking the input to see if it falls within a reason range of values. For example, if you ask for someone's age and get a response of 422, it's pretty likely that the user meant some other value. Your code should prompt the user to reenter the value.

4. **Length checking:** Often a response requires a specific number of characters as input. Common examples are two-character state abbreviations, zip codes, and phone and Social Security numbers. Sometimes simply checking the length of the user's input can detect errors that are missed by other checks.

The rule is pretty simple: assume the user's input is *always* incorrect.

Limit User Input

You've doubtless run programs in which you've made a choice from a given list. Common input techniques are to present you with a list of options in the form of a listbox or combination box object. While you may see this approach as a convenience provided by the programmer, the driving force was not your convenience, but rather a desire to restrict your choice to the options in the list.

Programmers know users can screw up program input. By presenting you with a limited list of options rather than letting you type something into a textbox, the programmer is limiting you to input that is at least consistent with the expected data. True, the user can still select the wrong option, but at least the answer is consistent with the processing that's to follow. For example, you could present a textbox with a label that reads: "Enter Gender (M, F)". Clearly, you are expecting a M or F to be entered by the user. However, you've given the user at least 24 chances to mess things up (and that's assuming that she gets the case correct.)

Radio Buttons

A better choice would be to use radio buttons. Figure 11-1 shows a simple program that exercises several input objects that can be used to force users into more consistent program input.

Figure 11-1

The program shown seems to suggest that the user should select either Male or Female and then select either Senior or Junior. Unfortunately, that's not the way the code works. As the form is currently laid out, if the user clicks on the Male radio button, a small dot appears in that selection (see Figure 11-1). Having made that selection, the user then moves onto the next input and clicks on Senior, which causes a small dot to appear in that selection. The bad news is that the selection of Male disappears, which is probably not what the programmer had in mind.

The problem is that radio buttons objects are associated with mutually exclusive choices. The program views all the radio buttons on the form as belonging to the same set of options. Therefore, selecting one option turns all the rest of the buttons off. This is precisely the behavior expected from radio button objects, but not what the programmer expected. So how do you fix the problem?

Group Box

The solution is simple: place each group of related radio button choices in its own GroupBox object. To add a GroupBox object to a form, select the Containers option in the Toolbox and drag a GroupBox object onto the form. Change the Text property of the object to Gender:. Now drag a second GroupBox object onto the form and make its Text property read Membership group: Now, while holding down the Shift key, click the Male and Female radio buttons. Now press Ctrl+X to cut those two radio buttons from the form. Click in the GroupBox to which you applied the Gender text and press Ctrl+V. The two radio buttons should now be copied inside the GroupBox with the Gender: heading. Repeat for the Membership radio buttons. Your form should now look like the one in Figure 11-2.

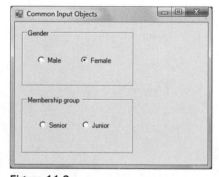

Figure 11-2

As you can see in Figure 11-2, the GroupBox arranges the radio buttons in two groups, each of which can have its appropriate choice. (You can tell this is the case because both Male and Senior are selected.)

The code for processing radio button choices is essentially as follows:

```
int choice;

if (rbMale.Checked == true)
{
    choice = MALE;
}
else
{
    choice = FEMALE;
}
```

275

(I use `rb` as a prefix for radio buttons, which is a break from my normal three-character prefixes for Toolbox objects. The reason for a two-character prefix is . . . I don't have a reason. It just seems to make sense to me. If this bothers you, try `rbt` or `rbn`.) A radio button object has a `Checked` property that is logic `True` if the button is selected and logic `False` if it is not. (The program assumes that symbolic constants for `MALE` and `FEMALE` have been defined elsewhere in the program.) If the list of choices is greater than two, you can use nested `if` statements to process the selection.

Default Choices

Quite often you'll want to have a default choice for a series of radio buttons. It makes sense to have the default choice be the expected choice for most users. If you expect most users to be female, you can add the following code to the form's constructor:

```
public frmMain()
{
    InitializeComponent();
    rbFemale.Checked = true;
}
```

The `InitializeComponents()` method is used to build a memory image of the form. When control returns from that method call, the complete form object has been built in memory. If you wish to change the default state of that form object, the constructor is the place to do it. When the form is displayed, it has the Female option selected.

Check Boxes

Another way to restrict the input from a user is to employ `CheckBox` objects. Figure 11-3 shows an example of `CheckBox` objects.

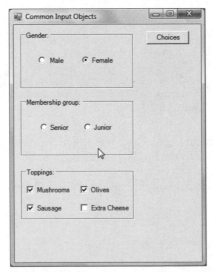

Figure 11-3

Unlike radio buttons, checkbox selections are not mutually exclusive. The user is free to check as many as he feels are appropriate. The GroupBox object that holds the CheckBox objects in Figure 11-3 is not required. However, it is not uncommon for the range of options depicted by the checkboxes to apply to some overriding choice. If that is the case, using a GroupBox helps to focus the user's attention on those choices.

Because each checkbox object can be selected, your code needs to examine the state of each one. One way to do this would be to use code similar to the following (I tend to use ckb as a prefix for checkbox objects):

```
Array.Clear(toppings, 0, toppings.Length);

if (ckbMushroom.Checked == true)
{
    toppings[MUSHROOMS] = 1;
}

if (ckbOlives.Checked == true)
{
    toppings[OLIVES] = 1;
}

if (ckbSausage.Checked == true)
{
    toppings[SAUSAGE] = 1;
}

if (ckbExtraCheese.Checked == true)
{
    toppings[EXTRACHEESE] = 1;
}
```

The code uses the Clear() method of the Array class to initialize all elements of the array to 0. Then a series of if statements records the choices made by the user. Again, symbolic constants are used to help document the choices and make subsequent processing easier for the programmer to understand. You could, of course, use a discrete variable for each topping choice. However, an array makes sense here because the choices all pertain to a single entity and an array will likely simplify subsequent code. If you wish to set a default set of choices, you can set the desired checkboxes' Checked properties to true in the constructor.

Combination Boxes

Combination boxes, or *combo boxes*, are similar to list boxes except that the user can also type in a response if she wishes. Normally, however, the user selects an option from the list presented in the combo box object. Figure 11-4 shows a typical use for a combo box.

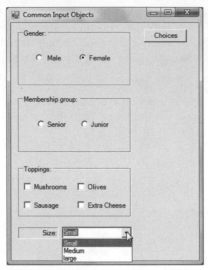

Figure 11-4

As you can see in Figure 11-4, combo boxes are similar to listboxes. Because of this, you can initialize the list in the combo box either by using the Property window in design mode or by setting the list under program control. Figure 11-5 shows how you can use the `Items` property from the Property window to add items to the list.

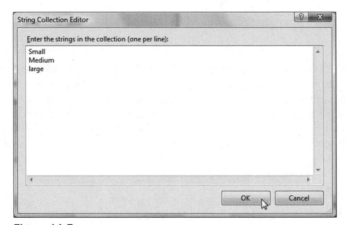

Figure 11-5

Using the `Items` property in the Property window presumably means that you know the list of items that you wish to place in the combo box before the program is run. However, in many cases you will want to populate the combo with a list that is determined at runtime rather than at compile time. For example, you might be reading a list of names from a database and wish to place a subset of those names in a combo box from which the user will choose a specific name. To create the list shown in Figure 11-5, you could use the following code:

```
cmbSize.Items.Add("Small");
cmbSize.Items.Add("Medium");
cmbSize.Items.Add("Large");
```

If you have an array of names that you want to add to the combo box, you might use something like this:

```
int i;

// Assume names[] filled in here...

for (int i = 0; i < names.Length; i++)
{
    cmbPeople.Items.Add(names[i]);
}
cmbPeople.SelectedIndex = 0;
```

This code fragment simply adds the list of names stored in the names array to the combo box. The SelectedIndex property of the combo box determines which of the items added to the combo box is displayed as the default choice when the program is run. Because the list of items in the combo box is a zero-based list, the preceding code displays the first item in the list. You should set SelectedIndex to be the default item from the list. If you do not set the SelectedIndex property, the combo box is empty and looks similar to an empty textbox waiting for the user to type something into it. You can also retrieve the SelectedIndex property from the combo box.

Note that you can also have the object sort the contents of the list of items added to the combo box. Often this makes it easier for the user to locate which item she wishes to select from the list. Keep in mind, however, that sometimes the order in which the items are added to the combo box has an impact on subsequent code. For example, if the names array selection will be used later to index into the database for details about the person selected, that person's position in the names array may determine how to locate him in the database. In that case you would not want to set the Sorted property to true.

If you wish to retrieve the text from a combo box, use something like this:

```
string buff = cmbPeople.Text;
```

Combo Boxes with or Without User Input

If you wish, you can turn off the user's ability to type a value into the combo box by setting the DropDownStyle property to DropDownList in the Property window. This style makes the combo box a read-only object.

If you do wish to accept user input, then set the type to DropDown. This is the default style of behavior for a combo box.

Date and Time Input

Another common input is a date. Having the user enter a date is also a good way to get bogus input data because there are so many different date formats in use (military, European, and so on). The same confusion can arise for time, too, because time can be represented by a 12 or 24-hour clock.

You can standardize such information by using the `DateTimePicker` object. If you drag a `DateTimePicker` object onto a form and run the program, it will look similar to what is shown in Figure 11-6.

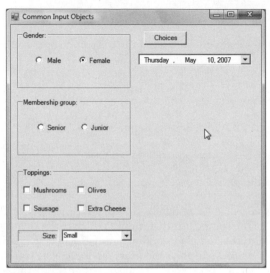

Figure 11-6

As you can see, the `DateTimePicker` object looks very similar to a combo box, but with a date in the `Text` property of the object. However, if you click the down arrow on the object, the output changes to look like that shown in Figure 11-7.

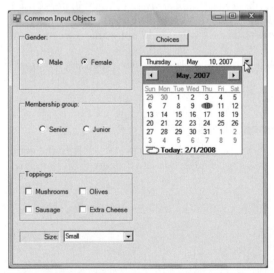

Figure 11-7

The Format and ShowUpDown Properties

The state of the object shown in Figure 11-7 assumes that the Format property of the object is set to Long and the ShowUpDown property is set to false. If you set the Format property to Short, the date would be shown as 5/10/2007.

Add a second DateTimePicker object to the form and set its ShowUpDown property to true. The form now looks like the one shown in Figure 11-8.

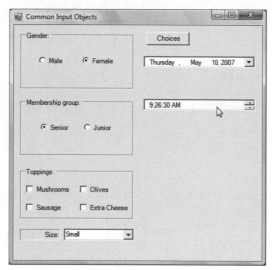

Figure 11-8

In the second DateTimePicker object, the user can use the spin controls at the end of the object to change the hour displayed in the Text property. The user can also type a time into the Text property should he choose to do so.

To extract the information from a DateTimePicker object, use the following code:

```
string date = dtpDate.Value.ToShortDateString();
string time = dtpTime.Value.ToShortTimeString();
```

You can select different date and time methods to alter the format of the data extracted from the DateTimePicker object to suit your needs. The statements above yield 5/10/2007 for date and 9:26 AM for time.

While the various objects discussed in this section can force the user to input program data in a specific format, things can (and do) still go wrong. With that in mind, let's examine some other techniques you can use to make your code more bulletproof.

Exception Handling

No matter how well you attempt to anticipate bad program input, the chance exists that something will slip through the cracks. When an error condition presents itself in a program, C# produces an exception. An *exception* is simply an undesired program state. Note that an exception really isn't a program bug. As I pointed out earlier, a bug is a programmer mistake and you must correct that yourself. Still, unexpected things can occur while the program runs even if there are no bugs in the program. For example, if you're writing a program that copies data to a CD and the user forgot to load a blank CD into the CD drive, the program generates an exception. The simple program shown in Listing 11-1 illustrates an exception.

Listing 11-1

```
using System;
using System.Windows.Forms;

public class frmMain : Form
{
    private Button btnCalc;

    #region Windows code

    public frmMain()
    {
        InitializeComponent();
    }

    public static void Main()
    {
        frmMain main = new frmMain();
        Application.Run(main);
    }

    private void btnCalc_Click(object sender, EventArgs e)
    {
        int exp1 = 0;
        int exp2 = 5;
        int result;

        result = exp2 / exp1;

    }
}
```

The program is just a standard C# form with a single button object on it. In the click event for the button object, note that exp1 is set to 0 and exp2 to 5. Dividing a value by zero produces a divide-by-zero exception. As it stands, if you run this program outside the Visual Studio environment, the program pops up the exception notification shown in Figure 11-9. (If you run the program within the Visual Studio environment, you'll get a similar message, but the precise statement where the exception occurred is highlighted.)

Figure 11-9

This is an ugly thing for the user to see! The message is telling everyone who sees it that the programmer didn't expect the program to reach this (divide-by-zero) state, but let it happen anyway. Not good.

How can you prevent such ugliness?

try-catch Statement Blocks

A `try-catch` statement block is used to "trap" program exceptions. The general syntax for a `try-catch` statement block is as follows:

```
try
{
    // try statement block
}
catch [(exception)]
{
    // catch statement block
}
[finally
{
    // finally statement block
}]
```

While this looks rather intimidating, it really isn't. The `try` block begins with the keyword `try` followed by an opening curly brace. Following the curly brace are the program statements that you think might cause an exception to be generated, or *thrown*, by the program. (Most programmers would say, "This code might *throw* an exception.") A closing curly brace for the `try` statement block appears after those program statements.

The `catch` block immediately follows the closing curly brace of the `try` block. The purpose of the `catch` block is to execute one or more statements if the exception is thrown. The brackets indicate that you can also follow the keyword `catch` with a specific exception if you wish. (I'll show an example of this in a moment.) The closing curly brace marks the end of the `catch` statement block.

The optional `finally` statement block represents a block of code you want to have executed whether an exception is thrown or not. For example, you might have activated some resource in the `try` statement block (for example, you might have opened a file or database, or maybe a network or printer connection) that needs to be closed when you're finished using it. By placing the required statements in the `finally` statement block you are assured that, regardless of the exception or lack of one, those statements will be executed. Not all `try-catch` blocks use the (optional) `finally` block.

Try It Out   **An Exception Example**

Let's modify the code in Listing 11-1 to include a `try-catch` block. Only the click event code for the button object is presented in Listing 11-2, because the rest of the code is unchanged.

Listing 11-2

```
private void btnCalc_Click(object sender, EventArgs e)
    {
        int exp1 = 0;
        int exp2 = 5;
        int result;

        try
        {
            result = exp2 / exp1;
            MessageBox.Show("Never get here");
        }
        catch
        {
            MessageBox.Show("Something went terribly wrong.",
                            "Exception Thrown");
        }
    }
```

How It Works

Now, when the program is run and the Calculate button is clicked, the program looks like what is shown in Figure 11-10.

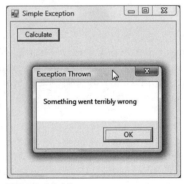

Figure 11-10

Now, when the divide-by-zero exception occurs, the `catch` statement block is executed to present a message to the user.

It is important to realize that the message box that appears in the `try` block after the divide-by-zero exception occurs is never executed. Once program control is passed to a `catch` block, the code path does *not* automatically return to the `try` block code.

While the solution is less ugly than what happened with Listing 11-1, it's still not going to win any beauty contest. We can remove a few of the remaining warts by considering what the code is trying to do.

Anticipating a Specific Exception

One of the ways you can add improvements is by considering what exceptions might occur given what the `try` statement block is doing. It's pretty obvious that one possible exception is the divide-by-zero exception with which we have been experimenting. So how can you find out what other possible exceptions might be thrown?

If you use the Debug ⇨ Exceptions menu sequence (or Ctrl+D, E), then expand the Common Language Runtime Exceptions heading, and finally expand the System heading, you will see a list similar to that shown in Figure 11-11.

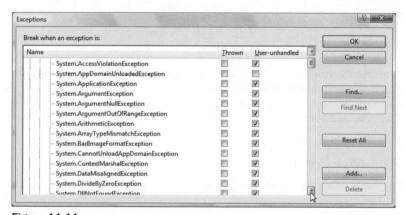

Figure 11-11

Realizing that a certain type of error could occur, I can modify Listing 11-2 to include the following code fragment:

```
try
{
    result = exp2 / exp1;
    MessageBox.Show("Never get here");
}
catch (DivideByZeroException)
{
    MessageBox.Show("Divide by zero error.", "Exception Thrown");
}
```

Note that the `catch` statement block is now prefaced by a parenthesized expression that uses the `DivideByZeroException` exception seen at the bottom of Figure 11-11. Because you have anticipated the error with greater precision, you can give a more meaningful error message to the user. Ah yes, you can hear the warts hitting the floor . . .

Alas, all the warts are not gone. For example, if the values for exp1 and exp2 are coming from other input sources, it is possible that they could overflow the values allowed by an int. Or perhaps there's some kind of hardware failure that throws an exception. In those cases, you may wish to provide multiple catch blocks. For example:

```
try
{
    result = exp2 / exp1;
    MessageBox.Show("Never get here");
}
catch (DivideByZeroException)
{
    MessageBox.Show("Expression 1 is zero. Please reenter.",
                    "Exception Thrown");
    txtExpression1.Focus();
    return;
}
catch
{
    MessageBox.Show("Something went terribly wrong.",
                    "Exception Thrown");
}
```

The code now catches the specific divide-by-zero exception, but can also catch an unspecified exception should one occur. For the divide-by-zero exception we can give a more helpful error message and even ask the user to reenter the value, as shown in the preceding code snippet. The error message for the unspecified exception, however, is not very helpful to the user. You need another way to get rid of a few more warts.

Fuzzy Exception Messages

Although you might not be able to nail the exact exception that occurs, you can provide a little more help to the user with the following modification:

```
try
{
    result = exp2 / exp1;
}
catch (DivideByZeroException)
{
    MessageBox.Show("Expression 1 is zero. Please reenter.",
                    "Exception Thrown");
    txtExpression1.Focus();
    return;
}
catch (Exception ex)
{
    MessageBox.Show("Error: " + ex.Message, "Exception Thrown");
}
```

In this code you define an Exception object variable named ex. In the message box you use the Message property of the Exception object to provide a more precise message about the exception that occurred. I call such messages *fuzzy exception messages* because they are better than no message, but often not precise enough to enable you to take some specific corrective action (as you did with the divide-by-zero exception). While this may not resolve the problem for the user, at least the fuzzy message is better than the generic message you gave before.

Given that your code now handles fuzzy exceptions, how can you test it?

Testing Fuzzy Exceptions

You can test an exception by throwing that exception using the throw keyword. (catch...throw...get it?) To illustrate this, let's modify our click event code again as follows:

```
try
{
    throw new ArgumentOutOfRangeException();
    result = exp2 / exp1;
}
catch (DivideByZeroException)
{
    MessageBox.Show("Expression 1 is zero. Please reenter.",
                    "Exception Thrown");
    txtExpression1.Focus();
    return;
}
catch (Exception ex)
{
    MessageBox.Show("Error: " + ex.Message, "Exception Thrown");
}
```

Note the first statement in the try block. In this case, I simply picked a sample exception to try from the list of possibilities shown in Figure 11-11. As you probably expected, the parentheses at the end of the ArgumentOutOfRangeException() expression mean that the program is going to "construct" an ArgumentOutOfRangeException and then throw that exception. (The term *throw* simply means that the program produces that exception at the moment the constructor is executed.) Because the exception is not a DivideByZeroException, the fuzzy exception handler is called. The message that is actually displayed by the call to the Show() method is presented in Figure 11-12.

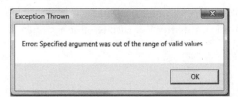

Figure 11-12

Clearly, this Exception object message is better than the generic message Something went terribly wrong. The ex.Message property is not the only useful property of the Exception object. You can also use the StackTrace property (ex.StackTrace) to show the methods that you called up to the point at which the exception occurred. (The methods are displayed in reverse order, with the last method called at the top of the list.) While it probably is not a good idea to display stack trace messages to the user, they can be useful for debugging complex programs.

The finally Statement Block

As I mentioned earlier, the `finally` statement block is used when you have a sequence of statements that you want executed regardless of the presence or absence of an exception. Again, let's modify the click event code for the button object, as follows:

```
try
{
    result = exp2 / exp1;
}
catch (DivideByZeroException)
{
    MessageBox.Show("Expression 1 is zero. Please reenter.",
                    "Exception Thrown");
    txtExpression1.Focus();
    return;
}
catch (Exception ex)
{
    MessageBox.Show("Error: " + ex.Message, "Exception Thrown");
}
finally
{
    MessageBox.Show("In finally");
}
```

The code throws a divide-by-zero exception and displays the appropriate message. The code then says to place the cursor in the `txtExpression1` textbox object and return from the subroutine. If you run the program, however, after the error message is displayed and you click the OK button another message box is displayed with the `In finally` message.

The important thing to notice is that, even though a `return` statement follows the divide-by-zero exception message box, control is passed to the `finally` statement block rather than returning from the click event. It should be clear that the `finally` block is executed regardless of the intent of other code in the method block. Also remember that program control never returns to the `try` block after an exception is thrown.

Even though there are over a hundred defined exceptions, you can write code for custom exceptions. I am going to postpone that topic until after I've discussed inheritance, however.

Program Debugging

The best way to solve program debugging is to never write a program with a bug in it. Since that's probably not going to happen anytime soon, your next best approach is to know how to use a program debugger effectively. Although you can write C# program code in other environments, I assume you are using Visual Studio. However, most of the debugging techniques discussed here apply to any programming environment.

The Nature of the Beast

I've already discussed syntax and semantic errors and how they are different from one another. Logic errors are the third type of program error, or bug, and it is this type of error I want to examine here. There are three steps in fixing a program error: 1) detection, 2) isolation, and 3) correction.

Detection

Strange as it sounds, detecting a program error isn't as easy as it might seem. If it were, no program would ever be released to the public with an error in it. For example, my company produced a statistics package named Microstat, which we sold for over 20 years. After almost seven years in the field with thousands of users, the Stepwise Multiple Regression component failed on one particular data set. The problem was caused when US Gross National Product (GNP) was entered *in dollars* and the program was calculating the sums of squares of cross products. The GNP data set was sufficiently large that the sums of squares overflowed the range of a floating-point number. (Floating-point values for the language back then had a smaller range than a C# `double` type does today.) Once we detected the error that had lain hidden for seven years, it took about three minutes to fix it. The real problem was producing a circumstance that caused the bug to manifest itself.

Most program bugs don't produce a numeric overflow exception the way the GNP data set did. More often, the program runs to completion and produces program output. Stated differently, the program manages to execute all Five Program Steps without fail. Given that the program runs to completion, how do you detect an error?

Test Data Sets

The key to program detection is test data sets. To create these sets, you take a known set of inputs (the Input Step) and process that set of inputs by hand (the Process Step). You then record the data from the Process Step, the results of which become the Output Step. These hand-generated test results serve as the yardstick by which you measure the output of your program.

How do you decide what data to test? In other words, how do you select the inputs by which to judge the output produced by the computer? First, select a "typical" data set that a user might be expected to use. For example, if you're writing a program that figures out the sales tax to apply to a purchase, you might test the method by supplying a purchase of 10 units at a price of $100 each and seeing if the computer produces the same sales tax figure as your hand-generated calculations. Such "typical" test data sets produce "typical" results. However, typical data rarely exercise those places where the bugs lurk.

Program bugs love to hide in what I call *boundary conditions.* Boundary conditions are those that lie at the extremes of the test data set. In the sales tax example, one test of a boundary condition is to determine what your method does if the sales tax rate is zero. Another boundary condition is when the quantity purchased is zero or the price is zero. Even if your sales tax method does properly handle a zero sales tax boundary condition, do subsequent methods called after this boundary condition handle the situation properly? A zero sales tax boundary is not as unusual as it sounds, especially when some purchases are exempt from sales tax. For example, some states exempt educational institutions from sales taxes while other states exempt certain products (such as food).

Likewise, you should enter extremely large values that exercise the upper-boundary conditions of a test data set. A minimum test data set should target the smallest expected value (zero), some typical value(s), and the largest expected value. One upper-limit test is to have input values that run at or near the range limit for the data type being used in the test. For example, if `byte` data sets are being used, try running an upper-limit test using an input value of `255`. Likewise, if textboxes are expecting numeric data to be entered, what does the program do if the user types in her first name? Good programs handle dumb data gracefully.

Simply stated, test data sets are the only means by which you can determine if your program is properly processing its data. Whenever possible, make sure you include test data sets that exercise the program's boundary conditions as well as more typical values. If your program uses arrays, exercise data sets for the lowest and highest index values allowed for the arrays.

It's also important that your test data exercise every code path. This means that programs with `if-else` code paths must have data sets that exercise both paths as part of the test suite. Too often programmers never test all of their code paths: that's a train wreck just waiting to happen.

Other boundary situations can exist. For example, in the advanced OOP programming course I teach, one of the first things I do at the beginning of the semester is have the students write a program in which the computer tries to determine the number the user is thinking of. The program asks for the lower and upper values for the game and then proceeds to guess the number. The computer displays its guess and the user clicks the appropriate button (Too High, Too Low, or Correct!). If the limits are 0 and 100, even a nonbinary search algorithm using RDC can guess the number in 100 tries, right? Wrong. Because the limits are inclusive, it would take 101 guesses to be sure you include all values in the search. Indeed, when the students tell me they are ready for me to test their programs, the first numbers I try are 0 and 100. A disappointingly large number of their programs fail to function properly with these boundary numbers.

Another reason for having a suite of test data sets is to increase the chance that you can make the bug repeatable. Absolutely the most difficult bug to fix is one that cannot be repeated consistently. Some programming languages (such as C and C++) suffer from stray pointer problems that can make program bugs especially difficult to track down. (This is one reason C# discourages the use of the pointer data type.)

It's not uncommon for users to enter a set of input values, click a Calculate (or similar) button, and then have the program either crash or generate incorrect answers. When you ask what values produced the error, the user can't remember what he typed in. Sometimes only a particular value or sequence of values triggers a program state that produces output errors. It's frustrating when those values cannot be recalled by the user, especially when you cannot duplicate the error. (In order to aid program debugging, some programs have error-logging methods that are called in `catch` blocks to write to disk specific program values.)

Whatever test data sets you use, save them. They will likely come in handy later on.

Isolation

Assuming you have a repeatable bug, the next step to removing it is to isolate it. In the bad ol' days before OOP techniques were used, erroneous output values could be caused almost anywhere in the program. There was no such thing as "private" data or scope. Every variable was visible and available at all points in the program. Therefore, trying to pinpoint exactly where a particular variable was going south was extremely difficult.

With OOP designs, it's usually pretty simple to at least figure out the class in which the program bug is hiding. Still, program classes can have a lot of code in them, so you can use any help you can find to simplify the discovery process. This is where a program debugger is invaluable.

While this section discusses the Visual Studio program debugger specifically, most debuggers have the same general set of features. Therefore, while the mechanics of running debuggers may differ, their use and purpose are universally the same.

The Visual Studio Debugger

Perhaps the greatest benefit of a debugger is as an aid in isolating a program bug. The starting point for isolating a bug is the breakpoint. While I've used the Visual Studio debugger before, I want to make a slightly more formal examination here. A *breakpoint* is a place in the program's source code at which you wish to force a pause in the execution of the program. By pausing program execution, you can examine the values of various data items that are in scope at that moment.

You already know that you can set a breakpoint by setting the cursor on the statement where you wish the breakpoint to occur and then pressing the F9 key (or clicking in the left margin of the Source window). The background color of the statement line immediately changes to red and a red dot appears in the program margin. This can be seen in Figure 11-13.

```
        {
            frmMain main = new frmMain();
            Application.Run(main);
        }

        private void btnCalc_Click(object sender, EventArgs e)
        {
            int exp1 = 0;
            int exp2 = 5;
            int result;

            try
            {
                throw new ArgumentOutOfRangeException();
                result = exp2 / exp1;
            }
            catch (DivideByZeroException)
            {
                MessageBox.Show("Divide by zero error.", "Exception Thrown")
                return;
            }
            catch (Exception ex)
            {
                MessageBox.Show("Error: " + ex.StackTrace, "Exception Thrown"
            }
            finally
            {
                MessageBox.Show("In finally");
            }
        }
```

Figure 11-13

When you run the program, it runs as usual until the breakpoint statement is reached. At that moment, the program pauses. The red background color is replaced with a yellow background color and the program is ready to execute the breakpoint statement. Note that the breakpoint statement has not yet been processed.

At this point, you can move the cursor over different variables that are in scope and examine their values.

The Locals Window

You can see all of the locally scoped variables by opening the Locals window. To do this, simply use the Debug ⇨ Windows ⇨ Locals menu sequence (or Ctrl+D, L). The display changes to something similar to what is shown in Figure 11-14.

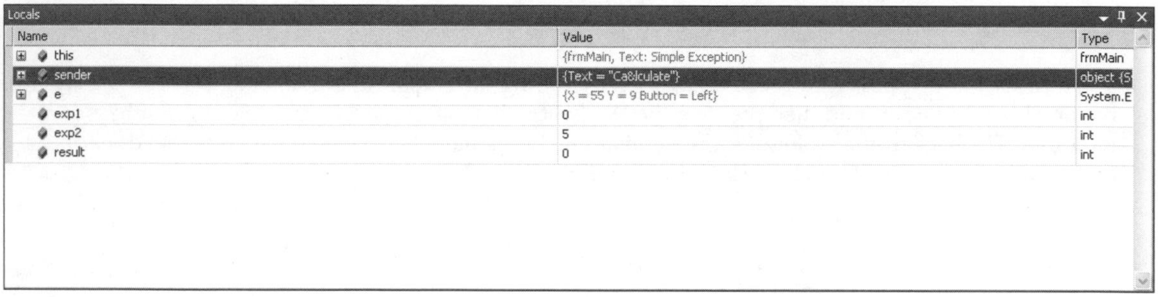

Name	Value	Type
⊞ this	{frmMain, Text: Simple Exception}	frmMain
⊞ sender	{Text = "Ca&lculate"}	object {S
⊞ e	{X = 55 Y = 9 Button = Left}	System.E
exp1	0	int
exp2	5	int
result	0	int

Figure 11-14

The Locals window shows all variables that have local scope, as discussed in Chapter 9. Generally it is easier to use the Locals window than to move the cursor to each variable to inspect its value. Notice that reference data types (such as sender) can be expanded if you want to inspect the properties associated with their objects.

The Immediate Window

The Immediate window can be activated by means of the Debug ⇨ Windows ⇨ Immediate menu sequence (Ctrl+D, I). The purpose of the Immediate window is to enable you to type in an expression and examine its impact on the code. For example, in Figure 11-15 I type in exp1 = 2, thereby changing its coded value from 0 to a new value of 2. Therefore, the Immediate window enables you to immediately change the value of a local variable and assess its impact on the behavior of the code. This is much quicker than editing the source code to change the value of exp1, recompile, and run the program.

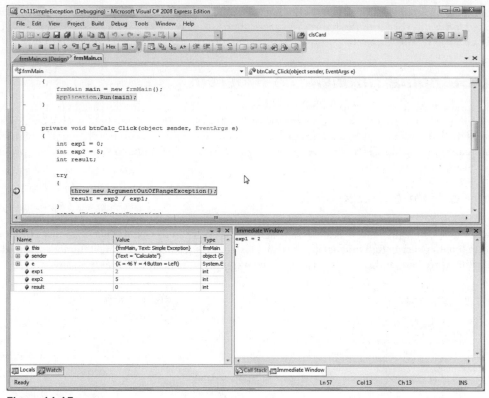

Figure 11-15

The Watch Window

The Watch window is activated by means of the Debug ⇨ Windows ⇨ Watch menu sequence (Ctrl+D, W). The Watch window enables you to evaluate an expression, even using variables that are currently not in scope (such as variable `main` in Figure 11-16) but that may be in scope at some other breakpoint. You can almost use the Watch window as though it were a scratch pad for evaluating interim expressions.

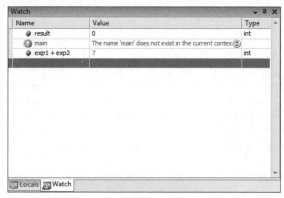

Figure 11-16

Notice that the Watch window overlays the Locals window in Figure 11-16, as indicated by the tabs in the lower left-hand corner of the figure. You can switch between the Locals and Watch windows by simply clicking on the tab for the window you wish to use.

Single-Stepping Through the Program

I've discussed how to single-step through a program before. However, in this case I want to mention some additional tools that the debugger makes available to you. First, when you reach a breakpoint you can press the F10 or F11 keys to advance to the next statement to be executed. When you advance to the next statement, the yellow arrow in the left margin moves to the next line to show you were program execution is at any moment.

Backing up from a Breakpoint

What may not be obvious is that you can back up program execution, too. Figure 11-17 shows the yellow arrow in the left margin as well as a message stating that you can drag the (yellow arrow) cursor to a previous line to execute that line again. This enables you to execute a program statement without having to restart the program and run it to the current breakpoint, which can be a real time-saver.

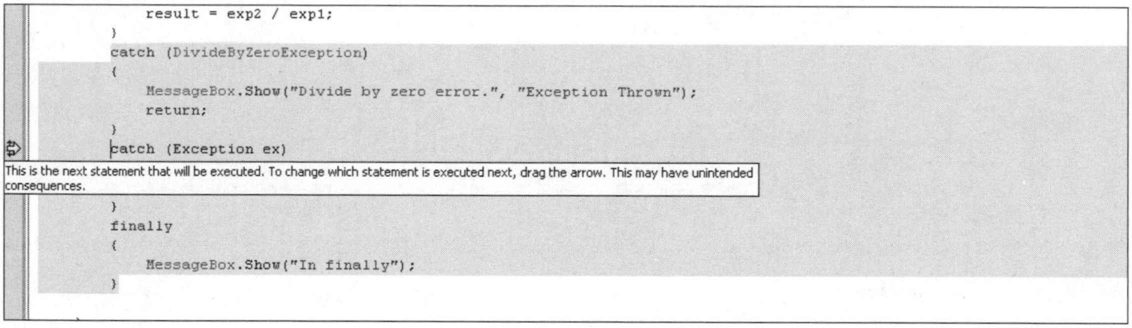

```
            result = exp2 / exp1;
        }
        catch (DivideByZeroException)
        {
            MessageBox.Show("Divide by zero error.", "Exception Thrown");
            return;
        }
        catch (Exception ex)
```
This is the next statement that will be executed. To change which statement is executed next, drag the arrow. This may have unintended consequences.
```
        }
        finally
        {
            MessageBox.Show("In finally");
        }
```

Figure 11-17

Although the message doesn't say so, you cannot advance the yellow arrow. To do so might mean bypassing needed statements to properly determine the values of the variables that are in scope. This is not a serious limitation, since you can simply set a breakpoint further down in the source file and press F5 to execute "at full speed" to that breakpoint.

The Debug Toolbar

The Debug toolbar is shown in Figure 11-18, along with callouts for the meaning of each icon on the toolbar. The Go icon simply causes the program to resume execution at normal speed from a breakpoint. The Break All icon provides a pause that enables you to enter the debug mode manually as the program executes. The Stop icon terminates the current run of the program. The Restart icon simply restarts the program. The Show Next icon shows the next statement to be executed. But perhaps the most interesting debugging features are associated with the Step icons, which I'll discuss in a little more detail now.

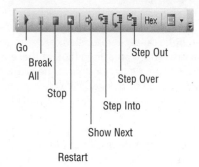

Figure 11-18

Step Into

With the Step Into icon, if the statement about to be executed is a method call for which the source code is available, program execution proceeds into that method's source code. This enables you to single-step through that method's source code.

Step Over

With the Step Over icon, if the statement about to be executed is a method call for which the source code is available, program execution skips over the method's source code and proceeds with the next statement after the current one. Stepping over a method is useful when you know the method that is about to be called is working correctly and you don't want to waste time single-stepping through its source code.

Step Out

Finally, suppose you have single-stepped into a method's source code and you get halfway through and decide you want to return to the method's caller. By clicking the Step Out icon, you bypass the remaining source-code lines in the method and return to the point at which the method was called. This too can be a real time-saver.

The Hex icon enables you to view the debugger information as hexadecimal values rather than their default base 10 representations. This could be useful for assembly language programmers. The final icon (Output) on the Debug toolbar presents additional information about the currently executing program. None of the information is terribly useful at this juncture.

Finding the Bug

The purpose of breakpoints and single-stepping through a program is to enable you to watch the values of the data change as the program executes. With the aid of your test data, you should be able to see how you progress from good input values (assuming those values are correct) to bad output values. If you have sufficient granularity in your input test data (such as intermediate values for complex calculations), you should be able to isolate exactly where the bug lies. (This is another argument for cohesive methods. If you write Swiss Army methods that try to do too many things, it makes debugging more difficult because multipurpose methods take longer to test and debug.)

Usually, fixing a bug is fairly simple. You simply change the offending program statement(s) that generate the error. Sometimes you may need to change the way the calculation is done (that is, its algorithm).

Scaffold Code

Back in the bad ol' days before symbolic debuggers existed, programmers were forced to print out the values of variables as the program ran. You would then look at those intermediate values and try to figure out where things were going wrong. Once you found the error, you had to go back and remove all the print statements that you used in the code. This was a very error-prone process because it was easy to miss a print statement or two or to accidently remove a line that should remain in the program.

Subsequent languages (such as C) allowed programmers to add preprocessor directives to the source code and let the compiler toggle debug statements into or out of the code. This debug code that was added or removed based on preprocessor directives was sometimes referred to as *scaffold code*. Letting the compiler toggle the code was much less likely to result in error.

C# enables you to use some preprocessor directives. You've already used the `#region-#endregion` directive in your programs. Now consider the following code:

```
#define DEBUG
// many lines of code.
// Now you're at a place where things often go amiss, so you add:
#if DEBUG
        MessageBox.Show("Value of exp1 = " + exp1.ToString());
#endif
```

Note that the `#define` preprocessor directive must be the *first line* in the source code file. In this example, the `#define DEBUG` preprocessor directive causes DEBUG to be added to the symbol table. Because it is defined outside of any method, it has class scope. This also means that DEBUG is known throughout all elements of the program, including other source files.

You can place as many lines of code as you wish between `#if` and `#endif`. You can also use the following variation:

```
#if DEBUG
        val = 3;
#else
        val = 0;
#endif
```

This enables you to toggle test values based upon the `#define` directive. A nice touch is that, if you look at this code fragment using Visual Studio, the statement that is currently not compiled is displayed in grayed out text. In other words, if DEBUG is defined, the statement `val = 0;` is grayed out.

Toggling Scaffold Code

The easiest way to toggle scaffold code into and out of a program is with the following two lines at the very top of the source file:

```
#define DEBUG
//#undef DEBUG
```

By means of these two lines, the DEBUG symbol is defined for the program. If you uncomment the second line, the `#undef` preprocessor directive has the effect of removing the DEBUG symbol from the symbol table. (Note that you should leave the `#define DEBUG` directive in the source file.) In the earlier code fragment, this would cause `val` to equal `0`.

Using the preprocessor directives in this manner enables you to leave scaffold test code in the source files permanently, yet toggle them into and out of the program as needed.

Defensive Coding

Sometimes it's difficult to determine exactly which variable is responsible for generating an erroneous result. It's common to find complex expressions like the following:

```
delta = a * (b -1) + (h * math.pow(1+r, x) + 2 * d) / left + right;
```

All you know here is that something is wrong with `delta`. Such complex expressions make judging intermediate values very difficult, even with a Watch window. Understanding and debugging this statement would be much easier if it were broken down into several smaller statements that generated intermediate values. It might take a few more lines of (less complex) code to arrange this, but the time you'll save testing and debugging will amply make up for it. Defensive coding simply means writing code in a manner that makes it easier to debug and maintain a program.

I've presented other defensive coding techniques in earlier chapters that should help make your debugging sessions more productive. I've suggested that you define all your properties using the `private` access specifier. If you do this, only your getter and setter property methods should be able to change the state of a property. I have also encouraged you to use symbolic constants in your programs to make the code easier to read. I have made other stylistic suggestions throughout the text that should help to either prevent bugs or make them easier to detect and isolate — use `default` in a `switch` even if it's not required, always use curly braces with `if` and `for` statements, don't rely on silent casts, and so on.

Other ideas about defensive coding techniques will appear in later chapters. As you write your own programs, try to practice defensive coding techniques. Perhaps the easiest to implement is to write your code with the idea that someone else will have to fix it. Clever and obtuse code never wins in the long run. If you think a piece of clever code is warranted because it enhances performance enough to make it worthwhile, just make sure you comment the code so someone else can understand it. Believe it or not, that someone else may well be you six months from now.

Summary

In this chapter you learned about the various types of errors and bugs that can creep into your programs. By now you have probably advanced to the point that you make relatively few syntax or semantic errors. You have moved up to the big time: logic errors. Some errors throw exceptions and you now know how to safeguard yourself against those using exception handlers. You also learned how to force an exception, which can be helpful in testing your exception handlers.

Your biggest ally in correcting program errors is the program debugger. You should know how to set breakpoints, single-step through your programs, and use the various debugging windows to watch key variables as the program executes.

Finally, I mentioned how defensive programming can ease the burden of testing and debugging a program. Writing clear, concise code makes it much easier for you or anyone else to debug your code. Always write your code as though someone else will be responsible for maintaining it.

Exercises

1. The following code fragment generates a compile error. What's the problem with the code?

```
private int TestCode()
{
    int j;
    int x;

    j = 4;
    if (j == 4)
        x = 5;

    return x;
}
```

2. The present value of a future asset is determined by the number of years into the future at which the asset will be received and the current market rate of interest. For example, if I promise to pay you $100 a year from now and the current interest rate is 5%, the present value of the asset is $95.23. Stated differently, placing $95.23 in the bank today at 5% interest would yield you $100 a year from now. The equation is:

$$p = \frac{a*1}{(1+i)^y}$$

where p is the present value, a is the future amount, i is the interest rate, and y is the number of years into the future the asset is deferred. How would you code this formula and why?

3. C# enables you to use code like the following, in which several variables are defined with a single statement:

```
long number, val, len;
```

What are the pros and cons of this type of variable definition statement?

4. You've written a very long and complex program that compiles and executes, but produces an incorrect solution. You've tried to locate the error, but so far without success. What would you do to fix the program bug(s)?

5. Most of my students are loath to place `try-catch` blocks in their code on their own. That is, unless I remind them to do so, I rarely see `try-catch` blocks in their assignments. If you were grading their assignments and were going to be dictatorial about it, where would you absolutely insist they use `try-catch` blocks or get a failing grade on the assignment?

Generics

This chapter discusses generics, a feature that has been a part of C# since its 2005 release. While Microsoft still has a few hiccups to remove, generics have the potential to save you a ton of programming effort. In this chapter, you will learn about the following:

1. Generics

2. The advantages generics offer

3. Boxing and unboxing

4. Runtime type checking

5. Interfaces

6. Recursion

Generics offer you a way to stretch your programming time in ways that just make sense. Let's examine what this relatively new OOP feature has to offer.

What are Generics?

The best way to appreciate what generics bring to the programming table is with an example. Sorting data is a very common programming problem. I once was interviewed for a consulting job and part of the interview was a programming test in which I was expected to generate a series of random numbers, display them in a listbox, sort them into ascending order, and redisplay them in a second listbox. The interviewers weren't happy when I bypassed writing my own sort routine and simply turned on the Sorted property in the second listbox. Moral: know your toolkit. But suppose you have to sort a series of integer data into ascending order and you can't use the listbox trick. How would you write the solution?

Try It Out   Quicksort

While volumes have been written on sorting algorithms, one of the fastest general-purpose sorts is the Quicksort. The algorithm uses a divide-and-conquer approach to partitioning the data and then calls itself recursively to perform the sorting task. A sample run of the program is shown in Figure 12-1.

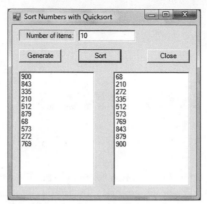

Figure 12-1

The listbox object on the left shows the "raw" data produced by the generation of 10 integer values using the pseudo-random number class (Random). After the user clicks the Sort button, that same list of numbers is sorted and then displayed in the second listbox object. (No, I didn't take the shortcut and simply set the Sorted property to true.)

How It Works

As usual, frmMain performs four of the five Program Steps, leaving the Process Step for the code found in clsSort. The code for frmMain is shown in Listing 12-1.

Listing 12-1

```
#define DEBUG
#undef DEBUG

using System;
using System.Windows.Forms;

public class frmMain : Form
{
    private const int MAXVAL = 1000;      // Max random number to generate

    private int[] data;                   // Data array to sort
    private int number;                   // Number of elements in array

    private TextBox txtNumber;
    private Button btnGen;
    private ListBox lstOutput;
    private Button btnClose;
    private Button btnSort;
    private ListBox lstSorted;
```

```
    private Label label1;

    #region Windows code

    public frmMain()
    {
        InitializeComponent();
    }

    public static void Main()
    {
        frmMain main = new frmMain();
        Application.Run(main);
    }

    private void btnGen_Click(object sender, EventArgs e)
    {
        bool flag;
        int i;

        flag = int.TryParse(txtNumber.Text, out number);
        if (flag == false)
        {
            MessageBox.Show("Enter whole digits only.", "Input Error");
            txtNumber.Focus();
            return;
        }

#if DEBUG
    Random rnd = new Random(number);     // For testing purposes
#else
    Random rnd = new Random();
#endif

        data = new int[number];

        lstOutput.Items.Clear();              // Clear listbox objects
        lstSorted.Items.Clear();

        for (i = 0; i < data.Length; i++)  // Set random values
        {
            data[i] = rnd.Next(MAXVAL);
            lstOutput.Items.Add(data[i].ToString());
        }
    }

    private void btnSort_Click(object sender, EventArgs e)
    {
        int i;
        clsSort mySort = new clsSort(data);

        mySort.quickSort(data.Length - 1);   // Sort the data

        for (i = 0; i < data.Length; i++)     // Show it
```

```
        {
            lstSorted.Items.Add(data[i].ToString());
        }
    }

    private void btnClose_Click(object sender, EventArgs e)
    {
        Close();
    }
}
```

In the listing, I've taken advantage of the scaffold coding technique that was mentioned in Chapter 11. In particular, notice the lines at the very top of the listing and the scaffolding that follows:

```
#define DEBUG
#undef DEBUG

// Omitted lines of code. . .

#if DEBUG
    Random rnd = new Random(number);     // For testing purposes
#else
    Random rnd = new Random();
#endif
```

Because of the #undef preprocessor directive, the #if test later in the program is logic False, which means that the constructor for the Random class is called without an argument. This causes rnd to produce a differing set of pseudo-random numbers on each run of the program. (It's called *pseudo-random* because the distribution of numbers only approximates a true random distribution of numbers.) When you are developing the code, it is often useful to have a repeatable series of numbers produced so you have a stable test dataset while debugging and testing. To establish that testing environment, simply comment out the #undef DEBUG line that toggles in the parameterized constructor for the Random class. When you're done testing, remove comment characters for the #undef, as shown in Listing 12-1.

The line

```
        data[i] = rnd.Next(MAXVAL);
```

simply generates a series of random numbers that fall within the domain of 0 to MAXVAL, which is a symbolic constant set to a value of 1000. The set of random values is then added to the listbox object.

The following statements define a clsSort object named mySort and then call the quickSort() method to sort the data:

```
        clsSort mySort = new clsSort(data);

        mySort.quickSort(data.Length - 1);    // Sort the data
```

Notice that the constructor is passed the raw data as an argument. The code for clsSort is shown in Listing 12-2.

Listing 12-2

```
using System;
using System.Collections.Generic;
using System.Text;

class clsSort
{
    int[] data;

    public clsSort(int[] vals)
    {
        data = vals;      // Copies the rvalue
    }

    /*****
     * Purpose: This method sorts an array of integers values into
     *          ascending order via recursive calls to quickSort().
     *
     * Parameter list:
     *   int first         the first value to sort
     *   int last          the last value to sort
     *
     * Return value:
     *   void
     *****/
    public void quickSort(int first, int last)
    {
        int start;      // Index for left partition
        int end;        // Index for right partition

        start = first;  // Keep copy of first element of array...
        end = last;     // ...and the last one.

        if (last - first >= 1)   // Make sure there's enough data to sort
        {
            int pivot = data[first];    // Set partitions

            while (end > start)             // While indexes don't match...
            {                               // Do left partition
                while (data[start] <= pivot && start <= last && end >
                                                 start)
                    start++;
                                           // Do right partition
                while (data[end] > pivot && end >= first && end >= start)
                    end--;
                if (end > start)    // If right partition index smaller...
                    swap(start, end); // ...do a swap
            }
```

```
            swap(first, end);      // Swap last element with pivot
            quickSort(first, end - 1); // Sort around partitions
            quickSort(end + 1, last);
        }
        else
        {
            return;
        }

    }


    /*****
     * Purpose: This method performs the data swap for quickSort()
     *
     * Parameter list:
     *    int pos1           the array index to first value
     *    int pos2           the array index to second value
     *
     * Return value:
     *    void
     *****/
    public void swap(int pos1, int pos2)
    {
        int temp;

        temp = data[pos1];
        data[pos1] = data[pos2];
        data[pos2] = temp;
    }
}
```

There are several things to notice about the class. First, in the constructor, the following statement does a normal rvalue-to-rvalue assignment:

```
            data = vals;     // Copies the rvalue
```

However, if you recall, the rvalue of a reference variable is a memory address pointer to the memory location where the data reside, so the end result is that the variables data and vals now both refer to the same data. This also means, however, that the original sequence of random values will be lost after the data are sorted. If you need to preserve that sequence for some reason, you could define the data as an array of the same size and copy those values in the constructor's statement block:

```
        public clsSort(int[] vals)
        {
            int[] data = new int[vals.Length];
            Array.Copy(vals, data, vals.Length);
        }
```

Recursion

The theory behind the Quicksort algorithm is to partition the set of numbers into two pieces around what's called a *pivot point* in the data. The code looks at the data around the two partitions and calls a `swap()` method to exchange values to reorder the data. The code then calls the same `quickSort()` method from within itself. The process of a method calling itself is called *recursion*.

The good news about recursion is that you are, in effect, reducing the amount of code by reusing the same method call rather than by writing some form of loop to accomplish the same task. The bad news is that it's pretty easy to get the code wrong, especially when determining that you've hit the last recursive call. Because a recursive method call creates a new set of local variables each time the method is called, a runaway recursion can eventually run out of memory and the program will die an ugly death. Also, because calling a method involves a certain amount of overhead each time the method is called (such as the overhead of pushing and popping data off the stack), recursion is often a little slower than a non-recursive solution to the problem.

However, most Quicksort implementations use recursion so that's what we've done here. You can see the two recursive calls toward the end of Listing 12-2. As mentioned earlier, the `swap()` method simply exchanges two values when the algorithm requires it.

Many sorting algorithms have performance factors that are dictated by what's called *big-O notation* (for example, the notation $O(N^2)$). This type of notation suggests that if the number of values to sort increases tenfold, it takes a hundred times longer to sort the data. The Quicksort, on the other hand, is bound by the relationship $O(N * LogN)$ which makes the sort time almost linear (that is, ten times the data takes about ten times as long). A piece of trivia: most programmers feel that the Bubble Sort is the slowest sorting algorithm on the planet. Actually, if the data are already in sorted order and a new item is added to the data set, the Bubble Sort can be one of the fastest algorithms to sort that new data set. (You can dazzle your friends at your next cocktail party when this topic comes up.) Conclusion: very few laws in programming are etched in stone.

Okay. Now you have a class that is capable of sorting data with good performance. You save the code somewhere for later use. After all, one of the real bennies of OOP is code reuse, right? Well, it depends.

Data Problems

Fast-forward a few months: a client comes to you with a programming problem. Part of the solution requires that you sort the data prior to the final processing of the data. A few neurons fire and you remember the sorting code you wrote a while back. Cool! Time to drag out the `clsSort` code and integrate it into the solution. You read the rest of the client's specs for the program and . . .

Uh-oh.

The client's specs require sorting of the `double` data type, but your `clsSort` code works only with `int` data. Of course, you could rewrite the code, changing everything to use a `double` data type, but then you will lose the ability to sort integer data. Or you could copy the code and have separate `int` and `double` sorting methods within the class. However, if you do that you have twice as much code to test, debug, and maintain. Man . . . wouldn't it be nice if one sorting method could be used to sort both types of data? This is exactly the type of problem that generics are designed to solve.

What are Generics?

Simply stated, *generics* enable you to create "typeless" data structures in C#. In the Quicksort example presented earlier, you defined an instance of the clsSort object with the following syntax:

```
clsSort mySort = new clsSort(data);
```

As you saw, the problem is that the algorithm is based upon using an int data type for the processing. With a generic class, the definition becomes:

```
clsSort<T> mySort = new clsSort<T>(data);
```

The data type you wish to use is substituted for the term T within the enclosing angle brackets. For example, if you wish to sort the int data values stored in the data array, you would use this code:

```
clsSort<int> mySort = new clsSort<int>(data);
```

In some later project that uses the double data type, you would use this code:

```
clsSort<double> mySort = new clsSort<double>(data);
```

One of the key advantages of generics is that the same code can process different data types *without the source code being changed* for each data type! If you write a class using the generic model, that class can process different data types without your having to craft methods for each data type. The Visual Studio compiler generates the necessary code to handle the different data types for you.

Generics Versus ArrayLists

You might be saying, "Wait a minute! Can't ArrayLists do the same thing?" Well, not really. ArrayLists suffer from a few messy limitations. Consider the following code fragment:

```
ArrayList a = new ArrayList();
int i = 5;

a[0] = i;
a[1] = "t";
```

The preceding code compiles without complaint. So what's the problem? The problem is that it *doesn't* complain when it should. The good news about ArrayLists is that they are designed to hold anything. The bad news is that ArrayLists can hold anything. In the snippet you just saw, I assigned an integer into the ArrayList and followed that with the assignment of a string literal into the same ArrayList. While this provides for a flexible means of storing things, it also means that no type checking is being performed on the data. Further, how can you safely read back the data from the ArrayList? You give up the safety of data type checking with ArrayLists.

Now consider what happens if you add this statement for processing in the previously defined `Arraylist`:

```
i = a[0];
```

The compiler complains about this statement, saying

```
Cannot implicitly convert type 'object' to 'int'. An explicit conversion
exists (are you missing a cast?)
```

The compiler removes the error message only if you change the statement to implement an explicit cast:

```
i = (int) a[0];
```

Casting everything from an `ArrayList` to its final destination type is tedious at best. Losing the benefits of data type checking is tantamount to writing code now that will produce a train wreck later. Finally, as I mentioned in Chapter 5, there are some performance issues with the underlying way that `ArrayLists` work.

Boxing and Unboxing

Recall from Chapter 5 that C# surrounds all value types with object "wrappers" so that you can treat value types as though they were objects. Essentially, everything in C# derives from `System.Object`, and `ArrayLists` make use of this fact in performing their magic of allowing virtually any object to be stored in an `ArrayList`. However, anytime you use a value type as an object, C# must convert that value type into an object in a process called *boxing*. Likewise, the process of converting a boxed object back into its value type is called *unboxing*. It is this boxing/unboxing ability that enables you to use methods like `ToString()` with a value type.

However, there is no such thing as a free lunch and the flexibility that wrappers bring to the party is paid for in performance. It has been estimated that there is about a 100 percent performance penalty associated with the boxing-unboxing process.

Generics overcome many of these limitations. Perhaps one of the greatest benefits of generics is that they provide strong type checking, yet enable you to avoid type casting every time you use a data item. To illustrate the use of generics, let's implement our Quicksort algorithm using them.

Try It Out   A Generic Quicksort

The user interface for our generic version of the sort program is presented in Figure 12-2. The program asks the user to specify the data type she wishes to use and a click of the Show Unsorted button shows the raw data that is generated. In this example, the program has generated 10 random `double` data values. Clicking the Show Sorted button presents the same `double` data, but in sorted order. See Figure 12-2.

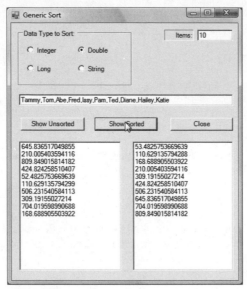

Figure 12-2

If you select the String radio button, the program asks the user to enter a list of comma-separated strings in the textbox object. The `string` data are sorted using the same code as was used to sort the `double` data. A sample run for string data is shown in Figure 12-3.

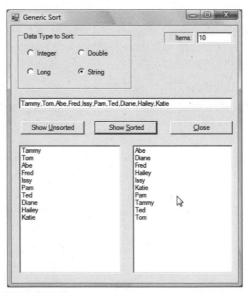

Figure 12-3

As you will see in a moment, you can have such data sorting flexibility yet keep the strong data type checking protection without a heavy performance hit because of boxing and unboxing. You also don't have to mess around with type casts. Clearly, generics are a worthy addition to your programming toolkit.

How It Works

Let's first examine the source code in `frmMain` that drives the sorting tests. This is shown in Listing 12-3.

Listing 12-3

```
using System;
using System.Windows.Forms;

public class frmMain : Form
{
    const int INTEGER = 1;              // Symbolic constants
    const int LONG = 2;
    const int DOUBLE = 3;
    const int STRING = 4;

    const int UNSORTED = 1;
    const int SORTED = 2;

    const int MAXVALUE = 1000;

    int items;                          // Values to generate
    int choice;                         // Which data type selected
    int whichListbox;                   // Which listbox getting this data

    int[] iData;                        // Data arrays
    long[] lData;
    double[] dData;
    string[] sData;

    Random rnd = new Random();

    private GroupBox groupBox1;
    private RadioButton rbString;
    private RadioButton rbDouble;
    private RadioButton rbLong;
    private Label label1;
    private TextBox txtItems;
    private TextBox txtString;
    private ListBox lstUnsorted;
    private ListBox lstSorted;
    private Button btnRaw;
    private Button btnSort;
    private Button btnClose;
    private RadioButton rbInt;
    #region Windows code

    public frmMain()
```

```
    {
        InitializeComponent();
        rbInt.Checked = true;          // Set defaults
        choice = INTEGER;
    }

    public static void Main()
    {
        frmMain main = new frmMain();
        Application.Run(main);
    }

    private void btnClose_Click(object sender, EventArgs e)
    {
        Close();
    }

    // Show the raw data first
    private void btnRaw_Click(object sender, EventArgs e)
    {
        bool flag;
        int i;

        flag = int.TryParse(txtItems.Text, out items);
        if (flag == false)
        {
            MessageBox.Show("Numeric only. Re-enter", "Input Error");
            txtItems.Focus();
            return;
        }

        lstUnsorted.Items.Clear();    // Clear old data
        lstSorted.Items.Clear();

        whichListbox = UNSORTED;

        switch (choice)                     // Select the data type in use
        {
            case INTEGER:                   // Integer

                iData = new int[items];
                for (i = 0; i < items; i++)
                {
                    iData[i] = rnd.Next(MAXVALUE);
                }
                break;
            case LONG:                      // Long
                lData = new long[items];
                for (i = 0; i < items; i++)
                {
                    lData[i] = (long)rnd.Next(MAXVALUE);
                }
                break;
            case DOUBLE:                    // Double
```

```
                    dData = new double[items];
                    for (i = 0; i < items; i++)
                    {
                        dData[i] = rnd.NextDouble() * MAXVALUE;
                    }
                    break;
            case STRING:                        // String
                    sData = txtString.Text.Split(',');   // Split into strings
                    break;
        }
        ShowData();                             // Show data in listbox object

    }

    private void btnSort_Click(object sender, EventArgs e)
    {
        whichListbox = SORTED;

        switch (choice)
        {
            case INTEGER:                       // Data types again. . .

                    clsQuickSort<int> iSort = new clsQuickSort<int>(iData);
                    iSort.Sort();
                    break;
            case LONG:
                    clsQuickSort<long> lSort = new clsQuickSort<long>(lData);
                    lSort.Sort();
                    break;
            case DOUBLE:
                    clsQuickSort<double> dSort = new
                                            clsQuickSort<double>(dData);
                    dSort.Sort();
                    break;
            case STRING:
                    clsQuickSort<string> sSort = new
                                            clsQuickSort<string>(sData);
                    sSort.Sort();
                    break;
        }
        ShowData();
    }

    private void ShowData()     // Simply displays the data
    {
        int i;

        switch (choice)
        {
            case INTEGER:                       // Data types again. . .
                    for (i = 0; i < items; i++)
                    {
                        if (whichListbox == SORTED)
                            lstSorted.Items.Add(iData[i].ToString());
```

```
                else
                    lstUnsorted.Items.Add(iData[i].ToString());
            }
            break;
        case LONG:
            for (i = 0; i < items; i++)
            {
                if (whichListbox == SORTED)
                    lstSorted.Items.Add(lData[i].ToString());
                else
                    lstUnsorted.Items.Add(lData[i].ToString());
            }
            break;
        case DOUBLE:
            for (i = 0; i < items; i++)
            {
                if (whichListbox == SORTED)
                    lstSorted.Items.Add(dData[i].ToString());
                else
                    lstUnsorted.Items.Add(dData[i].ToString());
            }
            break;
        case STRING:
            for (i = 0; i < sData.Length; i++)
            {
                if (whichListbox == SORTED)
                    lstSorted.Items.Add(sData[i].ToString());
                else
                    lstUnsorted.Items.Add(sData[i].ToString());
            }
            break;
    }
}

private void rbInt_Click(object sender, EventArgs e)
{
    choice = INTEGER;
}

private void rbLong_Click(object sender, EventArgs e)
{
    choice = LONG;
}

private void rbDouble_Click(object sender, EventArgs e)
{
    choice = DOUBLE;
}

private void rbString_Click(object sender, EventArgs e)
{
    choice = STRING;
}
}
```

The code starts with the definition of several symbolic constants, followed by a series of array reference objects. These arrays ultimately hold the data that is to be sorted. The frmMain constructor sets the default data type to be an integer for the radio button choices and the current choice (choice = INTEGER). The default number of values to generate for the numeric data types is 10, as seen in Figure 12-2.

Using the Split() Method for Strings

The count when string data types are selected is set by the number of comma-delimited string entries that are made in the txtString textbox object. This is accomplished with the statement:

```
sData = txtString.Text.Split(',');
```

The Split() method examines txtString looking for the comma character. Each time it finds a comma, it creates a new string for the characters leading up to (but not including) the comma. After all substrings have been read, the array of strings is assigned into sData. The Split() method can use multiple separator characters if you need them. You can find the details using the online help. (That is, double-click the word Split in the source code to highlight it and then press the F1 key.)

If the user selects something other than the default INTEGER option, the variable choice is set in the appropriate radio button click event code. For example, if the user clicks on the Double radio button, the following code is executed, setting choice to the appropriate value:

```
private void rbDouble_Click(object sender, EventArgs e)
{
    choice = DOUBLE;
}
```

The variable choice is used to select the appropriate code via the various switch statements.

Generating the Data

Depending upon the value of choice, the appropriate array is filled with data. How this is done can be seen in the following code fragment:

```
switch (choice)                          // Select the data type in use
{
    case INTEGER:                        // Integer

        iData = new int[items];
        for (i = 0; i < items; i++)
        {
            iData[i] = rnd.Next(MAXVALUE);
        }
        break;
    case LONG:                           // Long
        lData = new long[items];
        for (i = 0; i < items; i++)
```

(continued)

(continued)

```
                        {
                            lData[i] = (long)rnd.Next(MAXVALUE);
                        }
                        break;
                    case DOUBLE:                    // Double
                        dData = new double[items];
                        for (i = 0; i < items; i++)
                        {
                            dData[i] = rnd.NextDouble() * MAXVALUE;
                        }
                        break;
                    case STRING:                    // String
                        sData = txtString.Text.Split(',');  // Split into strings
                        break;
                }
```

For the INTEGER and LONG data types, the parameterized Next() method is used to generate a pseudo-random number inside a for loop. The number of passes through the loop is determined by the items variable entered by the user. Passing in the value MAXVALUE means that the values generated fall within the range of 0 and MAXVALUE (exclusively). For the DOUBLE data type, the method NextDouble() returns a value between 0 and 1 (exclusively). Therefore, multiplying the fractional value returned from the NextDouble() method by MAXVALUE sets the same range for the double data type. For string data, the Split() method populates the sData array, as explained earlier.

After the values have been generated, the call to ShowData() moves the data into the listbox to show the values that were generated.

Using a Generic Class

After the raw data have been generated and displayed in the listbox object, you are ready to pass the unsorted data to the generic version of the Quicksort method. The following code fragment shows how the sort method is called for the differing data types:

```
private void btnSort_Click(object sender, EventArgs e)
{
    whichListbox = SORTED;

    switch (choice)
    {
        case INTEGER:                    // Integer
            clsQuickSort<int> iSort = new clsQuickSort<int>(iData);
            iSort.Sort();
            break;

        case LONG:
            clsQuickSort<long> lSort = new clsQuickSort<long>(lData);
            lSort.Sort();
            break;

        case DOUBLE:
```

```
                    clsQuickSort<double> dSort = new
                                      clsQuickSort<double>(dData);
                    dSort.Sort();
                    break;

              case STRING:
                    clsQuickSort<string> sSort = new
                                      clsQuickSort<string>(sData);
                    sSort.Sort();
                    break;
        }
        ShowData();
}
```

In each case, the code uses the generic syntax to create an object of the clsQuickSort class. That is, the statement to instantiate the object has the following form:

```
clsQuickSort<T> typeSort = new clsQuickSort<T>(typeData);
```

Therefore, depending upon the value of choice , the four objects are instantiated using one of the following four statements:

```
clsQuickSort<int> iSort = new clsQuickSort<int>(iData);
clsQuickSort<long> lSort = new clsQuickSort<long>(lData);
clsQuickSort<double> dSort = new clsQuickSort<double>(dData);
clsQuickSort<string> sSort = new clsQuickSort<string>(sData);
```

After the appropriate object has been instantiated, the code calls the object's Sort() method to sort the data (such as iSort.Sort()). Once that code has executed, the data have been sorted and the sorted data are displayed in the second listbox object.

Now let's see what changes we had to make to the Quicksort code.

Generic Quicksort

The code for clsQuickSort is presented in Listing 12-4. Note the second using statement in the listing that makes generics possible in the clsQuickSort class. This Generic namespace contains generic classes, structures, and interfaces to support generic dictionaries, lists, queues, and stacks. In this section we draw upon generics only as they relate to the implementation of a generic class.

The third line in Listing 12-4 —

```
public class clsQuickSort<T> where T : IComparable
```

— uses the generic angle bracket notation that surrounds the data type (T) that is being used by the object of the class. Recall that when you instantiated an object of a generic class, perhaps for the double data type, it took the following form:

```
clsQuickSort<double> dSort = new clsQuickSort<double>(dData);
```

Therefore, the dSort object is of type double and that becomes the T type in the opening statement of the class definition. In other words, instantiating object dSort makes the statement

```
public class clsQuickSort<T> where T : IComparable
```

appear as though the class is written as

```
public class clsQuickSort<double> where double : IComparable
```

The compiler generates the necessary code to accommodate the data types that might be passed to the generic clsQuickSort class. For the moment we'll ignore the expressions that follow the where keyword in the statement. They are discussed a little later in the chapter.

Listing 12-4

```
using System;
using System.Collections.Generic;


public class clsQuickSort<T> where T : IComparable
{
    // ================= instance member ====================
    T[] data;

    // ================= constructor ====================
    public clsQuickSort(T[] values)
    {
        data = values;    // copy rvalue of unsorted data
    }
    // ================= Property methods ====================

    // ================= Helper methods ====================

    /*****
     * Purpose: This method gets the initial pivot point for the sort and then
     *          calls itself recursively until all values have been set.
     *
     * Parameter list:
     *   int first          index of first element of partition
     *   int last           index of last element of partition
     *
     * Return value:
     *   void
     *****/
    private void doSort(int first, int last)
    {
        if (first == last)
        {
            return;    // Done
        }
        else
        {
```

```
            int pivot = getPivotPoint(first, last);

            if (pivot > first)
                doSort(first, pivot - 1);
            if (pivot < last)
                doSort(pivot + 1, last);
        }
}

/*****
 * Purpose: This method sets the pivot point for the sort.
 *
 * Parameter list:
 *   int start           index to start of partition
 *   int end             index to end of partition
 *
 * Return value:
 *   void
 *****/
private int getPivotPoint(int first, int last)
{
    int pivot = first;

    int start = first;  // Keep copies
    int end = last;

    if (last - first >= 1)
    {
        while (end > start)
        {
            while (data[pivot].CompareTo(data[start]) >= 0 &&
                              start <= last && end > start)
                start++;
            while (data[pivot].CompareTo(data[end]) <= 0 &&
                              end >= first && end >= start)
                end--;
            if (end > start)
                swap(start, end);
        }
        swap(first, end);
        doSort(first, end - 1);
    }
    return end;
}


/*****
 * Purpose: This method performs the data swap for quickSort()
 *
 * Parameter list:
 *   int pos1              index to first value to swap
```

(continued)

Listing 12-4 (continued)

```
 *   int pos2              index to second value to swap
 *
 * Return value:
 *   void
 *****/
private void swap(int pos1, int pos2)
{
    T temp;

    temp = data[pos1];
    data[pos1] = data[pos2];
    data[pos2] = temp;
}



// ================= General methods ====================
/*****
 * Purpose: This is the user interface entry point for the Quicksort
 *
 * Parameter list:
 *   n/a
 *
 * Return value:
 *   void
 *
 * CAUTION: This routine assumes constructor is passed unsort data
 *****/
public void Sort()
{
    int len = data.Length;
    if (len < 2)      // Enough to sort?
        return;
    doSort(0, data.Length - 1);
}


}
```

You might think that it would be a fairly simple process to convert the code shown in Listing 12-2 to use generics. A complication, however, arises with statements like

```
while (data[start] <= pivot && start <= last && end > start)
```

Unlike some other languages that support similar constructs (such as templates in C++), C# does not like the use of relational operators with a generic type T. Because of that limitation, the C# compiler complains about the expression

```
data[start] <= pivot
```

in the while statement because you are trying to compare two operands of type T. Because the pivot point for the data array plays an important part in the Quicksort algorithm, I had to modify the code to work around this limitation.

Fortunately, the points of complaint by the compiler center on the comparison of the pivot point with a particular element of the array. You can fix that.

Using Generics with Constraints and Interfaces

If you had written the first line of the class as

```
public class clsQuickSort<T>
```

you would be saying that this class works with *any* data type you can think of. That is, you could use an object of this class with all value types and all reference types, including any custom objects you may have created yourself. Such a class signature means that clsQuickSort is useable with any type of data on the planet. Such a generic class is known as an *unbounded* generic class. Unbounded generic classes are not limited, or constrained, to any particular type of data.

As you might imagine, however, there might be data types that don't lend themselves to the Quicksort algorithm. Indeed, I have chosen to limit the use of the class to those data types that support the ICompare interface. The following expression uses the `where` keyword to introduce a *constraint* for the class:

```
where T : IComparable
```

The expression begins with the `where` keyword followed by the generic data type indicator (T), a colon (:), and an interface name. You can verbalize the complete class signature

```
public class clsQuickSort<T> where T : IComparable
```

as "The clsQuickSort may be used with any data type T subject to the constraint that data type T implements the IComparable interface." In other words, I am providing tight type checking on the types of data that may use this class. If the data type supports the ICompare interface, that data type can be sorted by our implementation of the Quicksort algorithm. It should be clear, therefore, that the `where` keyword is used to constrain the class to only those data types that support the ICompare interface. Therefore, clsQuickSort is known as a *constrained* generic class.

Interfaces

Okay, but what is an interface? An *interface* is a reference object that has no implementation, or code, associated with it. Recall from Chapter 4 that we made a strong distinction between the terms *define* and *declare*. Programmers use those two terms as if they are the same. They are not and it's just plain sloppy to use them interchangeably. I went on to say that a data definition must have memory allocated for the data. This also means that an lvalue for that data exists in the symbol table. Conversely, I said that a data declaration does *not* cause memory to be allocated for the data. The purpose of a data declaration serves only to fill in an attribute list for the data item in the symbol table. Data declarations do not provide memory for the data itself. Interfaces may include declarations for method signatures, properties, and events. They do *not*, however, provide the code to implement those methods, properties, or events. As you will see, an interface is a declaration precisely because no code is associated with the interface.

The IComparable interface used in Listing 12-4 supports only one method in the interface. You can write this interface as follows:

```
public interface IComparable
{
    int CompareTo(Object obj);
}
```

Each of the value types supports the IComparable interface, which means that the wrapper class around each value type has a CompareTo() method that you can use to compare one data item of that type against another data item of the same type. If the int value returned from CompareTo() is less than 0, it means that the current instance is less than obj. If the return value is 0, the two instances are equal. If the return value is positive, the current instance is greater than obj.

For example, given an object named obj,

```
obj.CompareTo(obj)
```

is required to return 0 if the two objects are the same. Likewise, if a different object named whatever is different from obj, then

```
obj.CompareTo(whatever)
```

must return a value other than 0 and

```
whatever.CompareTo(obj)
```

must return a value of the opposite sign. That is, if obj.CompareTo(whatever) returns 1 then whatever.CompareTo(obj) must return –1.

Keep in mind that an interface is really a promise that you make as a programmer to anyone who uses the code in the class that implements the IComparable interface, including the C# compiler. If you wish to use the IComparable interface with a class that you write that doesn't provide the CompareTo() method, your class must write the code for that method, assuring that it obeys the return value rules for the interface.

Why Use an Interface?

Recently I flew in a private plane with a friend who has his pilot's license. About 40 years ago I also had my pilot's license, but ran out of money as a broke graduate student and didn't fly a plane after that. What amazed me the most a few weeks ago were the avionics (radar and other electronics) that I saw in my friend's plane. One of the questions that crossed my mind during the flight with my friend was "Could I fly this plane with all these new electronic thingies?"

The fact is, the basics of flying haven't changed much. You have a yoke and pedals that control the basic movements of the plane. Therefore, a basic plane class might have

```
public clsPrivatePlane : IControls
```

and you might declare the IControls interface as:

```
public interface IControls
{
    int Yoke(int pitch, int yaw);
    int Pedals(int direction);
    int Throttle(int rateOfFuelFlow);
}
```

With these basic controls defined, a pilot could "fly" an object of the class, although the FAA might have dozens of citations for rules that might be broken along the way. Over the years, as new avionics were added, you could upgrade your private plane class to reflect the new stuff today's planes have. You might change the class to

```
public clsPrivatePlane : IControls, IAvionics
```

where IAvionics provides for the methods and members that are necessary to reflect today's avionics. If my friend later wants to do stunt flying, which may require certain devices to equip the plane, the class could again be expanded:

```
public clsPrivatePlane : IControls, IAvionics, IStunts
```

(By convention, most interface declarations begin with the capital letter I.) The key thing to notice here is that earlier versions of the plane class can still exist if classes are created that don't implement the newer interfaces or "empty" methods are used for the new interfaces. These empty interface methods simply mean the current plane object doesn't support these advanced features. Perhaps more importantly, an upgraded plane doesn't "break" the code for the earlier versions of the plane. This is the real strength of interfaces: if done correctly, interfaces decouple the user interface from the underlying code.

For example, consider the IControls that I used when I was flying. All the control surfaces for the plane were connected to the cockpit with steel cables. The IControls for many private planes today are based on a system of hydraulics for the control surfaces. The IControls for modern military aircraft are fly-by-wire and the control surfaces are computer-controlled. However, as a pilot using an object of the class, I can view IControls as a black box because I don't care *how* the control surfaces are moved. That is, I don't care about the implementation of the controls. I only care that the controls *do* move the control surfaces when I touch them. (It's a big problem if the control surfaces stop moving while you're flying a plane!) Using an interface means that I can still use the same code to call the Yoke(), Pedals(), and Throttle() methods regardless of whether I'm flying a canvas-covered Piper J2 or the F/A-22 Raptor.

Using an Interface

If you look closely at the code in Listing 12-4, you find two statements:

```
while (data[pivot].CompareTo(data[start]) >= 0 &&
                  start <= last && end > start)
```

and

```
while (data[pivot].CompareTo(data[end]) <= 0 &&
                  end >= first && end >= start)
```

Each of these uses the `CompareTo()` method of the `IComparable` interface for examining the pivot values in the data arrays. Because the wrapper classes for value types implement the `CompareTo()` method, you don't have to write the code yourself! Again, this is one of the nice features of interfaces. The .NET Framework provides the code you need to use the `IComparable` interface.

If you wish to compare objects of classes that you've written yourself, you will probably have to write your own `CompareTo()` method. However, even if you do have to write the code to implement an interface, you still gain the flexibility provided by interfaces.

How Do You Know an Interface is Implemented for a Data Type?

In Figure 12-3, the `btnSort_Click()` event uses a `switch` statement to determine which data object to create for the sort method. This means that only the four data types presented in the radio button objects can be selected. But how can you determine if a data type you are using implements a specific interface? There are four ways to do this.

Implement the Interface Yourself

First, if the data type is an object that you created, you must specify the interface(s) it supports. This is what we did for the `clsQuickSort` class. We simply wrote the class stating as part of the class signature that the class is constrained for those data types that support the `IComparable` interface. You are free, of course, to add your own interfaces to a class. If you do that, then you must provide the interface declaration and its supporting code yourself. (The `IControls` interface mentioned earlier in this chapter is an example of how to implement an interface with your own code.)

Use the C# Documentation

The second way to determine if a data type supports a given interface is to examine its documentation. Using the C# documentation, you can look up the relevant data types to see if they support the `IComparable` interface.

For example, if you select Help ⇨ Index from the C# main menu, you can search the `int` keyword. The search provides you with information about that data type. Figure 12-4 shows what you see when you index on the `int` keyword.

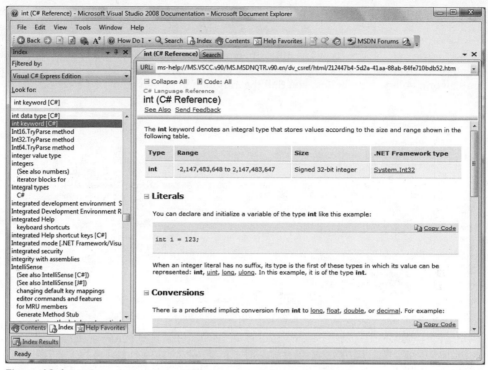

Figure 12-4

On the right-hand side of the figure, in the middle, you can see the table heading .NET Framework Type. Immediately under that column heading is the link System.Int32. If you click that link, you'll see the information presented in Figure 12-5.

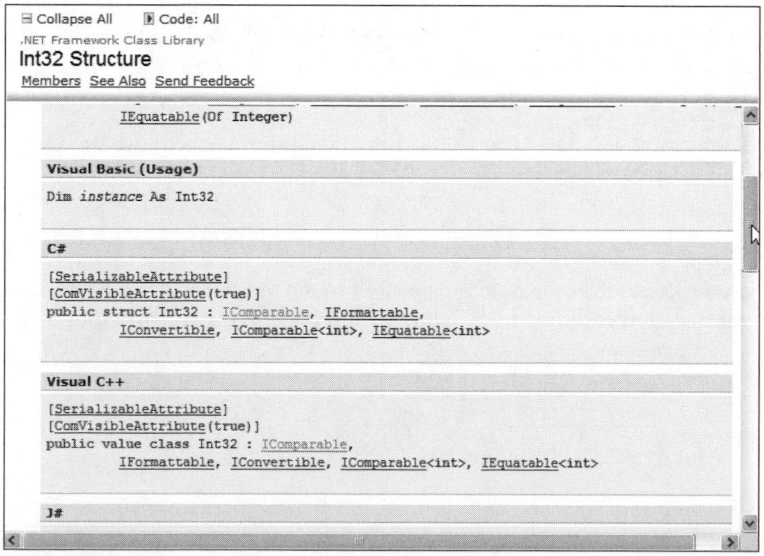

Figure 12-5

In the C# section, you can see that `System.Int32` supports the `IComparable` interface (along with several others).

The process for the `string` data type is a little different because a `string` is a reference type to begin with. If you perform an index search on `string`, you are told that it is an alias name for `String` in the .NET Framework. Following that link, you find the information presented in Figure 12-6.

Figure 12.6

This also confirms that the `string` data type supports the `IComparable` interface. Using the C# documentation is a pretty easy way to determine if a specific C# data type supports a specific interface. However, these two methods are not runtime ways to determine whether a data type supports a certain interface. How can you make the determination at runtime?

Use the is Operator

The third way to determine if a data type supports a given interface is to use the `is` operator. The syntax for the `is` operator is as follows:

```
TypeInQuestion is InterfaceInQuestion
```

For example, if you wished to see if a data type passed to the `clsQuickSort` constructor supports the `IComparable` interface, you could add the following test code to the constructor presented in Listing 12-4:

```
public clsQuickSort(T[] values)
{
    data = values;    // copy rvalue of unsorted data
    if (data[0] is IComparable)
    {
        Console.WriteLine("data[0] is IComparable");
    }
}
```

Note the use of the is operator in the if statement. If you set a breakpoint on the if statement, you can check each data type passed to the class to see if it supports the IComparable interface. In the final version of the code you would probably want to flag a data set that fails the if test and returns an error message to the caller.

Using the IComparable interface in clsQuickSort enables us to get around the fact that generics currently don't directly support the relational operators. If you take a little time, you will find that the code functions the same way it did in the non-generic form of the class code.

Use the as Operator

Fourth, you can use the as operator to determine if an object supports a specific interface. The as operator has the following syntax form:

```
expression as type
```

The as operator is actually used to perform conversions between compatible reference data types. However, if the conversion cannot be made, it produces null as the outcome of the expression. This is kind of nice because if the conversion fails the result is null rather than an exception being thrown.

For example, ArrayList data types support only the IList interface. You could check this fact using code similar to that shown in the following code fragment:

```
ArrayList val = new ArrayList();
IComparable val1 = val as IComparable;
if (val1 == null)
{
    Console.WriteLine("val1 doesn't support IComparable");
}
```

In this example, I defined an ArrayList reference named val and then used the as operator to see if I could convert val into an IComparable object named val1. If ArrayList objects don't support the IComparable interface, the conversion fails and val1 is null. Because ArrayLists do not support the IComparable interface, the conversion fails and the failure message is written to the console.

If you modify the code to define val using the following statement —

```
int val = 5;
```

— the conversion is made successfully and the failure message is not displayed. (You have to assign a value to val or the compiler issues an uninitialized local variable error message.)

Generics and interfaces can often team up to make a given class much more flexible in terms of the data types it can process. Obviously, the time to think about generics is during the design phase of a project. While the design time might increase slightly, you will be rewarded with a much more robust class for those that do implement generics.

Summary

In this chapter you learned how generics can be used to reduce the code burden of developing a new application. We concentrated on how generics enable you to write classes and methods in a way that makes them capable of processing different data types. Not only do generics provide code flexibility, they do it with strongly typed data yet without the hassles involved in having to cast every expression. You also learned how interfaces can be used to simplify your code. Interfaces guarantee the user that specific functionality is provided by the code. Entire books have been written on interfaces and their related topics and they are worth your study.

Exercises

1. What are the major advantages of generics?

2. Listing 12-3 shows a method named ShowData() that is used to fill the listbox objects with the appropriate data. How would you modify that method to take advantage of generics?

3. What are the major advantages of interfaces?

4. The swap() method in clsQuickSort is a little sloppy because we rely on class scope for the data being swapped. Rewrite the swap() method so it can still swap any type of data of the class, but without relying on class scope.

5. One of the major banes of writing commercial software is adding new features without breaking older versions. Do any of the topics discussed in this chapter cause you to rethink software versioning?

Part IV
Storing Data

Using Disk Data Files

This chapter shows you how to use disk data files. If you think about it, computers would lose much of their functionality if there wasn't a way to permanently store, or *persist,* the data generated by a computer. Things that we take for granted today, such as making an airline reservation, must have been a nightmare before computers were in widespread use. In this chapter, you will learn about the following:

- ❑ Two basic file types: text and binary
- ❑ The advantages and disadvantages of each file type
- ❑ Computer streams
- ❑ Sequential files
- ❑ Random access files
- ❑ Serialization and deserialization
- ❑ Multiple document interface (MDI) programs
- ❑ Writing program menus

Up to this point you have written programs whose usefulness ended when the program ended. Once you've mastered the contents of this chapter, you'll be able to write programs that can store data, enabling you to recall that data at some later time. Programs take on a whole new light when you know how to persist data.

Let's get started.

Directories

Anytime I want to explore a new area in C#, the first thing I do is find out which namespaces are involved with that area. Since we're going to discuss file input and output (I/O), I simply typed in using System. at the top of the program and started looking for namespaces that may apply.

Sure enough, up popped `System.IO`. Just highlight `IO` and press the F1 key and you'll get information about the IO namespace. All kinds of interesting things come up, but let's concentrate first on those classes that deal with directory and drive information.

The DriveInfo Class

Just as Ed McMahon used to say on the Johnny Carson show, "Everything you could ever possibly want to know . . ." about a disk drive is in the `DriveInfo` class. A few of the more useful methods and properties are presented in Table 13-1.

Table 13-1

Method or Property	Description
GetDrives()	Returns an array with all of the logical drives of the computer
AvailableFreeSpace	Gives the amount of free disk space (in bytes) on a drive
DriveFormat	Returns the format for the drive (such as NTFS or FAT32)
DriveType	Returns the type of drive (such as fixed, removable, RAM, etc.)
Name	Gives the name of the drive
TotalFreeSpace	Gives the amount of unused space on the drive
TotalSize	Gives the capacity of the drive

If you look in the IO namespace, you will also discover that there are classes named `Directory` and `DirectoryInfo`. These two classes present related, albeit different, information.

Directory Class

Table 13-2 presents a partial listing for methods found in the `Directory` class. (You can always get more complete information using the online help for the class.)

Table 13-2

Methods	Description
CreateDirectory()	Creates a directory for a given path name
Delete()	Deletes a specified directory
Exists()	Determines if a specified directory exists
GetCreationTime()	Returns a DateTime type with the time a directory was created
GetCurrentDirectory()	Gets the current working directory of an application
GetFiles()	Returns the file names in a given directory

Methods	Description
GetLastAccessTime()	Returns the date and time the directory was last accessed
GetLastWriteTime()	Returns the data and time the directory was last written to
GetParent()	Returns the parent directory for a given path name
Move()	Moves a file or directory to a new location
SetCreationTime()	Sets the time for the creation of a file or directory
SetLastWriteTime()	Sets the date and time the file or directory was last written to

DirectoryInfo Class

Finally, Table 13-3 presents the methods and properties for the DirectoryInfo class. Note that the DirectoryInfo class implements the FileSystemInfo interface. This means that you should also check the FileSystemInfo interface to see what properties and methods that interface requires.

Table 13-3

Methods or Property	Description
Create()	Creates a directory.
CreateSubdirectory()	Creates a subdirectory.
Delete()	Deletes a given directory.
Equals()	Compares directory objects.
GetDirectories()	Returns the subdirectories for the current directory.
GetFiles()	Returns the files in the current directory. This is overloaded so you can do searches easily.
GetFileSystemInfos()	Returns strongly typed FileSystemInfo for files and subdirectories.
MoveTo()	Moves a DirectoryInfo object's contents to a specified path.
Exists	Returns a value to indicate if a directory exists.
Extension	Returns a string that represents the extension component of a file name.
FullName	Returns the full path of a directory or path.

With the properties and methods presented in the three preceding tables, you can obtain just about all the information you need to manipulate directories.

Try It Out   Using Directories

The program shown in Figure 13-1 uses some of the directory methods and properties presented in the previous tables. The user types in a drive and directory (that is, a *path name*) he is interested in and clicks the List button to show the directories in that directory. The program then presents a list of the directories and subdirectories. By the way, you may not want to type in just the drive name, like c:\. My Windows directory by itself has Over 2,700 directories in it!

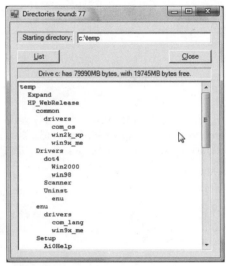

Figure 13-1

How It Works
The code for the user interface is presented in Listing 13-1.

Listing 13-1

```
using System;
using System.IO;
using System.Collections;
using System.Windows.Forms;

public class frmMain : Form
{
    private ListBox lstDirectories;
    private Label label1;
    private TextBox txtStartingPath;
    private Button btnClose;
    private Label lblDriveInfo;
    private Button btnList;
    #region Windows code

    public frmMain()
```

```
{
    InitializeComponent();
}

public static void Main()
{
    frmMain main = new frmMain();
    Application.Run(main);
}

private void btnList_Click(object sender, EventArgs e)
{
    string startingPath;
    int count;
    int i;
    ArrayList dirs = new ArrayList();

    startingPath = @txtStartingPath.Text;

    try
    {
        DirectoryInfo myDirInfo = new DirectoryInfo(startingPath);

        if (myDirInfo.Exists == false)
        {
            MessageBox.Show("Cannot find directory. Re-enter.",
                            "Directory Not Found");
            txtStartingPath.Focus();
            return;
        }
        clsDirectory myDirs = new clsDirectory();

        ShowDriveInfo();

        lstDirectories.Items.Clear();

        count = myDirs.ShowDirectory(myDirInfo, 0, dirs);
        for (i = 0; i < dirs.Count; i++)
        {
            lstDirectories.Items.Add(dirs[i]);
        }
        this.Text = "Directories found: " + count.ToString();

    }
    catch (Exception ex)
    {
        MessageBox.Show("Error: " + ex.Message, "IO Error");
        return;
    }
}

/*****
 * Purpose: This shows some size info about the drive selected.
 *
```

```
        * Parameter list:
        *   n/a
        *
        * Return type:
        *   void
        ******/
     private void ShowDriveInfo()
     {
         int pos;
         long driveBytes;
         string buff;

         try
         {
             pos = txtStartingPath.Text.IndexOf('\\');// Get drive name
             buff = txtStartingPath.Text.Substring(0, pos);

             DriveInfo myDrive = new DriveInfo(@buff);   // Get its info

             driveBytes = myDrive.TotalSize / 1000000;
             lblDriveInfo.Text = "Drive " + buff + " has " +
                               driveBytes.ToString() + "MB bytes, with "
                               +   myDrive.TotalFreeSpace/1000000
                               + "MB bytes free.";
         }
         catch
         {
             txtStartingPath.Text = "";
         }

     }
     private void btnClose_Click(object sender, EventArgs e)
     {
         Close();
     }
 }
```

The program begins by including the Collections and IO namespaces. The real action, however, takes place in the btnList_Click() event code. The starting path name entered by the user is assigned into the variable startingPath. Note the use of the at symbol (@) to tell the compiler that the backslashes are not to be treated as escape sequences. The program instantiates a DirectoryInfo object named myDirInfo, passing the user's path information to the constructor.

If you wanted to get a list of all the drives currently available, you could use the following code:

```
        DriveInfo[] listDrives = DriveInfo.GetDrives();
```

This statement creates a string array of all of the drives on the system. You could use this information to check that the user typed in a valid drive name.

The code then calls the ShowDriveInfo() method. The ShowDriveInfo() method is simply a helper method that collects some statistics about the disk drive that the user entered. The code creates a DriveInfo object named myDrive, passing the drive name to its constructor. The code then gathers some statistics about the drive and displays them in a label object. The storage statistics are divided by one million simply to express the stats in terms of megabytes. You could also use

```
driveBytes = myDrive.AvailableFreeSpace;
```

to display the free space on the drive. We did it the hard way just to show how to use those methods.

The program then creates a clsDirectory object named myDirs and calls the ShowDirectory() method. The code for the clsDirectory class is shown in Listing 13-2.

Listing 13-2

```
using System;
using System.Collections;
using System.IO;


class clsDirectory
{
    const string TAB = " ";
    static private int visits;  // How many times here

    //============================= Instance variables ====================
    private int dirCounter;      // How many directories

    //============================= Constructor ==========================
    public clsDirectory()
    {
        dirCounter = 1; // The directory passed in
    }
    //============================= Property methods =====================

    public int DirectoryCount    // Make it read-only
    {
        get
        {
            return dirCounter;
        }
    }

    /*****
     * Purpose: This method creates a directory list at a given path
     *
     * Parameter list:
     *   DirectoryInfo curDir        the current directory info
     *   int inLevel                 how deep in list
     *   ArrayList dirs              array of directory strings
     *
     * Return value:
     *   int                         directory count or -1 on error
     *
     *****/
    public int ShowDirectory(DirectoryInfo curDir, int inLevel,
                             ArrayList dirs)
```

```
    {
        int i;
        string indent = "";

        try
        {
            for (i = 0; i < visits; i++)      // Indent subdirectories
            {
                indent += TAB;
            }

            dirs.Add(indent + curDir.Name); // Add it to list
            visits++;

            foreach (DirectoryInfo subDir in curDir.GetDirectories())
            {
                dirCounter++;
                ShowDirectory(subDir, visits, dirs);   // Recurse
                    // FileInfo[] files = subDir.GetFiles();
            }
            visits--;     // Go back to previous directory level

            if (indent.Length > 0)   // Adjust the indent level accordingly
                indent.Substring(0, indent.Length - TAB.Length);
        }
        catch (Exception ex)
        {
            return -1;   // Could do something with ex.Message
        }
        return dirCounter;
    }
}
```

Most of the code in Listing 13-2 should look familiar by now. The ShowDirectory() method is passed three arguments: 1) a DirectoryInfo object, 2) an integer that keeps track of where we are in the directory structure, and 3) an ArrayList variable to store the directory names. Note that ShowDirectory() is called recursively each time a directory is read. That way we can get a list of subdirectories and traverse those, too. The variable named visits keeps track of how far down the directory tree we are at any given moment. The visits variable is also used to indent the directory names for display in the listbox object. The recursive calls are performed by the loop:

```
        foreach (DirectoryInfo subDir in curDir.GetDirectories())
        {
            dirCounter++;
            ShowDirectory(subDir, visits, dirs);   // Recurse
                // FileInfo[] files = subDir.GetFiles();
        }
```

You also keep a count of the directories read with the variable `dirCounter`. After all the directories have been read, this number is displayed in the title bar of the form. If you want to get a list of the files in a given subdirectory, uncomment the line in the `foreach` loop. You can then look at the files variable to see the files in each directory.

I would encourage you to single-step through this program using the debugger to inspect each of the variables as the program is run. This gives you a better feel for how the `DirectoryInfo` class works.

File Namespace

The File namespace presents you with a number of useful methods that you will want to use in your programs. A partial list of the methods in the File namespace is presented in Table 13-4.

Table 13-4

Method	Description
AppendAllText()	Appends a string of text to a specified file. The method is overloaded so that different encoding schemes may be used.
AppendText()	Uses a `StreamWriter` object to append UTF-8-encoded text to a specified file. UTF-8 is an eight-bit Unicode Transformation Format that is backward-compatible with the ASCII character set.
Copy()	Copies a specified file.
Create()	Creates a specified file.
CreateText()	Creates or opens a file for UTF-8 encoded text
Delete()	Deletes a specified file.
Exists()	Checks to see if a specified file exists.
GetCreationTime()	Returns the date and time a file was created.
Move()	Moves a specified file to a specified location.
Open()	Uses a `FileStream` object to open a specified file.
OpenRead()	Opens an existing file for reading.
OpenText()	Opens a UTF-8 file for reading.
OpenWrite()	Opens an existing file for writing.
ReadAllBytes()	Opens a binary file and copies the contents into a byte array. (Each `ReadAll*()` method has a corresponding `WriteAll*()` method.)

Table 13-4 (*continued*)

Method or Property	Description
ReadAllLines()	Opens a text file, reads all lines in the file into a string array, and closes it.
ReadAllText()	Opens a text file, reads the contents into a string, and closes it.
Replace()	Replaces the content of one file with that of another file, deleting the original file and making a backup of the replaced file.
SetAttributes()	Sets the attributes of a file.

Keep in mind that the entries in Table 13-4 are just a partial listing of the methods available to you. If you find yourself wishing that a specific File method existed, check the online help before writing the method yourself.

FileInfo Class

In Listing 13-2, I commented out a statement that uses the FileInfo class. This class provides a lot of details about the files you find on the system. Some of the more important properties and methods are presented in Table 13-5.

Table 13-5

Method or Property	Description
AppendText()	Appends text for the current FileInfo object using a StreamWriter
CopyTo()	Copies an existing file to a new file
Create()	Creates a new file
CreateText()	Creates a StreamWriter object that writes a new text file
Delete()	Deletes a file
Equals()	Determines if two FileInfo objects are equal
MoveTo()	Moves a file to a new location with the option to rename it
Open()	Opens a file with various read/write privileges
Replace()	Replaces a specified file with contents of current FileInfo file
Attributes	Gets the file attributes of a specified file
CreationTime	Gets or sets the creation time for a file

Method or Property	Description
Directory	Gets an instance of the parent directory
DirectoryName	Returns the full path name as a string
Exists	Determines if a file exists
Extension	Returns a string representation of a file's extension
FullName	Returns the complete path of a file or directory
LastAccessTime	Returns the last time the file was accessed
Length	Returns the number of bytes in a file
Name	Returns the name of the current file

The tables and their associated methods and properties should give you enough information about directories and files for you to manipulate them in your programs. I draw on several of these properties and methods later in this chapter. Before I do that, however, you need to understand the basic types of files that C# supports.

Types of Files

From a programming language point of view, there are two basic types of files: those that contain textual data and those that contain binary data. Often you can determine if a given file is a text or binary file by its name. File names are stored on disk using a primary and secondary file name. For example, a file named PamAtParty.jpg has a *primary* name of PamAtParty and a *secondary* file name of jpg. (Many people refer the primary file name as *the* file name and the secondary file name as the file's *extension*.) The secondary file name often gives a clue as to its type. For example, a file extension of txt is normally a textual data file while those ending in jpg are binary image files. While there is nothing that requires you to use common file extensions, it's usually a good idea to employ them in your own programs.

Textual Versus Binary Data Files

Files that contain textual data are usually built from strings appended to the file. When a user types text into a textbox, that data is stored in memory as plain text in a string format. If you wish to save that information permanently on disk, it means moving the strings from memory to a disk data file. If the user types a number into a textbox and that number is used numerically (for example, if the square root of that number is taken), the number is stored in memory in a binary format. For that number to be saved in a text file, it must be converted to a string and *then* written to disk. In other words, text files contain nothing but strings.

One of the nice things about text files is that it is easy to read the content of a text file. You can use a simple program like Notepad (which comes free with Windows) to read a text file. Because text files are so easy to read, programs that read and write text files are usually easier to debug. Figure 13-2 shows the output of a text file using Notepad to read it.

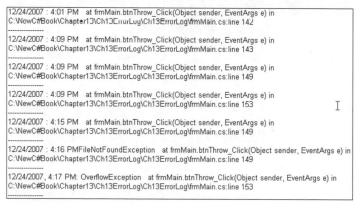

Figure 13-2

Binary files are a little different from text files. If a number is written to a binary file, no conversion of that number to a string occurs. If an `int` variable has the value 50, that value is written to the binary file as four bytes of data even though it would only take two bytes if it were written as a string. Because `int` value types are stored in memory as hexadecimal (base-16) values, the number 50 would be stored as 32 00 00 00 in a binary file. If that same value were a `decimal` data type, it would require 16 bytes to store that value in a binary file.

If some numbers (such as 50) take more bytes to store in memory than their string equivalents, why use binary files? First, if the value were 1 billion instead of 50, a string would require 10 bytes to store it as text but still would take only four bytes to store it as a binary value. Second, and more importantly, values stored as binary can be moved into memory and used without their values having to be converted from the string format stored on disk to the hexadecimal format used in the program. Avoiding this conversion process makes binary files a little faster when reading data from a disk file into a program.

If you take the same file shown in Figure 13-2 and read it using a program that displays that file in a binary format, the output will look like that shown in Figure 13-3.

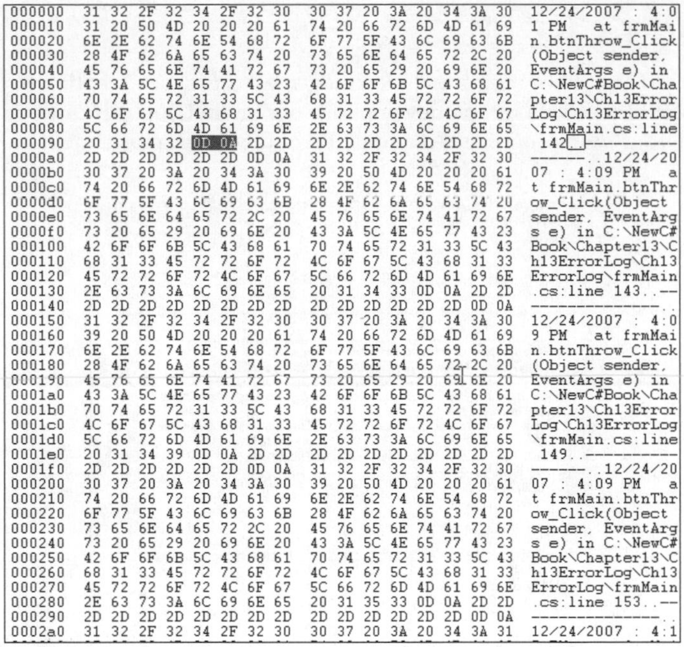

```
000000  31 32 2F 32 34 2F 32 30   30 37 20 3A 20 34 3A 30   12/24/2007 : 4:0
000010  31 20 50 4D 20 20 20 61   74 20 66 72 6D 4D 61 69   1 PM    at frmMai
000020  6E 2E 62 74 6E 54 68 72   6F 77 5F 43 6C 69 63 6B   n.btnThrow_Click
000030  28 4F 62 6A 65 63 74 20   73 65 6E 64 65 72 2C 20   (Object sender,
000040  45 76 65 6E 74 41 72 67   73 20 65 29 20 69 6E 20   EventArgs e) in
000050  43 3A 5C 4E 65 77 43 23   42 6F 6F 6B 5C 43 68 61   C:\NewC#Book\Cha
000060  70 74 65 72 31 33 5C 43   68 31 33 45 72 72 6F 72   pter13\Ch13Error
000070  4C 6F 67 5C 43 68 31 33   45 72 72 6F 72 4C 6F 67   Log\Ch13ErrorLog
000080  5C 66 72 6D 4D 61 69 6E   2E 63 73 3A 6C 69 6E 65   \frmMain.cs:line
000090  20 31 34 32 0D 0A 2D 2D   2D 2D 2D 2D 2D 2D 2D 2D   142 ----------
0000a0  2D 2D 2D 2D 2D 2D 0D 0A   31 32 2F 32 34 2F 32 30   ------..12/24/20
0000b0  30 37 20 3A 20 34 3A 30   39 20 50 4D 20 20 20 61   07 : 4:09 PM   a
0000c0  74 20 66 72 6D 4D 61 69   6E 2E 62 74 6E 54 68 72   t frmMain.btnThr
0000d0  6F 77 5F 43 6F 67 6C 69   63 6B 28 4F 62 6A 65 63 74 20  ow_Click(Object
0000e0  73 65 6E 64 65 72 2C 20   45 76 65 6E 74 41 72 67   sender, EventArg
0000f0  73 20 65 29 20 69 6E 20   43 3A 5C 4E 65 77 43 23   s e) in C:\NewC#
000100  42 6F 6F 6B 5C 43 68 61   70 74 65 72 31 33 5C 43   Book\Chapter13\C
000110  68 31 33 45 72 72 6F 72   4C 6F 67 5C 43 68 31 33   h13ErrorLog\Ch13
000120  45 72 72 6F 72 4C 6F 67   5C 66 72 6D 4D 61 69 6E   ErrorLog\frmMain
000130  2E 63 73 3A 6C 69 6E 65   20 31 34 33 0D 0A 2D 2D   .cs:line 143..--
000140  2D 2D 2D 2D 2D 2D 2D 2D   2D 2D 2D 2D 2D 2D 0D 0A   ----------------
000150  31 32 2F 32 34 2F 32 30   30 37 20 3A 20 34 3A 30   12/24/2007 : 4:0
000160  39 20 50 4D 20 20 20 61   74 20 66 72 6D 4D 61 69   9 PM    at frmMai
000170  6E 2E 62 74 6E 54 68 72   6F 77 5F 43 6C 69 63 6B   n.btnThrow_Click
000180  28 4F 62 6A 65 63 74 20   73 65 6E 64 65 72 2C 20   (Object sender,
000190  45 76 65 6E 74 41 72 67   73 20 65 29 20 69 6E 20   EventArgs e) in
0001a0  43 3A 5C 4E 65 77 43 23   42 6F 6F 6B 5C 43 68 61   C:\NewC#Book\Cha
0001b0  70 74 65 72 31 33 5C 43   68 31 33 45 72 72 6F 72   pter13\Ch13Error
0001c0  4C 6F 67 5C 43 68 31 33   45 72 72 6F 72 4C 6F 67   Log\Ch13ErrorLog
0001d0  5C 66 72 6D 4D 61 69 6E   2E 63 73 3A 6C 69 6E 65   \frmMain.cs:line
0001e0  20 31 34 39 0D 0A 2D 2D   2D 2D 2D 2D 2D 2D 2D 2D   149..----------
0001f0  2D 2D 2D 2D 2D 2D 0D 0A   31 32 2F 32 34 2F 32 30   ------..12/24/20
000200  30 37 20 3A 20 34 3A 30   39 20 50 4D 20 20 20 61   07 : 4:09 PM   a
000210  74 20 66 72 6D 4D 61 69   6E 2E 62 74 6E 54 68 72   t frmMain.btnThr
000220  6F 77 5F 43 6C 69 63 6B   28 4F 62 6A 65 63 74 20   ow_Click(Object
000230  73 65 6E 64 65 72 2C 20   45 76 65 6E 74 41 72 67   sender, EventArg
000240  73 20 65 29 20 69 6E 20   43 3A 5C 4E 65 77 43 23   s e) in C:\NewC#
000250  42 6F 6F 6B 5C 43 68 61   70 74 65 72 31 33 5C 43   Book\Chapter13\C
000260  68 31 33 45 72 72 6F 72   4C 6F 67 5C 43 68 31 33   h13ErrorLog\Ch13
000270  45 72 72 6F 72 4C 6F 67   5C 66 72 6D 4D 61 69 6E   ErrorLog\frmMain
000280  2E 63 73 3A 6C 69 6E 65   20 31 35 33 0D 0A 2D 2D   .cs:line 153..--
000290  2D 2D 2D 2D 2D 2D 2D 2D   2D 2D 2D 2D 2D 2D 0D 0A   ----------------
0002a0  31 32 2F 32 34 2F 32 30   30 37 20 3A 20 34 3A 31   12/24/2007 : 4:1
```

Figure 13-3

This first row in Figure 13-3 has the value 000000. This is a count of the number of bytes being displayed in hexadecimal (often abbreviated to "hex") format. After that, you see the number 31. Because that number is being expressed as a hex number, you need to convert it to the base-10 numbering system we are familiar with. Therefore, 3 * 16 + 1 = 48 + 1 = 49. If you look up the ASCII value for 49, you will find it represents the digit character 1. The next value in the row is 32, so 3 * 16 + 2 = 50. If you look that ASCII value up, you'll find that it is the character 2. Next, 2F is 2 * 16 + 15 = 47 which is the ASCII value for a slash character (/). (The hex numbering system counts the values 0 through 9 as standard numbers, but 10 through 15 are the letters A through F. Because 0 through F can represent 16 values, it is called a base-16, or hex, numbering system. Therefore, F has a numeric value of 15 in a hex numbering system.) At the extreme right of the first row, you can see the hex values displayed as their ASCII character equivalents.

If you look closely at Figure 13-3, you can see the hex values 0D 0A are highlighted. These two characters form a carriage return-linefeed (CRLF) pair of characters. Think of a carriage return (CR) as moving the cursor to the extreme left of the screen. The linefeed (LF) moves the cursor down one line. Taken together, the CRLF combine to form the *newline* character, which is represented as \n in a string format. Simply stated, the CRLF sequence causes the subsequent text to appear on a new output line.

| Try It Out | **Writing a Text File** |

In Chapter 11 you read about how using error log messages as part of exception handling can be a useful debugging technique. This section develops a program that you can easily modify to work as an error log class in your own programs. A sample run of the program is shown in Figure 13-4.

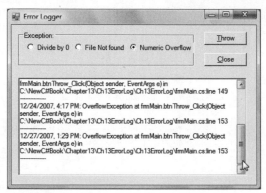

Figure 13-4

The program lets the user select the type of error she wishes to throw to test the error-logging feature. Once the selection is made, the user clicks the Throw button, which throws the appropriate exception. That exception is then written to an error log file. The content of the error log file is then displayed in a listbox object shown in Figure 13-4. Because the error log file is a text file, you can use other programs, such as Notepad, to display its contents.

How It Works

As usual, there are two parts to the program. `frmMain` provides the shell for testing the class that actually processes the error log file (`clsErrorLog`). The code for `frmMain` is presented in Listing 13-3.

Listing 13-3

```
using System;
using System.Windows.Forms;
using System.IO;

public class frmMain : Form
{
    string err;

    private RadioButton rbNumericOverflow;
    private RadioButton rbFileNotFound;
    private RadioButton rbDivideBy0;
    private Button btnThrow;
    private Button btnClose;
    private TextBox txtErrorMsgs;
    private GroupBox groupBox1;

    #region Windows code

    public frmMain()
```

```csharp
{
    InitializeComponent();
    rbDivideBy0.Checked = true;
}

public static void Main()
{
    frmMain main = new frmMain();
    Application.Run(main);
}

private void btnThrow_Click(object sender, EventArgs e)
{

    try
    {
        // To use a general catch, uncomment the next line
        // throw new System.OutOfMemoryException();

        if (rbDivideBy0.Checked == true)
        {
            throw new System.DivideByZeroException();
        }
        else
        {
            if (rbFileNotFound.Checked == true)
            {
                throw new System.IO.FileNotFoundException();
            }
            else
            {
                throw new System.OverflowException();
            }
        }
    }
    catch (DivideByZeroException ex)
    {
        MessageBox.Show("DivideByZeroException thrown.",
                        "Exception Error");
        err = "DivideByZeroException: " + ex.StackTrace;
    }
    catch (FileNotFoundException ex)
    {
        MessageBox.Show("FileNotFoundException thrown.",
                        "Exception Error");
        err = "FileNotFoundException" + ex.StackTrace;
    }
    catch (OverflowException ex)
    {
        MessageBox.Show("OverflowException thrown.",
                        "Exception Error");
        err = "OverflowException" + ex.StackTrace;
    }
    catch (Exception ex)
```

```
        {
            MessageBox.Show(ex.StackTrace, "Exception Error");
            err = ex.Message + " " + ex.StackTrace;
        }
        finally
        {
            clsErrorLog myErrLog = new clsErrorLog(err);
            myErrLog.PathName = Application.StartupPath;

            myErrLog.WriteErrorLog();
            txtErrorMsgs.Text = myErrLog.ReadErrorLog();
        }

    }

    private void btnClose_Click(object sender, EventArgs e)
    {
        Close();
    }
}
```

Most of the work is done in the btnThrow_Click() event code. Based upon the type of exception selected by the user, a series of nested if statements causes the appropriate exception to be thrown. The exception then triggers its associated catch block to be processed. For example, if the user selects the divide-by-zero exception, that exception is thrown and the catch block is executed:

```
catch (DivideByZeroException ex)
{
    MessageBox.Show("DivideByZeroException thrown.",
                    "Exception Error");
    err = "DivideByZeroException: " + ex.StackTrace;
}
```

A message is shown to the user and then the string variable err records the type of exception plus the StackTrace information from the Exception object ex.

The finally block instantiates an error log object named myErrorLog, passing in the error string (err) to the constructor. Finally, the WriteErrorLog() method appends the error string to the error log file. The ReadErrorLog() method simply displays the contents of the error log file in a multiline textbox object.

Managing the error log file itself is done through the clsErrorLog class. The code for the error log class is shown in Listing 13-4.

Listing 13-4

```
using System;
using System.Collections.Generic;
using System.IO;

class clsErrorLog
```

```csharp
{
    //==================== Instance members ====================
    private string fileName;
    private string pathName;
    private string errorMessage;
    private int errorFlag;

    StreamWriter sw = null;
    StreamReader sr = null;

    //==================== Constructor =========================
    public clsErrorLog(string msg)
    {
        errorMessage = msg;
        errorFlag = 0;
        fileName = "ErrorLog.txt";
    }
    //==================== Property Methods ====================
    public string FileName
    {
        get
        {
            return fileName;
        }
        set
        {
            if (value.Length > 0)
                fileName = value;
        }
    }
    public string Message
    {
        get
        {
            return errorMessage;
        }
        set
        {
            if (value.Length > 0)
                errorMessage = value;
        }
    }

    public string PathName      // Set the path name thingie
    {
        get
        {
            return pathName;
        }

        set
```

```
                {
                  if (value.Length > 0)
                    pathName = value;
                }
        }
        //=================== Helper Methods =====================
        //=================== General Methods ====================

        /*****
        * Purpose: This reads the error log file.
        *
        * Parameter list:
        *   n/a
        *
        * Return value
        *   string          the contents of the error log message file
        *****/
        public string ReadErrorLog()
        {
            string buff;
            try
            {
                        string pfn = Path.Combine(pathName, fileName);
                    if (File.Exists(pfn) == true)
                    {
                        sr = new StreamReader(pfn);

                        buff = sr.ReadToEnd();
                        sr.Close();
                        return buff;
                    }
            }
            catch
            {
            return "";
            }
            return "";
        }

        /*****
        * Purpose: This writes an error log message to the error log file.
        *          The message has the date and time, the type of error,
        *          and the stack trace for the error.
        *
        * Parameter list:
        *   n/a
        *
        * Return value
        *   int          0 = no errors, 1 otherwise
        *****/
```

```
public int WriteErrorLog()
{
    errorFlag = 0;
    DateTime currentDT = DateTime.Now;

    try
    {
            // Do we have all the stings need?
            if (errorMessage.Length != 0 && pathName.Length != 0 &&
                        fileName.Length != 0)
            {
                    sw = new StreamWriter(Path.Combine(pathName,
                                                fileName), true);
                    sw.WriteLine(currentDT.ToShortDateString() + ", " +
                                currentDT.ToShortTimeString() + ": " +
            errorMessage);
                                    sw.WriteLine("----------------");
                    sw.Close();
            }
            else
            {
                    errorFlag = 1;  // Something bad happened
            }
    }
    catch (Exception ex)
    {
            errorMessage = ex.Message;
            errorFlag = 1; // Something bad happened
    }
    return errorFlag;
}

/*****
 * Purpose: This writes an error log message to the error log file.
 *
 * Parameter list:
 *   string msg       the error message to write
 *
 * Return value
 *   int              0 = no errors, 1 otherwise
 *****/
public int WriteErrorLog(string msg)
{
    errorMessage = msg;              // Copy the message
    errorFlag = WriteErrorLog();     // Now call original one
    return errorFlag;
}
}
```

The StreamWriter Object

The code makes use of a `StreamWriter` object to write the error message and related information to a disk file named ErrorLog.txt. (See the constructor code in Listing 13-4.) The statement

```
sw = new StreamWriter(Path.Combine(pathName, fileName), true);
```

calls the `StreamWriter` constructor to instantiate the `sw` `StreamWriter` object. The constructor is overloaded and the version you are using here has two arguments.

The first argument, `Path.Combine(pathName, filename)`, combines the pathname and the file name to form a single argument. By default, if you do not supply a path name for the file, C# assumes you want to place the file in the same directory as the executable file for the program. If you stored this program in a folder named `TestCode` on the `C` drive and named the project `ErrorLogger`, the default path name supplied to the constructor would be

```
"C:\\TestCode\\ErrorLogger\\bin\\Debug\\ErrorLog.txt"
```

The second argument is a Boolean with the value `true`. If the second argument is `true`, all new text data is appended to the end of the file. If the file does not exist, the file is created. If the second argument is `false` and the file exists, any current data in the file is overwritten. If the file does not exist and the second argument is `false`, the file is created and the new string data is written to the file.

Notice that we have overloaded the `WriteErrorLog()` method for the class. The signatures for the two methods are as follows:

```
public int WriteErrorLog()

public int WriteErrorLog(string msg)
```

In `frmMain`, we passed in the error message to the constructor. That error message is then assigned into class member named `errorMessage`. However, if an object of `clsErrorLog` has already been instantiated and the user then wants to write another error message to the file, he can use the second `WriteErrorLog()` method that accepts a string as its argument. The code for this version shows that the error message passed in is assigned into `errorMessage` and then the no-parameter version of `WriteErrorLog()` is called. The appropriate return value is maintained in either call.

```
public int WriteErrorLog(string msg)
{
    errorMessage = msg;                // Copy the message
    errorFlag = WriteErrorLog();       // Now call original one
    return errorFlag;
}
```

The code for the `WriteErrorLog()` that does the real work is embodied within a `try-catch` block. This is always a good idea, because electromechanical devices are the Achilles heel of most computer systems. The `WriteLine()` method of the `StreamWriter` object is used to write the error message to the file. The `WriteLine()` method differs from the `Write()` method in that `WriteLine()` appends a newline character at the end of the string currently being saved to disk. The statements are these:

```
sw.WriteLine(currentDT.ToShortDateString() + ", " +
              currentDT.ToShortTimeString() + ": " + errorMessage);
sw.WriteLine("---------------");
sw.Close();
```

The first call to `WriteLine()` writes the current date and time to the file, followed by the error message that has been passed to the class. The second call to `WriteLine()` simply writes out a series of dashes to make the end of each error message entry easier to differentiate. The final statement closes the file by a call to the `Close()` method of the `StreamWriter` object.

Reading the Data

After the data has been written to the disk, control eventually returns to the statement:

```
txtErrorMsgs.Text = myErrLog.ReadErrorLog();
```

This statement uses the `ReadErrorLog()` method to read the contents of the error log file. (You could, of course, use Notepad or some equivalent program to read the file.) The code for reading the file is:

```
public string ReadErrorLog()
{
    string buff;
    try
    {
        string pfn = Path.Combine(pathName, fileName);
        if (File.Exists(pfn) == true)
        {
            sr = new StreamReader(pfn);

            buff = sr.ReadToEnd();
            sr.Close();
            return buff;
        }
    }
    catch (Exception ex)
    {
        return ex.Message;
    }
    return "";
}
```

Again, the code is surrounded by a `try-catch` block to prevent an ungraceful death by the program. The program builds the path and file name and assigns them into the variable `pfn`. The code then uses a `File` object to determine if that file exists. (You can use `File.Exists(pfn)` directly without explicit instantiation because it is a `static` method.) Assuming the file does exist, we instantiate a `StreamReader` object named `sr`. The `ReadToEnd()` method of the `StreamReader` class reads all the string data in the file and assigns it into `buff`, which is returned to the caller. In the code, you simply copy the string to the `listbox` object.

Using clsErrorLog

Unlike most of our previous programs, the `clsErrorLog` class is actually useful in its own right. If you use `try-catch` blocks in your code or use `if` statements to sense error conditions other than exceptions, you can use this class to record what happened. Because you are free to pass in any string you wish, its contents can vary according to your information needs when a given error occurs. If it is in a commercial product and someone is calling for product support, you can have the caller read the `ErrorLog.txt` file with Notepad and at least have some idea of what went wrong.

True, the program's pretty simple, but you can always add functionality if you need it. That's one of the nice things about OOP . . . you can always extend the class to suit your specific needs.

Sequential Versus Random Access Files

The error log program presented in Listing 13-3s and 13-4 writes textual data to a disk file named ErrorLog.txt. If the log file doesn't exist, it is created and the new data is written to the file. If the file exists and already has information stored in it, new data is appended to the end of the existing file. Over the years, this file could grow fairly large if errors continue to be added. Typically, when reading a text file, the reading program starts at the beginning of the file and reads the data in the file to the end.

Sequential Files

The process of continually adding new data to the end of an existing file creates what is called a *sequential file*. With sequential files, new data is added on to the end of the file. There are no gaps in the data. Indeed, one of the advantages of sequential files is that they are dense. That is, every byte of storage space in a sequential file is filled with a piece of information.

Sequential files are like the old cassette music tapes. If you like song number nine on the tape, you had to fast-forward the tape to that particular song in order to play it. If you were good at it, you could press the fast-forward button on the cassette player, count the required number of seconds in your head, and then press the play button. With practice, you could get pretty close to your desired song. The DVD players of today make this "timed search" seem pretty archaic. You simply skip over the tracks you don't want to hear and immediately begin listening to the song of choice. No wonder we're turning into a nation of softies!

If you can visualize a disk file like a music tape, it would look something like Figure 13-5.

Figure 13-5

The first thing to notice in the figure is that each song is free to be longer or shorter than any other song. The BOF in Figure 13-5 stands for *Beginning Of File*, while EOF stands for *End Of File*. You can think of the File Pointer as the ceramic read/write head of disk hardware. Sequential files are read sequentially from BOF to EOF. Therefore, to read the sequential file, the File Pointer is placed at BOF when the file is opened and it moves towards EOF as the file is read. To get to song five, you must read through the first four songs. (While the fast-forward button sped things up, you still had to read the intervening songs.) Sequential files have an EOF marker written at the end of the file so the end of the file can be sensed by the program code. When the File Pointer has read through the file and reads the EOF marker, you know that the entire contents of the file have been read.

Advantages and Disadvantages of Sequential Files

When it comes to sequential files, the good news is that the files are dense: they waste no disk space. The bad news is that you are forced to read through unwanted data to get to the data you actually want to use. Also, editing the information in a sequential file is awkward at best. In most cases, editing some part of a sequential file means reading the old file into memory, rewriting the old file information up to the point of the edit to a new file, writing the new information to the new file, and then appending the remaining part of the old file onto the new file. Yep . . . it's as clumsy as I've described it.

Sequential files are often used for information that rarely requires editing or updating. E-mail messages, error logs, documents, letters, and similar types of data are good candidates for sequential files because they are used to store information that isn't often updated. However, the bulk of business transactions often employ information that needs to be updated frequently, so sequential files just aren't suited to the task. That's where random access files come in.

Random Access Files

Random access files are based upon the concept of a fixed record size. For example, when you open a credit account with a store, it records your name and home and work addresses, plus some credit information. Because people do move, change jobs, improve (or ruin) their credit history, get married, and do dozens of other things, such information needs to be updated fairly often. Because information of this nature does require frequent updating, software engineers make sure each record is the same size. This is shown in Figure 13-6.

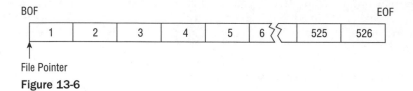

Figure 13-6

Whereas Figure 13-5 shows records of differing length, the byte length of each record in Figure 13-6 is identical. You can visualize a random access record as a line of bricks laid end to end, in which each brick represents the information about one customer. Because each brick has the same size, it's easy to pick up brick number five (perhaps the information about Ms. Melton) from the line, change the information written on the brick, and replace the brick at position number five in the line of bricks.

Fixed Record Sizes

So . . . big deal. What's the advantage of random access files? I can show the advantage with a simple example. Suppose the information about each customer takes 300 bytes. This means the length of each "information brick" in Figure 13-6 is 300 bytes. Each information brick forms what is called a *record* for one customer. The advantage of random access files is that we can pick up the File Pointer and *skip over* the four bricks (that is, records) you don't want to read and drop the File Pointer down at the exact beginning of brick five. By our not having to read the information contained in the first four bricks, physically getting to brick five is significantly faster.

C# provides you with a file method named Seek() that lets you scoot the File Pointer to any point in the file you wish. The Seek() method can move the File Pointer virtually instantaneously, and significantly faster than you can move the File Pointer by reading the records between its current position and the record you wish to read. The general syntax for the Seek() method is as follows:

```
Seek((desiredRecord - 1) * RECORDSIZE, SeekOrigin.Begin);
```

As with almost everything in computer programming, the first record in a random access file is actually record 0. Therefore, if each RECORDSIZE is 300 bytes and we wish to read record number five, we need to position the File Pointer at a spot that is 1,200 bytes into the file, as measured from BOF. Because the desired record is record number five, the actual position in the file must be calculated as follows:

```
Seek((desiredRecord - 1) * RECORDSIZE, SeekOrigin.Begin);
Seek((5 - 1) * 300, SeekOrigin.Begin);
Seek(4 * 300, BOF);
Seek(1200, BOF);
```

You can read this last statement as "Use the Seek() method to position the File Pointer with a byte offset of 1,200 bytes relative to the beginning of file." This position can be viewed as shown in Figure 13-7.

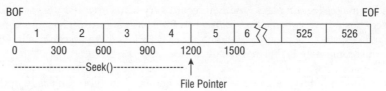

Figure 13-7

The first argument in the Seek() method is the *byte offset* that the File Pointer is to be moved expressed as a long data type. The second argument for Seek() is the *relative position* from which the File Pointer is to move. The second argument of the Seek() method provides three relative points for moving the File Pointer. The first, SeekOrigin.Begin, positions the File Pointer with the byte offset relative to BOF. This is what is shown in Figure 13-7: the File Pointer is offset 1,200 bytes relative to BOF.

Second, SeekOrigin.Current moves the File Pointer relative to the current location of the File Pointer. For example, if you have read record number five, the File Pointer's current position would be at the start of record number six (byte offset 1,500 relative to BOF). If you wish to now read record number four, you could use

```
Seek(-600, SeekOrigin.Current);
```

Because the byte offset is negative, the File Pointer is moved 600 bytes *back* from its current position, which would be at the start of record number four (byte offset = 900 in Figure 13-7). A negative offset, therefore, means that you wish to move the File Pointer towards the BOF.

The third relative point for the File Pointer is the end. The statement

```
Seek(0, SeekOrigin.End);
```

would place the File Pointer at the end of file (EOF). Where does Seek(-300, SeekOrigin.End) place the File Pointer? In terms of Figure 13-7, your code would be ready to read record number 526. If you think about it, it is an error to have a positive byte offset when SeekOrigin.End is used and you are reading the file. A positive byte offset would mean you are trying to read past the end of the file. Likewise, it is an error to have a negative byte offset when using SeekOrigin.Begin. This would imply placing the File Pointer at a location that is "in front of" the beginning of the file.

Advantages and Disadvantages of Random Access Files

The biggest advantage of random access files is that you can get to a particular record much faster than you can with sequential files. In fact, it's common to tie a customer's record location in the file to some unique piece of information associated with the customer. For example, imagine a customer's last name is Smith. The ASCII code for the letter S is 83. Therefore, you could write this customer at record position 83 in the file. If each record is 300 bytes, this person's information would be stored at byte offset 24,900 bytes relative to BOF. The process of using one piece of information (an S) to derive a second piece of information (record 83) is called *hashing*. Using a hash code algorithm for record positions within a random access file makes locating an individual record very fast. Obviously, if a second Smith is added to the file, this creates what's called a *hash collision* and the hash algorithm has to accommodate such things. (If you're interested, C# provides a `HashAlgorithm` class that you can use in your own programs. Use the online help for further details.)

Because each record in a random access file is exactly the same size, you can easily update a particular record and rewrite that record without having to copy the entire file. Record updating is *much* faster with random access files because you have to rewrite only the record that has been changed.

The bad news is that you must design the record size in terms of a worst-case scenario. Even though you know that most peoples' first names do not exceed 10 characters, you might have to design the number of bytes devoted to the customer's first name to be 15 bytes because of that one oddball whose parents thought it would be cute to name their son Guyfromtazmania. The same is true for all of the information in the record. Street addresses, city names, e-mail addresses, and so on all have to be designed for the largest possible size. Obviously, the trick to designing the byte size for each piece of string data is a balancing act between wasting bytes and being able to record the requisite information.

Because of this worst-case design philosophy, random access files are not dense like sequential files. If a customer has a short name and lives at an address like 1 Elm St., and has no e-mail address, that customer might only use 100 bytes of the 300 bytes you've allowed for him in his record in the file. This means there are information "gaps" in the file where no data are stored. Such a random access file might look like that shown in Figure 13-8.

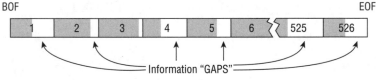

Figure 13-8

The shaded portion of each record contains the actual data for a customer, while the unshaded portion is a gap where no useful information is present. However, if the person moves from 1 Elm St. to 657 Debbie Lane, you have enough room in the gap to update the customer's information with the longer street address.

Most programmers agree that the wasted bytes in the information "gaps" is a small price to pay for the increased performance and ease of updating that random access files bring to the table. Back in the early 1980s, I bought an IBM PC *5MB* hard disk drive for $1,500. At that time, a megabyte of disk storage cost about $300. The price today is approaching 25 *cents* per megabyte! While you still need to think about storage requirements, the cost constraints today are much less severe than in the past. As a result, random access rules for files that may require frequent updating.

Try It Out   Random Access Files

Let's write an electronic phone book to maintain a record of your friends (or customers, or . . . whomever). The user interface for the program is shown in Figure 13-9.

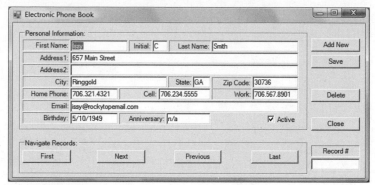

Figure 13-9

Two groupbox objects are present in the user interface. The first group is used to collect the personal information about the person via a collection of textbox objects. The second groupbox object contains several button objects that may be used to navigate through the records stored in the file.

How It Works

Because this program is a little more complex than earlier programs, I used the `#region-#endregion` preprocessor directives to hide sections of code after they have been written, tested, and debugged. A picture of my source code window when I was finished is shown in Figure 13-10.

```
using System;
using System.Windows.Forms;

public class frmMain : Form
{
    const string TESTDATAFILE = "Friends.bin";
    clsRandomAccess myData = new clsRandomAccess(TESTDATAFILE);
    long recs;
    long currentRecord = 1;

    Initialization Step code

    Reading-Displaying data

    Navigation buttons code

    Save-Add-Delete buttons code

    Close button code
```

Figure 13-10

By clicking on the plus sign for any given region, you can expand the code associated with that section. Using regions can save you a lot of scrolling time for programs that have a lot of source code.

frmMain

The complete listing for `frmMain` is presented in Listing 13-5.

Listing 13-5

```csharp
using System;
using System.Windows.Forms;

public class frmMain : Form
{
    const string TESTDATAFILE = "Friends.bin";

    long recs;
    long currentRecord = 1;
    clsRandomAccess myData = new clsRandomAccess(TESTDATAFILE);

    #region Initialization Step code
    private GroupBox groupBox1;
    private Label label2;
    private TextBox txtMI;
    private Label label1;
    private Label label6;
    private TextBox txtZip;
    private Label label7;
    private TextBox txtState;
    private Label label8;
    private TextBox txtCity;
    private Label label5;
    private TextBox txtAddr2;
    private Label label4;
    private TextBox txtAddr1;
    private Label label3;
    private TextBox txtLastName;
    private TextBox txtWork;
    private Label label11;
    private TextBox txtCell;
    private Label label10;
    private TextBox txtHome;
    private Label label9;
    private Label label13;
    private Label label12;
    private TextBox txtEmail;
    private CheckBox chkStatus;
    private TextBox txtAnniversary;
    private Label label14;
    private TextBox txtBirthday;
    private Button btnAdd;
    private Button btnSave;
    private Button btnDelete;
    private Button btnClose;
    private GroupBox groupBox2;
```

```csharp
private Button btnFirst;
private Button btnLast;
private Button btnPrevious;
private Button btnNext;
private Label label15;
private TextBox txtRecord;
private TextBox txtFirstName;

#region Windows code

public frmMain()
{
    InitializeComponent();
}

public static void Main()
{
    frmMain main = new frmMain();
    Application.Run(main);
}
#endregion

#region Reading-Displaying data

/*****
 * Purpose: Read a record and display the results
 *
 * Parameter list:
 *   n/a
 *
 * Return value:
 *   void
 *****/
private int ReadAndShowRecord()
{
    int flag = 1;

    try
    {
        myData.Open(myData.FileName);
        flag = myData.ReadOneRecord(currentRecord - 1);
        if (flag == 1)
        {
            ShowOneRecord();
            txtRecord.Text = currentRecord.ToString();

        }
        else
        {
            MessageBox.Show("Record not available.", "Error Read");
            flag = 0;
        }
    }
    catch
```

(continued)

Listing 13-5 (continued)

```
        {
            flag = 0;
        }
        myData.Close();
        return flag;
    }

/*****
 * Purpose: Move the record data into the textboxes
 *
 * Parameter list:
 *   n/a
 *
 * Return value:
 *   void
 *****/
private void ShowOneRecord()
{
    txtFirstName.Text = myData.FirstName;
    txtLastName.Text = myData.LastName;
    txtAddr1.Text = myData.Address1;
    txtAddr2.Text = myData.Address2;
    txtCity.Text = myData.City;
    txtState.Text = myData.State;
    txtZip.Text = myData.Zip;
    txtHome.Text = myData.HomePhone;
    txtCell.Text = myData.CellPhone;
    txtWork.Text = myData.WorkPhone;
    txtEmail.Text = myData.Email;
    txtBirthday.Text = myData.Birthday;
    txtAnniversary.Text = myData.Anniversary;
    if (myData.Status == 1)
        chkStatus.Checked = true;
    else
        chkStatus.Checked = false;
}

/*****
 * Purpose: Copies data from textboxes to class members.
 *
 * Parameter list:
 *   n/a
 *
 * Return value:
 *   void
 *****/

private void CopyData()
{
    myData.FirstName = txtFirstName.Text;
    myData.MiddleInitial = txtMI.Text;
    myData.LastName = txtLastName.Text;
```

```csharp
        myData.Address1 = txtAddr1.Text;
        myData.Address2 = txtAddr2.Text;
        myData.City = txtCity.Text;
        myData.State = txtState.Text;
        myData.Zip = txtZip.Text;
        myData.HomePhone = txtHome.Text;
        myData.CellPhone = txtCell.Text;
        myData.WorkPhone = txtWork.Text;
        myData.Email = txtEmail.Text;
        myData.Birthday = txtBirthday.Text;
        myData.Anniversary = txtAnniversary.Text;
        if (chkStatus.Checked == true)
            myData.Status = 1;
        else
            myData.Status = 0;
}
#endregion

#region Navigation buttons code

private void btnFirst_Click(object sender, EventArgs e)
{
    int flag;

    currentRecord = 1;
    flag = ReadAndShowRecord();
}

private void btnNext_Click(object sender, EventArgs e)
{
    int flag;

    currentRecord++;
    flag = ReadAndShowRecord();
    if (flag == 0)
    {
        currentRecord--;
    }
}

private void btnPrevious_Click(object sender, EventArgs e)
{
    int flag;

    currentRecord--;
    flag = ReadAndShowRecord();
    if (flag == 0)
    {
        currentRecord++;
    }
}

private void btnLast_Click(object sender, EventArgs e)
```

(continued)

Listing 13-5 (continued)

```csharp
    {
        int flag;

        myData.Open(myData.FileName);
        currentRecord = myData.getRecordCount();
        if (currentRecord > -1)
        {
            flag = ReadAndShowRecord();
        }
    }
    #endregion

    #region Save-Add-Delete buttons code
    /*****
     * Purpose: Save textbox info as a record.
     *
     * Parameter list:
     *   object sender     control that caused the event
     *   EventArgs e       details about the sender
     *
     * Return value:
     *   void
     ******/
    private void btnSave_Click(object sender, EventArgs e)
    {
        CopyData();
        if (myData.Open(TESTDATAFILE) == 1)
        {
            recs = myData.getRecordCount();
            myData.Open(TESTDATAFILE);
            myData.WriteOneRecord(recs);
            myData.Close();
            MessageBox.Show("Data written successfully.");
        }
        else
        {
            MessageBox.Show("Could not open file " + TESTDATAFILE,
                            "File Error");
            return;
        }
    }

    /*****
     * Purpose: Clears out the textboxes and gets ready to accept new
     *          record
     *
     * Parameter list:
     *   object sender     control that caused the event
     *   EventArgs e       details about the sender
     *
     * Return value:
     *   void
     ******/
```

```
private void btnAdd_Click(object sender, EventArgs e)
{
    ClearTextboxes();
    if (myData.Status == 1)
        chkStatus.Checked = true;
    else
        chkStatus.Checked = false;

    txtFirstName.Focus();
}

/*****
 * Purpose: Clear textboxes.
 *
 * Parameter list:
 *   n/a
 *
 * Return value:
 *   void
 *****/
private void ClearTextboxes()
{
    txtFirstName.Text = "";
    txtMI.Text = "";
    txtLastName.Text = "";
    txtAddr1.Text = "";
    txtAddr2.Text = "";
    txtCity.Text = "";
    txtState.Text = "";
    txtZip.Text = "";
    txtHome.Text = "";
    txtCell.Text = "";
    txtWork.Text = "";
    txtEmail.Text = "";
    txtBirthday.Text = "";
    txtAnniversary.Text = "";
}
/*****
 * Purpose: Deletes a record by changing the status member
 *
 * Parameter list:
 *   object sender    control that caused the event
 *   EventArgs e      details about the sender
 *
 * Return value:
 *   void
 *****/
private void btnDelete_Click(object sender, EventArgs e)
{
    DialogResult ask;

    ask = MessageBox.Show("Are you sure you want to delete
            this record?", "Delete Record", MessageBoxButtons.YesNo);
    if (ask == DialogResult.Yes)
```

(continued)

Listing 13-5 (continued)

```
            {
                myData.Status = 0;
                myData.Open(myData.FileName);
                myData.WriteOneRecord(currentRecord - 1);
                MessageBox.Show("Record deleted", "Delete Record");
            }
        }
        #endregion

        #region Close button code

        private void btnClose_Click(object sender, EventArgs e)
        {
            Close();
        }
        #endregion

    }
```

The program begins by defining a number of working variables and constants:

```
        const string TESTDATAFILE = "Friends.bin";

        long recs;
        long currentRecord = 1;
        clsRandomAccess myData = new clsRandomAccess(TESTDATAFILE);
```

These variables have class scope so they are available to all methods within frmMain. As the TESTDATAFILE file name might suggest, a binary file is used to store the information about each friend. Although we know that file records begin with record 0, we initialize the currentRecord variable to 1 (the N − 1 Rule again) so the user can think of the first record as record number one. I administer the actual record number ourselves.

Testing Tip

If you type in the code for this program, change the Text property of each textbox to give that variable a sample test value. This saves you from having to type in data for each textbox each time you test the program. To add a new person, you can view the last person, add 01 to her last name, and then press the Save button. (Don't press the Add New button as it clears all the textbox objects.) On each run, just increment the value by one to differentiate it from the others.

You should use such test values anytime there is a lot of input information that you must enter in order to test the program.

Enter the requested information into the appropriate textbox objects and then click the Save button. The btnSave_Click() event code calls the CopyData() method to copy the contents of the textboxes into the appropriate members of the clsRandomAccess object named myData:

```
private void btnSave_Click(object sender, EventArgs e)
{
    CopyData();
    if (myData.Open(TESTDATAFILE) == 1)
    {
        recs = myData.getRecordCount();
        myData.WriteOneRecord(recs);
        myData.Close();
    }
    else
    {
        MessageBox.Show("Could not open file " + TESTDATAFILE,
                        "File Error");
        return;
    }
}
```

The program then opens the data file and, if there is no error opening the file, calls the getRecordCount() method of the clsRandomAccess class. This method simply determines where the new record should be placed in the file. The call to WriteOneRecord() writes the new data to the file and the file is closed. (Instead of displaying the MessageBox.Show() message, you could use the error log program discussed earlier in this chapter to record the information about the error.)

Navigating the Records

The navigation buttons allow the user to roam around the records that are stored in the file. The code to provide this feature is pretty simple. For example, if the user clicks the First button, the code sets the currentRecord variable to 1 and calls ReadAndShowRecord() to read and display the information in the appropriate textbox objects:

```
private void btnFirst_Click(object sender, EventArgs e)
{
    int flag;

    currentRecord = 1;
    flag = ReadAndShowRecord();
}

private void btnNext_Click(object sender, EventArgs e)
{
    int flag;

    currentRecord++;
    flag = ReadAndShowRecord();
    if (flag == 0)
    {
        currentRecord--;
    }
}
```

The Next button is similar, but it increments `currentRecord` before calling `ReadAndShowRecord()`. If the user tries to use the Next button on the last record in the file, an appropriate error message is displayed. Similar checks are made for the Previous button, too.

Delete a Record

To refer to "deleting" a record is a little misleading because the record isn't actually deleted. Instead, change the `status` member of the `clsRandomAccess` member to `0`, thus marking it as an inactive record. Why not actually delete the record from the file?

There are several reasons for not deleting a record. First, ask yourself why you want to delete the record. Is this person no longer a friend? Was there a fight where all will be forgiven a few days later and you're just doing it now in a fit of pique? In other words, what is the reason for deleting the record? Most people would say it's to free up disk space. Aw, come on! At $.25/MB, are you *really* worried about 300 bytes? With a cost of $.0000075 per member, chances are you can afford to store a few inactive members.

Second, deleting information is just not a good idea . . . period. For example, you might reuse the `clsRandomAccess` code as part of a membership program. Perhaps you have a second file that records membership dues payments, which uses a member club record number to tie the payments to the member. If you delete them from the membership file, you now have *"orphan records"* in the membership dues file that can no longer be linked back to a member . . . active or not. Just as soon as you delete such a record, your luck might be such that the IRS comes in the next day and wants to audit your membership dues records. Now what do you do? If you use a status variable rather than physically deleting the record, such requests are easily fulfilled. Transactions-based programs rarely delete such information because without it, constructing a complete audit trail is very difficult at best.

I would suggest you always use an `int` variable to record the status of a client. Don't make the status variable a `bool`. Often customer records appear to have either an active or inactive state, but other states are more common that you might think. For example, a golf club I've done some programming for has membership status states of: 1) inactive, 2) active, 3) financial leave of absence, and 4) medical leave of absence. Had I elected to use a two-state `bool`, I would not have been able to record all data states for member status.

If you delete a record in the program, you can still see the record displayed as you scroll through the file using the navigation buttons. However, the status flag checkbox object changes its state according to the status flag of the friend being reviewed. If you wanted to prevent the display of inactive friends, a minor change to the `ReadAndShowRecord()` method would do the trick. (See the exercises at the end of this chapter.)

clsRandomAccess

Now let's take a peek at the code for the `clsRandomAccess` class. The code is presented in Listing 13-6.

Listing 13-6

```
using System;
using System.IO;

class clsRandomAccess
```

```
{
          // ------------------ Constants --------------------
     const int NAMESIZES = 20;
     const int ADDRESSSIZES = 30;
     const int PHONESIZES = 12;
     const int EMAILSIZE = 100;
     const int DATESIZES = 10;
     const int STRINGSINFILE = 14;

     const int RECORDSIZE = NAMESIZES          // First name
                    + 1                        // Middle Initial
                    + NAMESIZES                // Last name
                    + ADDRESSSIZES * 2         // Both addresses
                    + NAMESIZES                // City
                    + 2                        // State abbreviation
                    + 5                        // Zip
                    + PHONESIZES * 3           // Phone numbers
                    + EMAILSIZE                // Email address
                    + DATESIZES * 2            // Birthday & anniversary
                    + sizeof(int)              // Status
                    + STRINGSINFILE;           // String's length byte

     // ---------------------- Instance variables ------------------
     private string firstName;          // Demographics
     private string middleInitial;
     private string lastName;
     private string address1;
     private string address2;
     private string city;
     private string state;
     private string zip;
     private string homePhone;
     private string cellPhone;
     private string workPhone;
     private string email;
     private string birthday;
     private string anniversary;

     private int status;                        // Active = 1, inactive = 0

     private string errorMessage;
     private string fileName;

     private FileStream myFile;
     private BinaryReader br;
     private BinaryWriter bw;

     // ---------------------- Constructor --------------------

     public clsRandomAccess()
```

(continued)

Listing 13-6 (continued)

```
    {
        // initialise instance variables
        myFile = null;
        errorMessage = "";
        fileName = "Friends.bin";                 // Default file name
        status = 1;
    }
    public clsRandomAccess(string fn):this() // Call no-arg constructor
                                             // first
    {
        fileName = fn;
    }
    #region Property Methods
    // -------------- Property Methods --------------------

    public string FirstName
    {
        get
        {
            return firstName;
        }
        set
        {
            if (value.Length > 0)                     // Do we have a string?
            {
                firstName = value;
                if (firstName.Length > NAMESIZES)  // Too long
                {                                    // Trim it.
                    firstName = firstName.Substring(0, NAMESIZES);
                }
            }
        }
    }

    public string MiddleInitial
    {
        get
        {
            return middleInitial;
        }
        set
        {
            if (value.Length > 0)                  // Do we have a string?
            {
                middleInitial = value;
                if (middleInitial.Length != 1)    // Too long?
                {
                    middleInitial = "n/a";
                }
            }
        }
    }
```

```
public string LastName
{
    get
    {
        return lastName;
    }
    set
    {
        if (value.Length > 0)                    // Do we have a string?
        {
            lastName = value;
            if (lastName.Length > NAMESIZES)     // Too long?
            {
                lastName = lastName.Substring(0, NAMESIZES);
            }
        }
    }
}

public string Address1
{
    get
    {
        return address1;
    }
    set
    {
        if (value.Length > 0)                    // Do we have a string?
        {
            address1 = value;
            if (address1.Length > ADDRESSSIZES)    // Too long?
            {
                address1 = address1.Substring(0, ADDRESSSIZES);
            }
        }
        else
        {
            address1 = "n/a";
        }
    }
}
public string Address2
{
    get
    {
        return address2;
    }
    set
    {
        if (value.Length > 0)                    // Do we have a string?
        {
            address2 = value;
            if (address2.Length > ADDRESSSIZES)    // Too long?
```

(continued)

Listing 13-6 (continued)

```
                {
                    address2 = address2.Substring(0, ADDRESSSIZES);
                }
            }
            if (address2 == null)    // None given?
            {
                address2 = "n/a";
            }
        }
    }
    public string City
    {
        get
        {
            return city;
        }
        set
        {
            if (value.Length > 0)                 // Do we have a string?
            {
                city = value;
                if (city.Length > NAMESIZES)    // Too long?
                {
                    city = city.Substring(0, NAMESIZES);
                }
            }
        }
    }
    public string State
    {
        get
        {
            return state;
        }
        set
        {
            if (value.Length > 0)                 // Do we have a string?
            {
                state = value;
                if (state.Length != 2)    // Must be 2
                {
                    state = "";   // Error
                }
            }
        }
    }
    public string Zip
    {
        get
        {
            return zip;
        }
```

```
        set
        {
            if (value.Length > 0)        // Do we have a string?
            {
                zip = value;
                if (zip.Length != 5)     // Must be 5
                {
                    zip = "";  // Error
                }
            }
        }
    }
}
public string HomePhone
{
    get
    {
        return homePhone;
    }
    set
    {
        if (value.Length > 0)        // Do we have a string?
        {
            homePhone = value;
            if (homePhone.Length > PHONESIZES)
            {
                homePhone = homePhone.Substring(0, PHONESIZES);
            }
        }
        if (homePhone == null)
        {
            homePhone = "n/a";
        }
    }
}

public string CellPhone
{
    get
    {
        return cellPhone;
    }
    set
    {
        if (value.Length > 0)        // Do we have a string?
        {
            cellPhone = value;
            if (cellPhone.Length > PHONESIZES)
            {
                cellPhone = cellPhone.Substring(0, PHONESIZES);
            }
        }
        if (cellPhone == null)
```

(continued)

Listing 13-6 (continued)

```csharp
            {
                cellPhone = "n/a";
            }
        }
    }

    public string WorkPhone
    {
        get
        {
            return workPhone;
        }
        set
        {
            if (value.Length > 0)        // Do we have a string?
            {
                workPhone = value;
                if (workPhone.Length > PHONESIZES)
                {
                    workPhone = workPhone.Substring(0, PHONESIZES);
                }
            }
            if (workPhone == null)
            {
                workPhone = "n/a";
            }
        }
    }

    public string Email
    {
        get
        {
            return email;
        }
        set
        {
            if (value.Length > 0)        // Do we have a string?
            {
                email = value;
                if (email.Length > EMAILSIZE)
                {
                    email = email.Substring(0, EMAILSIZE);
                }
            }
            if (email == null)
            {
                email = "n/a";
            }
        }
    }

    public string Birthday
```

```
    {
        get
        {
            return birthday;
        }
        set
        {
            if (value.Length > 0)        // Do we have a string?
            {
                birthday = value;
                if (birthday.Length > DATESIZES)
                {
                    birthday = birthday.Substring(0, DATESIZES);
                }
            }
            if (birthday == null)
            {
                birthday = "n/a";
            }
        }
    }
    public string Anniversary
    {
        get
        {
            return anniversary;
        }
        set
        {
            if (value.Length > 0)        // Do we have a string?
            {
                anniversary = value;
                if (anniversary.Length > DATESIZES)
                {
                    anniversary = anniversary.Substring(0, DATESIZES);
                }
            }
            if (anniversary == null)
            {
                anniversary = "n/a";
            }
        }
    }

    public int Status
    {
        get
        {
            return status;
        }
        set
        {
            if (value == 1)        // Active
```

(continued)

Listing 13-6 (continued)

```
                    {
                        status = value;
                    }
                    else
                    {
                        status = 0;        // Inactive
                    }
                }
            }

            public string FileName
            {
                get
                {
                    return fileName;
                }

                set
                {
                    if (value.Length > 0)
                        fileName = value;
                }
            }

            public FileStream MyFile
            {
                get
                {
                    return myFile;
                }

                set
                {
                    myFile = value;
                }
            }

            public BinaryReader BinReader
            {
                get
                {
                    return br;
                }

                set
                {
                    br = value;
                }
            }

            public BinaryWriter BinWriter
            {
                get
```

```
        {
            return bw;
        }

        set
        {
            bw = value;
        }
    }

    public String ErrorText
    {
        get
        {
            return errorMessage;
        }
    }
    #endregion

    // -------------- General Methods --------------------
    /****
     * This creates a random access file.
     *
     * Parameter list:
     *    fn        a string that holds the file name to use
     *
     * Return value:
     *    int       0 if error, 1 otherwise
     ****/
    public int Create(String fn)
    {
        try
        {
            myFile = new FileStream(fn, FileMode.OpenOrCreate);
            bw = new BinaryWriter(myFile);
            fileName = fn;
        }
        catch
        {
            return 0;
        }
        return 1;
    }

    /****
     * This opens a file for reading
     *
     * Parameter list:
     *    fn        the file name
     *
     * Return value:
     *    int       0 if error, 1 otherwise
     ****/
```

(continued)

Listing 13-6 (continued)

```
public int Open(string fn)
{
    if (bw == null)
    {
        return Create(fn);
    }
    else
    {
        myFile = new FileStream(fn, FileMode.OpenOrCreate);
    }

    return 1;
}


/****
 * This closes the currently-open file.
 *
 * Parameter list:
 *     n/a
 *
 * Return value:
 *     void
 ****/

public void Close()
{
    if (myFile != null)
        myFile.Close();
    if (bw != null)
        bw.Close();
    if (br != null)
        br.Close();
}

/**
 * This writes one record to the currently-open file
 *
 * Parameter list:
 *     num             an integer that holds the record number
 *
 * Return value:
 *     int      0 if error, 1 otherwise
 *
 * CAUTION: this method assumes that the properties contain the
 * record to be written.
 */

public int WriteOneRecord(long num)
```

```
{
    int errorFlag = 1;

    try
    {
        if (myFile != null && bw != null)
        {   // Position the file pointer
            myFile.Seek(num * RECORDSIZE, SeekOrigin.Begin);
            bw = new BinaryWriter(myFile);

            bw.Write(firstName);          // Write the data
            bw.Write(middleInitial);
            bw.Write(lastName);
            bw.Write(address1);
            bw.Write(address2);
            bw.Write(city);
            bw.Write(state);
            bw.Write(zip);
            bw.Write(homePhone);
            bw.Write(cellPhone);
            bw.Write(workPhone);
            bw.Write(email);
            bw.Write(birthday);
            bw.Write(anniversary);
            bw.Write(status);
            bw.Close();
        }
    }
    catch (IOException ex)
    {
        errorMessage = ex.Message;    // In case they want to view it.
        errorFlag = 0;
    }
    return errorFlag;
}

/**
 * This reads one record and returns it as a string
 *
 * Parameter list:
 *   num              an integer that holds the record number
 *
 * Return value
 *   int              0 if error, 1 otherwise
 */

public int ReadOneRecord(long num)
{
    try
    {
        if (myFile != null)
            myFile.Close();

        myFile = new FileStream(fileName, FileMode.Open);
```

(continued)

Listing 13-6 (continued)

```
            br = new BinaryReader(myFile);

            if (myFile != null && br != null)
            {
                // Position the file pointer
                myFile.Seek(num * RECORDSIZE, SeekOrigin.Begin);
                firstName = br.ReadString();
                middleInitial = br.ReadString();
                lastName = br.ReadString();
                address1 = br.ReadString();
                address2 = br.ReadString();
                city = br.ReadString();
                state = br.ReadString();
                zip = br.ReadString();
                homePhone = br.ReadString();
                cellPhone = br.ReadString();
                workPhone = br.ReadString();
                email = br.ReadString();
                birthday = br.ReadString();
                anniversary = br.ReadString();
                status = br.ReadInt32();
                br.Close();

            }
        }
        catch (IOException ex)
        {
            errorMessage = ex.Message;
            return 0;
        }

        return 1;
    }
    /**
    * Purpose: This determines the number of records currently in the file
    *
    * Parameter list:
    *    void
    *
    * Return value
    *    long            the number of bytes in the file
    */
    public long getRecordCount()
    {
        long records = 0;
        long remainder;

        try
        {
            if (myFile != null)
```

```
                    {
                        // Position the file pointer
                        records = myFile.Seek(0, SeekOrigin.End);
                        Close();
                    }
                }
                catch (IOException ex)
                {
                    //MessageBox.Show("Error: " + ex.Message);
                    return -1;
                }
                remainder = records % RECORDSIZE;      // Is there a partial record
                records = records / RECORDSIZE;        // Calculate the records
                if (remainder > 0)                     // Partial record...
                    records++;                         // ...account for it.

                return records;
            }
        }
```

While the listing seems quite long, a good part of its length is due to the Property methods' code, which is fairly repetitious.

Determining a Record Size

The first order of business is to determine the record size necessary to store our data. Near the top of Listing 13-6 you find this:

```
// ----------------- Constants --------------------
const int NAMESIZES = 20;
const int ADDRESSSIZES = 30;
const int PHONESIZES = 12;
const int EMAILSIZE = 100;
const int DATESIZES = 10;
const int STRINGSINFILE = 14;


const int RECORDSIZE = NAMESIZES          // First name
                     + 1                  // Middle Initial
                     + NAMESIZES          // Last name
                     + ADDRESSSIZES * 2   // Both addresses
                     + NAMESIZES          // City
                     + 2                  // State abbreviation
                     + 5                  // Zip
                     + PHONESIZES * 3     // Phone numbers
                     + EMAILSIZE          // Email address
                     + DATESIZES * 2      // Birthday & anniversary
                     + sizeof(int)        // Status
                     + STRINGSINFILE;     // String's length byte
```

The constants are used to set the maximum (worst-case) number of characters for various strings used to store the data. The property methods use these constants to truncate any string that exceeds the prescribed length. You can, of course, adjust these if you wish and the appropriate code reflects the changes once the program is recompiled.

A couple of expressions need some explanation. The expression

```
sizeof(int)
```

uses the `sizeof()` operator to determine the number of bytes necessary to store an `int` value type. You can use the `sizeof()` operator with any value type. Simply place the value type within the enclosing parentheses.

The Length of a String in a Binary File

What's with the expression `STRINGSINFILE` near the end of the list of constants? The simple explanation is that there are 14 string variables being stored in each record. To understand why this is necessary needs a little more detailed explanation.

The purpose of adding all the constants together is to determine the number of bytes each record uses. This total is then stored in `RECORDSIZE` and is used at several places in the class when the File Pointer is being moved around in the file. Figure 13-11 can help explain why the 14 variables are necessary.

```
000000  04 49 73 73 79 01 43 05   53 6D 69 74 68 0F 36 35   ⎕Issy.C.Smith.65
000010  37 20 4D 61 69 6E 20 53   74 72 65 65 74 03 6E 2F   7 Main Street.n/
000020  61 08 52 69 6E 67 67 6F   6C 64 02 47 41 05 33 30   a.Ringgold.GA.30
000030  37 33 36 0C 37 30 36 2E   33 32 31 2E 34 33 32 31   736.706.321.4321
000040  0C 37 30 36 2E 32 33 34   2E 35 35 35 35 0C 37 30   .706.234.5555.70
000050  36 2E 35 36 37 2E 38 39   30 31 16 69 73 73 79 40   6.567.8901.issy@
000060  72 6F 63 6B 79 74 6F 70   65 6D 61 69 6C 2E 63 6F   rockytopemail.co
000070  6D 09 35 2F 31 30 2F 31   39 34 39 03 6E 2F 61 01   m.5/10/1949.n/a.
000080  00 00 00 00 00 00 00 00   00 00 00 00 00 00 00 00   ................
000090  00 00 00 00 00 00 00 00   00 00 00 00 00 00 00 00   ................
0000a0  00 00 00 00 00 00 00 00   00 00 00 00 00 00 00 00   ................
0000b0  00 00 00 00 00 00 00 00   00 00 00 00 00 00 00 00   ................
0000c0  00 00 00 00 00 00 00 00   00 00 00 00 00 00 00 00   ................
0000d0  00 00 00 00 00 00 00 00   00 00 00 00 00 00 00 00   ................
0000e0  00 00 00 00 00 00 00 00   00 00 00 00 00 00 00 00   ................
0000f0  00 00 00 00 00 00 00 00   00 00 00 00 00 00 00 00   ................
000100  00 00 00 00 00 00 00 00   00 00 00 00 00 00 00 00   ................
000110  00 00 00 00 00 00 00 00   00 00 00 00 00 00 00 00   ................
000120  00 00 00 00 00 00 00 00   00 00 00 00 00 00 04 49   ...............I
000130  73 73 79 01 43 07 53 6D   69 74 68 30 32 0F 36 35   ssy.C.Smith02.65
000140  37 20 4D 61 69 6E 20 53   74 72 65 65 74 06 41 70   7 Main Street.Ap
000150  74 2E 20 33 08 52 69 6E   67 67 6F 6C 64 02 47 41   t. 3.Ringgold.GA
000160  05 33 30 37 33 36 0C 37   30 36 2E 33 32 31 2E 34   .30736.706.321.4
000170  33 32 31 0C 37 30 36 2E   32 33 34 2E 35 35 35 35   321.706.234.5555
000180  0C 37 30 36 2E 35 36 37   2E 38 39 30 31 16 69 73   .706.567.8901.is
000190  73 79 40 72 6F 63 6B 79   74 6F 70 65 6D 61 69 6C   sy@rockytopemail
0001a0  2E 63 6F 6D 09 35 2F 31   30 2F 31 39 34 39 03 6E   .com.5/10/1949.n
0001b0  2F 61 00 00 00 00 00 00   00 00 00 00 00 00 00 00   /a..............
0001c0  00 00 00 00 00 00 00 00   00 00 00 00 00 00 00 00   ................
0001d0  00 00 00 00 00 00 00 00   00 00 00 00 00 00 00 00   ................
0001e0  00 00 00 00 00 00 00 00   00 00 00 00 00 00 00 00   ................
0001f0  00 00 00 00 00 00 00 00   00 00 00 00 00 00 00 00   ................
000200  00 00 00 00 00 00 00 00   00 00 00 00 00 00 00 00   ................
000210  00 00 00 00 00 00 00 00   00 00 00 00 00 00 00 00   ................
000220  00 00 00 00 00 00 00 00   00 00 00 00 00 00 00 00   ................
000230  00 00 00 00 00 00 00 00   00 00 00 00 00 00 00 00   ................
000240  00 00 00 00 00 00 00 00   00 00 00 00 00 00 00 00   ................
000250  00 00 00 00 00 00 00 00   00 00 05 43 61 72          ...........Car
000260  6F 6C 01 4E 08 41 6E 64   65 72 73 6F 6E 17 31 31   ol.N.Anderson.11
000270  31 20 57 69 6E 64 69 6E   67 20 54 72 61 69 6C 20   1 Winding Trail
000280  44 72 69 76 65 07 41 70   74 2E 20 32 31 0C 49 6E   Drive.Apt. 21.In
000290  64 69 61 6E 61 70 6F 6C   69 73 02 49 4E 05 34 36   dianapolis.IN.46
0002a0  32 31 31 0C 33 31 37 2E   33 33 33 2E 32 32 32 32   211.317.333.2222
```

Figure 13-11

The first line in the figure has the following values:

```
000000   04 49 73 73 79 01 43 05     53 6D 69 74 68 0F 36 35
```

If you decode these hex values into their appropriate ASCII values, you get

```
000000   04 49 73 73 79 01 43 05    53 6D 69 74 68 0F 36 35    (Hex)
            I  s  s  y     C          S  m  i  t  h     6  5    (ASCII)
         4              1     5                          15     (Decimal)
```

Notice the binary values that precede each string. The number 4 precedes Issy, 1 precedes C, 5 precedes Smith, 15 precedes 657 Main Street. Why . . . could it be? Does the number in front of each string tell how many bytes are necessary to store the string? Yep, it does. When you store strings in a binary data file, the low-level file I/O code needs to know how many bytes are associated with each piece of string data. In some programming languages, the information necessary to store a string in a binary file is a little more complex and is called a *string descriptor block*. In C#, the string descriptor block is simply called the *length byte*. Because each string has one length byte and we have 14 strings in the file, we need to account for those length bytes in our total record size calculation. Hence, the STRINGSINFILE (because of the 14 strings) at the end of the record size calculation.

If you add up all the byte requirements for all the data in a friend record, you find that RECORDSIZE equals 302 bytes. Therefore, after a few records are written to the file, the file is going to look very similar to that shown in Figure 13-7.

Writing a Record

When the user wants to save a record, she clicks the Save button in frmMain. This causes the following methods to be called:

```
recs = myData.getRecordCount();
myData.Open(TESTDATAFILE);
myData.WriteOneRecord(recs);
```

The code in getRecordCount() uses the Seek() method to position the File Pointer at the end of the file (EOF). When the File Pointer has reached that position, it returns the number of bytes (as a long) that are in the file from its current position. If you divide the number of bytes in the file by its record size, you get the number of records that have already been written to the file. However, you need to refine the calculation to account for the fact that there could be an "information gap" in the last record. (See Figure 13-8.) If that is the case, the record counter must be incremented by one.

Next, the data file is opened and the code calls WriteOneRecord(), passing in the record position (recs) that is used for the new file. The code for WriteOneRecord() is fairly straightforward:

```
public int WriteOneRecord(long num)
{
    int errorFlag = 1;

    try
    {
        if (myFile != null && bw != null)
        {   // Position the file pointer
            myFile.Seek(num * RECORDSIZE, SeekOrigin.Begin);
            bw = new BinaryWriter(myFile);
            bw.Write(firstName);        // Write the data
```

(continued)

(continued)

```
                bw.Write(middleInitial);
                bw.Write(lastName);
                bw.Write(address1);
                bw.Write(address2);
                bw.Write(city);
                bw.Write(state);
                bw.Write(zip);
                bw.Write(homePhone);
                bw.Write(cellPhone);
                bw.Write(workPhone);
                bw.Write(email);
                bw.Write(birthday);
                bw.Write(anniversary);
                bw.Write(status);
                bw.Close();
            }
        }
    catch (IOException ex)
    {
        errorMessage = ex.Message;     // In case they want to view it.
        errorFlag = 0;
    }
    return errorFlag;
}
```

The code checks to make sure we have a valid `FileStream` object (`myFile`) and then positions the File Pointer at the spot in the file where the new record is to be written (that is, `num * RECORDSIZE` bytes into the file). The code then creates a `BinaryWriter` object (`bw`) and proceeds to write the data to the file. The file is then closed and you're done. (It's a good idea to close a file when you're done with it. In a networking environment, some files cannot be accessed if someone else is using them.) The code is encapsulated within a `try-catch` block just in case something goes wrong. You could work in the error-logging functionality in the `catch` block to make a more robust application.

Keep in mind that each string that is written by the `BinaryWriter` object bw automatically writes the length byte for each string. What about `status`? It's an `int`, not a string, so it has no length byte. How does bw know how many bytes to write? The Common Language Runtime knows how many bytes are associated with each value type, so bw writes four bytes for `status`.

Reading a Record

Reading a record is almost a mirror image of writing the record. The code for the `ReadOneRecord()` is shown here:

```
public int ReadOneRecord(long num)
{
    try
    {
        if (myFile != null)
            myFile.Close();

        myFile = new FileStream(fileName, FileMode.Open);
        br = new BinaryReader(myFile);
```

```
        if (myFile != null && br != null)
        {
            // Position the file pointer
            myFile.Seek(num * RECORDSIZE, SeekOrigin.Begin);
            firstName = br.ReadString();
            middleInitial = br.ReadString();
            lastName = br.ReadString();
            address1 = br.ReadString();
            address2 = br.ReadString();
            city = br.ReadString();
            state = br.ReadString();
            zip = br.ReadString();
            homePhone = br.ReadString();
            cellPhone = br.ReadString();
            workPhone = br.ReadString();
            email = br.ReadString();
            birthday = br.ReadString();
            anniversary = br.ReadString();
            status = br.ReadInt32();
            br.Close();

        }
    }
    catch (IOException ex)
    {
        errorMessage = ex.Message;
        return 0;
    }

    return 1;
}
```

Once again, a `FileStream` object named `myFile` is used to scoot the File Pointer to the location in the file from which you wish to read the data. The code then creates a `BinaryReader` object (`br`) for use when reading the data. The `BinaryReader` class provides methods for reading each of the value types offered by C#. The last two statements show how a `string` is read followed by reading an `int` data type:

```
        anniversary = br.ReadString();
        status = br.ReadInt32();
```

Each read statement assigns its data into the appropriate member of the class. Note that the order of the read statements *must* match the order used in the write statements. If you mess up the sequence of variables and their data types, don't be surprised that the data appears messed up as well. After the data are read, the file is immediately closed.

The best way for you to understand this program is to type it in and single-step through the writing and reading of the data. Make sure you use the Step Into (F11) feature of the debugger so you can see how each method works.

Serialization and Deserialization

In OOP programs, reading and writing an object's data (like myData in the previous section) is so common that C# provides a simple mechanism for those tasks. After all, in the previous program, each time you wrote a new friend's information to disk you were actually saving the state of the clsRandomAccess object named myData to disk. Simply stated, *serialization* is the act of saving, or persisting, an object's state to disk. *Deserialization* is the act of reconstructing an object's state by reading the information stored on disk back into an object of that class.

Because the primitive data types (byte, char, int, long, double, string, and so on) are not serializable by default, you must explicitly state that the object can be serialized using the [Serializable] attribute at the top of the class source file of the object to be serialized.

Time-Saving Tip

If you fail to mark a class as serializable using the [Serializable] attribute *before* you compile the program, the program will fail. The error message tells you that one (or more) of the class members does not have the [Serializable] attribute set. If you see this error message, going back and adding [Serializable] to the class file does no good. Moral of the story: don't forget to add the [Serializable] attribute to the class file *before* you compile it.

Try It Out   Serialization-Deserialization

Figure 13-12 shows a sample run of a program that uses serialization.

Figure 13-12

The program gathers the class information (such as name, e-mail address, and status) and serializes the data to a disk file named Test.bin when the user clicks the Serialize button. Clicking the Display button deserializes the data from the disk file and displays it in a listbox object.

How It Works

The source code for frmMain is presented in Listing 13-7.

Listing 13-7

```
using System;
using System.Windows.Forms;

public class frmMain : Form
{
    clsSerial myFriend = new clsSerial();    // Object to serialize

    private Label label1;
    private TextBox txtName;
    private TextBox txtEmail;
    private TextBox txtStatus;
    private Label label3;
    private Button btnSerial;
    private Button btnDisplay;
    private Button btnClose;
    private ListBox lstOutput;
    private Label label2;
    #region Windows code

    public frmMain()
    {
        InitializeComponent();
    }

    public static void Main()
    {
        frmMain main = new frmMain();
        Application.Run(main);
    }

    private void btnSerial_Click(object sender, EventArgs e)
    {
        int flag;

        MoveTextToClass(myFriend);        // Move from textboxes to data

        flag = myFriend.SerializeFriend(myFriend);
        if (flag == 1)
        {
            MessageBox.Show("Data Serialized successfully", "Data Write");
        }
        else
        {
            MessageBox.Show("Serialization failure", "Data Error");
        }
    }

    private void btnDisplay_Click(object sender, EventArgs e)
```

```
    {
        clsSerial newFriend = new clsSerial();
        newFriend = newFriend.DeserializeFriend();
        lstOutput.Items.Clear();
        lstOutput.Items.Add(newFriend.Name);
        lstOutput.Items.Add(newFriend.Email);
        lstOutput.Items.Add(newFriend.Status.ToString());

    }

    private void MoveTextToClass(clsSerial obj)
    {
        bool flag;
        int val;

        obj.Name = txtName.Text;
        obj.Email = txtEmail.Text;
        flag = int.TryParse(txtStatus.Text, out val);
        if (flag == false)
        {
            MessageBox.Show("Must be 1 or 0", "Input Error");
            txtStatus.Focus();
            return;
        }
        obj.Status = val;
    }

    private void btnClose_Click(object sender, EventArgs e)
    {
        Close();
    }
}
```

The user types in the data via the three textbox objects. (To keep the program short, no validation is done on the inputs, except for the variable status.) The method MoveTextToClass() simply copies the three properties to their associated members of the myFriend object. The SerializeFriend() method serializes the information to disk. (Listing 13-8 shows the clsSerial code.)

The Display button calls the DeserializeFriend() method to deserialize the data from the disk file. The members of the class are then displayed in the listbox object.

Listing 13-8 shows the source code for the clsSerial class.

Listing 13-8

```
using System;
using System.IO;
using System.Runtime.Serialization;
using System.Runtime.Serialization.Formatters.Binary;

[Serializable]          // DON'T FORGET THIS
class clsSerial
```

```
{
    //------------------- Instance members -----------------
    private string name;
    private string email;
    private int status;

    //------------------- Property methods -----------------
    public string Name
    {
        get
        {
            return name;
        }
        set
        {
            name = value;
        }
    }
    public string Email
    {
        get
        {
            return email;
        }
        set
        {
            email = value;
        }
    }
    public int Status
    {
        get
        {
            return status;
        }
        set
        {
            status = value;
        }
    }
    //------------------- Helper methods -----------------
    //------------------- General methods -----------------

    /*****
     * Purpose: To serialize the contents of this class
     *
     * Parameter list:
     *   clsSerial myFriend      Serialize an instance
     *
     * Return value:
     *   int                     0 on error, 1 otherwise
     *****/
    public int SerializeFriend(clsSerial myFriend)
```

```
{
    try
    {
        BinaryFormatter format = new BinaryFormatter();
        FileStream myStream = new FileStream("Test.bin",
                                 FileMode.Create);
        format.Serialize(myStream, myFriend);
        myStream.Close();
    }
    catch (Exception ex)
    {
        string buff = ex.Message;
        return 0;
    }
    return 1;
}

/*****
 * Purpose: To deserialize an instance of this class from a file
 *
 * Parameter list:
 *   n/a
 *
 * Return value:
 *   clsSerial       an instance of the class with the data
 *****/
public clsSerial DeserializeFriend()
{
    clsSerial temp = new clsSerial();
    try
    {
        BinaryFormatter format = new BinaryFormatter();
        FileStream myStream = new FileStream("Test.bin",
                                 FileMode.Open);
        temp = (clsSerial)format.Deserialize(myStream);
        myStream.Close();
    }
    catch (Exception ex)
    {
        string buff = ex.Message;
        return null;
    }
    return temp;
}
}
```

Note the various include files that must be added to the top of the file. These make the various elements of the Serialization namespace available for use in the class. Once again, it is important that you add [Serializable] immediately before the class signature. Failure to do this is frustrating, as you have to start over if you compile the file without it.

Most of the code in the file should look familiar to you by now, so we will concentrate on the two methods that do most of the serialization work. In the following code fragment from Listing 13-8, it is the responsibility of the BinaryFormatter object format to convert the data held in the myFriend object into its required binary form:

```
public int SerializeFriend(clsSerial myFriend)
{
    try
    {
        BinaryFormatter format = new BinaryFormatter();
        FileStream myStream = new FileStream("Test.bin",
                                    FileMode.Create);
        format.Serialize(myStream, myFriend);
        myStream.Close();
    }
    catch (Exception ex)
    {
        string buff = ex.Message;
        return 0;
    }
    return 1;
}
```

A Filestream object (myStream) is used to open the test file named Test.bin. If the file does not exist, it is created automatically. (If you change FileMode.Create to FileMode.Append, you can append more than one object's state to the file.) The program then uses the Serialize() method of the BinaryFormatter class to store myFriend's state to disk. Because exceptions can occur, you should enclose the code in a try-catch block.

Deserialization is little more than serialization in reverse:

```
public clsSerial DeserializeFriend()
{
    clsSerial temp = new clsSerial();
    try
    {
        BinaryFormatter format = new BinaryFormatter();
        FileStream myStream = new FileStream("Test.bin",
                                    FileMode.Open);
        temp = (clsSerial)format.Deserialize(myStream);
        myStream.Close();
    }
    catch (Exception ex)
    {
        string buff = ex.Message;
        return null;
    }
    return temp;
}
```

A `BinaryFormatter` object is instantiated and a `FileStream` object is also instantiated, but using the `Open` file mode. The `Deserialize()` method of the `BinaryFormatter` class reads the data from the disk file and formats into the `clsSerial` object. The explicit cast `(clsSerial)` is required because `Deserialize()` returns a plain object type. The `FileStream` is then closed and control returns to the caller. Back in `frmMain`, the returned object's data is displayed in the `listbox`.

To Serialize or Not to Serialize

Given how simple it is to serialize and deserialize an object, why wouldn't you use this kind of program rather than the random access program discussed earlier? After all, the random access program is also saving the state of an object to disk, but it requires quite a bit more code to do so.

First, the random access program is not specifically designed to simply serialize an object. Rather, it's intended to serve as a transactions-based structure where the object is permanently stored. Serialization of an object is more often used to temporarily store the state of an object so it can be restored later. That object's state might be passed along to some other user of the object (such as a session state in a web app) or used to reestablish the state of an application when the application is reloaded.

Second, you may not want to have all the information in a class serialized. There could be sensitive information in the class that you don't want others to see. Even though the serialized file is in binary form, you can still read a good part of it with Notepad.

If you want to exclude a specific member of a class from being serialized as part of the object's state, you can use the following statement in the class definition:

```
[NonSerialized] string cellPhone;
```

This syntax marks the cell phone number as being excluded from the properties that are to be serialized to disk.

A third issue is that, if your class includes other (non-primitive) data types, like custom classes you've defined, those classes must also be compiled with the `[Serializable]` attribute set. This may not be a problem if you have access to the source code for these classes. However, if you are using a class from a commercial product for which you don't have the source, you may not be able to mark that object as serializable.

MDI, Menus, and File Dialogs

In this section I want to show you how to use the Multiple Document Interface, the C# menu object, and the file dialog objects. Start by creating the project as you have all the others. With the `frmMain` form showing in the Design window, set the form's `IsMdiContainer` property to `true`. When you do this, the style of the form changes and the client area of the form changes to a dark shade of gray. Scroll to the bottom of the form's property list and set the `WindowState` property to `Maximized`.

Adding a Menu

Now go to the Toolbox window, open up the Menu & Toolbars section, and double-click on the MenuStrip object. Your Design window should look like the one in Figure 13-13. Notice that the MenuStrip object (named menuStrip1 by default) appears in the System Tray area at the bottom of the screen. (It is not viewable in Figure 13-13.) The object also causes a blank menu strip to appear just under the title bar of frmMain, as can be seen in Figure 13-13.

Figure 13-13

Place the cursor in the textbox on the menu strip where it says Type Here, type in &File, and press the Enter key. Your screen should look like Figure 13-14.

Figure 13-14

In Figure 13-14 there are two Type Here boxes. While it may not be obvious, the lower textbox is tied to the File menu option you just entered. The second Type Here box is intended for additional menu options that you wish to appear to the right of the File menu option. If you wanted the menu bar to look similar to that for Visual Studio, you would type Edit in that textbox. However, we will instead concentrate on submenus for the File menu option. In the textbox that is below File, type in &Open and press the Enter key. Move the cursor back into the &Open textbox and change the Name property in the Properties window to mnuOpen.

Immediately below the <u>O</u>pen menu option, type in &Edit and change its Name property to mnuEdit. Immediately below the <u>E</u>dit option, type in a dash. This serves as a menu separator. Finally, in the empty textbox below the menu separator line type in E&xit and press the Enter key. Change its name to mnuExit. Your screen should look similar to what is shown in Figure 13-15.

Figure 13-15

Adding a File Open Dialog

Let's examine the code for the program as it exists at this point. The code is shown in Listing 13-9.

Listing 13-9

```
using System;
using System.Windows.Forms;

public class frmMain : Form
{
    string selectFile;

    private ToolStripMenuItem mnuFile;
    private ToolStripMenuItem mnuOpen;
    private ToolStripMenuItem editToolStripMenuItem;
    private ToolStripSeparator toolStripMenuItem1;
    private ToolStripMenuItem mnuExit;
    private OpenFileDialog openFileDialog1;
    private MenuStrip menuStrip1;
    #region Windows code

    public frmMain()
```

```
    {
        InitializeComponent();
    }

    [STAThread]                  // Something new
    public static void Main()
    {
        frmMain main = new frmMain();
        Application.Run(main);
    }

    private void mnuFile_Click(object sender, EventArgs e)
    {

    }

    private void mnuOpen_Click(object sender, EventArgs e)
    {
        OpenFileDialog fileOpen = new OpenFileDialog();

        fileOpen.Title = "Select file to open:";
        fileOpen.Filter = "(*.bin)|*.bin|(*.txt)|*.txt|All files
                          (*.*)|*.*";

        if (fileOpen.ShowDialog() == DialogResult.OK)
        {
            selectFile = fileOpen.FileName;
        }
    }
}
```

Notice the statement just before the Main() method:

```
    [STAThread]                  // Something new
```

This statement is needed when the program is run with the debugger. It tells the compiler to generate the code using what is called a *Single Thread Apartment*. Without going into details, C# enables you to have multiple threads, or processes, running simultaneously. Using this statement insures that a single thread is used for communication with the FileOpenDialog object. If you wish to use the debugger while working on this program, you need this attribute statement in the program. You can leave it out, but you'll need to run the program outside the debugger (that is, with Ctrl+F5 rather than F5). For now, I'd suggest that you leave it in.

In the mnuOpen_Click() event code, the first statement creates an instance of an OpenFileDialog object named fileOpen. The Title property for the object simply sets the text that appears in the title bar of the file dialog box. The Filter property sets the file types that you wish to see when the dialog is run. The filter shown here establishes the default file type to *.bin files because that is the first file type that appears in the filter list. The user can opt to change this to view only text file (*.txt) or any file type, if she wishes. These different file types appear in the familiar dropdown listbox object that is common to many Windows programs. A sample run of the code to this point is shown in Figure 13-16.

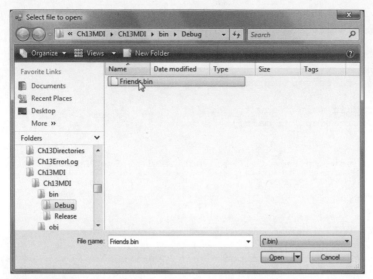

Figure 13-16

When you run the program, click on File ⇨ Open. The result is the dialog you see in Figure 13-16. (When you run the program, notice that frmMain fills the entire display screen. This is because you set the WindowState property for frmMain to Maximize.) Assuming the user clicks the Open button in Figure 13-16, the selectFile variable holds the name of the file, including its full path name. That is, the string might be something like this:

```
"C:\\C#Code\\DataFiles\\Friends.bin"
```

Obviously, this string can be used to open and read the file using the data held in selectFile. You can use the debugger to examine the file name that is returned by the OpenFileDialog object.

Calling Another Form

Let's add another form to the project and name it frmEditFriend. Use Project ⇨ Add New Item to add the new form. Once the form is created and the stub code is visible in the Source window, delete *all* the stub code that appears in frmEditFriend. Now go to where you stored the random access program code shown in Listing 13-5. Using Notepad, open the frmMain.cs file and highlight all of the code seen in Listing 13-5. Now paste that code into the frmEditFriend source file in the Source window. Change the name of the class from frmMain to frmEditFriend and delete the following code:

```
public static void Main()
{
    frmMain main = new frmMain();
    Application.Run(main);
}
```

After all, a program can only have one Main() method, and you already have one named frmMain in this project. Now make the clsRandomAccess code available to the project. You can do this either by using Project ⇨ Add Exiting Item and selecting clsRandomAccess from the old project, or using Project ⇨ Add Class and copying the code into the new file.

Add the following code to Listing 13-9:

```
private void mnuEdit_Click(object sender, EventArgs e)
{
    frmEditFriend frm = new frmEditFriend();
    frm.ShowDialog();
}
```

This code creates a frmEditFriend object named frm and then uses the ShowDialog() method to display that object on the screen. This is shown in Figure 13-17.

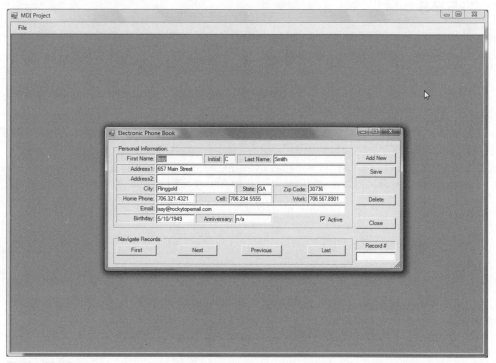

Figure 13-17

Look familiar? It should, since this was the main input form used in the random access file project.

Notice how simple it was to write this application. You "borrowed" (stole?) most of the work from an earlier project by simply copying the code. The result is a Multiple Document Interface program that could be used as the starting point to build a more robust electronic phone book application. Many Windows programs use the MDI interface to give a familiar look and feel to a suite of programs. Microsoft Office is but one example.

Try adding some additional menu options to the program, like a form that displays the contents of a friend's data file.

Summary

We covered a lot of ground in this chapter. You should feel comfortable using both text and binary files in either a sequential or random access format. You also know how to serialize and deserialize an object to disk. You learned how to create an MDI program and a system of menus. Finally, you saw how easy it is to reuse a Windows form object in a different program. Indeed, we reused the `clsRandomAccess` class without modification! But then, that's what OOP is all about.

Exercises

1. How might you change the code in Listing 13-5 so it would not show inactive records?

2. Looking at the information in Table 13-5, could you use any of the `FileInfo` class properties or methods in the `getRecordCount()` method shown in Listing 13-6?

3. If you are designing a program that must persist a specific set of information, how would you decide whether to use sequential or random access files?

4. Which approach would you use to persist the state of an object to disk: serialization, or standard read/write methods of your own design?

5. Many program use an About box to convey information about the software (version number, company name, etc.) How would you add an About box to your programs?

Using Databases

In Chapter 13 you learned how to persist data using several different types of data files. In this chapter I expand on that topic, but persist the data using database techniques. In this chapter you will learn:

- ❏ What a relational database is
- ❏ What tables, fields, records, and keys are
- ❏ What normalization is
- ❏ How to use the database Structured Query Language
- ❏ What DDL is
- ❏ How to use ADO.NET with databases
- ❏ How to use bound controls
- ❏ What LINQ is

It's been said that of all the programs that are under development, over 80 percent of them use a database in one form or another. Clearly, this is one tool that must hang from your tool belt.

What is a Database?

A *database* is simply a collection of information. In fact, if you wanted to, you could use the topics covered in Chapter 13 to construct your own database. However, if you value your time at more than two cents an hour, it's silly to reinvent the wheel. It is far wiser to use a commercially available database system than to attempt to write one yourself.

A *relational database* is a collection of information in which the data within the database are associated with one another in some way. Managing the interrelationships in a relational database can get rather complex. For that reason, most people prefer to use a commercially available *database management system* (DBMS) to manage a database. A DBMS is a suite of programs that simplifies the tasks associated with building and using a relational database. Many major software companies (such as Oracle, IBM, Microsoft, and others) market DBMS software for use with their databases.

C# embodies the Microsoft Jet DBMS and is designed to work directly with Microsoft Access database (`*.mdb`) files. However, Visual Studio 2008 also comes with support for a new language component named LINQ that provides some interesting features for manipulating data. The C# Express version directly supports the use of LINQ only with Microsoft's SQL Server databases. (You can get around this, however, quite easily.) The Professional version of C# also supports other commercially available DBMSes. (I explore both Jet and LINQ in this chapter.)

The Structure of a Database

A relational database is normally a collection of two or more database tables.

Database Tables, Fields, and Records

A database table is constructed of data arranged in rows and columns. Each row in a database table is called a *record*. Each column in a database table is called a *field*. A database table may have zero or more rows. If the table has zero rows, the database table is said to be *empty* and contains no useful information. Database tables almost always have at least two or more fields in them.

You can think of a database field as being similar to a property for a class. Each field is used to store values for a particular data item. For example, in Chapter 13 your electronic phone book program had properties for your friend's first name, middle initial, last name, addresses, city, state, zip, and so on. Each of these properties could be used to construct a field in a database table. It follows, then, that each row in the database table would become a record for one of your friends in the phone book database. Figure 14-1 summarizes these relationships.

In Figure 14-1, the database is shown to hold two database tables named Friends and Cards. If the database is an Access DMBS database, it might be named Friends.mdb. We have assumed that the Friends table is constructed to hold the same information as class clsRandomAccess from Chapter 13 (Listing 13-6). Note that each field in the Friends database table corresponds to a property in the clsRandomAccess class. (I have not shown all of the properties in Figure 14-1 because of space limitations.)

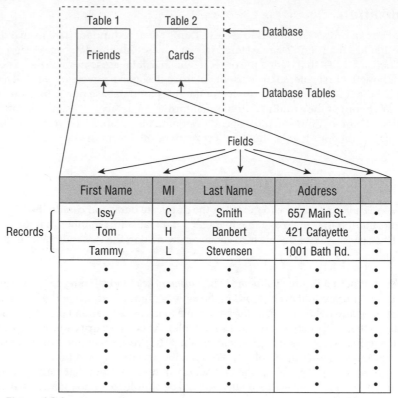

Figure 14-1

Designing Fields for a Database Table

The Cards table might be a database table you add to the database to keep track of which friends you sent a birthday card and which friends sent you a birthday card. You think about the information that you need to store in the table and you come up with the following fields for the table:

❑ firstName: The first name of the friend

❑ MI: The friend's middle initial

❑ lastName: The friend's last name

❑ dateSent: The date you sent the friend a birthday card

❑ dateReceived: The date you received a card from the friend

You sit back, admire your work for a moment, and then it hits you: This is an RDC approach to the problem. You now have two tables (Friends and Cards) that store similar information. That is, both tables store the first name, middle initial, and last name of the friend under consideration. Not good.

Data Normalization

Data normalization is a process designed to remove duplicate or redundant data from a database. Because my current design has the friend's name stored in two tables, I say my database design is not normalized. There are rules that define the order in which a database is normalized. The current design doesn't even follow the first rule, so the current database design isn't even *first normal form*. While I can't afford the space here for a complete discussion of the rules for database normalization, most programmers are happy if they fulfill "third normal form for a database design. The higher the degree of normalization, the more time you must spend designing the database. (If you ever find yourself in jail with a lot of time on your hands, shoot for a seventh normal form in your design. It will help pass the time!)

Primary Key

You need to redesign your database to get rid of the duplicate data. You can do that if you can find a way to relate the information in the `Cards` table to the `Friends` table in a manner that forms a unique relationship. The easiest way to do this is to create a new field in the `Friends` table that is unique to each friend in the table.

Fields in a table that hold a unique value are called *primary key* fields. If a record has a unique value in one of its fields, we can say that each record in the table is unique because of the primary key field. You can use this primary key field value in a different table (such as the `Cards` table) to refer back to the information in another table (such as the `Friends` table). A Social Security number would do the trick, but your friends might be reluctant to give that to you. (They're not *that* good of friends.) Then…shazam! Lightning strikes and you have an epiphany. Why not just use their row numbers as ID numbers? You add a new field to the `Friends` table named ID, which stores a number that corresponds to the friend's row number in the `Friends` table. This ID field would be simple to administer since its value is simply the previous record ID plus one.

With this change, you redesign the fields in the `Cards` table to be an identification number (ID) associated with each friend, the date you sent him a card (`dateSent`), and the date you received a card from him (`dateReceived`).

Let's assume that Issy sent you a card on April 30 and you sent her a card on May 5. If you record this information in the `Cards` table, it might look similar to that shown in Table 14-1.

Table 14-1

Id	DateSent	DateReceived
1	4/30/2008	5/5/2008

The `ID` field value in the `Cards` table tells you which friend in the `Friends` table exchanged cards with you. That is, the information in the `Cards` table now relates to the friends stored in the `Friends` table, but you are no longer duplicating that information in both tables. This is why such databases are called *relational* databases: relationships exist between tables for the data stored in the database.

Over the years, you and Issy could exchange birthday cards many, many times. This forms what is called a *one-to-many* database relationship between the `Friends` and `Cards` tables. That is, one friend (Issy in the `Friends` table) has sent many cards (as recorded in the `Cards` table) to you. There are a number of such potential database relationships possible (one-to-one, many-to-many, and so on).

Enhancing Functionality

While the table design shown in Table 14-1 fulfills our goal, adding one new field to the `Cards` table increases its functionality significantly. Suppose we change the design to that shown in Table 14-2.

Table 14-2

Id	DateSent	DateReceived	CardType
1	4/30/2008	5/5/2008	1

Let's further assume that the integer stored in the `cardType` field serves as a proxy for the type of card that is being sent. While you could decode the interpretation of what `cardType` means as part of the program code, why not let the database take care of it for you? You could store the interpretation of the list of potential card types in a third table named `CardType` using a design similar to that shown in Table 14-3.

Table 14-3

CardType	CardName
1	"Birthday"
2	"Anniversary"
3	"Sympathy"
4	"Mother's Day"
5	"Father's Day"
6	"Christmas"
7	"Arbor Day"
8	"Guy Fawkes' Day"
9	"Jack Purdum's birthday"

The primary key field in the `CardType` table would be the value in field `cardType` and would form a relationship to the `Cards` table that is a many-to-one relationship. (That is, the `Cards` table can have many different types of cards, but it must be one of the cards specified in the `CardType` table.)

By creating a third table named `CardType`, you have extended the functionality of the `Cards` table. Where the `Cards` table was originally limited to just birthday cards, it can now record eight additional card types. Further, if the need arises in the future, you could extend the `CardType` table to include new card types by simply adding new records to the CardType table. Figure 14-2 summarizes how the tables relate to one another. In Figure 14-2, the infinity sign is a standard notation for the term "many" in discussions of database table relationships.

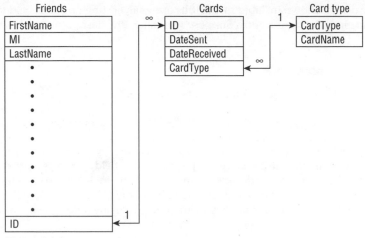

Figure 14-2

Foreign Keys

In Figure 14-2, the field named ID serves as the primary key, but it also is used in the second table (Cards) to relate the information in the Cards table back to the friend in the Friends table. Therefore, the field named ID in the Cards table serves as a *foreign key* that tells us whom this card relates to in the Friends table. It follows that a field that serves as a foreign key in one table must have some established relationship with another table. The relationship between the Friends and Cards tables is one-to-many. This is simply a geeky way of saying that a friend can send multiple cards.

Finally, there is a relationship between the Cards and CardType tables. Each row in the Cards table must have one card type defined in its row, but it can be any of the card types.

Using Your Own Databases

There are many different types of commercially available databases. Microsoft offers Access and SQL Server, IBM offers DB2, MySQL (which is open source), Oracle, and probably dozens of others. You can use C# to communicate with any of them. In this section, however, we are going to use Access to illustrate how you use C# with commercial databases. There are several reasons for this choice. First (and foremost), you don't have to buy or install additional software to use the programs that follow in this chapter. Visual Studio comes with Access support built in. Second, Access is capable of serving almost any database application need, provided you don't have too many users accessing the database at the same time. Access is capable of performing serious work as long as you don't bog it down with more than four or five users at one time.

ADO.NET

Before you jump into the code that you will use to create your own databases, you need to understand how C# interacts with a database. The primary vehicle for this interaction is ADO.NET, which stands for the underlying technology for *ActiveX Data Objects*. While this technology has been around for some time, it has undergone a substantial evolution over the years. In its current form, ADO.NET provides an efficient means for interacting with any database.

You can think in terms of ADO.NET as consisting of two primary elements: 1) a *data provider* element and 2) a *datasets* element.

Data Provider

A number of classes work in concert to act as a data provider for ADO.NET. As you might imagine, every database vendor has its own way of storing data in its database. Even something as seemingly simple as an `int` data type can be stored different ways in a database. The vendor is free to use whatever it thinks is best for its own DBMS. Therefore, there is no one single class that has a one-size-fits-all connection to a vendor's database.

Microsoft, however, has created a means by which other database vendors can communicate with Microsoft's database classes. Microsoft created Object Linking and Embedding for Databases, or *OLE DB*, to serve as a bridge between external data sources and Microsoft's database classes. This approach is a win-win situation because all a database vendor needs to do is provide a link to its database that uses the OLE DB standard. The programmer wins because all she needs to learn is how to use OLE DB and she can "talk" to any external database. I use OLE DB to illustrate how all the classes work together to make database programs much easier to write. (If you are using some other database, you can look for its provider information and bypass the OLE DB provider. This normally provides better performance because the database vendor can tweak the objects for optimum performance. The OLE DB provider objects, however, will work with any database using the common routines shown here, as long as the database vendor supplies the OLE DB provider objects.)

The OLE Connection Object

In order to communicate with a database, you must first establish a connection with that database. Because you are going to use OLE DB to work with your database, you use the `OleDbConnection` class to provide the connectivity we need to communicate with the database. Once you have instantiated an `OleDbConnection` object, that object is used to issue commands to the database via an `OleDbCommand` object. You can also use the `OleDbConnection` object to read the content of the database through an `OleDbReader` object. Therefore, the `OleDbConnection` object serves as the launch point for performing most database operations via other OLE objects.

The OLE Command Object

The `OleDbCommand` object is used to process Structured Query Language (SQL) commands. SQL is standard language written to work with relational databases. You will learn enough SQL later in this chapter to manipulate a database in ways that produce the results you want. You will also learn SQL commands to create a new database, create tables within that database, create fields within each table, and add and delete records in a table, and learn how to construct queries to fetch data from a database. Once you have learned some of the SQL commands, you can feed those commands to the database via the `OleDbCommand` object in a way that interacts with the database.

Data Definition Language (DDL)

SQL includes a language subset called *the Data Definition Language*, or DDL. You use the DDL commands to establish the structure of a database when it is first created. For example, you use DDL to create a database, add tables to the database, and add fields to the database tables. Once that structure is defined, additional DDL commands are used to add, edit, or delete rows in the database. Most of the other SQL operators are used to manipulate the data that already resides in the database.

The OLE Reader Object

After you have used the `OleDbCommand` object to fetch data from the database, you use an `OleDbReader` object to loop through the data produced by an SQL command. It is the output from the reader object that ultimately produces the data you wish to view.

Datasets

The *dataset classes* provide the means to manipulate the data contained within the database. Dataset objects are generic in the sense that they do not vary among databases so their use does not vary because of the underlying database. Each dataset can be associated with a `DataTable` object that has columns (fields) and rows (records). From the `DataTable` object it is possible to construct a `DataView` object. The `DataView` object usually represents a data set that has been filtered by an SQL command. For example, you might issue an SQL command to return all records where the zip code is 46214. You can also use a `DataRow`, a `DataColumn`, or a `DataRowView` object to refine the data even more should you need to.

No doubt all of this seems overwhelming right now. But as you shall soon see, it ties together nicely and makes sense when you see how all the objects relate to one another. Before you do that, however, you need a short crash course in the SQL language.

Using SQL

The Structured Query Language was developed in the early 1970s by Donald Chamberlin and Ray Boyce of IBM. It was designed to be a universal database language that could create, manage, and maintain relational databases. Entire books have been written on various SQL topics, so I cannot give it full coverage here. Rather, I will concentrate on a useful subset of SQL that you can use in your programs. Once you get comfortable with the basics, there are plenty of online sources that you can use to expand your SQL prowess.

The SELECT Statement

Perhaps the most used part of SQL is the query features that enable you to retrieve specific subsets of data from a database. Most queries are initiated with the SELECT statement. Its syntax is

```
SELECT fieldList FROM tablename
```

In this case, `fieldList` is a comma-separated list of the fields that you wish to retrieve from the database. For example, suppose you want to retrieve the first and last names from the phone book database using fields that are similar to those used in Chapter 13. Suppose the table that holds the relevant information is the Friends table. The SQL command would be written like this:

```
SELECT firstName,lastName FROM Friends
```

(It is a common practice to use uppercase letters for the SQL keywords, like SELECT and FROM in the preceding statement. This is not a requirement, but simply a convention most programmers use.) The sample SELECT statement generates a dataset that contains the first and last names of everyone in the database.

You can also use the wildcard character in lieu of a fieldList:

```
SELECT * FROM Friends
```

This query returns a dataset that contains all the field data for every row in the Friends table...and that's the problem: the dataset contains everyone in the database. Most of the time you want some subset of the database. Perhaps it's all the people with a specific last name. Or maybe everyone who lives in a certain zip code. What you want, therefore, is a way to filter the dataset that comes back from a SELECT query.

The WHERE Predicate

You can use the WHERE predicate to filter the dataset returned from a database. For example, the query

```
SELECT firstName,lastName FROM Friends WHERE Zip = 80120
```

returns a dataset that contains all of the first and last names for people who live in the 80120 zip code. You can also apply basic conditional operators to a WHERE predicate. For example:

```
SELECT firstName,lastName FROM Friends WHERE Zip > 46214 AND Zip < 46254
```

This allows somewhat less restrictive datasets to be formed.

The ORDER BY Clause

The ORDER BY clause enables you to reorganize the datasets into ascending or descending order. For example, the query

```
SELECT * FROM Friends WHERE Zip = 80120 ORDER BY lastName
```

returns the dataset sorted in ascending order by the lastName field. If you want the same list, but in descending order, you would use

```
SELECT * FROM Friends WHERE Zip = 80120 ORDER BY lastName DESC
```

Note the SQL keyword DESC at the end of the SELECT statement. It should be clear that the default ordering using the ORDER BY clause is ascending order. If you do not use the ORDER BY clause, the dataset returns the data in the order in which it is read from the database.

Finally, we mentioned that most programmers capitalize the SQL keywords in a query. Another popular style that's often used when formatting SQL queries is this:

```
SELECT *
FROM Friends
WHERE Zip = 80120
ORDER BY lastName
DESC
```

This format places all SQL operators on their own lines with the actual database arguments to the right of the appropriate SQL operators. Use whatever form makes sense to you...the choice is yours.

Aggregates

Some database operations are so common that SQL provides methods, called *aggregates,* to perform specific calculations on a database. Most databases, at a minimum, support the aggregates found in Table 14-4.

Table 14-4

Aggregate Name	Description
AVG	Returns the numeric average of a selected field:
	`SELECT AVG(Age) FROM Friend`
	Assuming field Age has each person's age, this returns the average age of the people.
COUNT	Returns the number of items found in a selected field:
	`SELECT COUNT(lastName) FROM Friend WHERE Status = 1`
	This tells how many active people are in the Friend table.
MIN	Finds the smallest value in a field:
	`SELECT MIN(Age) FROM Friend`
MAX	Finds the largest value in a field:
	`SELECT MAX(Age) FROM Friend`
SUM	Returns the sum of the values in a field:
	`SELECT SUM(Status) FROM Friend`
	If Status is 1 for active friends and 0 for inactive, this would return the number of active people in the table.

The aggregate methods don't give you anything you couldn't construct yourself from other (multiple) SQL queries. They do, however, make such information easier to get.

That's it! You will be surprised how much work you can do with databases building queries from these simple commands. Before we demonstrate the power of such queries, we need a database. That's the topic of the next section.

Try It Out   Writing Your Own Mini-DBMS

You can use SQL and ADO.NET to build and manipulate your own databases. In this section I create an MDI program capable of creating an Access database, adding tables to that database, and adding, editing, and deleting row data. I also show how to bind a database to a grid control for quick and easy reporting. Because I have drawn upon a lot of the code features I discussed in previous chapters, only code that is unfamiliar is presented here. You can download the complete code from the Wrox web site. Figure 14-3 shows how the Database MDI menu appears when the program is run.

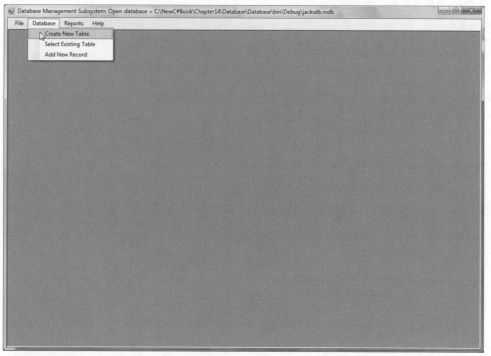

Figure 14-3

How It Works

The File menu option in Figure 14-3 is used to create a new database, open and close an existing database, and exit the program. The Database menu option enables you to create a new table or select an existing table. Once a table is selected, you can add a new record or edit an existing record. For reasons mentioned in Chapter 13, deleting a record doesn't actually delete it. Instead, you can change the status of a record from active to inactive.

Creating a New Database

Most of the default database settings in Visual Studio are geared toward working with Microsoft's SQL Server. I thought it would be more instructive, however, if I don't take the default (i.e. easy) way of doing things. Instead, I use the Access database engine that is built into Visual Studio. I use a few additional SQL statements to create and build a new database from scratch.

Adding the ADOX Reference

The OLE DB features discussed earlier in this chapter do not provide the ability to create a new database. Therefore, we use ADOX, an extension to the standard ADO, to give us the ability to create a new database. The ADOX reference must be added to the project for this to work properly. Simply go to the Project ⇨ Add Reference menu option in Visual Studio, click the COM (Component Object Model) tab, and select the Microsoft ADO Ext. 2.8 for DDL and Security reference. After that reference has been added to the project, you can provide the `CreateNewDB()` method to the `clsDB` class. The code is presented in Listing 14-1.

Listing 14-1

```
/*****
 * Purpose: To create a new database
 *
 * Parameter list:
 *   string name      the name of the new database
 *
 * Return value:
 *   int              1 on success, 0 otherwise
 *****/
public int CreateNewDB(string name)
{
    int index;
    string newDB;

    try
    {
        // No DB name given?
        if (name.Length == 0 && dbName.Length == 0)
        {
            return 0;
        }
        index = name.LastIndexOf('.');
        if (index == -1)        // No secondary file name?
        {
```

```
                dbName += ".mdb";        // Assume Access DB
                name = dbName;
            }
            // Where to put new database
            combinedName = Path.Combine(pathName, name);

            ADOX.CatalogClass myCat = new ADOX.CatalogClass();

            newDB = CONNECTSTRING + combinedName + ";" +
                    CONNECTSTRINGPART2;
            myCat.Create(newDB);
            myCat = null;

        }
        catch (Exception ex)
        {
#if DEBUG
            // Don't put user I/O in a non-form class except for debugging
            MessageBox.Show("Error: " + ex.Message);
#endif
            return 0;
        }
        return 1;
    }
```

The code expects the new name for the database to be passed into the method. The method is called from frmMain via a menu option, with the same basic syntax you used in Chapter 13:

```
private void mnuNew_Click(object sender, EventArgs e)
{
    frmCreateDB myNewDB = new frmCreateDB(dbName);
    myNewDB.ShowDialog();
}
```

The form frmCreateDB is shown in Figure 14-4.

Figure 14-4

The user types in the name of the new database and clicks the Create New DB button, which executes the following statements:

```
clsDB myDB = new clsDB(txtDBName.Text); // Pass in new name
flag = myDB.CreateNewDB(txtDBName.Text);
```

These statements end up calling the code in Listing 14-1. Note in Listing 14-1 that the code combines the path name with the database name. Because a file path defaults to the path where the program executable is located, that seems to be a good place to put the database by default. If the path name provided does not exist, an exception is thrown, which is one reason for using a `try-catch` block in Listing 14-1. Because Listing 14-1 is taken from `clsDB` and is not code associated with a Windows form, I use the preprocessor `#define DEBUG` directive to toggle the code for the `MessageBox()` method. Assuming no errors occur, an empty database exists in the chosen directory with the `.mdb` extension.

Creating a New Table (CREATE TABLE)

If you select the first menu option in Figure 14-3, Create New Table, the form shown in Figure 14-5 appears. The figure is shown after you entered in the field names and types you wish to have in the new table named `Friend`.

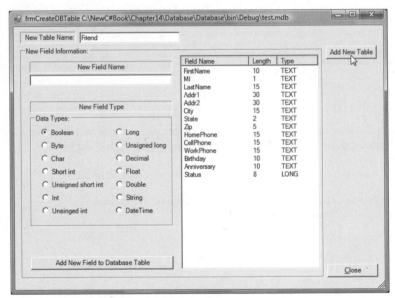

Figure 14-5

In this example I have added 13 string fields to the table plus one `long` variable. If you make a mistake while entering a field (such as misspelling the field name or perhaps selecting the wrong data type), you can double-click the offending item in the listview control to remove it. The code to remove an entry is shown in Listing 14-2.

Listing 14-2

```
private void lstFieldsToAdd_DoubleClick(object sender, EventArgs e)
{
    ListView.SelectedIndexCollection indexes =
        lstFieldsToAdd.SelectedIndices;

    foreach (int index in indexes)
```

```
        {
            lstFieldsToAdd.Items[index].Remove();
        }
    }
```

If you're satisfied with the fields that you wish to add to the table, click the Add New Table button. The code for the Add New Table button is shown in Listing 14-3.

Listing 14-3

```
private void btnWrite_Click(object sender, EventArgs e)
{
    int i,j;
    int flag;
    string sqlCommand;
    string buff;
    string temp;

    try
    {
      clsDB myDB = new clsDB(dbName);
      sqlCommand = "CREATE TABLE " +
          txtTableName.Text + " (ID COUNTER, "; // Automatically add

      for (i = 0; i < lstFieldsToAdd.Items.Count; i++)
      {
        temp = "";
        for (j = 0; j < lstFieldsToAdd.Items[i].SubItems.Count; j++)
        {
          buff = lstFieldsToAdd.Items[i].SubItems[j].Text;
          switch (j)
          {
            case 0:   // The field name
              sqlCommand += buff + " ";
              break;

            case 1:   // The field length
              temp = buff;
              break;

            case 2:   // The field type
              if (buff.Equals("TEXT") == true)
              {                              // Need length if strings
                sqlCommand += "TEXT(" + temp + "), ";
              }
              else
              {
                sqlCommand += buff + ", ";
              }
              break;
          }
        }
      }
    }
```

(continued)

Listing 14-3 (continued)

```
            i = sqlCommand.LastIndexOf(",");
            sqlCommand = sqlCommand.Substring(0, sqlCommand.Length - 2);
            sqlCommand += ")";
            flag = myDB.ProcessCommand(sqlCommand);
            if (flag == 1)     // Table created OK, so...
            {
              // ...create the primary key
              sqlCommand = "CREATE INDEX idxID ON " + txtTableName.Text +
                 "(ID) WITH PRIMARY";
              flag = myDB.ProcessCommand(sqlCommand);
              if (flag == 1)
              {
                MessageBox.Show("Table created successfully.");
              }
            }
            else
            {
              MessageBox.Show("Failed to create table.", "Process Error");
            }

        }catch (Exception ex)
        {
          MessageBox.Show("Error: " + ex.Message);
        }
      }
```

SQL (actually DDL) supports the creation of new database tables with the CREATE TABLE statement. In Listing 14-3, the code builds the CREATE TABLE command from the information entered by the user. However, the following lines automatically create a field called ID, which is an Access auto-increment (COUNTER) variable:

```
    sqlCommand = "CREATE TABLE " +
        txtTableName.Text + " (ID COUNTER, ";   // Automatically add
```

A *counter-type variable* is little more than an integer data type that increments itself each time a new row is added to the table. This field ensures that each row in the table is unique.

The for loop iterates through the contents of the listview control to build the CREATE TABLE command. For example, imagine you enter the following into the listview control for a new database table named Dodah:

```
    FirstName       10      TEXT
    MI              1       TEXT
    LastName        15      TEXT
```

The resultant sqlCommand string would be

```
    "CREATE TABLE Dodah (ID COUNTER, FirstName TEXT(10), MI TEXT(1),
    LastName TEXT(15))"
```

Note that the first field in the table is the one we sneaked into the field list.

The statement

```
flag = myDB.ProcessCommand(sqlCommand);
```

calls the `ProcessCommand()` method of class `clsDB` to execute the SQL command to create the table. If `flag` returns 1, everything went okay and the table now exists. The following statements build another SQL command to create a database index for the new table and make `ID` the primary key for the table:

```
if (flag == 1)    // Table created OK, so...
{
  // ...create the primary key
  sqlCommand = "CREATE INDEX idxID ON " + txtTableName.Text +
      "(ID) WITH PRIMARY";
  flag = myDB.ProcessCommand(sqlCommand);
  if (flag == 1)
  {
    MessageBox.Show("Table created successfully.");
  }
}
```

While you can live without adding a primary key, creating the index does improve query performance. If you have Microsoft's Access program, you can open the newly created table and verify that everything's as it should be.

All the SQL commands are processed by the same method of the `clsDB` class. Its code is presented in Listing 14-4.

Listing 14-4

```
/*****
 * Purpose: Process an SQL command.
 *
 * Parameter list:
 *   string sqlCommand      a command string that holds the SQL command
 *                          directives
 *
 * Return value:
 *   int               1 on success, 0 otherwise
 *
 * CAUTION: The connect string assumes an Access database. It will need
 *          to be changed for other databases.
 *****/
public int ProcessCommand(string sqlCommand)
{
    int flag = 1;
    OleDbConnection myDB = new OleDbConnection();
    OleDbCommand command;
    connectString = CONNECTSTRING + dbName;

    try
```

(continued)

Listing 14-4 (continued)

```
        {
            myDB.ConnectionString = connectString;          // Initialize
            myDB.Open();                                     // Open DB

            command = new OleDbCommand(sqlCommand, myDB);    // Set command
            command.ExecuteNonQuery();                       // Do it
        }
        catch (Exception ex)
        {
#if DEBUG                                                     // Only for debugging
            MessageBox.Show("Error: " + ex.Message);
#endif
            flag = 0;
        }
        finally
        {
            myDB.Close();                                    // Close it
        }
        return flag;
    }
```

The code instantiates an OLE DB connection object named myDB and an OLE command object named command. The constant CONNECTSTRING is defined as follows:

```
    private const string CONNECTSTRING =
            "Provider=Microsoft.Jet.OLEDB.4.0;Data source =";
```

This defines the database as an Access database. This connection string needs to be changed for other databases. If you need to find the connection string for a database other than Access, try visiting

```
    http://www.connectionstrings.com
```

At the time of this writing, this site had the connection strings for most popular databases.

The following statements open the database and instantiate the OLE DB command object.:

```
    myDB.Open();                                         // Open DB

    command = new OleDbCommand(sqlCommand, myDB);        // Set command
    command.ExecuteNonQuery();                           // Do it
```

The OLE DB ExecuteNonQuery() method is used when an SQL command is not expected to return a result. In our case, if something goes wrong, the try-catch block lets us know.

At this point you have a new database with a new table and fields in it, but no records in the table. Obviously, the next step is to start adding data to a database table.

Adding Records to a Table (INSERT INTO)

We made life a little easier for adding data to the table by "borrowing" and slightly modifying the form shown in Figure 13-9 in Chapter 13. The modified form is shown in Figure 14-6.

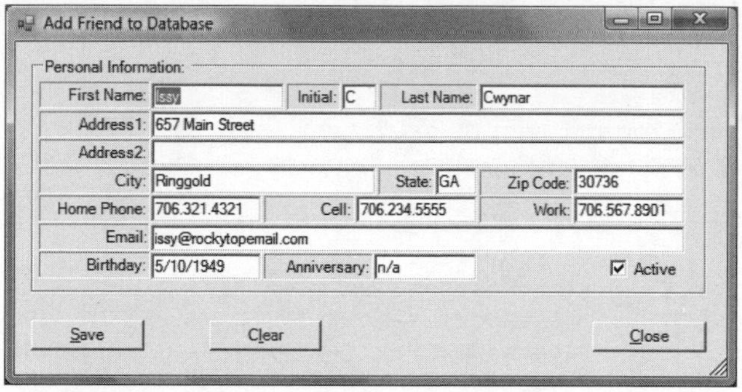

Figure 14-6

The user supplies the necessary information for the textboxes and, when finished, clicks the Save button. The code for the Save button appears in Listing 14-5.

Listing 14-5

```
/*****
 * Purpose: Save textbox info as a record.
 *
 * Parameter list:
 *  object sender      control that caused the event
 *  EventArgs e        details about the sender
 *
 * Return value:
 *  void
 ******/
private void btnSave_Click(object sender, EventArgs e)
{
    int status;
    int flag;
    int i;
    string sqlCommand;
    string[] colNames = new string[MAXCOLUMNS];

    clsDB myDB = new clsDB(dbName);
    myDB.GetColumnInfo(colNames);

    if (chkStatus.Checked == true)
        status = 1;
    else
        status = 0;

    // Build INSERT command
```

(continued)

413

Listing 14-5 (continued)

```
            sqlCommand = "INSERT INTO " + dbTableName + " (";
            for (i = 1; i < colNames.Length; i++)
            {
              if (colNames[i] == null)
                break;
              sqlCommand += colNames[i] + ",";
            }
            i = sqlCommand.LastIndexOf(',');
            sqlCommand = sqlCommand.Substring(0, i) + ") VALUES ('";
                                            // Now add the values
            sqlCommand += txtFirstName.Text + "','" +
                          txtMI.Text + "','" +
                          txtLastName.Text + "','" +
                          txtAddr1.Text + "','" +
                          txtAddr2.Text + "','" +
                          txtCity.Text + "','" +
                          txtState.Text + "','" +
                          txtZip.Text + "','" +
                          txtHome.Text + "','" +
                          txtCell.Text + "','" +
                          txtWork.Text + "','" +
                          txtEmail.Text + "','" +
                          txtBirthday.Text + "','" +
                          txtAnniversary.Text + "'," +
                          status.ToString() + ")";

        flag = myDB.ProcessCommand(sqlCommand);
        if (flag == 1)
        {
            MessageBox.Show("Record added successfully.");
        }
        else
        {
            MessageBox.Show("Failed to add data.", "Process Error");
        }

    }
```

The code begins by creating a string array named colNames and defines it with MAXCOLUMNS elements. I defined MAXCOLUMNS as a symbolic constant equal to 1000. While you could use an ArrayList object to avoid a constant array size, it seems reasonable that a table won't hold more than a thousand fields. The method GetColumnInfo() is used to fetch the names of the columns from the database. The code for GetColumnInfo() of class clsDB is shown in Listing 14-6. Note that the System.Data namespace must be imported because of the DataTable, DataRow, and DataColumn objects.

Listing 14-6

```
/*****
 * Purpose: This method fills in the column names for a database table.
 *
 * Parameter list:
 *   string sqlCommand    a command string that holds the INSET INTO
 *                        directive
 *   string whichTable    the table for which to get the info
 *
 * Return value:
 *   int                  1 on success, 0 otherwise
 *
 * CAUTION: The connect string assumes an Access database. It will need
 *          to be changed for other databases.
 *****/
public int GetColumnInfo(string[] colNames, string whichTable)
{
    int flag = 1;
    int i;
    string buff = "";
    string index = "";
    bool err;
    OleDbConnection myDB = new OleDbConnection();
    connectString = CONNECTSTRING + dbName;

    try
    {
      myDB.ConnectionString = connectString;         // Initialize
      myDB.Open();                                   // Open DB

      string[] elements = new string[] {null, null, whichTable, null};
      DataTable table = myDB.GetSchema("Columns", elements);

      foreach (DataRow row in table.Rows)
      {
        foreach (DataColumn col in table.Columns)
        {
          // Get position...
          if (col.ColumnName.Equals("ORDINAL_POSITION") == true)
              index = row[col].ToString();

          // ... and the name
          if (col.ColumnName.Equals("COLUMN_NAME") == true)
              buff = (string)row[col];
        }
        err = int.TryParse(index, out i);
        colNames[i - 1] = buff;    // Adjust for ordinal values and copy
      }
    }
    catch (Exception ex)
    {
```

(continued)

Listing 14-6 (continued)

```
#if DEBUG
        MessageBox.Show("Error: " + ex.Message);
#endif
        flag = 0;
    }
    finally
    {
        myDB.Close();                                    // Close it
    }
    return flag;
  }
```

The `GetSchema()` method returns all kinds of information about the database. The second parameter for `GetSchema()` is used to restrict the schema information returned from the call. These restrictions are as follows:

```
TABLE_CATALOG       1
TABLE_SCHEMA        2
TABLE_NAME          3
TABLE_TYPE          4
```

Because I am interested in one specific table, I initialize the `elements` array to `null` for the four elements, except for position 3, which I set to the table I am interested in (`whichTable`). The table name is passed in as a parameter to the `GetColumnInfo()` method. When the method finishes execution, the `colNames` array contains the field names for the table. In the column collection, the `ORDINAL_POSITION` element tells me the position of each field in the table.

If you refer back to Listing 14-5, you can see how you use the column names to align with the textbox objects and the information they contain. For example, the `sqlCommand` string might look something like this (I've omitted most of the fields for brevity):

```
"INSERT INTO Friend (FirstName,MI,LastName,Status) VALUES ('Fred', 'C',
'Smith',1)
```

The code calls `ProcessCommand()` to execute the SQL command on the database. Assuming no errors occur, the new record is written to the `Friend` table in the database.

Edit a Record (UPDATE)

Once you have added a record to the database, you can edit it using the SQL UPDATE command. The edit form is shown in Figure 14-7. It is very similar to the form used to add a record, except that it has a textbox object at the top that allows the user to enter a record number. This number corresponds to the `ID` field in the `Friend` table. You can observe the `ID` value in the report form discussed later in this chapter. However, you can also type in the friend's last name and use that for the query in lieu of the `ID` number.

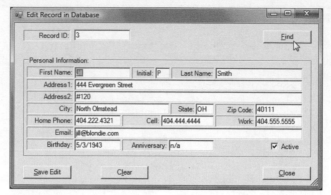

Figure 14-7

The Find button is used to read the record from the database and move the information into the appropriate textbox objects. The code for the Find button is presented in Listing 14-7.

Listing 14-7

```
private void btnFind_Click(object sender, EventArgs e)
{
    int status = 0;
    int record;
    string sql;
    DialogResult answer;
    OleDbConnection myDB = new OleDbConnection();
    OleDbDataReader myReader;
    OleDbCommand myCommand;
    clsDB myData = new clsDB(dbName);

    try
    {
        myDB.ConnectionString = myData.getConnectString + dbName;
        myDB.Open();
        sql = "SELECT * FROM " + dbTableName + " WHERE ";

        // Construct appropriate WHERE predicate
        if (txtLastName.Text.Length != 0)
            sql += "LastName = '" + txtLastName.Text + "'";
        else
            sql += "ID = " + txtRecordID.Text;

        ClearFields();

        myCommand = new OleDbCommand(sql, myDB);
        myReader = myCommand.ExecuteReader();
```

(continued)

Listing 14-7 (continued)

```
            while (myReader.Read() == true)
            {
                record = (int)myReader[0];
                txtRecordID.Text = record.ToString();
                txtFirstName.Text = (string) myReader[1];
                txtMI.Text = (string) myReader[2];
                txtLastName.Text = (string)myReader[3];
                txtAddr1.Text = (string)myReader[4];
                txtAddr2.Text = (string)myReader[5];
                txtCity.Text = (string)myReader[6];
                txtState.Text = (string)myReader[7];
                txtZip.Text = (string)myReader[8];
                txtHome.Text = (string)myReader[9];
                txtCell.Text = (string)myReader[10];
                txtWork.Text = (string)myReader[11];
                txtEmail.Text = (string)myReader[12];
                txtBirthday.Text = (string)myReader[13];
                txtAnniversary.Text = (string)myReader[14];
                status = (int)myReader[15];
                if (status == 1)
                    chkStatus.Checked = true;
                else
                    chkStatus.Checked = false;

                // Correct Record??
                answer = MessageBox.Show("Correct record:",
                        "Find",MessageBoxButtons.YesNo);
                if (answer == DialogResult.Yes)
                {
                  txtFirstName.Focus();
                  break;
                }
            }
            myReader.Close();
    }
    catch (Exception ex)
    {
        MessageBox.Show("Could not query database: " + ex.Message,
                    "Process Error");
        return;
    }
}
```

Most of the statements in Listing 14-7 are very similar to the other events you've studied. However, the following statements are our first example of using a SELECT statement to retrieve information from the database:

```
sql = "SELECT * FROM " + dbTableName + " WHERE ";

// Construct appropriate WHERE predicate
if (txtLastName.Text.Length != 0)
    sql += "LastName = '" + txtLastName.Text + "'";
else
    sql += "ID = " + txtRecordID.Text;

ClearFields();

myCommand = new OleDbCommand(sql, myDB);
myReader = myCommand.ExecuteReader();
```

If you are looking into the Friend table, sql equals

```
sql = "SELECT * FROM Friend WHERE ";
```

at the outset. Depending upon whether the user has entered a last name or a record number, the WHERE predicate is calculated. If a record number is entered, sql might equal

```
sql = "SELECT * FROM Friend WHERE ID = 4";
```

if the user wants to find record 4. If the last name field has Smith in it, the sql string becomes

```
sql = "SELECT * FROM Friend WHERE LastName = 'Smith'";
```

Notice that string literals must be surrounded by single quotes but that numeric values do not use quotes.

The sql string is then passed as a parameter to the OleDbCommand() constructor to instantiate a command object. ExecuteReader() uses the command object (myCommand) to instantiate an OleDbDataReader object (myReader), which ultimately reads the information from the database. A while loop is used to read the database data, because there could be more than one record with the same last name. The appropriate textbox objects are filled in with the database information.

To edit the information, simply change the text in the appropriate textbox object. (Or change the checkbox object if the friend's status has changed.) Then click the Save button to rewrite the edited data to the database. The code for the Save button is presented in Listing 14-8.

Listing 14-8

```
private void btnSave_Click(object sender, EventArgs e)
{
    int status;
    string sqlCommand;

    OleDbConnection myDB = new OleDbConnection();
```

(continued)

Listing 14-8 (continued)

```
OleDbCommand myCommand;
clsDB myData = new clsDB(dbName);

try
{
    myDB.ConnectionString = myData.getConnectString + dbName;
    myDB.Open();

    if (chkStatus.Checked == true)
        status = 1;
    else
        status = 0;

    // Build UPDATE command for this form
    sqlCommand = "UPDATE " + dbTableName + " SET ";
    sqlCommand += "FirstName = '" + txtFirstName.Text + "'," +
                  "MI = '" +  txtMI.Text + "'," +
                  "LastName = '" +  txtLastName.Text + "'," +
                  "Addr1 = '" + txtAddr1.Text + "'," +
                  "Addr2 = '" + txtAddr2.Text + "'," +
                  "City = '" + txtCity.Text + "'," +
                  "State = '" + txtState.Text + "'," +
                  "Zip = '" + txtZip.Text + "'," +
                  "HomePhone = '" + txtHome.Text + "'," +
                  "CellPhone = '" + txtCell.Text + "'," +
                  "WorkPhone = '" + txtWork.Text + "'," +
                  "Email = '" + txtEmail.Text + "'," +
                  "Birthday = '" + txtBirthday.Text + "'," +
                  "Anniversary = '" + txtAnniversary.Text + "'," +
                  "Status = " + status.ToString() +
                  " WHERE ID = " + txtRecordID.Text;
    myCommand = new OleDbCommand(sqlCommand, myDB);
    myCommand.ExecuteNonQuery();
    MessageBox.Show("Record added successfully.");
    myDB.Close();
} catch (Exception ex)
{
    MessageBox.Show("Failed to save edit data. Error: " +
                    ex.Message, "Process Error");
}
}
```

Once the database is reopened, an SQL command string (sqlCommand) is built from the data contained in the textbox objects. Again, in an abbreviated form, the command string looks like this (assuming that record 4 is the record being edited):

```
UPDATE Friend SET
FirstName='Fred',MI='C',LastName='Smith',Status=1 WHERE ID = 4
```

The command string is then used to instantiate a command object (myCommand) and ExecuteNonQuery() is called to write the edited data back into the database.

Delete a Record (DELETE)

The command to delete a record from a database is very similar to the other SQL commands.
For example, if you want to delete record 4 from the Friend database, the syntax would be as follows:

```
DELETE FROM Friend WHERE ID = 4
```

If you pass this command to the ExecuteNonQuery() method of the OleDbCommand object, record 4 is permanently deleted from the Friend table.

However, as I mentioned in Chapter 13, I'm not a big fan of permanently deleting information from a database. Instead, a better alternative is to have an integer status flag as one of the fields in the table. If a value of 1 is active and 0 inactive, you can perform your queries using a WHERE predicate with something like this:

```
SELECT * FROM Friend WHERE Status = 1
```

This query would return only active friends in the database. You could perform the same query but change the Status value to 0 and get a list of inactive friends.

If you look back at Figure 14-2, you can see that the primary key (ID) appears in both the Friend and Cards tables. If you delete record 4 from the Friend table, you likely will leave records for ID = 4 "dangling" in the Cards table. While relational databases can delete associated records, doing so completely erases any audit trail you might need to reconstruct at a later date. Given how cheap storage is these days, you should consider simply flagging records as inactive rather than actually deleting them.

Database Queries

Okay. . . so now you know how to create a database and its associated tables, add fields to a table, and add or update a record in a table. How do you retrieve the information in a useful way? Obviously, that's the "query" part of SQL. Figure 14-8 shows the form for generating a query.

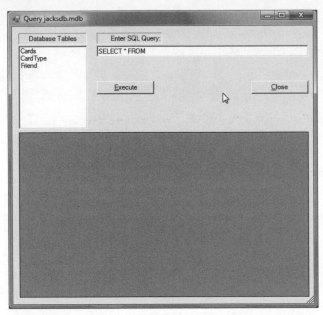

Figure 14-8

The figure shows the state of the form after the Do Query menu option is selected. The form cannot be loaded if the user has not opened a database. The code that ensures the database is open is in the mnuQuery_Click() event code in frmMain:

```
private void mnuQuery_Click(object sender, EventArgs e)
{
    if (dbName == null)       // See if they opened a DB
    {
        MessageBox.Show("You must open a database first");
        return;
    }
    frmReport myFriendReport = new frmReport(dbName, tableName);
    myFriendReport.ShowDialog();
}
```

If variable dbName is not set, a message is issued asking the user to select a database. Assuming that he has selected a database, the form shown in Figure 14-8 appears. The listbox object on the left side of the figure lists the tables that are in the currently opened database. When the user double-clicks one of the table names, the code performs a nonrestrictive query on the database based upon the table selected. The SELECT statement is copied into the textbox and the query is run. A sample result is shown in Figure 14-9.

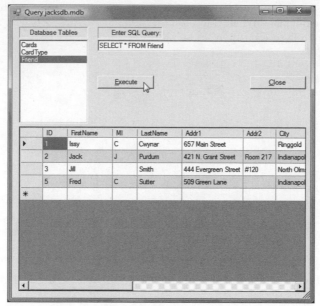

Figure 14-9

One of the nice things about this approach is that the user can then make a more restrictive query since all of the field names are visible as column heads in the data grid object (DataGridView). The bad news is that it *is* an unrestrictive query (that is, one with no WHERE predicate), so the contents of the entire table are dumped to the grid control. You can turn off the auto-query feature by not calling DoQuery() in the code:

```
private void lstTables_DoubleClick(object sender, EventArgs e)
{
    dbTable = (string)lstTables.SelectedItem;
    txtQuery.Text = "SELECT * FROM " + dbTable;

    DoQuery();      // Comment this call out to stop auto-query
}
```

If you do turn off the auto-query feature, you could use the GetColumnInfo() method in clsDB to display a list of the field names for the selected table. Those field names could then be used in a more restrictive query.

Binding a DataGridView Object to a Database

The trick to making things work properly in the program is feeding the proper database information to the DataGridView object. You can select a DataGridView object (which I will simply call *grid control* from now on) from the Data subheading of the Toolbox.

Once you have the grid control on your form, you can use the `DataSource` property of the grid control to bind the control to the database. When you select the `DataSource` property, you are presented with the option dialog shown in Figure 14-10.

Figure 14-10

Click Add Project Data Source. This invokes another dialog, shown in Figure 14-11.

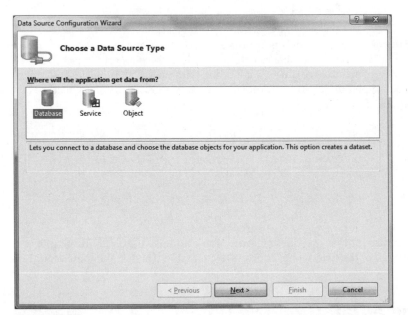

Figure 14-11

The default option is to select a database, which is what you wish to do. Click Next. The dialog updates itself and asks you for the data connection you wish to use. You should opt for a new connection by clicking the New Connection button. A new dialog appears, as shown in Figure 14-12.

Figure 14-12

In Figure 14-12, the default database is Microsoft's SQL Server. However, since we wish to use an Access database, click the Change button, as shown in Figure 14-13. This causes the dialog box shown in Figure 14-14 to be loaded.

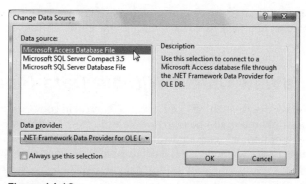

Figure 14-13

Now select the Microsoft Access database option and click OK. A modified dialog is now shown in which you can browse to the location of the database that you wish to use with the grid control. See Figure 14-14.

Figure 14-14

Once you have selected the database, you can click the Test Connection button to see if the connection to the database is working. Assuming it is, simply click OK, then Next, and then Finish. When you are done, the database you named during this process is bound to the grid control. You can then use the OleDbCommand object to issue queries on the database. As you can see, while there are quite a few steps in setting things up to bind the grid to a database, once you have done it, it takes very little code to fetch data from the database.

Alas . . . I don't like bound controls.

My primary objection is that binding the grid control to the database is not very flexible. If you want to work with another database, you have to go back through the entire process again and reconfigure everything. Not good.

Using a DataGridView Object Without Data Binding

For our query generator, we opt to do things with the grid control in code. That way, if I want to work with the phone book database, all I have to do is select it from the File menu and then select the Report ⇨ Do Query menu option. If I want to do a query on the Northwind sample database, all I have to do is select it instead of the phone book database and I can immediately start querying that database. I don't have to mess around with binding that database to the grid control. True, I have to write a little more code up front, but not much.

Listing 14-9 presents the frmQuery code.

Listing 14-9

```
using System;
using System.ComponentModel;
using System.Data;
using System.Data.OleDb;
using System.Windows.Forms;

public class frmQuery : Form
{
    private const int MAXCOLUMNS = 1000;    // Probably safe

    string conString;             // Instance members of class
    string name;
    private string dbName;
    private string dbTable;
    clsDB myDB;
    OleDbConnection conn;
    OleDbCommand command;
    OleDbDataAdapter adapter;
    DataSet ds;

    private DataGridView dataGridView1;
    private Label label1;
    private TextBox txtQuery;
    private Button btnExecute;
    private ListBox lstTables;
    private Label label2;
    private Button btnClose;

    #region Windows code

    public frmQuery(string dbN) // Constructor
    {
        int index;

        InitializeComponent();
        dbName = dbN;

        index = dbName.LastIndexOf("\\");   // Get just table name
        name = dbName.Substring(index + 1);

        // Copy DB name and table to title bar
        this.Text = "Query " + name;

        myDB = new clsDB(dbName);             // Instantiate objects
        conString = myDB.getConnectString + dbName;
        conn = new OleDbConnection(conString);
```

(continued)

427

Listing 14-9 (continued)

```
        command = conn.CreateCommand();

        txtQuery.Text = "SELECT * FROM "; // Default query

    }

    private void btnExecute_Click(object sender, EventArgs e)
    {
        DoQuery();
    }

    private void DoQuery()
    {
        try
        {
            ds = new DataSet();       // Instantiate DataSet object
            conn.Open();
            command.CommandText = txtQuery.Text;

            adapter = new OleDbDataAdapter(command);
            adapter.Fill(ds);
            dataGridView1.DataSource = ds.Tables[0];

            command.ExecuteNonQuery();
            conn.Close();
        }
        catch (Exception ex)
        {
            MessageBox.Show("Error: " + ex.Message);
        }
    }

    private void btnClose_Click(object sender, EventArgs e)
    {
        Close();
    }

    private void frmQuery_Load(object sender, EventArgs e)
    {
        int i = 0;
        string[] colNames = new string[MAXCOLUMNS];

        myDB.GetTableInfo(colNames);     // Get table names from database

        while (true)
        {
            if (colNames[i] != null)
                lstTables.Items.Add(colNames[i++]); // Show tables
```

```
                else
                    break;
            }
        }

        private void lstTables_DoubleClick(object sender, EventArgs e)
        {
            dbTable = (string)lstTables.SelectedItem;
            txtQuery.Text = "SELECT * FROM " + dbTable;
            DoQuery();          // Comment this call out to stop auto-query
        }

    }
```

The constructor code is a little more complex than you've normally seen:

```
        public frmQuery(string dbN) // Constructor
        {
            int index;

            InitializeComponent();
            dbName = dbN;

            index = dbName.LastIndexOf("\\");    // Get just table name
            name = dbName.Substring(index + 1);

            // Copy DB name and table to title bar
            this.Text = "Query " + name;

            myDB = new clsDB(dbName);                // Instantiate objects
            conString = myDB.getConnectString + dbName;
            conn = new OleDbConnection(conString);
            command = conn.CreateCommand();

            txtQuery.Text = "SELECT * FROM "; // Default query

        }
```

The InitializeComponent() method is called as usual to build the form in memory. Note that I pass in the name of the database as a parameter named dbN, which is copied to dbName. However, since dbName contains the full path name and the database name, I use LastIndexOf() to extract just the database name, which I then place in the form's title bar.

The code then instantiates a clsDB object named myDB and creates a connection string (connString). The connection string then creates an OleDbConnntion object (conn), which feeds a OleDbCommand object (command). I then partially fill in the txtQuery object.

The constructor code completes its tasks before anything appears on the display. That is, a constructor is part of the Initialization Step of the Five Programming Steps. However, in this example, the frmQuery_Load() event executes after the constructor code finishes. It is this load event that actually moves the memory images to the display screen. The load event also gives you an opportunity to execute additional code beyond that of the constructor. (You could, however, place the code in the frmQuery_Load() event into the constructor, but you would need to make sure that the InitializeComponent() call is performed before the code is executed.)

If you look at the code in the frmQuery_Load() method, you can see that it fetches the names of the tables in the currently selected database and populated the lstTables listbox object with those table names. The user then can double-click the table name and the query in the txtQuery object is completed. The user can then add a WHERE (or other) predicate and click the Execute button to see the results of the query. (See Figure 14-9.) The real work is done in the DoQuery() method:

```
private void DoQuery()
{
    try
    {
        ds = new DataSet();       // Instantiate DataSet object
        conn.Open();
        command.CommandText = txtQuery.Text;

        adapter = new OleDbDataAdapter(command);
        adapter.Fill(ds);
        dataGridView1.DataSource = ds.Tables[0];

        command.ExecuteNonQuery();
        conn.Close();
    }
    catch (Exception ex)
    {
        MessageBox.Show("Error: " + ex.Message);
    }
}
```

The reference objects are declared at the top of the form's code. However, the objects actually become defined in the DoQuery() method. First a DataSet object (ds) is defined and the connection is opened via the connection object (conn) that was instantiated in the constructor. The command object (command) has its CommandText property set via the query entered by the user (txtQuery.Text). The query is then passed to the OleDbDataAdapter() constructor to instantiate a data adapter object named adapter. The Fill() method of the data adapter passes the DataSet object, ds, for storing the results of the query. It is this DataSet object that ends up serving as the data source for the DataGridView object. Now that everything has been set up, you can actually execute the query using the ExecuteNonQuery() method of the command object.

It may seem odd to call ExecuteNonQuery() to perform a query, but that's just a nomenclature anomaly. It's called a *non-query* because the method is not designed to return the actual data of the query. Instead, it returns the results in the DataSet object, ds, which your code has tied to the grid control. When the query finishes, the connection is immediately closed.

That's all there is to it. While DoQuery() does contain code that establishes the link between the database and the grid control, the benefit is that you can use this form to communicate with any Access database. If you modify the connection string, you can query *any* database! In fact, with a little thought and effort, this code could serve as the basis for a point-and-click query builder for users who don't know SQL at all.

DataViewGrid Properties

Before we leave this example, you should know that there are a ton of properties that you can set to alter the way the DataViewGrid appears. In fact, I doubt if there is one person who knows all the permutations that you can have using the DataViewGrid object. (If there is such a person, my guess is that he is in a padded room somewhere.) The best way to test these many properties is to simply review the documentation you can find online and try changing them. However, I almost always change the following two properties any time I use this grid object.

AutoSizeColumnMode

By default, the column widths for the grid are fixed for all columns, regardless of data content. If you change this property to AllCells from the AutoSizeColumnMode dropdown combination box, the column widths automatically resize themselves to a width that accommodates the longest item in the data set for that field.

While this does make some columns wider than you might prefer them, other columns (such as zip codes, middle initial, state abbreviations, and so on) use much less display real estate than they would otherwise. Often this means seeing more data without having to scroll the display horizontally.

AlternatingRowsDefaultCellStyle

If you select this property for the grid object, you are presented with a dialog similar to that shown in Figure 14-15.

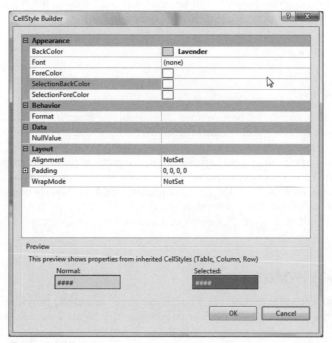

Figure 14-15

As you can see, there are a number of cell style attributes that you can set. At the top you can see that I have set the background color to Lavender. I picked this color for a very good reason: it's my favorite color. If you would like the display to look like the old IBM-style printout, click the BackColor box, click the down arrow, click the tab named Web, and select PaleGreen.

The Behavior attribute allows you to format the content of a cell in a manner that is consistent with the column type. For example, if you select Numeric, you are free to fix the number of decimal places that are displayed. Commas are automatically inserted where appropriate. If you select Currency, a dollar sign appears before the numbers and negative amounts are displayed using the accounting convention of surrounding the value with parentheses.

The Data attribute enables you to specify how null values are to be displayed in the cell. If your data source allows null values, you might set this to n/a or some other value that makes sense for your application.

The Layout attribute has several properties that you can change. If you are displaying currency values, you could right-justify the values. Most of the time I leave these properties unchanged, but they are there if you need them.

Of course, the user can resize the columns widths by default if she wishes. (You can turn this ability off if you wish by changing AllowUserToResizeColumns to false.)

Of course, the grid object assumes many functions that you find with other Microsoft products. For example, double-clicking a column header sorts the grid data according to the values in the column selected. You should experiment to see if your favorite "functionality" is implemented in the grid's default settings. If not, you should examine the properties for the grid object to see if that process can be adjusted.

Using LINQ

SQL is so simple to use, wouldn't it be nice if we could apply its simplicity to data structures other than databases? That's what Microsoft's latest creation, LINQ, is designed to do. LINQ stands for *Language INtegrated Query* and is a new feature with Visual Studio 2008. While SQL may be used with relational database objects, LINQ is also capable of querying object types where the data source is not a database. You can use LINQ to query any object type, including arrays, class objects, and XML, in addition to relational databases. Visual Studio incorporates the LINQ query engine directly, but also has defined an extension definition that allows third-party data sources to tie into the engine via a translator. Just as SQL queries result in datasets that are stored in memory, LINQ returns a collection of memory-based objects.

LINQ Query Keywords

SQL has specific keywords that are used in query statements, and LINQ provides a similar set of keywords. Perhaps the easiest way to begin explaining LINQ is to use a simple example.

A LINQ Program Example

In this example, the program generates MAXNUM (such as 100) random numbers and displays them in a listbox object. The program then uses LINQ to query that data for values that fall within a specified range. A sample run of the program can be seen in Figure 14-16.

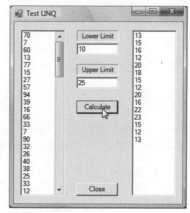

Figure 14-16

The specified range is set by the values in the two textbox objects. The result of the query is shown in the right listbox object in Figure 14-16.

How It Works

The code for the program is shown in Listing 14-10.

Listing 14-10

```
using System;
using System.Collections.Generic;
using System.Linq;
using System.Windows.Forms;

public class frmMain : Form
{
    private const int MAXNUM = 100;      // Symbolic constant

    static List<int> numbers = new List<int>(); // static member

    private Button btnClose;
    private ListBox lstOutput;
    private ListBox lstFull;
    private TextBox txtLow;
    private Label label1;
    private Label label2;
    private TextBox txtHi;
```

(continued)

Listing 14-10 (continued)

```csharp
    private Button btnCalc;

    #region Windows code

    public frmMain()
    {
        InitializeComponent();
    }

    public static void Main()
    {
        frmMain main = new frmMain();
        Application.Run(main);
    }

    private void btnCalc_Click(object sender, EventArgs e)
    {
        bool flag;
        int temp;
        int lo;
        int hi;
        DateTime current = DateTime.Now;
        Random rnd = new Random((int)current.Ticks);
        List<int> numbers = new List<int>();

            lstFull.Items.Clear();                    // Clear out old
            lstOutput.Items.Clear();

        flag = int.TryParse(txtLow.Text, out lo);    // Input validation
        if (flag == false)
        {
            MessageBox.Show("Numeric only, 0 to 100", "Input Error");
            txtLow.Focus();
            return;
        }
        flag = int.TryParse(txtHi.Text, out hi);
        if (flag == false)
        {
            MessageBox.Show("Numeric only, 0 to 100", "Input Error");
            txtHi.Focus();
            return;
        }

        for (int i = 0; i < MAXNUM; i++)             // Random values
        {
            temp = rnd.Next(MAXNUM);
            numbers.Add(temp);                       // Copy into list
            lstFull.Items.Add(temp.ToString());
        }
```

```
        var query = from p in numbers              // The "Query"
                    where p > lo && p < hi
                    select p;

        foreach (var val in query)                 // Display results
            lstOutput.Items.Add(val.ToString());

    }

    private void btnClose_Click(object sender, EventArgs e)
    {
        Close();
    }

}
```

Namespaces and References for LINQ

In this example we use a generic `List` object, so you need to include the collections-generic namespace in the program. The necessary `using` statements for the sample program are as follows:

```
using System;
using System.Collections.Generic;
using System.Linq;
using System.Windows.Forms;
```

In order to have the proper references available, you need to add a few new references to the standard list. Your reference list should include these:

```
System
System.Core
System.Data
System.Data.DataSetExtensions
System.Data.Linq
System.Drawing
System.Windows.Forms
```

The new references provide the necessary libraries to use LINQ.

The `btnCalc_Click()` event code does all the work. You begin by validating the upper and lower limits for the domain of random numbers that are generated by an object named `rnd` of the `Random` class. Recall that the statement

```
        List<int> numbers = new List<int>();
```

simply defines an object (`numbers`) that is capable of storing a list of `int` data. The first `for` loop simply defines a random number between 0 and `MAXNUM` and sets it into the `numbers` `List` object and copies the value to the `lstFull` listbox object.

The var Keyword

The following query statement defines a variable named `query`, which is of type var:

```
var query = from p in numbers                    // The "Query"
                where p > lo && p < hi
                select p;
```

A type `var` appears to enable you to define a variable without specifying what it is. You can, for example, have a definition like this:

```
var myVar = 61;
```

This leads some programmers to conclude that `var` is the same as the `object` data type. But `var` is truly different from `object`. You can prove this to yourself with the following statements:

```
var myVar = 61;
object myObj = 61;

myVar += 1;
myObj += 1;
```

The last line generates a compiler error stating that the `+=` operator can't be applied to types `object` and `int`. You can further confirm that `var` is different from an `object` by attempting to assign `myVar` and `myObj` into a primitive value type, such as:

```
long big1 = myVar;
long big2 = myObj;
```

The first statement compiles without complaint, but the second draws a type mismatch error and suggests using a cast to fix the problem.

Finally, try to compile the statements:

```
myVar = "Alice Parker";
myObj = "Tom Bangert";
```

Variable `myObj` sails through the compiler without causing complaint, but `myVar` draws an error message stating that it cannot convert a `string` to an `int`. This is the key difference between the `var` type and an `object` type: `var` is strongly typed. It also means that `var` infers its type from the context in which it is used.

So how does the compiler infer `var`'s type? Its type is set at the time it is initialized. In fact, you cannot define a `var` type without initializing it as part of its definition. That is, the statement

```
var myVar;                       // Causes compiler error!
```

draws a compiler error stating:

```
    Implicitly-typed local variables must be initialized
```

Therefore, the actual type that `var` assumes is dictated by the expression that initializes it.

Using var in a Query

Consider this extract from Listing 14-10:

```
var query = from p in numbers               // The "Query"
              where p > lo && p < hi
              select p;
```

Because `numbers` is defined generically as a list of type `int` data, `query` assumes a type `int` type. The statement works like a `FROM-WHERE` clause in SQL to examine the `numbers` data set and extract those values that fall between `lo` and `hi`. Think of the values that fall within the specified range as becoming part of a temporary data set named `p`, which is then assigned into `query`.

The statement

```
foreach (var val in query)                  // Display results
     lstOutput.Items.Add(val.ToString());
```

defines a second `var` type named `val` that, because of the initialization context in which it is defined, assumes the same type as `query`. The `foreach` loop simply iterates over the query collection and adds the values in `query` to the `lstOutput` listbox object.

While LINQ doesn't give you anything that you couldn't write yourself, it sure makes it easier. The added bonus is that its syntax mimics SQL's, making it easier to use if you already know SQL.

Try It Out   **Another LINQ Example Using String Data**

Let's try another LINQ example. In this example, let's assume that the data are names followed by that person's state. The user types in a state abbreviation for the state she wishes to examine from those shown in the left-hand listbox object and then clicks the Calculate button. The right-hand listbox object then displays those entries that match the selected state abbreviation. Figure 14-17 shows a sample run of the program.

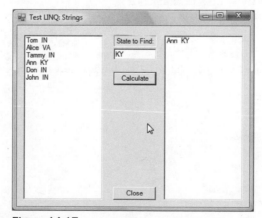

Figure 14-17

How It Works

The code for the program is shown in Listing 14-11. The code is similar to that shown in Listing 14-10, so I limit my comments to those sections that are different. First, note that I define two `static` variables (`passes` and `count`) near the top of the listing. I use the `static` specifier because I want those variables available the instant the program loads. After the `frmMain()` constructor builds the form's image in memory and initializes its data, the left listbox object is filled in via a call to `ShowAll()`.

Listing 14-11

```
using System;
using System.Linq;
using System.Windows.Forms;

public class frmMain : Form
{
    static int passes = 0;
    static int count;

    private Button btnClose;
    private ListBox lstOutput;
    private ListBox lstFull;
    private Label label1;
    private TextBox txtState;
    private Button btnCalc;

    #region Windows code

    public frmMain()
    {
        InitializeComponent();
        ShowAll();
    }

    public static void Main()
    {
        frmMain main = new frmMain();
        Application.Run(main);
    }


    private void btnCalc_Click(object sender, EventArgs e)
    {
        ShowAll();
    }

    private void ShowAll()
    {
        int i;

        var friends = new[] {
            new {name = "Tom", state = "IN"},
            new {name = "Alice", state = "VA"},
```

```
                new {name = "Tammy", state = "IN"},
                new {name = "Ann", state = "KY"},
                new {name = "Don", state = "IN"},
                new {name = "John", state = "IN"},
                new {name = "Debbie", state = "IN"},
            };
            if (passes == 0)
            {
                count = friends.GetUpperBound(0);
                i = 0;
                for (i = 0; i < count; i++)
                {
                    lstFull.Items.Add(friends[i].name + " " +
                                        friends[i].state);
                }
                passes++;
            }
            else
            {
                lstOutput.Items.Clear();          // Clear out old results

                var query = from p in friends      // The "Query"
                            where p.state == txtState.Text
                            select p;

                foreach (var val in query)         // Display results
                    lstOutput.Items.Add(val.name + " " + val.state);
            }
        }

        private void btnClose_Click(object sender, EventArgs e)
        {
            Close();
        }
    }
```

The ShowAll() method constructs a test data set using the var type and names it friends. (It would be nice to define friends as static data with class scope, but var types can assume only local scope, remember?) If passes is 0, the call was from the constructor, so the code moves the friends data to the left listbox object (lstFull) and increments passes. The next time ShowAll() is called after a button click event, filling in lstFull is bypassed because passes is no longer 0. In that case, the else statement block is executed. The right-hand listbox object (lstOutput) is cleared and the query is processed.

The following query statement uses a LINQ where predicate to restrict the result of the query to the state selected by the user:

```
            var query = from p in friends      // The "Query"
                        where p.state == txtState.Text
                        select p;

            foreach (var val in query)         // Display results
                lstOutput.Items.Add(val.name + " " + val.state);
```

The `foreach` statement block then iterates through the result of the LINQ query (as stored in `query`) and displays the relevant information in the right-hand listbox object (`lstOutput`).

Of course, the test data set can consist of more complex objects. For example, you could extend the set to something like

```
var friends = new[] {
    new {name = "Tom", state = "IN", age = 48},
    new {name = "Alice", state = "VA", age = 59},
    new {name = "Tammy", state = "IN", age = 46},
    new {name = "Ann", state = "KY", age = 59},
    new {name = "Don", state = "IN", age = 60},
    new {name = "John", state = "IN", age = 61},
    new {name = "Debbie", state = "IN", age = 58},
};
```

and change the query to

```
var query = from p in friends            // The "Query"
                where p.age < age
                select p;
```

where `age` is set from a textbox object and used as the `where` predicate in a search by age.

Other SQL-like keywords and operators are also available in LINQ. While I am not prepared to discuss all of them given our limited look at SQL, Table 14-5 gives you a list of some of the more important keywords and operators.

Table 14.5

Keyword/Operator	Description
select, selectmany	Like SELECT in SQL. selectmany may be used with another collection and allows the result set to return pairs.
where	Similar to the WHERE predicate in SQL.
join, groupjoin	Allows result sets to span multiple tables based upon matching keys in the tables.
take, takewhile	Selects the first N objects from a collection. takewhile uses a predicate to further refine the query.
skip, skipwhile	A compliment of the take operator. The set skips the first N objects in the collection. skipwhile is the compliment of takewhile.
oftype	Enables you to select elements of a certain type.
concat	Enables concatenation of two collections.
orderby, thenby	Specifies the primary sort order for a collection. The default is ascending order. You can use orderbydescending to reverse the default order. thenby enables subsequent orders after the primary sort key.

Keyword/Operator	Description
reverse	Reverses the current order of the collection.
groupby	Returns a collection of object that supports the IGrouping<*key, values*> interface.
distinct	Removes all duplicates from the result set.
union, intersect, except	Used to perform specialized operations on two sequences.
equalall	Checks to see if all elements in two collections are equal.
first, firstordefault, last, lastordefault	Uses a predicate to return the first element for which the predicate is logic True. An exception is thrown if no match is found in the collection. firstordefault is like first, but returns the first item in the collection if no match is found (that is, if no exception is thrown). last works in a similar fashion, but looks for the last match in the collection.
single	Uses a predicate to find a match but throws an exception if none is found.
elementat	Returns an element of the collection at the specified index.
any, all, contains	Uses a predicate to see if there are any matches (returns logic True or False), or if they all match, or if the collection contains a match (returns logic True or False)
count, sum, min, max, average, aggregate	Like the aggregate functions in SQL.

Table 14-5 is not exhaustive. You can use the online help to get a more complete list if you wish, but Table 14-5 will get you started.

LINQ is an important addition to C# and can make some programming tasks significantly easier to develop. You might try experimenting with some of the operators in Table 14-5, using the code in Listing 14-11 as a starting point.

Summary

You covered quite a bit of ground in this chapter. You should have a pretty good idea of what a database is, how one can be created and expanded, and how otherwise to manipulate the data within the database. You also got a brief introduction to LINQ, which brings a lot of SQL query functionality to data structures other than databases. I encourage you to experiment with the sample programs in this chapter and try to create a different database on your own. Once you have done that, add data to the tables so they use LINQ instead of SQL to query the database. This should solidify your understanding of the database concepts in this chapter as well as LINQ.

Exercises

1. Suppose you define a `Friends` table using the data structure suggested in Chapter 13. Give two SQL commands that would return the number of active members of the `Friends` table.

2. Again using the `Friends` data structure from Chapter 13, construct an SQL statement that returns all the active members who live in Indiana (or whatever state you might use) and whose second address is not empty.

3. The code in `frmAddFriend` is a bit of a hack because it is tightly coupled with the user interface:

```
sqlCommand = "INSERT INTO " + dbTableName + " (";
for (i = 1; i < colNames.Length; i++)
{
  if (colNames[i] == null)
    break;
  sqlCommand += colNames[i] + ",";
}
i = sqlCommand.LastIndexOf(',');
sqlCommand = sqlCommand.Substring(0, i) + ") VALUES ('";
// Now add the values
sqlCommand += txtFirstName.Text + "','" +
              txtMI.Text + "','" +
              txtLastName.Text + "','" +
              txtAddr1.Text + "','" +
              txtAddr2.Text + "','" +
              txtCity.Text + "','" +
              txtState.Text + "','" +
              txtZip.Text + "','" +
              txtHome.Text + "','" +
              txtCell.Text + "','" +
              txtWork.Text + "','" +
              txtEmail.Text + "','" +
              txtBirthday.Text + "','" +
              txtAnniversary.Text + "'," +
              status.ToString() + ")";
```

    The reason it is tightly coupled is that I have tied the inputs to the textbox objects used to gather the information from the user. Because you don't want end user interface objects like textboxes in a non-UI class, the current code shouldn't be moved into class `clsDB`. However, it would be nice to move the database `INSERT` command out of the user interface code in `frmAddFriend` and move it into the `clsDB` class where it belongs. How might you do that?

4. Using the `Friends` table as an example, how could you use LINQ to process a database query?

5. If you're at a cocktail party and someone approaches you and asks, "Why should I use LINQ instead of SQL in my code?" what would you say? (What? This couldn't happen?)

Inheritance and Polymorphism

In this chapter I expand on the concept of inheritance. Although you have been using inheritance since the first chapter of this book, I haven't said much about it. In this chapter you learn the details of inheritance that are necessary to use it properly in your own programs. In this chapter you will learn the following:

❑ What inheritance is

❑ How inheritance simplifies program code

❑ What base classes and derived classes are

❑ What the `protected` access specifier is

❑ What polymorphism is

❑ How polymorphism can simplify your programs

As you read this chapter, keep in mind that inheritance was added to OOP languages to make the programmer's life easier. While the end user may not see any advantages to inheritance and polymorphism, you will have a greater appreciation of how much simpler they can make program code.

What is Inheritance?

Up until now, inheritance has been a concept sitting in the background, making your life easier every time you designed a user interface for your programs. Indeed, you have probably glossed over the fact that the program line

```
public class frmMain : Form
```

enabled you to inherit all of the basic functionality of a Windows form without having to write that code yourself. In fact, the colon in the preceding statement could be verbalized as "inherits from." The concept of inheritance is built upon the notion that many objects share similar properties. In the preceding statement, you are stating that you wish to create a new class named `frmMain` that inherits all of the functionality of a basic Windows form. Being able to inherit this functionality means that you don't have to write, test, debug, and maintain that inherited code yourself. Therefore, the driving force behind inheritance is to simplify writing code. Inheritance makes it possible for your code to extend one class to suit your specific needs. Simply stated, *inheritance* is the ability to take one class and extend that class to suit a similar, albeit different, purpose. An example will help explain inheritance.

An Inheritance Example

Some time ago I was contracted to write a program for a real estate investor. The type of real estate the investor purchased could be classified as apartments, commercial properties (such as small strip malls), and residential homes. I sat down with her and asked her to describe the type of information that she needed to track with her investments. Table 15-1 is taken from my notes as she described her needs.

Table 15-1

Apartments	Commercial	Residential
Purchase price	Purchase date	Address
Purchase date	Address	Purchase price
Address	Rent per month	Purchase date
Monthly mortgage payment	Purchase price	Square feet
Insurance	Property taxes	Number of bedrooms
Property taxes	Insurance	Number of bathrooms
Covered parking	Mortgage payment	Basement?
Storage units	Parking spaces	Fireplace(s)
Number of bedrooms	Restroom facilities	Garage size (cars)
Number of bathrooms	Handicap parking	Rent per month
Rent per month		Lot size

Given the data requirements presented in Table 15-1, I could design the three classes with properties that would track the information she required. Looking at the information she needed, you can simplify each property type by removing those pieces of information that are common to all investment types. These are shown in Table 15-2.

Table 15-2

Information Common to All Properties
Purchase price
Purchase date
Address
Property taxes
Insurance
Mortgage payment
Rent per month

If you remove these common pieces of information from each investment type, you can simplify Table 15-1 to what is shown in Table 15-3.

Table 15-3

Apartments	Commercial	Residential
Covered parking	Parking spaces	Square feet
Storage units	Restroom facilities	Number of bedrooms
Number of bedrooms	Handicap parking	Number of bathrooms
Number of bathrooms		Basement?
		Fireplace(s)
		Garage size (cars)
		Lot size

Less information is contained in Table 15-3 than in Table 15-1 because of the common information all three property types share in Table 15-2 is removed. You can express the relationships for the data as shown in the UML class diagrams in Figure 15-1.

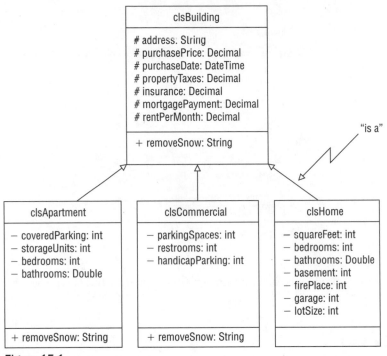

Figure 15-1

The Base and Derived Classes

As you can see in Figure 15-1, I used our UML notation to give a first approximation of how I wanted to organize the data for the investment types. At the top of the figure is clsBuilding. clsBuilding contains all the properties common to all the investment types, and is called the *base class*. You can think of the base class as a common denominator of data for all the classes. Any classes that wish to use the properties and methods of the base class are called a *derived class*. In terms of Figure 15-1, clsBuilding is the base class and classes clsApartment, clsCommercial, and clsHome are derived classes. You will also hear the base class referred to as the *parent class* and a derived class as a *child class*. The interpretations are the same.

In Figure 15-1 you will notice that three arrows point from the derived classes to the base class. Each of these arrows can be verbalized as "is a." That is, clsApartment is a clsBuilding. Using straight English, you can say, "An apartment object is a kind of building object." Likewise, a commercial object is a kind of building object. The arrows in the UML diagram are used to indicate the nature of the inherited relationships that exist between classes.

The protected Access Specifier

In Figure 15-1 I placed the seven common properties all investment types share in clsBuilding and have indicated the data type for each property. However, unlike the public (+) and private (-) access specifiers you learned in Chapter 9, Figure 15-1 uses a new access specifier (#). The sharp sign (#) is used to denote the protected access specifier. The protected access specifier is needed because of the symbiotic relationship ("is a") that is formed between the base class and the derived classes.

To understand why the protected class is used, consider how things would work if you were limited to either a public or a private access specifier. First, consider the private access specifier. If you use the private access specifier in clsBuilding, each method and property has class scope. As you already know, this means that those properties and methods would not be visible outside the class. Therefore, nothing in the program would have access to those properties and methods, including the derived classes. If you can't access them, they are virtually worthless to the derived classes.

Now consider the other alternative: making all the properties and methods public. If you do that, you just threw away all the benefits that encapsulation brings to the party. Not only can the derived classes gain access to the properties and methods of the base class, so can every other object in the program. As you learned in earlier chapters, encapsulation enables you to protect your data from evil agents who want to wreak havoc on your program.

Using either the public or private access specifier poses a true dilemma: two choices, both bad. The *protected access specifier* solves this problem. The protected access specifier allows all derived classes to have access to those properties and methods that are defined with the protected access specifer in the base class. By your using the sharp sign in Figure 15-1 before the properties defined in clsBuilding, all three derived classes have access to those properties. However, any object in the program that is not derived from the base class does not have direct access to those protected properties. The protected access specifier is sort of like a high school clique in that the base and derived classes can share information that people outside the clique don't know about. This allows the base and derived classes to encapsulate the data that they need without exposing it outside those symbiotic classes.

Just to drive the point home, given a line in clsBuilding:

```
protected decimal purchasePrice;
```

You could have the line

```
purchasePrice = 150000M;
```

in clsHome and it would be perfectly acceptable. The reason is that the protected keyword for the definition of purchasePrice in clsBuilding is completely in scope within clsHome. Therefore, protected data definitions in the base class are within scope for any of its derived classes.

Advantages of Inherited Relationships

You might be asking yourself what inheritance gets you. Well, to begin with, if you didn't have the inherited relationships shown in Figure 15-1, each of the derived classes would have to have its own copy of the data shown in Table 15-2. That would also mean that each of those properties would have to have its own get and set property methods. The same would be true for any methods that might be shared in the derived classes, like RemoveSnow(), shown in Figure 15-1.

Inheritance enables you write less code by sharing properties and methods between the base and derived classes. Writing less (duplicate) code means less testing, debugging, and maintenance. It also follows that if you need to change a protected property or method, you have to change it in only one place and all the derived classes can immediately take advantage of it.

Try It Out   Inheritance Example

Let's write a simple version of the real estate investor program. Figure 15-2 shows a sample run of the program you are writing.

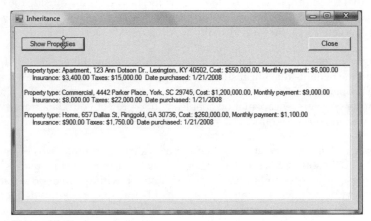

Figure 15-2

At the present time, all I want the program to do is display a description of each property type. You show the sample investment properties by clicking the Show Properties button.

How It Works

I begin the program discussion with the base `clsBuilding` class, the code for which is shown in Listing 15-1.

Listing 15-1

```
using System;

public class clsBuilding
{
    //-------------------- Symbolic constants -------------------
    public const int APARTMENT = 1;
    public const int COMMERCIAL = 2;
    public const int HOME = 3;

    //-------------------- Instance variables -------------------
    protected string address;
    protected decimal purchasePrice;
    protected decimal monthlyPayment;
    protected decimal taxes;
```

```csharp
protected decimal insurance;
protected DateTime datePurchased;
protected int buildingType;

string[] whichType = {"", "Apartment", "Commercial", "Home" };

//-------------------- Constructor -------------------------
public clsBuilding()
{
        address = "Not closed yet";
}

public clsBuilding(string addr, decimal price, decimal payment,
                   decimal tax, decimal insur, DateTime date,
                   int type):this()
{
        if (addr.Equals("") == false)
              address = addr;
      purchasePrice = price;
      monthlyPayment = payment;
      taxes = tax;
      insurance = insur;
      datePurchased = date;
      buildingType = type;
}
//-------------------- Property Methods --------------------

public string Address
{
    get
    {
        return address;
    }
    set
    {
        if (value.Length != 0)
              address = value;
    }
}
public decimal PurchasePrice
{
    get
    {
        return purchasePrice;
    }
    set
    {
        if (value > 0M)
              purchasePrice = value;
    }
}
```

```
public decimal MonthlyPayment
{
    get
    {
        return monthlyPayment;
    }
    set
    {
        if (value > 0M)
            monthlyPayment = value;
    }
}

public decimal Taxes
{
    get
    {
        return taxes;
    }
    set
    {
        if (value > 0M)
            taxes = value;
    }
}

public decimal Insurance
{
    get
    {
        return insurance;
    }
    set
    {
        if (value > 0M)
            insurance = value;
    }
}

public DateTime DatePurchased
{
    get
    {
        return datePurchased;
    }
    set
    {
        if (value.Year > 2008)
            datePurchased = value;
    }
}
```

```
        public int BuildingType
        {
            get
            {
                return buildingType;
            }
            set
            {
                if (value >= APARTMENT && value <= HOME)
                    buildingType = value;
            }
        }
        //-------------------- General Methods ---------------------

        /*****
         * Purpose: Provide a basic description of the property
         *
         * Parameter list:
         *   string[] desc        a string array to hold description
         *
         * Return value:
         *   void
         *
         * CAUTION: Method assumes that there are 3 elements in array
         ******/
        public void PropertySummary(string[] desc)
        {
            desc[0] = "Property type: " + whichType[buildingType] +
                      ", " + address +
                      ", Cost: " + purchasePrice.ToString("C") +
                      ", Monthly payment: " + monthlyPayment.ToString("C");
            desc[1] = "      Insurance: " + insurance.ToString("C") +
                      " Taxes: " + taxes.ToString("C") +
                      " Date purchased: "+ datePurchased.ToShortDateString();
            desc[2] = " ";
        }

    }
```

The code begins by defining several symbolic constants followed by the property members of clsBuilding. As specified in your design, each property method uses the protected access specifier. The code also provides for the property get and set methods for each of the properties so the user can change the state of the object.

Symbolic Constants Versus Enumerated Types

I have used symbolic constants in many programs throughout this text. If you think about it, however, you could also use enumerated types in the same way. For example, you could replace the symbolic constants shown in Listing 15-1 with this:

```
public enum bldgType {APARTMENT = 1, COMMERCIAL, HOME}
```

Then you could use the enum in the BuildingType() like this:

```
set
{
    if (value >= (int) bldgType.APARTMENT &&
        value <= (int) bldgType.HOME)
    {
        buildingType = value;
    }
}
```

The int cast is required in the if statement because value is defined as an int for the property. Personally, I find the syntax using the enum clumsy and prefer the use of symbolic constants. Select the style you prefer and use it consistently.

The method PropertySummary() is used to provide a summary of the building's description using the properties associated with each property. The method builds an array of strings, which are then returned to the caller in frmMain to display the property description in a listbox object. (I present the frmMain code a little later in the chapter.) The output generated by the PropertySummary() method looks like that shown in Figure 15-2.

There are two constructors in Listing 15-1. The first constructor assumes that you wish to set the properties for the building by separate calls to the property methods:

```
public clsBuilding()
{
    address = "Not closed yet";
}
```

It also sets the default address to a message that suggests you haven't actually purchased the property yet. The second constructor assumes that you wish to initialize the properties when the building object is instantiated.:

```
public clsBuilding(string addr, decimal price, decimal payment,
                decimal tax, decimal insur, DateTime date,
                int type):this()
{
    if (addr.Equals("") == false)
        address = addr;
    purchasePrice = price;
    monthlyPayment = payment;
```

```
        taxes = tax;
        insurance = insur;
        datePurchased = date;
        buildingType = type;
    }
```

Note that I follow the good coding practice of calling the first constructor via the `this()` call to the first (no-argument) constructor. This also means that, if you pass in a property address in `addr`, the second constructor overwrites the "Not closed yet" string with the address.

Listing 15-2 shows the `frmMain` code that drives the application.

Listing 15-2

```
using System;
using System.Windows.Forms;

public class frmMain : Form
{
    DateTime myTime;                // instance members
    clsBuilding myBldg;
    clsApartment myApt;
    clsCommercial myComm;
    clsHome myHome;
    private string[] whichType = { "", "Apartment", "Commercial",
                                   "Home" };

    private ListBox lstMessages;
    private Button btnShow;
    private Button btnRemoveSnow;
    private Button btnClose;

    #region Windows code

    public frmMain()
    {
        InitializeComponent();      // Initialize the form

        myTime = DateTime.Now;
        myBldg = new clsBuilding();  // A base object

                                    // Derived objects
        myApt = new clsApartment("123 Ann Dotson Dr., Lexington, KY
                          40502", 550000, 6000, 15000, 3400,
                          myTime, 1);

        myComm = new clsCommercial("4442 Parker Place, York, SC 29745",
                          1200000, 9000, 22000, 8000, myTime, 2);

        myHome = new clsHome("657 Dallas St, Ringgold, GA 30736",
                          260000, 1100, 1750, 900, myTime, 3);
    }
```

(continued)

Listing 15-2 (continued)

```
        public static void Main()
        {
            frmMain main = new frmMain();
            Application.Run(main);
        }

        // Show each of the properties...
        private void btnShow_Click(object sender, EventArgs e)
        {
            string[] desc = new string[3];

                myApt.PropertySummary(desc);
                ShowProperty(desc);

                myComm.PropertySummary(desc);
                ShowProperty(desc);

                myHome.PropertySummary(desc);
                ShowProperty(desc);
        }

        private void ShowProperty(string[] str)
        {
            int i;

            for (i = 0; i < str.Length; i++)
            {
                lstMessages.Items.Add(str[i]);
            }
        }

        private void btnClose_Click(object sender, EventArgs e)
        {
            Close();
        }
    }
```

In a "real" program you would likely have textbox objects that would fill in each of the properties for the different types of buildings. In this code I simply initialize the buildings using the parameterized constructors. You can see the data in the frmMain() constructor method.

Notice how the descriptions are displayed in the listbox object. For example,

```
        myApt.PropertySummary(desc);
        ShowProperty(desc);
```

calls the PropertySummary() method using the myApt object.

The code for the three derived classes is shown in Listing 15-3. (I have separated the three class listings with double-dashed lines to make it easier to see where one class ends and another begins.) If you look closely, you'll notice that clsApartment does not have a method named PropertySummary(), yet Figure 15-2 shows the correct information for the apartment property. The same is true for clsCommercial and clsHome: neither has a PropertySummary() method. How does the program display the correct information for each building? Obviously, all three buildings are using the PropertySummary() method from the base class to display their properties.

Listing 15-3

```csharp
using System;

class clsApartment : clsBuilding
{
    //-------------------- Instance variables --------------------
    private int units;
    private decimal rentPerUnit;
    private double occupancyRate;

    //-------------------- Constructor --------------------------
    public clsApartment():base()
    {
    }
    public clsApartment(string addr, decimal price, decimal payment,
                        decimal tax, decimal insur, DateTime date,
                        int type) :
                        base(addr, price, payment, tax, insur, date, type)
    {
        buildingType = type;   // Apartment type from base
    }
    //-------------------- Property Methods --------------------
    public int Units
    {
        get
        {
            return units;
        }
        set
        {
            if (value > 0)
                units = value;
        }
    }
    public decimal RentPerUnit
    {
        get
        {
            return rentPerUnit;
        }
        set
        {
            if (value > 0M)
                rentPerUnit = value;
        }
    }
```

(continued)

Listing 15-3 (continued)

```
    public double OccupancyRate
    {
        get
        {
            return occupancyRate;
        }
        set
        {
            if (value > 0.0)
                occupancyRate = value;
        }
    }

    //-------------------- General Methods ----------------------
    public override string RemoveSnow()
    {
        return "Called John's Snow Removal: 859.444.7654";
    }
}
==========================================================================

using System;

class clsCommercial : clsBuilding
{
    //-------------------- Instance variables -------------------
    private int squareFeet;
    private int parkingSpaces;
    private decimal rentPerSquareFoot;

    //-------------------- Constructor ------------------------
    public clsCommercial(string addr, decimal price, decimal payment,
                         decimal tax, decimal insur, DateTime date,
                         int type) :
                         base(addr, price, payment, tax, insur, date, type)
    {
        buildingType = type;    // Commercial type from base
    }
    //-------------------- Property Methods --------------------
    public int SquareFeet
    {
        get
        {
            return squareFeet;
        }
        set
        {
            if (value > 0)
                squareFeet = value;
        }
    }
```

```
    public int ParkingSpaces
    {
        get
        {
            return parkingSpaces;
        }
        set
        {
            parkingSpaces = value;
        }
    }
    public decimal RentPerSquareFoot
    {
        get
        {
            return rentPerSquareFoot;
        }
        set
        {
            if (value > 0M)
                rentPerSquareFoot = value;
        }
    }

    //-------------------- General Methods ---------------------
    public override string RemoveSnow()
    {
        return "Called Acme Snow Plowing: 803.234.5566";
    }
}


=========================================================================
using System;


class clsHome : clsBuilding
{
    //-------------------- Instance variables -------------------
    private int squareFeet;
    private int bedrooms;
    private double bathrooms;
    private decimal rentPerMonth;

    //-------------------- Constructor ------------------------
    public clsHome(string addr, decimal price, decimal payment,
                   decimal tax, decimal insur, DateTime date,
                   int type) :
                   base(addr, price, payment, tax, insur, date, type)
    {
        buildingType = 3;       // Home type from base
    }
```

(continued)

Listing 15-3 (continued)

```
//-------------------- Property Methods --------------------
public int SquareFeet
{
    get
    {
        return squareFeet;
    }
    set
    {
        if (value > 0)
            squareFeet = value;
    }
}
public int BedRooms
{
    get
    {
        return bedrooms;
    }
    set
    {
        bedrooms = value;
    }
}
public double BathRooms
{
    get
    {
        return bathrooms;
    }
    set
    {
        bathrooms = value;
    }
}
public decimal RentPerMonth
{
    get
    {
        return rentPerMonth;
    }
    set
    {
        if (value > 0M)
            rentPerMonth = value;
    }
}

//-------------------- General Methods --------------------

}
```

Notice that each of the three building type begins with a line similar to

```
class clsApartment : clsBuilding
```

This is what establishes the "is a" relationship depicted in Figure 15-1. This also means that each derived class can use the `PropertySummary()` found in `clsBuilding`.

One more thing. Derived classes cannot inherit constructors. You must write a constructor for a derived class. If the base class doesn't have a default constructor, the constructor for the derived class must call the base constructor using the `base` keyword, as shown in `clsApartment`:

```
public clsApartment(string addr, decimal price, decimal payment,
                    decimal tax, decimal insur, DateTime date,
                    int type) :
                    base(addr, price, payment, tax, insur, date, type)
```

The keyword `base` is used here to pass parameters used to construct the `clsApartment` object on to the `clsBuilding` constructor. (The concept is similar to the `this` construct used with multiple constructors.)

Base Classes are Not Derived Classes

The ability for a derived class to use a method in the base class is a one-way relationship. That is, the derived class can call a base class method, but the base class cannot call a derived class method. For example, suppose `clsCommercial` contains a public method named `HouseCleaning()`. If `myBldg` is a `clsBuilding` object, you cannot use

```
myBldg.HouseCleaning();
```

The compiler throws an error and informs you that it cannot find a definition for `HouseCleaning()`. This conclusion is true even if you use the `public` access specifier for the `HouseCleaning()` method. The reason you can't perform a base-to-derived method call is that the "is a" relationship shown in Figure 15-1 is a one-way street. That is, a `clsCommercial` object assumes all of the property and methods of a `clsBuilding` object, but a `clsBuilding` object does not assume all the properties and methods of a `clsCommercial` object.

Abstract Classes

As I mentioned earlier, the base class is typically used to serve as a repository for all the properties shared among the derived classes. However, it is possible that the base class is so nondescript that instantiating an object of the base class doesn't make sense. For example, you might create a class called `clsDeciduous` that has the properties `leafColor`, `barkStyle`, `matureHeight`, and `ringCount`. The derived classes might be `clsOak`, `clsMaple`, `clsWillow` and so on. The problem is that, even though all of the derived classes have leaves, bark, a mature height, and a ring count, there are so many trees with these characteristics that it makes no real sense to instantiate a `clsDeciduous` object. Only the details found in the derived classes, in conjunction with the base class, have enough information to make an object useful.

To prevent instantiation of the base class, you use the `abstract` keyword:

```
public abstract class clsDecidious
{
        // The class code...
}
```

If a class is defined by means of the `abstract` keyword, as shown here, you cannot instantiate an object of that class. This means that a statement like the following draws a compiler error telling you that you cannot instantiate an object of an `abstract` class:

```
clsDecidious myLeafyTree = new clsDecidious();
```

If you can't instantiate an object of the class, why use it?

By defining a class using the `abstract` keyword, you are telling the users of the class two things. First, they cannot instantiate an object of this class, which tips them off to the second reason. Second, and more importantly, the user must define derived classes to capture the functionality embodied in the base class. Indeed, there is no reason to use the base class in the absence of derived classes.

If you define a method using the `abstract` keyword, the derived classes *must* implement the method. There is no code in the base class for the method. In this way, abstract classes and methods are similar to interfaces in that interfaces contain no code either. However, interfaces cannot contain constructors.

Polymorphism

I mentioned in Chapter 1 that polymorphism is one of the three pillars of object-oriented programming. At that time I dismissed the topic, saying that the word *polymorphism* is derived from the Greek meaning "many shapes." Now that you understand what inheritance is, you are ready to more completely appreciate what polymorphism is.

Instead of sticking with the concept of "many shapes," perhaps I should amend the definition to mean "many messages." In essence, *polymorphism* means that you can send the same message to a group of different classes and that each class will know how to respond correctly to that message.

Try It Out **Using Polymorphism**

Consider the following example. Where I live, if more than two inches of snow falls, you are supposed to get out and shovel your walkways. Let's further assume that our software should notify someone at each property location when our property manager sees that two or more inches of snow has fallen. (I will just pretend that there is an electrical hookup between the software and the phone system. I'll use things displayed in the listbox object as an indicator that the call(s) have been made.)

What we want to do is add a button that the manager can click when he sees that more than two inches of snow is on the ground. A sample run of the program is shown in Figure 15-3.

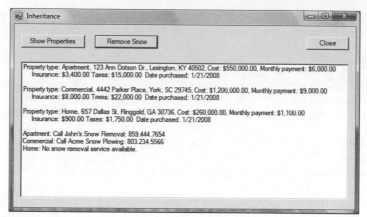

Figure 15-3

Notice that the apartment and commercial buildings are given a phone number to call for snow removal, but none is given for people who live in a rented home. The assumption is that, as part of their lease agreement, they are required to shovel the walks themselves.

How It Works

The first thing we need to do is modify the base class to process the snow-removal message. The code that is added to `clsBuilding` is as follows:

```
public virtual string RemoveSnow()
{
    return whichType[buildingType] +
            ": No snow removal service available.";
}
```

The virtual Keyword

The snow removal method in `clsBuilding`, `RemoveSnow()`, is defined via the keyword `virtual`. The word *virtual* is used to identify that the method may be overridden in a derived class. Stated differently, a virtual method can be replaced by a different definition of the method in any class that is derived from this class.

If you look back at Figure 15-1, you can see that we provide `RemoveSnow()` methods for both `clsApartment` and `clsCommercial` objects. The code for these two methods is as follows:

```
public override string RemoveSnow()      // clsApartment
{
    return "Apartment: Call John's Snow Removal: 859.444.7654";
}

public override string RemoveSnow()      // clsCommerical
{
    return "Commercial: Call Acme Snow Plowing: 803.234.5566";
}
```

461

Figure 15-1 also shows that there is no RemoveSnow() method for clsHome. People who rent homes were informed when they signed their lease that they were responsible for snow removal.

The override Keyword

As you might guess, the override keyword goes hand in hand with the virtual keyword. Whereas virtual tells the reader of the code that the method may be overridden, the override keyword tells her that this method is overriding a method found in the class from which it inherits.

Normally, the derived class overrides a virtual method defined in the base class. However, you can define a new class from a derived class. For example, you could add clsRecreational to clsHome, perhaps with new properties for lakeFrontage, boatRamp, availableFishingTackle, and so on. The definition of that class might be as follows:

```
public class clsRecreational : clsHome
{
    // Class code
}
```

You can keep extending the class definitions are far as you think you need them. (If you want to prevent further inheritance from a class, you can use the sealed keyword as a modifier in the class definition, as in public sealed clsLastClass.)

Most of the time, however, you will use override in conjunction with a virtual method that is defined in the base class.

Sending the Snow-Removal Message

The new user interface for frmMain now contains a button that issues the snow-removal messages. It is the responsibility of each class to figure out what to do. The button click event code for the snow removal message is as follows:

```
private void btnRemoveSnow_Click(object sender, EventArgs e)
{
    lstMessages.Items.Add(myApt.RemoveSnow());
    lstMessages.Items.Add(myComm.RemoveSnow());
    lstMessages.Items.Add(myHome.RemoveSnow());
    lstMessages.Items.Add("");
}
```

Each derived class is sent the same message via the method call to RemoveSnow(). However, the message displayed is dictated by whatever process the derived class wishes to attach to the method call.

Note that clsHome doesn't even *have* a RemoveSnow() method, yet it still displays the following message:

```
Home: No snow removal service available.
```

As you no doubt have already figured out, because clsHome has no RemoveSnow() method, the RemoveSnow() method in the base class is used. In other words, clsHome chose not to override the RemoveSnow() method, but instead to use the "default" method as written in the base class.

The nice thing about using inheritance and polymorphic behavior is that each object knows the specifics of how it is supposed to react to whatever events or methods are called, even though the objects share a common method name.

Summary

This chapter completed our study of the three pillars of object-oriented programming: encapsulation, inheritance, and polymorphism. Throughout this text I have stressed the importance of hiding your data inside a class or methods. In this chapter you learned how the `protected` access specifier permits you to encapsulate data, yet share it with derived classes as needed. You also learned how the base class serves as a common denominator for related, yet distinct, classes. Finally, you learned how polymorphism enables you to have each derived class react to messages in a way that is appropriate for it.

We've come to the end of our study. I have presented the essential parts of OOP, using C# as the vehicle to learn those concepts. Still, you can't really master a language until you take on a major coding project. The examples presented throughout the book were purposely kept simple so the concepts could be taught without our having to wade through a lot of complex code. Real life, however, is rarely so kind. If you have some project you've always wanted to write but used the excuse you couldn't find the time, *that* would be the project you should tackle to *really* learn C# and OOP.

If you are already coding in some other language and just stopped by to see what C# has to offer, I hope you agree that C# is a very nice language, capable of serious program development. Here, again, perhaps you might try your next project using C#. Personally, I think you'll be amazed at how fast you can develop serious applications in C#.

To all: give C# a serious workout. I think you'll like it.

Exercises

1. A golf club wants to set up a membership program capable of sending out mail, e-mails, and voting ballots to its members. The membership consists of junior, regular, and senior golfing members, plus a social membership, which excludes golf. The problem is that junior and social members are not allowed to vote on club issues. Also, social members should not receive mailings about golf tournaments since they are not allowed to use the course, only the pool and restaurant facilities. If you were to write the program, how would you organize it?

2. Suppose you see the following line of code in a program:

   ```
   public clsJunion(string addr, int status, decimal minimum)
                  : base(string addr, int status, decimal minimum)
   ```

   What can you tell me about the line of code?

3. Some programmers don't like the `protected` access specifier. What do you think might be their reasons?

4. How would you prevent other programmers from extending one of your classes via inheritance?

5. Does inheritance bring anything to the party that we couldn't do without it?

Exercise Solutions

Chapter 3

Exercise 1 Solution

The code for this solution is exactly the same as for the integer division solution provided earlier in the chapter, with the exception that the line that reads

```
answer = operand1 / operand2;
```

in the code should be changed to:

```
answer = operand1 * operand2;
```

The remainder of the program is the same. It is important to try very large and very small numbers to see what happens when your answer falls outside the range of the data type you selected.

Exercise 2 Solution

You can use most of the code shown in the chapter; the only difference is that you do not need to have the user enter two input values. In this program, you want to prompt them only for the Fahrenheit temperature. Therefore, the relevant code becomes

```
private void btnCalc_Click(object sender, EventArgs e)
{
    bool flag;
    double operand1;
    double answer;

        //                      Input Step
        // Check first input...
    flag = double.TryParse(txtOperand1.Text, out operand1);
```

```
        if (flag == false)
        {
          MessageBox.Show("Enter Fahrenheit temperature", "Input Error");
          txtOperand1.Focus();
          return;
        }


              //                        Process Step

        answer = 5.0 / 9.0 * (operand1 - 32);

              //                        Display Step
        txtResult.Text = operand1.ToString() + " is " +
                          answer.ToString() + " Celsius";
        txtResult.Visible = true;


        }
```

You can use the same textbox to display the answer. If you wrote the equation as:

```
        answer = .555555555555555 * (operand1 - 32);
```

treat yourself to an extra scoop of ice cream. Division is one of the slowest math operations a computer performs, and because the equation uses two constants, you can avoid the division by simply using the ratio 5/9 expressed as a constant.

Exercise 3 Solution

Again, use the first program as the starting point for this program, but with only one input from the user. We can use the modulo operator to determine whether the integer was odd or even. Recall that the modulo operator returns the remainder of division.

```
        private void btnCalc_Click(object sender, EventArgs e)
        {
          bool flag;
          int operand1;
          int answer;

              //                    Input Step
              // Check first input...
          flag = int.TryParse(txtOperand1.Text, out operand1);
          if (flag == false)
          {
            MessageBox.Show("Enter Fahrenheit temperature", "Input Error");
            txtOperand1.Focus();
            return;
          }


              //                        Process Step

        answer = operand1 % 2;
```

```
    //                      Display Step
If (answer == 0)
{
    txtResult.Text = " Your number was even ";
} else
{
    txtResult.Text = " Your number was odd";
}
}
```

By taking the number entered by the user and applying a modulo 2 operation, you get a remainder that is either 0 if the number is even or 1 if it is odd. Think about it.

Chapter 4

Exercise 1 Solution

This exercise is designed to make you use the debugger so you can examine the variables and their values while the program executes. You will notice that you cannot set a breakpoint on empty lines in the Source window.

Exercise 2 Solution

Relatively few changes are needed to the original code. You should add these lines:

```
const double FAHRENHEITFREEZINGPOINT = 32;
const double FIVENINTHS = .55555555555555555; // This is 5/9
```

Note the short comment to help explain the second symbolic constant. This helps to explain what the constant is. Now change the statement that calculates the temperature to

```
celciusTemp = FIVENINTHS * (fahrenheitTemp -
            FAHRENHEITFREEZINGPOINT);
```

This should make the code a little easier to understand.

Exercise 3 Solution

An lvalue for a variable is the memory address of where that variable resides in memory. The rvalue of a variable is what is stored at the lvalue memory location. If a variable does not have an lvalue, no memory has been allocated for it. This means that the variable serves informational purposes only in the symbol table and cannot be used to store program values.

Exercise 4 Solution

The size of the bucket is determined by the data type being defined. The analogy typically expresses the size of the bucket in terms of bytes. The number of bytes for C#'s value types is found in Chapter 3. The location of the bucket in memory is the bucket's lvalue, while the content of the bucket is the bucket's rvalue.

Chapter 5

Exercise 1 Solution

A value type variable has its data stored in its rvalue. A reference variable has an rvalue that holds either null or a memory address. If the reference variable currently holds null, it means that the reference variable is not associated with any useful information. If the reference variable holds a valid memory address (i.e., non-null), the rvalue tells you where in memory the information associated with the reference variable is stored.

Exercise 2 Solution

```
message = message.Replace("Frday", "Friday");
```

Exercise 3 Solution

There are several ways to solve the bug. First, you could do nothing and say that most people will never notice there's an extra space. Always keep in mind that doing nothing *is* a decision. Sometimes fixing a bug is so difficult and expensive, it's just not worth the effort. (A major chip manufacturer had a bug "etched" into the firmware for the chip. Because the error was so obscure, the manufacturer simply ignored the problem until enough people complained about it.) Fixing this bug, however, is pretty simple, so we should explore some other alternatives.

Second, you could pad the word to be removed with a leading blank space. As long as the word is not at the beginning of a sentence, this would probably work.

A third alternative is to leave the code as it is but follow it up with a call to the Replace() method. In this case, you would want to find the two blank spaces and replace them with a single blank space.

Which method is best? It all depends upon the exact nature of the data. For the example shown in this chapter, I obviously chose the first method. If I wanted to fix it given the string used in the example, the second solution provides the easiest fix.

Exercise 4 Solution

A constructor is a special method that always has the same name as the class in which it appears. The constructor is called as part of the process of instantiating an object of a class. You don't have a choice about calling a constructor; it is *always* called, one way or another. For example, in Chapter 2 you saw the statement:

```
clsPerson myFriend = new clsPerson();
```

On the left side of the assignment operator, you see that myFriend is going to be a reference to a clsPerson object. The expression on the right side of the assignment operator has the keyword new, which results in a memory allocation for the object. That is, the rvalue of myFriend gets filled in with a memory address of where the data associated with myFriend resides. Finally, the clsPerson()

constructor is called. We know it's the constructor because it shares the same class name and it is followed by the opening and closing parentheses . . . It is a special method called a constructor.

What's interesting is that, even if you don't write any code for the constructor, your program behaves as though you wrote a default constructor. A default constructor means that all value type properties in the class are initialized to 0 and all reference type properties are initialized to `null`.

Exercise 5 Solution

Again, there's more than one way to skin a cat, but one way would be as follows:

```
bool flag;
int age;
DateTime birthday;
DateTime currentDate = DateTime.Now;

flag = DateTime.TryParse(txtBirthday.Text, out birthday);
if (flag == false)            //Error!
{
    MessageBox.Show("Invalid date format. Use MM/DD/YY");
    txtBirthday.Focus();
    return;
}
age = currentDate.Year - birthday.Year;
txtAge.Text = age.ToString();
```

The program defines several working variables, including initializing `currentDate` to today's date. The call to the `TryParse()` method of the `DateTime` object checks to see if the user entered the birthday as a valid date. If `flag` is `false`, the user made an error and we use an `if` statement to call his attention to the error and give him a chance to re-enter the data. (You will cover `if` statements in detail in the next chapter. For now, just pretend you know what's going on!)

Assuming the data were entered correctly, the code subtracts the `Year` property of the `birthday` object from the `Year` property of the `currentDate` object. This is the age of the user. The program then simply uses the `ToString()` method to format the age value into the `Text` property of the `txtAge` textbox object.

Chapter 6

Exercise 1 Solution

The decision can be made using a single `if` statement:

```
price = FULLPRICE;
if (age < 13 || age > 64)
{
    price *= .5M;
}
```

The `if` statement checks for the child and senior price values and adjusts the price accordingly.

Exercise 2 Solution

The most important style consideration is consistency. The placement of curly braces is whatever you or your programming team decides works best for you. Personally, I think all if-else statement blocks should use curly braces, even when only a single statement is being controlled.

Exercise 3 Solution

It is appropriate to use cascading if statements anytime a single value can have multiple resolutions. Keep in mind that a switch might also be appropriate in lieu of a cascading if statement.

Exercise 4 Solution

```
if (x = y);
{
    price =* .06;
}
```

There are a number of problems. First, the if expression uses the assignment operator rather than a test for equality. Second, the semicolon after the if expression and before the opening curly brace of the if statement block is an error. Third, the shortcut assignment-multiplication operator is backwards (it should be *=). Fourth, assuming that price is a decimal data type, which it probably should be, the .06 literal needs the M type designator after the literal.

Exercise 5 Solution

One possible solution is:

```
const int SMALL = 1;
const int MEDIUM = 2;
const int LARGE = 3;

decimal smallPrice = 6.0M;
decimal mediumPrice = smallPrice + 1.0M;
decimal largePrice = mediumPrice + 1.0M;

decimal price;

int size;

// code for customer to select size

switch (size)
{
  case SMALL:
    price = smallPrice;
    break;

  case MEDIUM:
    price = mediumPrice;
    break;
```

```
    case LARGE:
      price = largePrice;
      break;

    default:
      price = -1;          // Error condition
      errorLog(size);
      break;
  }
```

The first three lines define constants for the three sizes of pizza. These symbolic constants are used only to make the code easier to read in the `switch` statement. While you could leave them out and just use `case1`, `case2`, and `case3` in the `switch`, I think using the constants makes the code easier to read. That is, the use of constants helps document what the code is doing.

The next three lines define the prices for the various sizes. Note how the prices are related to one another. That way, if the base price for a small pizza increases but the $1 add-on stays the same, you need to change only the `smallPrice` value. The new prices for the medium and large pizzas are adjusted automatically. The final purchase price is set using a `switch` statement. Note how the use of the constants makes it easier to read the `switch` code. While there are other, simpler ways of writing the solution, the code here is pretty easy to read and understand and, therefore, should be easy to maintain.

Chapter 7

Exercise 1 Solution

One possible solution is:

```
int factorial = 1;

for (i = num; i > 0; i--)
{
    factorial *= i;
}
lblAnswer.Text = factorial.ToString();
```

In the `for` loop, notice how the initial state of the loop is set to the number to factor (`expression1`) and how the loop control expression (`expression3`) uses the decrement operator to walk "backward" through the loop.

Exercise 2 Solution

The solution shown for Exercise 1 produces the correct answers . . . provided you don't enter a large number to factorial. Because factorials can produce very large numbers, one problem is using an `int` data type for variable `factorial`. Even a factorial as small as 13 overflows the range of an `int`. It would be better to use a `double` to extend its range.

A more subtle problem is that the test expression, `i > 0`, causes the loop to execute one more time than is really necessary. The reason is that the last iteration of the loop ends up multiplying the current value of `factorial` by 1 which, of course, has no impact on the result. You can correct this inefficiency by changing the second expression of the `for` loop to

```
i > 1
```

This does away with the unnecessary loop iteration that multiplies `factorial` by 1.

Exercise 3 Solution

One solution is

```
const int FOURPOUNDS = 48;
const double GRAMSPEROUNCE = 28.3495231;
int i;
double grams;
string buff;

for (i = 1; i <= FOURPOUNDS; i++)
{
    grams = (double) i * GRAMSPEROUNCE;
    buff = string.Format("{0, 4} {1, 15}", i, grams);
    lstResult.Items.Add(buff);
}
```

You could take this code and place it in the button click event.

Exercise 4 Solution

Because the table is constructed by increasing variable `i` by one on each pass through the loop, the expression:

```
grams = (double) i * GRAMSPEROUNCE;
```

could be replaced with the simpler:

```
grams += GRAMSPEROUNCE;
```

provided you change the definition of grams to

```
double grams = GRAMSPEROUNCE;
```

so it is initialized as part of its definition. Now you have a simple addition taking place within the loop where there used to be a multiply and a cast.

Exercise 5 Solution

Your program should input the percent and year values in the manner you've used for previous programs. Keep in mind that, because you want to use monetary values, the `TryParse()` method is the one for the `decimal` data type. Then:

```
int i;
int year = 10;
decimal percent = .06M;
decimal val = 100M;
string buff;
for (i = 1; i < year; i++)
{
    val *= (1.0M + percent);
    buff = string.Format("{0, 4} {1, 15:C}", i, val);
    lstResult.Items.Add(buff);
}
```

Note how I have used the `Format()` conversion for currency in the second formatting option.

Chapter 8

Exercise 1 Solution

The code has a user interface with two textboxes for getting the starting and ending heights for the table and a listbox or `ListView` object to present the results. The button click event code does most of the work and one solution using a listbox is shown here:

```
const double MININCHES = 36;
const double MAXINCHES = 96;

private void btnCalc_Click(object sender, EventArgs e)
{
    bool flag;
    int i;
    int j;
    double start;
    double end;
    double male;
    double female;
    double[,] idealWeights;
    string buff;

    //=================== Input ========================
    flag = double.TryParse(txtStart.Text, out start); // Table start
    if (flag == false)
    {
        MessageBox.Show("Numeric only.");
        txtStart.Focus();
        return;
    }
```

```
flag = double.TryParse(txtEnd.Text, out end);    // Table end
if (flag == false)
{
  MessageBox.Show("Numeric only.");
  txtEnd.Focus();
  return;
}

//=================== Validate Inputs ================
if (start < MININCHES || start > MAXINCHES)    // Check table limits
{
  MessageBox.Show("Table can only span " + MININCHES.ToString() +
                  " to " + MAXINCHES + " inches.");
  txtStart.Focus();
  return;
}
if (end < MININCHES || end > MAXINCHES)
{
  MessageBox.Show("Table can only span " + MININCHES.ToString() +
                  " to " + MAXINCHES + " inches.");
  txtStart.Focus();
  return;
}

if (end <= start)          // Can we display anything?
{
  MessageBox.Show("Starting value must be less than ending value");
  txtStart.Focus();
  return;
}
// Define the array for table data
idealWeights = new double[2, (int) (end - start) + 1];


//=================== Process =====================
female = 3.5 * start - 108;    // Set initial table values
male = 4.0 * start - 128;

for (i = (int)start, j = 0; i <= (int)end; i++, j++)
{// Since linear relationships...
  idealWeights[0, j] = (female += 3.5);
  idealWeights[1, j] = (male += 4.0);
}
 //=================== Display =====================
for (i = (int)start, j = 0; i <= (int)end; i++, j++)
{
  buff = string.Format("{0,5}{1,15}{2,15}", i, idealWeights[0, j],
                        idealWeights[1, j]);
  lstResults.Items.Add(buff);
}}
```

The program validates the input values for the table. Once the start and end values are determined, those variables can be used to set the array size:

```
idealWeights = new double[2, (int) (end - start) + 1];
```

Note that, because start and end are double data types, you must cast those values to an int to use them to set the array size. The code then calculates the initial ideal weights for males and females. However, since the code increments the value by one on each pass through the loop, you can simply add 3.5 to the current female value and 4.0 to the current male value to derive the new table values. Because adding numbers is a little faster than multiplication, you get a small performance improvement. Also note how you use the shorthand addition operators and the array reference to store the new values:

```
idealWeights[0, j] = (female += 3.5);
idealWeights[1, j] = (male += 4.0);
```

The second for loop simply displays the results in a listbox object. Obviously, you could move everything into a single loop and even do away with the arrays if you wanted to.

Exercise 2 Solution

Arrays of value types create a reference variable using the array name whose rvalue points to the starting memory address for the data array. Arrays of reference types, like strings, create a reference variable using the array name whose rvalue points to an array of memory addresses, not the actual data. The memory addresses in the array point to the actual data for the reference object.

Exercise 3 Solution

One solution is:

```
using System;
using System.Windows.Forms;

public class frmMain : Form
{
  const int MAXVAL = 52;
  const int MAXELEMENTS = 100;

  int[] data = new int[MAXELEMENTS];
  private Button btnSort;
  private Button btnClose;
  private ListBox lstResult;
  private Button btnCalc;

  #region Windows code


  public frmMain()
  {
    InitializeComponent();
  }
```

```
        public static void Main()
        {
          frmMain main = new frmMain();
          Application.Run(main);
        }

        private void btnClose_Click(object sender, EventArgs e)
        {
          Close();
        }

        private void btnCalc_Click(object sender, EventArgs e)
        {
          int i;
          Random rd = new Random(5);      // Define a random object

          for (i = 0; i < data.Length; i++)
          {
            data[i] = rd.Next(MAXVAL);   // Get a random value
            lstResult.Items.Add(data[i].ToString());   // Put in listbox
          }
        }

        private void btnSort_Click(object sender, EventArgs e)
        {
          int i;

          Array.Sort(data);                    // Sort the data

          lstResult.Items.Clear();             // Clear out old data

          for (i = 0; i < data.Length; i++)    // Show it
          {
            lstResult.Items.Add(data[i].ToString());
          }

        }
    }
```

Again, notice the use of symbolic constants. This makes it easy to change the number of items in the array. Also note that you always use the Length property of an array to control walking through the array. That way, if you do change the array's size, the code controlling the loop does not have to be changed. Finally, the statement:

```
        data[i] = rd.Next(MAXVAL);
```

uses the Next() method of the Random class to generate a random number between 0 and MAXVAL. Note that the set is exclusive of MAXVAL.

Exercise 4 Solution

This is actually very easy to do. First, place the following definition at the top of the class:

```
  static string stars = "*********************************************************";
```

You could change the `for` loop code in the `Calc` event to the following:

```
int i;
int j;
string buff;
Random rd = new Random(5);      // Define a random object

for (i = 0; i < data.Length; i++)
{
  data[i] = rd.Next(MAXVAL);  // Get a random value
  buff = "";
  for (j = 0; j < data[i]; j++)
  {
    buff += "*";
  }
  lstResult.Items.Add(data[i].ToString() + " " + buff);
}
```

However, a better solution is:

```
for (i = 0; i < data.Length; i++)
{
  data[i] = rd.Next(MAXVAL);  // Get a random value
  buff = data[i].ToString() + " " + stars.Substring(0, data[i]);
  lstResult.Items.Add(buff);  // Put in listbox
}
```

Note how I used the `Substring()` method of the `stars` string to display the proper number of stars. This is more efficient because I have done away with the inner `for` loop.

Exercise 5 Solution

Anytime you see an assignment statement, you should think in terms of rvalues. In this case, the rvalue of `str1` is assigned into `temp`. What this actually means is that you now have two reference variables that point to the same array of strings.

Chapter 9

Exercise 1 Solution

The definitions would be as follows:

```
//============ static members ===============
private static string[] daysOfWeek = new string[] {"", "Monday",
      "Tuesday", "Wednesday","Thursday", "Friday", "Saturday",
      "Sunday"};

//============ instance members ===============
private string lastName;
private string zipCode;
```

You would want the daysOfWeek array to be static since all instances of the class could then share this data. Also, we added an empty element at the front of the array because I tend to think of Monday as the first day of the week.

Exercise 2 Solution

One solution might be written like this:

```
/*****
 * Purpose: Return the number of days in a given month.
 *
 * Parameter list:
 *    int month      the month "        "
 *    int year       the year under consideration
 *
 * Return value:
 *    int            the number of days in the month or 0 on error
 *****/
public int getDaysInMonth(int month, int year)
{
    int days;

    if (month < 1 || month > 12 || year < 1 || year > 9999)
    {
        return 0;
    }
    if (month != 2)    // As long as it's not February
    {
        days = daysInMonth[month];
    }
    else
    {
        days = daysInMonth[2] + getLeapYear(year);
    }
    return days;
}
```

A discussion of this code appears in Chapter 10.

Exercise 3 Solution

I couldn't think of one, either.

Exercise 4 Solution

First, you would need to define a temporary string:

```
string buff;
```

Now replace the statement with this:

```
buff = year.ToString() + " is ";
```

```
        if (leap == 1)        // leap is 1 for a leap year
        {
            buff += "a leap year";
        } else
        {
            buff += "not a leap year";
        }
        lblLeapYearResult.Text = buff;
```

If I were writing the program, I would use the version shown here. While the first version tests your knowledge of the ternary operator, that is not the goal for commercial code. You should design your code so that it is as easy to read as possible. Making code easy to read makes testing and debugging easier. About the only valid reason for using complex code is when you can demonstrate that the easy-to-read code executes noticeably slower than more complex code. If that's the case, make sure you document clearly what the complex code is doing.

Exercise 5 Solution

You would create a new getLeapYear() method that overloads the existing getLeapYear() method. The new code would be as follows:

```
public int getLeapYear()
{
    return getLeapYear(year);
}
```

Because the new constructor for clsDates can be called for the year under consideration, you can call the earlier version of getLeapYear() using the class property year as the argument. Because the two method signatures are different, Visual Studio knows which one to call based upon whether the year argument is passed or not.

Using a snippet of the code from Listing 9-5, you would use

```
// clsDates myDate = new clsDates();        MOVE BELOW

// Convert validate integer
flag = int.TryParse(txtYear.Text, out year);
if (flag == false)
{
    MessageBox.Show("Digit characters only in YYYY format.",
                    "Input Error");
    txtYear.Focus();
    return;
}
clsDates myDate = new clsDates(year); // Place it here!

leap = myDate.getLeapYear();              // Call overloaded method
lblLeapYearResult.Text = year.ToString() + " is " +
            ((leap == 1)? "":"not ") + "a leap year";
lblEasterResult.Text = myDate.getEaster(year);
```

With this approach, myDate is constructed passing the year variable to the constructor. You can then call the overloaded version of getLeapYear().

Chapter 10

Exercise 1 Solution

Because the only difference is in the range of cards, no changes are needed to either the client (frmMain) or the server (clsCardDeck) objects. You do, however, need to change the way each card is viewed in the rules of the game. The change is quite simple: Force each ace to have a value greater than a king. This means modifying the code for getFirstCard(), getSecondCard(), and getDealtCard() to reflect the following type of change:

```
public void getFirstCard()
{
    lowCardIndex = myDeck.getOneCard();
    lowCard = lowCardIndex % 13;
    if (lowCard == 0)                  // A King
        lowCard = 13;
    if (lowCard == 1)                  // View an Ace as high card
        lowCard = 14;
}
```

The last two lines of code would have to be added to each method, reflecting the card in question. This means that six new lines of code change the way the game is played. No other changes are needed.

Exercise 2 Solution

The code shown in getFirstCard(), for example, has several magic numbers in it, which are usually not a good idea. Suppose we make the following changes to clsInBetweenRules:

```
// =============== symbolic constants ===================
const int CARDSINSUIT = 13;
const int ACE = 1;
const int KING = 13;
const int MAKEACEHIGH = 14;

// Other code in class...

public void getFirstCard()
{
    lowCardIndex = myDeck.getOneCard();
    lowCard = lowCardIndex % CARDSINSUIT;
    if (lowCard == 0)                  // A King
        lowCard = KING;
    if (lowCard == ACE)                // View an Ace as high card
        lowCard = MAKEACEHIGH;
}
```

The symbolic constants make it a little easier to read what the method is doing. Similar changes could be made to the other magic numbers in the clsInBetweenRules class code.

Exercise 3 Solution

The way clsCardDeck is presently designed, there is no way to prevent invalid cards (such as two through eight) from being dealt. Also, the current state of the deck assumes that an ace is viewed as the lowest card in a suit rather than the highest, as euchre would require.

Exercise 4 Solution

Any time you face an issue like this, you need to ask where the problem really lies. The way the question is phrased, it would appear that the issue is with clsCardDeck because it deals out cards that should not be used in a game of euchre. Indeed, when I pose this question to my students, one solution that is always offered is to add a method named getOneEuchreCard() to clsCardDeck. They suggest that the method can then be written so that only valid euchre cards are returned. While this might work, it detracts from clsCardDeck's purpose: to deal cards from a deck. Adding euchre functionality to clsCardDeck adds a Swiss Army knife element to the class and reduces its cohesiveness. For example, if there are a million card games in the world and each card game's quirkiness is added to clsCardDeck, how can you possibly hope to cope with its complexity?

A little thought reveals that it is the rules of euchre that dictate which cards are valid. It is not the responsibility of clsCardDeck to determine what rules apply to each card. The tasks for clsCardDeck remain the same: mainly, dealing a card from a shuffled deck. A new class, clsEuchreRules, should be written to enforce the valid cards returned from clsCardDeck.

Exercise 5 Solution

You could replaces the Shuffle button code in Listing 10-5 with the following code:

```
private void btnShuffle_Click(object sender, EventArgs e)
{
    int j;
    int cardIndex;
    int cardsShown;
    int deckSize;
    int passes;
    int card;
    string buff;
    string temp;
    clsCardDeck myDeck = new clsCardDeck();

    passes = myDeck.ShuffleDeck();
    lblPassCounter.Text = "It took " + passes.ToString() +
                          " passes to shuffle the deck";

    deckSize = myDeck.DeckSize;

    cardIndex = 1;
    cardsShown = 0;
    buff = "";
    while (cardIndex < deckSize + 1)
    {
        card = myDeck.getCurrentCardIndex();
        if (card % 13 < 9 && card % 13 != 0 && card % 13 != 1)
```

```
            {
                    cardIndex++;
                    myDeck.IncrementCardIndex();
                    continue;
            }
            temp = myDeck.getOneCard(cardIndex);
            buff += temp + " ";
            cardIndex++;
            cardsShown++;
            if (cardsShown % 6 == 0 && cardsShown > 0)
            {
                    lstDeck.Items.Add(buff);
                    buff = "";
            }
        }
        lstDeck.Items.Add(" ");        // Add an empty line

}
```

You also need to add two new methods to clsCardDeck:

```
/**
* Purpose: Get the index of current card.
*
* Parameter list:
*       void
*
* Return value:
*       int        the index into the pips array
*/
public int getCurrentCardIndex()
{
    return deck[nextCard];
}
/**
* Purpose: Advance card index to next card
*
* Parameter list:
*       void
*
* Return value:
*       void
*/
public void IncrementCardIndex()
{
    nextCard++;
    if (nextCard > DECKSIZE + 1)
    {
        ShuffleDeck();
    }
}
```

When you run the program, the output looks like that shown in Figure 10-A after two shuffles of the deck.

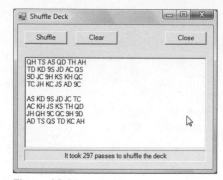

Figure 10-A

Chapter 11

Exercise 1 Solution

The error message is:

```
Use of unassigned local variable 'x'
```

The problem is that C# doesn't want you to return a variable that has not been explicitly assigned a value. In the code, x is assigned a value only when the if statement is true. To fix the problem, you must explicitly assign x a value. The easiest fix is to change the definition of x:

```
int x = 0;
```

Exercise 2 Solution

The issue here is not whether you can code the equation correctly, but whether you can make it readable for others. The first solution might be

```
p = a  * 1 / (Math.Pow(1 + i, y));
```

The code would compile and generate the correct values for p. However, which would you rather debug: the preceding statement or the following?

```
presentValue = futureAmount  * 1.0 / (Math.Pow(1.0
 + interestRate, yearsIntoFuture));
```

The primary difference is the use of meaningful variable names. Another benefit is the use of numeric constants (1.0) that reflect the fact that floating-point values are being used in the equation. You could make the argument that the decimal data type should be used since this is a financial calculation. However, the pow() method uses the double data type, so I would probably stuff this equation into a method that returned a double and let the user decide to cast it to a decimal if needed.

An alternative that makes debugging a bit easier would be:

```
discountFactor = 1.0 / (Math.Pow(1.0 + interestRate,
                                yearsIntoFuture));

presentValue = futureAmount  * discountFactor;
```

This form uses an intermediate value (discountFactor) to simplify the code. This variation also enables you to generate a present value discount factor, the values for which can be found in published tables. This makes generating test data easier.

Exercise 3 Solution

I have never used this style of variable definition because it discourages initialization and documentation of the variable. The pro is that it takes fewer keystrokes. In my mind, that's not a strong enough argument to use that style. You should use this:

```
long number = 2;  // The number of parameters
long val;         // The value of the solution
long len;         // The length of the steel bar
```

The single-statement definition discourages such comments. If you insist on using the short style, you could still comment the code using the following:

```
long number = 2,  // The number of parameters
     val,         // The value of the solution
     len;         // The length of the steel bar
```

Exercise 4 Solution

This could be an example of the "forest for the trees" problem. I'm assuming you've checked the obvious sources of error (such as bogus input values) and that those revealed nothing useful. It's not uncommon to look at the code so long that you are no longer actually reading the code closely enough to see what it does. That is, you've read the code so many times, your mind recognizes the patterns of the code and you are convinced the bug is not in those familiar lines. Perhaps . . . perhaps not.

My first action for the "impossible bug" problem is to have someone else look at the code. It's not uncommon for another programmer to spot a program bug in minutes even though you've been staring at it for days. If you don't have another programmer you can call upon, simply take a long (at least an hour) break. Sometimes that gets your mind off the problem long enough so that when you come back, you're actually reading the code again.

Another technique is to force an exception just before you display the (erroneous) answer and have a catch block that does a stack trace. Because a stack trace shows the method calls that were made to generate the answer, you should use your test data set to examine each method in the order in which they are presented in the stack trace. (Remember, a stack trace shows the method calls in reverse order from last to first. This means you are working from the Output Step toward the Input Step of the Five Program Steps.) By hand-calculating the value(s) that should be produced by each method call, you should be able to isolate the method causing the error. Then just concentrate on what test values should be generated in each method until you isolate the bug. Correcting the bug is typically a simple process. It's the isolation process that eats up time.

Exercise 5 Solution

I've reached the point where I insist my students use try-catch blocks in the Process Step of any program. That is the bare minimum. I also tell them that any method that does file or database I/O must be enclosed in a try-catch block. As a general rule, the two most dangerous places in a program where exceptions might lurk are in the Input and Process Steps of a program. I look for try-catch blocks in those two places.

I sometimes ask my students how they would rewrite their assignments if their codes were going to be part of a mission-critical software package that manages the space shuttle. They almost always offer ideas on how they could have "tightened up" their code to make it less error-prone in such circumstances. After they've presented all the improvements they *could* have made, I ask them, "Which is more important to you: the next shuttle mission or your grade in this class?" They usually get the point.

There is really no good reason not to cover each program you write in a protective coat of Kevlar whenever possible. It's just a good habit to get into.

Chapter 12

Exercise 1 Solution

The major advantage of generics is that they provide data flexibility without sacrificing strong type checking. Another advantage is that generics can avoid the overhead associated with boxing and unboxing the data. It's not uncommon for generics to provide a 100% performance increase over code that must exercise the boxing-unboxing process. Finally, the absence of generics almost always means that your code must use a lot of casts to accommodate more flexible coding practices. The "cast hassle" is avoided with generics.

Exercise 2 Solution

The first thing you would do is modify the ShowData() method along these lines:

```
private void ShowDataGeneric<T>(T[] val)
{
    int i;

    for (i = 0; i < t.Length; i++)
    {
        if (whichListbox == SORTED)
            lstSorted.Items.Add(val[i].ToString());
        else
            lstUnsorted.Items.Add(val[i].ToString());
    }

}
```

This enables you to pass in the data array that needs to be displayed. Note the use of the generic type specifier in the method's signature. Next, you would need to modify the code in the switch statements where ShowData() is used. For example, in btnSort_Click() event the code

```
case INTEGER:                     // Integer
    clsQuickSort<int> iSort = new clsQuickSort<int>(iData);
    iSort.Sort();
    break;
```

needs to add a call to the new generic method and remove the old call to ShowData(). The next code for the integer data type would be as follows:

```
case INTEGER:                     // Integer
    clsQuickSort<int> iSort = new clsQuickSort<int>(iData);
    iSort.Sort();
    ShowDataGeneric<int>(iData)
    break;
```

Exercise 3 Solution

This is kind of a trick question. As I have currently discussed interfaces, they indicate a guaranteed behavior or functionality as specified in the interface. I used the known behavior of the IComparable interface in our clsQuickSort code. I don't know *how* that functionality is implemented, only that I can rely on it being there. The trick part of the question comes into play because I discuss other advantages of interfaces when I discuss inheritance in Chapter 15.

Exercise 4 Solution

The solution means that you must pass the data to be swapped into the method. One solution is:

```
private void swap01<T>(T[] data, int pos1, int pos2)
{
    T temp;

    temp = data[pos1];
    data[pos1] = data[pos2];
    data[pos2] = temp;
}
```

Exercise 5 Solution

I would hope so. Just as with the role that interfaces could play in modernizing an aircraft (such as with IControls, IAvionics, and IStunts), the same concepts apply to software versioning. By encapsulating the new features inside interface declarations you ensure that the older version can still function; they simply don't have the newer enhancements available to them. This approach is especially useful when enhancements alter the underlying data structures (for example, the members of a class that are persisted to disk).

Chapter 13

Exercise 1 Solution

There's probably a bazillion different ways to accomplish this task, of which the following involves simple changes to the ReadAndShowRecord() method:

```
private int ReadAndShowRecord()
{
    int flag;

    try
    {
        myData.Open(myData.FileName);
        flag = myData.ReadOneRecord(currentRecord - 1);
        if (myData.Status == 0)
        {
            ClearTextboxes();
            txtRecord.Text = currentRecord.ToString() + " Not Active";
        }
        else
        {
            if (flag == 1)
            {
                ShowOneRecord();
                txtRecord.Text = currentRecord.ToString();

            }
            else
            {
                MessageBox.Show("Record not available.", "Error
                            Read");
                flag = 0;
            }
        }
    }
    catch
    {
        flag = 0;
    }

    myData.Close();
    return flag;
}
```

This solution displays the record position (currentRecord) in the txtRecord object, but appends a Not Active message after clearing out all the textboxes. Presenting the information this way doesn't leave the user in the dark when an inactive record is read.

You could also put Read Active and Read All radio buttons on the form to give the user more control over reading the data.

Exercise 2 Solution

Obviously you can, or I wouldn't have asked the question. In the getRecordCount() method from Listing 13-6, delete the following line:

```
records = myFile.Seek(0, SeekOrigin.End); // Position file pointer
```

Replace it with this:

```
FileInfo myInfo = new FileInfo(fileName);
records = myInfo.Length;
```

This exercise simply confirms that there are almost always multiple ways to accomplish a given task. Part of the journey to becoming an experienced programmer is learning what these alternatives are and which one offers the best solution for the task at hand.

Exercise 3 Solution

Once people learn how to use random access files, they tend to throw away sequential files. You should never throw away a programming tool. Sequential files are often used for persisting non-transactions-based information. By *non-transactions-based*, I am referring to those sets of data that do not require updating and editing. The density of sequential files makes them perfect for such data storage. However, when the data will likely need to be updated or otherwise edited, random access files are usually a better choice.

Exercise 4 Solution

This is sort of a trick question because there is no "right" answer. Without much conscious effort, I tend to use serialization techniques to pass an object's state to other applications that need it for their processing tasks. Because of this, it seems that I write one object to the file and pass it on to some other app, and that app hands it back to me with additional (or altered) information about the object's state. Perhaps it's just me and the type of programming I do, but most of the time I use serialization for temporary storage.

If I know that the object's information is going to hang around on a fairly permanent basis, like a client file, I tend to use standard read/write code. Therefore, the correct answer is: "It depends…"

Exercise 5 Solution

An About box is normally found under the rightmost menu option of MDI applications. Convention has Help as the rightmost menu option in MDI applications. Normally, the Help topic offers a means by which you can provide information about how to use the program. The last submenu item under Help is About. Therefore, the first thing you probably need in order to implement an About box is an application that implements the MDI interface.

Next, you need to create a new menu option, perhaps named mnuAbout. Finally, you need to add a new form to the project (frmAbout) and add labels that convey whatever information you deem desirable to the user. Finally, add the following code:

```
private void mnuAbout_Click(object sender, EventArgs e)
{
    frmAbout frm = new frmAbout();
    frm.ShowDialog();
}
```

. . . and recompile the program.

Chapter 14

Exercise 1 Solution

The two commands are:

```
SELECT * FROM Friends WHERE status = 1
```

and:

```
SELECT SUM(status) FROM Friends
```

The reason the aggregate SUM function works is that we assigned the value of 1 to an active member and 0 to inactive members. Therefore, SUM also produces a count of active members.

Exercise 2 Solution

The SELECT statement might be written as:

```
SELECT * FROM Friend WHERE status = 1 AND ADDR2 <> '' AND State = 'IN'
```

Note that the middle expression of the WHERE predicate is two single-quote marks, not a double-quote mark.

Exercise 3 Solution

There are several ways to do this. First, you could create a new static class (such as clsGlobalFriendData) and give it property members that match the data in the Friends data structure and use the property get and set methods to make the data available to clsDB. This would work because a static data item is instantiated at load time so there is always one (and only one) instance of the class. You could then copy the data from frmAddFriend into the static class object and then let clsDB retrieve it. While this works, it means that you always have a copy of that object hanging around chewing up resources when you may not need it. Also, there's just something about that approach that seems "messy" . . . sorta like using an H-bomb to kill an ant.

A less H-bombish approach would be to copy the contents of each textbox object into a string array and pass that string array to a new `InsertFriend()` method. A second parallel array would have to keep track of whether the string variable represented a string or a numeric value. Assuming `str` holds the data and `type` holds the data type, you might have something in the `InsertFriend()` method that looks like

```
public string InsertData(string[] str, int[] type, string sqlCommand)
{
    int i;

    for (i = 0; i < str.Length; i++)
    {
        switch (type[i])
        {
            case 0:            // Numeric data
                sqlCommand += str[i] + ",";
                break;
            case 1:            // String data
                sqlCommand += "'" + str[i] + "',";
                break;
            default:
                break;
        }
    }
    i = sqlCommand.LastIndexOf(',');    // Strip off last comma
    sqlCommand = sqlCommand.Substring(0, i) + ")";
    return str;
}
```

This assumes that the first part of the INSERT command has been built and only the textbox information needs to be added to the `sqlCommand` string.

Exercise 4 Solution

This is a short question with a fairly long answer. The necessary code is very similar to the code found in `frmQuery`, which currently is

```
private void DoQuery()
{
    try
    {
        ds = new DataSet();       // Instantiate DataSet object
        conn.Open();
        command.CommandText = txtQuery.Text;

        adapter = new OleDbDataAdapter(command);

        adapter.Fill(ds);
        dataGridView1.DataSource = ds.Tables[0];
        command.ExecuteNonQuery();
    }
    catch (Exception ex)
```

```
            {
                MessageBox.Show("Error: " + ex.Message);
            }
            finally
            {
                conn.Close();
            }
    }
```

To modify the SQL query to use LINQ instead, change the code to something like this:

```
        private void DoQuery()
        {
            string buff;

            try
            {
                ds = new DataSet();       // Instantiate DataSet object
                conn.Open();
                command.CommandText = txtQuery.Text;

                adapter = new OleDbDataAdapter(command);

                adapter.Fill(ds);
                dataGridView1.DataSource = ds.Tables[0];

                                                // New stuff starts here...
                DataTable buddies = ds.Tables[0];

                IEnumerable<DataRow> query =
                    from buddy in buddies.AsEnumerable()
                    select buddy;
                                                    // Sample output...
                foreach (DataRow myRow in query)
                {
                    buff = myRow.Field<string>("LastName") + " " +
                        myRow.Field<string>("Zip");
                }
            }
            catch (Exception ex)
            {
                MessageBox.Show("Error: " + ex.Message);
            }
            finally
            {
                conn.Close();
            }
        }
```

The only major change is the inclusion of the System.Collections.Generic namespace. You must include it because in this example we did not use the var data type, but instead chose to use the IEnumerable interface using a DataRow object for the generic. The string variable buff then simply picks off two of the fields that result from the dataset's using the Friends table.

Exercise 5 Solution

Perhaps the simplest answer is that LINQ enables you to query across all object types, whereas SQL is limited to databases. Therefore, programmers familiar with SQL can apply a good part of that knowledge directly to a LINQ implementation.

While there are ways to shoehorn SQL queries to "fit" all object types, this would normally involve a lot of explicit casts to make things work. LINQ gives you the ability to work with various object types yet retain strong typing of the data that comes from a query. As you saw earlier in the chapter, var types that are often used with LINQ are not objects, but assume the type of the data used to instantiate the var variable.

Chapter 15

Exercise 1 Solution

Clearly this is a problem that begs for an inherited solution. The base class would be called clsMembers and would contain all of the information that pertains to all members. That data would include name and mailing address, billing information, and the like. The derived classes would be clsSenior, clsRegular, clsJunior, and clsSocial. Each of these classes would have information that pertains to that class only (dues rate, voting privileges, monthly food minimums, and so on).

Exercise 2 Solution

You can tell that this line of code appears in the clsJunior class and is part of the constructor for the class. You can also tell that the base class has a similar constructor that the writer wants to call as part of setting the initial state of the object. As a general rule, the sequence displayed here is good, because it shows that the writer is being consistent with the initialization of new objects.

Exercise 3 Solution

Their concern is that the derived classes can directly change the value of a data item in the base class without having to be subject to any validation code that might be associated with that property's set method in the base class. This is a real concern.

However, I think the concern, while real, is not serious. Users of the class will still go through the property's set method and only the programmers of the derived classes can abuse this concern. If you can assume that your programming colleagues aren't out to sabotage your project, it's probably not going to be a serious problem.

Exercise 4 Solution

If you define a class using the `sealed` keyword, you are informing the compiler that it should not let this class be used as a base class for further inheritance. For example:

```
public sealed clsMyClass
```

prevents anyone from using `clsMyClass` as a base class for further inheritance.

Exercise 5 Solution

Most of the abilities of base-derived class behavior can be written without the use of inheritance. However, you do end up duplicating a lot of code by not using inheritance. Also, polymorphic behavior is not possible without the use of inheritance.

Index

Symbols

G

Get more from Wrox.

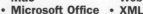